Hawthorne in Concord

Philip McFarland

Grove Press
New York

Published simultaneously in Canada
Printed in the United States of America

FIRST GROVE PRESS PAPERBACK EDITION

Library of Congress Cataloging-in-Publication Data

McFarland, Philip James.
    Hawthorne in Concord / Philip McFarland.
        p. cm.
    ISBN 0-8021-4205-2 (pbk.)
    1. Hawthorne, Nathaniel, 1804–1864—Homes and haunts—Massachusetts—
Concord.   2. Novelists, American—Homes and haunts—Massachusetts—
Concord.   3. Novelists, American—19th century—Biography.   4. Concord
(Mass.)—Biography.   I. Title.

PS1884.M395 2004
813'.3—dc22

                                                                                    [B]
                                                                         2003067661

Grove Press
an imprint of Grove/Atlantic, Inc.
841 Broadway
New York, NY 10003

05 06 07 08 09   10 9 8 7 6 5 4 3 2 1

Praise for *Hawthorne in Concord*:

"*Hawthorne in Concord* is an intimate, tender, and unusually attractive account of a great American writer. Vividly rendered, the high-minded and quirky community of Concord is itself a major actor in this superb narrative."
—Justin Kaplan

"I don't know when I have read a book as satisfying as *Hawthorne in Concord*. Not since Van Wyck Brooks's *The Flowering of New England* has anyone else so perfectly re-created the world of the New England Renaissance."
—David Herbert Donald

"McFarland focuses on the people and ideas that shaped the era as it moved from early industrialization to the turmoil of the Civil War. [He] illuminates Hawthorne's art and the intellectual ferment originating in that small, bucolic town." —*Publishers Weekly*

"McFarland . . . enters Hawthorne's milieu (his prose even echoes Hawthorne's textures, cadences, and grammar) and illuminates it with intelligence and affection." —*Booklist* (starred review)

"In this lyrical account of our first great novelist, Philip McFarland shows how central this reclusive writer was to the cultural and political life of antebellum New England." —Jerome Loving

"Enchanting." —Rebecca Pepper Sinkler, *American Scholar*

"[An] admirable book . . . McFarland . . . has found a way to bring [Hawthorne] into fresh perspective." —William H. Pritchard, *The Washington Times*

"McFarland manages to capture in his tone the flintiness of the brilliant minds that sparked off each other to ignite America's first great intellectual fire."
—Lucille Stott, *The Concord Journal*

"A novel historical spin . . . [McFarland's] innovative focus on Hawthorne's years in Concord, Massachusetts, enables him to reconsider Hawthorne's place in the history of the town's fascinating writers, intellectuals, and reformers. McFarland's important if implicit historical premise is that a biography of Hawthorne must also be a biography of his culture."
—Joel Pfister, *St. Petersburg Times*

"Warm and vivid. McFarland provides charming glimpses of Hawthorne's life in Concord." —Michael Kenney, *The Boston Globe*

Also by Philip McFarland

NONFICTION
The Brave Bostonians
Sea Dangers
Sojourners

FICTION
Seasons of Fear
A House Full of Women

for

Sarah Alice McFarland Boggs
Thomas Alfred McFarland, Jr.
John Sylvester McFarland

Sally, Tommy, and John

CONTENTS

THE FORTIES

Learning to Be Happy

Nathaniel Hawthorne in 1840, by Charles Osgood (oil on canvas), courtesy Peabody Essex Museum, Salem, Massachusetts.

I

WEDDING IN BOSTON

Both the groom and the bride were well past the bloom of their youth. Nathaniel Hawthorne had reached his late thirties, and Sophia Peabody was already thirty-two. Nor was it that either had been married before, the bride—sickly since infancy—never having expected to marry at all. As for the groom, others had assumed that he would have found a wife long before a certain summer day in July 1842. Years earlier, a college friend had made a bet to that effect and had done so very reasonably; for not only was the gentleman in the Peabodys' parlor this Saturday morning strikingly handsome. He was, as he himself might have put it, endowed as well "with the liveliest sensibility to feminine influence."*

Nearly two decades earlier a classmate at Bowdoin, Jonathan Cilley, had made the bet about Hawthorne's marrying within a dozen years. In due time Cilley had written his friend jocularly: "Bridge informs me that 'you are about to publish a book, and are coming into repute as a writer very fast.'" This was in 1836. "I am gratified to hear it; but just now it would have pleased me more to have heard that you were about to become the author and father of a legitimate and well-begotten boy than book. What! suffer twelve years to pass away, and no wife, no children, to soothe your care, make you happy, and call you blessed. Why, in that time I have begotten sons and daughters to the number of half a dozen, more or less."

* Sources of quotations appear on pages 303–30.

According to their friend Horatio Bridge, during the same long interval since leaving college Hawthorne had been writing, and through such effort was soon to be the author of a book. "I did not mistake your vein in that particular," Cilley had bantered his former classmate good-naturedly, "if I did in the line matrimonial. Damn that barrel of old Madeira; who cares if I have lost it! If only you and Frank Pierce and Joe Drummer and Sam Boyd and Bridge and Bill Hale were together with me, we would have a regular drunk, as my chum in college used to call it, on that same barrel of wine."

The collegians, once all chums together, were widely scattered now. Indeed, one of their number by Hawthorne's wedding morning in 1842—and he the writer of this very letter—was already four years dead. "What sort of a book have you written, Hath?" the doomed Cilley had been led to wonder before bringing his letter to an end.

The book comprised sketches and tales that had appeared anonymously in various newspapers, magazines, and annuals over most of a decade, some of them collected and published finally in 1837, the year before Jonathan Cilley, by then a member of Congress, was murdered in a duel that left his wife and those sons and daughters to the number of half a dozen husbandless, fatherless. Hawthorne would be deeply affected by the news. Meanwhile, the book, *Twice-Told Tales*, had been published in March 1837, leading to its author's introduction before year's end to the Peabody family, neighbors in his hometown of Salem, Massachusetts. A daughter in the family proved the belated choice of the handsome author for the wife who— fulfilling Cilley's hopes—might call him blessed and soothe his cares and make him happy.

The choice would have appeared imprudent for such purposes. The bride herself had doubted the wisdom of the union; her health remained too feeble to allow her to contemplate housework, and neither she nor her suitor had the means to set up a proper domestic establishment. Might they not better remain friends, she as his "sister," or the two of them no more than spiritual "husband" and "wife"? For his part, Hawthorne, though thoroughly in love, had nonetheless delayed for months and months telling his family of his secret engagement to Miss Peabody, who, as the summer of 1842 approached and the date was reset for their wedding, was increasingly tormented with bouts of her sometimes excruciating invalidism.

Even so, in the midst of a wet yesterday the groom had at last taken the decisive step of approaching the reverend brother of Sophia's friend Sarah Clarke. "My dear Sir," he had written, "Though personally a stranger to you, I am about to request of you the greatest favor which I can receive from any man. I am to be married to Miss Sophia Peabody tomorrow, and it is our mutual desire that you should perform the ceremony. Unless it should be decidedly a rainy day, a carriage will call for you at half past eleven oclock in the forenoon."

Accordingly, the Reverend James Freeman Clarke, then in his early thirties, arrived the next morning, July 9, 1842, at West Street between Tremont and Washington, just off the Common. Much of that area, now aggressively commercial in the heart of Boston, was residential then. In one such brick home, No. 13, celebrants had been rejoicing to see the sun pierce morning clouds, so that the wedding at noon was conducted in sunlight, happily enough, although the simplest of ceremonies sparsely attended. Only members of the bride's family were on hand, and the Reverend Mr. Clarke, of course, along with his sister Sarah as friend of Sophia's, a servant, and one other friend. "There were present," as the bride recorded later in her journal, "beside the family Cornelia and Sarah and the cook Bridget."

The groom's family did not attend. After the ceremony, the new Mr. and Mrs. Hawthorne boarded a carriage bound northwest into the countryside, toward the village of Concord some fifteen miles away. And it was a miracle. "Dear, dear Mother," the ecstatic bride wrote back to Boston the following day, "Every step the horses took, I felt better and not in the least tired. I was not tired at the tavern and not tired when I arrived. My husband looked upon me as upon a mirage which would suddenly disappear. It seemed miraculous that I was so well." Sophia's health, which had caused her agony as far back in the past as her teething days, was all at once blissfully untroublesome. In her new role the bride felt wonderful—woke next morning feeling wonderful still, though hardly more so than did the groom. Hawthorne found time that same Sunday, on the first full day of married life, to inform his younger sister of what had lately transpired. "The execution took place yesterday," he wrote Louisa at the family home in Salem. "We made a christian end, and came straight to Paradise, where we abide at this present writing. We are as happy as people can be, without making themselves ridiculous, and might be even happier; but, as a matter of taste, we choose to stop short at this point. Sophia is very well, and sends her love."

A weekly newspaper published in the couple's new home of Concord may help us retrieve the Hawthornes' wedding day. Crisp on the eve of the Boston wedding, the first of the four pages of the *Concord Freeman* for July 8, 1842, entertains its readers with a fictional tale, as anonymous tales by Nathaniel Hawthorne had earlier entertained readers of a similar newspaper in Salem. This present story, in the column farthest left, is entitled "The Night-Shriek," by one Charles Ollier, coolly lifted from an English periodical, *Bentley's Miscellany*: culture pirated from eastward overseas. At the same time, on the same front page appears a glance at the vast West, still hardly known, with an account of how North American Indians tame wild horses and buffalo calves. Included as well on page 1 are the text of President Tyler's veto of the Provisional Tariff Bill, dated June 29, and a report of a "Dreadful Storm in Philadelphia last evening," shared with Concord readers from Saturday's *Philadelphia Inquirer* (so the newsworthy storm in those more leisurely times had raged last Friday a week ago): "The rain poured down in torrents, the lightning flashed, and the thunder pealed in the most terrific manner."

Page 2 of the *Freeman* gives news of the arrival of the steamship *Caledonia* at Boston from Liverpool the previous Tuesday morning. The vessel had brought forty passengers and the London and Liverpool papers to June 19—three weeks old by then. From the pages of the latter, readers in Concord were to learn that the youth John Francis had been tried for high treason in London on Friday, June 17, for shooting at the queen; Francis was found guilty on two of three counts. "The prisoner, who was dreadfully affected, was sentenced in the usual form, to be hanged, drawn and quartered." Meanwhile, people in Cork, Limerick, and Ennis had rioted because of the high price of potatoes; four to five thousand miners had been thrown out of work in Truro; and at the Cheltenham Sessions, George Jacob Holyoke had been fined £100 for giving a lecture in which he denied the existence of God.

News from nearer home appears elsewhere in the *Freeman*: of a robbery in Dracut, of a murder in the public square in Nashville, and of the death by lightning in Elizabethtown, New Jersey, of a lovely young woman of eighteen. Mr. Lauriat made a beautiful balloon ascension from Taft's garden at Chelsea on Monday, descending safely in Lynn. And the *Louisville Sun* shares particulars of a duel, growing out of a love affair, "fought near that city between two boys of the ages of fifteen and thirteen! Upon their return home they were greeted with a sound spanking from their mothers for being out without permission—an excellent medicine for unruly children."

The times were different from ours. On the national scene, the paper reports that Secretary of State Webster and Lord Ashburton were about to sign a treaty that would settle the border between Maine and New Brunswick. Here in Concord, meanwhile, the criminal court was keeping busy; in a flawed world that much abides. On page 3 we learn of a larceny, of assault and battery, of highway robbery, and of a barn burning for which the young perpetrator will spend three years incarcerated. A shopbreaker in Waltham can ponder four years behind bars. Sarah Anne Willson of Lowell, having concealed the death of a child, is committed to the common jail for three months. Joseph Bulgar, guilty of lascivious cohabitation in the same town, has been sentenced to a year in state prison; and for the like offense Lucy Terrier of Lowell will spend six months in the House of Correction.

Burgeoning criminality in those nearby mill towns might have been read as a sign of change. But Concord itself appeared unalterable on the Saturday afternoon that was the Hawthornes' wedding day, a sleepy agricultural village of seventeen hundred souls with a history that reached back more than two hundred years already, back far before the birth of the Republic sixty-six years ago, back to the very settlement of New England.

Hawthorne had informed his sister in Salem that the bridal couple, having made a Christian end at their wedding, came straight to paradise. Paradise in this instance took the form of a clapboard house on the northwest edge of Concord, which Mr. and Mrs. Hawthorne laid claim to as tenants at about five on the afternoon of their wedding day. It stood, as it stands still, at the far end of a drive reaching to derelict gateposts at the public road; in view from the road were an old horse and a couple of cows munching the overgrown grass. Poplar trees lined the rutted avenue, the house at the end of the shaded path long faded from its original white to a sober grayish hue. A vegetable garden had been planted in the side yard to the left; an apple orchard was visible out back between the house and a little river a short walk away. Around the place sprawled shadows that lay glimmering between the front door and the highway, the light somehow creating an effect, it seemed to the groom, of a spot not quite belonging to the material world.

Set off in its accessible seclusion, this gray-hued paradise rose two stories to an attic under a gambrel roof. At its entrance, the wedding couple were stepping beyond the doorway into a hall that ran front to back, and into rooms filled with flowers that a neighbor had furnished in welcome. A lone servant girl was there to greet them as well: Sarah, still in her teens, whom the bride's eldest sister in Boston had provided to assist her with the unfamiliar matrimonial responsibilities that loomed. One such early chore was the wedding dinner. But the servant couldn't cook in that antiquated kitchen, didn't know how. Dinner accordingly was hours late, so that the first purchase needed would be an up-to-date stove to cook on.

Yet none of that mattered. Three years before, an enamored Hawthorne had written (in the ardent language of nineteenth-century love, which seems musty now, though it was fresh enough then): "Oh, beloved, if we had but a cottage, somewhere beyond the sway of the East Wind, yet within the limits of New-England, where we could be always together, and have a place to *be* in—" What more could the lovers want? "Nothing—save daily bread, (or rather bread and milk; for I think I should adopt your diet) and clean white apparel every day for mine unspotted Dove. Then . . . I could not be other than good and happy, when your kiss would sanctify me at all my outgoings and incomings, and when I should rest nightly in your arms."

The tardiness of dinner would have mattered scarcely at all that wondrous first evening, the two at last in their cottage long dreamed of, after their dinner retired at last in each other's arms. A month later, Hawthorne would return to dwell on the joys of their first intimacy—joys derived from a different kind of feasting—as he set down words for only Sophia to read. Would that she might allow him, he wrote, to record "the ethereal dainties" that a kind heaven had furnished the bridal couple on their magical day of arrival here! "Never, surely, was such food heard of on earth."

2

THE MANSE AND HISTORIC CONCORD

*T*his new tenant would make the house where he and his wife had moved on their wedding day famous around the world. To be sure, the Old Manse, as he called it, was not really a manse at all, not a domicile that the village church had provided its minister. Rather, it was a private residence where, before the Hawthornes moved in, ministers had happened to live from the beginning. The previous owner had lived in the place for over sixty years, during which time a new kitchen had turned antique and old Dr. Ripley (not always old, it is true, as Hawthorne himself would muse about it) was "gradually getting wrinkles and gray hairs, and looking more and more the picture of winter." Until last fall, when after having for so long reliably baptized, married, and buried the members of his Concord flock, the pastor in his nineties, his own time come, had finally left them. The Reverend Ezra Ripley had died downstairs in the front room early on Tuesday morning, September 21, 1841, by then having so long and with such anxious tenderness watched over his parishioners that he had made himself, as one who knew him noted, "universally respected and loved by the old and young."

Now strangers had moved into the late parson's home, secular tenants from Boston, a bridal couple. "I wish I could give a description of our house," the groom recorded soon after his and Sophia's arrival there, "for it really has a character of its own—which is more than can be said of most edifices in these days." When Hawthorne had first seen the place, on a visit with his betrothed early in May, eight or nine weeks before the wedding, it had looked as it had during Dr. Ripley's lifetime, showing the disarray and dust of sixty years of occupancy. But through busy days around the wedding, gloomy dilapidation had been transformed into what was now a comfortable modern residence. Dr. Ripley's bedroom on the ground floor had been turned into a parlor; "and by the aid of cheerful paint and paper, a gladsome carpet, pictures and engravings, new furniture, *bijouterie,* and a daily supply of flowers, it has become," according to this grateful newlywed, "one of the prettiest and pleasantest rooms in the whole world. The shade of our departed host will never haunt it," so cheerily unecclesiastical was the renovated atmosphere.

Behind the parlor, looking out over orchard, meadow, and river, lay the bright room where husband and wife were taking their meals. We may, incidentally, see all of this still, may stand in the little room with its window facing north toward the adjoining fields, its two windows on the adjacent wall looking west over the orchard and the river at its edge. Across a hallway is the kitchen, no longer quite as it was when those nineteenth-century tenants with their new stove put it to use. But the hallway survives intact in its generous dimensions downstairs and up, "occupying more space," as Hawthorne noted, "than is ever devoted to such a purpose, in modern times. This feature contributes to give the whole house an airy, roomy, and convenient appearance; we can breathe the freer for the sake of this broad passage-way."

Three rooms had been fitted out upstairs. The Hawthornes' bedroom was in front, over the parlor. Opposite, across the hall, was the guest room, containing the most presentable of Dr. Ripley's ancient furniture. And in the rear of the house, above the dining room, was the author's study, embellished with a bride's touches: a vase of flowers on the bookcase, a larger bronze vase of ferns on the bureau. Then—this being Hawthorne's house, at least for a while—"there are dark closets," he added in completing his description of the interior, "and strange nooks and corners, where the ghosts of former occupants might hide themselves in the day time, and stalk forth, when night conceals all our sacrilegious improvements." In truth, on many evenings during their early residence at the Manse, these present occupants heard strange noises, in the kitchen mostly, sometimes as of paper being crumpled, or felt a breeze that couldn't be accounted for, like someone passing; "and last night my wife heard thumping and pounding, as of somebody at work in my study."

That would have been the Reverend Dr. Ripley's ghost, still composing sermons of which its living incarnation had written so many hundreds over a diligent lifetime. As long ago as 1780 Ezra Ripley had come into possession of this house by marrying the widow who was living here then. Phebe Bliss, herself the daughter of an earlier Concord minister, had first wed her father's successor in the parish, so that Parson Bliss's daughter had become first the wife of Parson Emerson, before marrying, a couple of years after that young cleric's untimely death, the long-lived Parson Ripley. It was the Reverend William Emerson, thus, who over seventy years earlier had moved his family—the former Miss Phebe Bliss and their infant son, Billy—into the then-new home (its deed dated April 6, 1770) now occupied by Mr. and Mrs. Hawthorne.

William Emerson had come to Concord when he was twenty-one, in 1765, the year of the Stamp Act crisis. Already more than a century old at the time, Concord had been the first inland settlement in the English colonies, the first to be founded away from tidewater. At tidewater in Boston as long ago as 1635 a small group of Puritans had been given leave to start a plantation at a place that the Indians called Musketaquid, or Grassy Brook. Those early seventeenth-century settlers had accordingly lunged forth—Peter Bulkeley and Simon Willard with about twelve families—over torturous days hacking a path through the wilderness for their teams and their wives and children, in search of the spot a few miles inland on which to erect their future. From the Indians they had acquired, for hatchets, hoes, knives, and the like, "six myles of land square," which they had renamed Concord, to acknowledge the goodwill of the transaction and the Puritans' own continued unity of spirit. And despite severe initial hardships, those few early settlers had survived and prospered, their descendants living in concord through the seventeenth century and far into the century that followed. Thus the settlement appeared well named, undoubtedly so until the 1760s, until His Majesty's Parliament overseas saw fit to pass the Stamp Act in 1765, the year of young William Emerson's arrival as the new minister. Thereafter, from that fateful year forward for nearly two decades, the records of Concord are filled with defiance, breathing (in the words of a nineteenth-century student of them) "a resolute and warlike spirit, so bold from the first as hardly to admit of increase."

From the start, then, the Reverend Mr. Emerson's ministry had unfolded amid strife. The Stamp Act had been passed and was violently protested and repealed. The hated Townshend duties, the posting of British troops to Boston, the Massacre, the Tea Party, all accompanied the cleric's first decade in the village. By the autumn of 1774 an extralegal Provincial Congress had met in the Concord meetinghouse. There the Congress had elected John Hancock president. Parson Emerson as chaplain opened each session with prayer, and within those same walls were heard the voices of Otis, Cushing, Dr. Warren, and Samuel Adams. Having adopted measures for the colony's defense against English encroachments on its liberties, the Congress would meet here again the following spring, its activities and the town's provoking Governor Gage back in Boston to send forth spies to determine Concord's vulnerability to a military strike.

For, in addition to entertaining the Congress, citizens of this New England village had been mustering and drilling militia and accumulating military stores: bell tents, lead balls, field pieces. Concord was a shire town, its location central in the west country with good roads in and out. Besides, almost all of its citizens appeared vigorously opposed to the policies of His Majesty's government. Thus stern logic lay behind the role that the village was about to play in an imminent, world-shaking episode.

The action commenced in the morning of April 19, 1775, and of the many eyewitness accounts of happenings in Concord that day, the most accurate proves to have been the Reverend William Emerson's: "This Morning between 1 & 2 O'clock we were alarmed by the ringing of ye Bell, and upon Examination found that ye Troops, to ye No. of 800, had stole their March from Boston in Boats and Barges from ye Bottom of ye Common over to a Point in Cambridge, near to Inman's farm, & were at Lexington Meeting House, half an hour before Sunrise." A messenger had ridden out to warn the Concord Minutemen, who, with supporters from neighboring settlements, hastened to assemble above the North Bridge. At the bridge the first English blood would be spilled, as redcoats were fired on and fell, survivors fleeing in panic back to the clamorous

center of the village. Suddenly Britain's vaunted army was in retreat, following the road out of Concord under patriot fire for fifteen terrifying miles toward the distant safety of Charlestown, which
weary remnants of His Majesty's forces reached only as nighttime
was falling.

Thus this earliest inland village took its place in history. In
Hawthorne's time the old North Bridge had been washed away, but
its western abutment could be seen still; and near there, after a
protracted delay, a grateful progeny had at last erected, in 1836, a
monument to commemorate the historic clash: a shaft carved from
a granite boulder found within the original "six myles of land
square" that had been purchased two centuries earlier from the
Indians. On property that the Reverend Dr. Ezra Ripley had given
the town, the shaft was dedicated on July 4, 1837, in a ceremony
where Concord's leading citizen, Squire Samuel Hoar, delivered
a thrilling address that was said to awaken the true patriotic spirit,
and a choir sang to the tune of "Old Hundred" words that another
villager, the patriot Reverend William Emerson's grandson, had
written for the occasion:

> By the rude bridge that arched the flood,
>   Their flag to April's breeze unfurled;
> Here once the embattled farmers stood
>   And fired the shot heard round the world.

Five years later, Nathaniel Hawthorne in the Old Manse might
lift his eyes and gaze through his study window down upon that
plain granite obelisk at the river's edge.

Concord's Reverend William Emerson had exulted in the rousing
times that followed upon the skirmish at the bridge on the edge of
his village. In June 1775 the colonists fought bravely at Bunker Hill;
in early July General Washington reached Cambridge to take command of the Continental forces; and on the 11th, "Breakfast with
General Washington and General Lee at Headquarters this morning," Emerson wrote in his diary. "Tarried this week in the Army
as Chaplain." For this was a fighting parson, not inclined to linger
in the vestry when he could be out among his congregants leading,
inspiring. Thus, a year later, after the Congress in Philadelphia had

issued the Declaration of Independence, Emerson bade a hasty farewell to his family, leaving them behind in the Manse while he set out to serve as chaplain with colonial forces at Ticonderoga.

But Chaplain Emerson had hardly reached that outpost on Lake Champlain before he came down with a mongrel fever that soon forced him to seek release from his new duties. Reluctantly he was obliged to mount his horse once more, to retrace the long path across Vermont toward his distant home. He got as far as Rutland, five days after his discharge, and could go no farther. He was thirty-three years old. From the residence of the local minister, who had taken him in, Emerson wrote his wife a last time to tell her that he was on his way, although very uncertain of arriving. Thereafter for nearly a month he lingered moribund in a stranger's house before dying finally on a Sunday morning, October 20, 1776. Among Chaplain Emerson's last words were these, written to his wife:

"My dear, strive for Patience, let not a murmuring Thought, and sure not a murmuring Word drop from your Lips. Pray against Anxiety—don't distrust God's making Provision for You. He will take care of You and by Ways you could not think of."

How God provided for Phebe Emerson was through the agency of the new young pastor whom Concord called to succeed its departed minister. Young Ezra Ripley came to the village in 1778, two years after his predecessor's death, and two years later married the widow and moved into her house. Phebe Bliss Emerson became Phebe Bliss Emerson Ripley, the couple living out their years together in the Manse that was later to be the bridal home of Mr. and Mrs. Nathaniel Hawthorne.

It was Chaplain Emerson's grandson, the son of the Revolutionary parson's eldest child, Billy, who had urged the Hawthornes to settle in Concord. Billy had grown up to become another Reverend William Emerson, beginning his own ministry in the village of Harvard before being called, as the century turned, to the pastorate of Boston's First Church. There this second William Emerson served until his death in his early forties, in 1811. Ralph Waldo Emerson was two weeks shy of eight when his father died.

Waldo (as the young man chose to be called from his college years onward) had been born thus in Boston, like his four brothers, and like three of them he took a degree from Harvard College. After briefly teaching school, Waldo Emerson in his turn entered the ministry, in January 1829 becoming junior pastor at Boston's Second Church. But young Emerson grew uncomfortable in his clerical role. In September 1832, he preached a final sermon to his congregation and resigned from his pastorate. His adored young wife had died of tuberculosis a year and a half earlier, after less than eighteen months of marriage. In dismay, in poor health himself, shattered and adrift, Waldo Emerson on Christmas Day 1832 set sail for Europe.

The voyage cured him of his illness; and the travels that followed, through Italy, France, and England, lifted the young American's spirits as they introduced him to stimulating European company. In the fall of 1833, a rejuvenated Emerson embarked for home, and in the next year or two he would make a career of sorts lecturing in Boston on such topics as Water, and The Naturalist, and The Uses of Natural History.

Emerson's mother all this while had remained close to her departed husband's mother, Phebe Emerson Ripley, as well as to Dr. Ezra Ripley of Concord. In the autumn of 1834, that sociable village parson invited the widower Waldo and his mother, who had been living in various temporary homes in and around Boston, to reside with the Ripleys in Concord. Accordingly, in October the two moved in, remaining in the Manse as guests of Emerson's grandmother and stepgrandfather for most of a year. During the stay, in the same upstairs room that Hawthorne would later choose for his study, Emerson was to draft and refine *Nature,* a little book of some ninety pages containing the kernel of ideas that would mark their author as the most compelling American thinker of his age.

Before long, in 1835, Emerson would purchase a home in Concord, on the other side of the village from the Manse. Settled for good with his second wife, he proceeded to assemble around him a little society of like-minded friends as neighbors: poets, thinkers, conversationalists. Some came on their own, drawn by the growing fame of the author of *Nature;* others Emerson encouraged to come. As for the Hawthornes, although he hardly knew Mrs. Hawthorne's husband, he was well acquainted with the family of the bride; so that when Emerson's stepgrandfather died and the Ripley home was left standing empty, Miss Peabody and Mr. Hawthorne were urged to consider starting their married life there. The two rode out from Boston to Concord to look at the parsonage in the spring of 1842, and a couple of months later, on their wedding day, they moved in.

With that, Mr. Emerson lost no time in getting to know his new neighbors better.

3

AN END TO SOLITUDE

*T*he newlyweds were both natives of Salem, a town on the coast north of Boston and some twenty-five miles east of Concord. Nathaniel Hawthorne's father, a ship's captain, had died of fever in South America in 1808, when his only son and namesake was not yet four. The captain's death had left the family poorly provided for; so the Hathornes (as the name was spelled then) had moved in with maternal relatives in Salem: the Mannings, commercial people, operators of a stagecoach line. Nathaniel had been born on Independence Day 1804. His older sister, Elizabeth, or Ebe, was nearly six when her father died; his younger sister, Louisa, was three months old; and their mother, Betsey, was in her late twenties when she was widowed.

Hawthorne's fatherless childhood appears in most respects to have been unexceptional until age nine, when he injured his leg, as his older sister recalled, while playing bat-and-ball. Nathaniel stayed out of school for more than two years, during his prolonged convalescence developing a lifelong habit of reading. He would never become a bibliophile, never owned many books and seldom read systematically. But from that early age he did read continually, often whatever came to hand, and very widely, too, with Shakespeare, Spenser, Milton, Bunyan, and Scott as particular favorites.

His leg healed. In due time Hawthorne attended Bowdoin College, out on the frontiers of Maine. Back then, in 1821, the college was barely a quarter century old; but for all its newness, its curriculum was demanding. Exposed to such rigor for four years, young Hathorne graduated eighteenth in a class of thirty-eight. He had hardly been diligent, and in later life professed to regret the time he had wasted as a student. He had read what he wanted, done well at what he enjoyed—English, Latin—been regularly fined for various venial transgressions, and made some lifelong friends. Jonathan Cilley was one such. Horatio Bridge was another. Frank Pierce was a third. Those three would all leave Bowdoin after commencement and plunge into the practical business of earning a livelihood, swept up in a nation-building America that provided abundant space to exercise their considerable talents. All three friends studied law, Bridge ending by following a long career in the navy. The other two, Pierce and Cilley, stepped from the bar into politics.

As for the twenty-one-year-old Hawthorne, it was his "fortune or misfortune," as he later wrote, "to have some slender means of supporting myself; and so, on leaving college, in 1825, instead of immediately studying a profession, I sat myself down to consider what pursuit in life I was best fit for." A father's career on the quarterdeck or various uncles' in the countinghouse held no allure. "Oh that I was rich enough to live without a profession. What do you think"—he had posed the question earlier, at sixteen, to his mother—"of my becoming an Author, and relying for support upon my pen. Indeed I think the illegibility of my handwriting is very authorlike. How proud you would feel to see my works praised by the reviewers."

Yet wealth did not lie in the path of American literature in 1825. Such literature as existed then, in a predominantly commercial and agricultural society, was regarded as matter for idle moments. Moreover, much of the literature that did exist was still being copied from the English, either directly by means of pirated texts or through imitation. True, the age had already been subjected to considerable discussion about the desirability of cultivating a genuine native literature, something nonimitative and homegrown. Hawthorne— or Hathorne as he still was; he would change the spelling of his name soon after leaving college—had, in fact, been listening at his Bowdoin commencement, on September 25, 1825, to yet another contribution to the ongoing national debate. On that festive Sunday a member of the senior class, addressing the subject "Our Native Writers," had acknowledged the utilitarian society in which he and his fellow graduates were about to take their place. Yet the speaker discerned out there a love of the arts, if only just now emerging. What had delayed the progress of literature in America had been a lack of serious commitment to it. People bent over their plows and ledgers had no time to develop belles lettres. Even so, this New World was rich in literary materials, and in a bright future, the speaker predicted, such wealth would cause America to become "the land of song." Meanwhile, our citizenry must support its artists, and aspiring writers (the young orator being one such) must hold "a deep and thorough conviction of the glory of their calling—an utter abandonment of everything else—and a noble self-devotion to the cause of literature."

Did Hawthorne take such devotion with him home to Massachusetts? After commencement at Bowdoin he did go back to Salem and settled into a room under the eaves in the Manning household on Herbert Street, where his mother and sisters were living. "And year after year," he later attempted to explain in accounting for what happened then, "I kept on considering what I was fit for, and time and my destiny decided that I was to be the writer that I am."

Year after year turned into twelve—twelve long years after his graduation before the Salem recluse had a palpable success. The first book bearing Hawthorne's name appeared in the spring of 1837, whereupon the author made sure that *Twice-Told Tales* was sent to that senior orator at Bowdoin who had articulated a need for such contributions to a budding American literature. In the intervening years the speaker, Harry Longfellow, had gone on to become a fairly well known writer himself, the author of poems and a book of travel prose. "Dear Sir," the newly published Hawthorne wrote Longfellow from Salem on March 7, 1837: "The agent of the American Stationers Company will send you a copy of a book entitled 'Twice-told Tales'—of which, as a classmate, I venture to request your acceptance. We were not, it is true, so well acquainted at college, that I can plead an absolute right to inflict my 'twice-told' tediousness upon you; but I have often regretted that we were not better known to each other, and have been glad of your success in literature, and in more important matters."

Longfellow, who by then was professor of modern languages at Harvard, would accept his unexpected gift graciously and go on to praise the book in the influential *North American Review*.

Meanwhile, Hawthorne had written his acquaintance a second, quite remarkable letter, alluding to the strange life that he had been leading since their Bowdoin days. The second letter to Longfellow, of early June, refers to the "owl's nest" in which he had been living; for like an owl, Hawthorne wrote, "I seldom venture abroad till after dusk. By some witchcraft or other—for I really cannot assign any reasonable why and wherefore—I have been carried apart from the main current of life, and find it impossible to get back again." Since leaving college he had been secluding himself from society, "and yet I never meant any such thing, nor dreamed what sort of life I was going to lead. I have made a captive of myself, and put me into a dungeon; and now," Hawthorne confessed, "I cannot find the key to let myself out—and if the door were open, I should be almost afraid to come out."

Perhaps he was exaggerating his isolation during those twelve years after Bowdoin, the fiction writer overdramatizing. Yet in late life his sister Ebe confirmed that Hawthorne's postcollege period was different from what had preceded it. In old age she wrote that her brother had begun to withdraw into himself only after finishing college and returning to Salem, "when he felt as if he could not get away from there and yet was conscious of being utterly unlike every one else in the place."

According to a family source, a feeling of superiority was a curse besetting the Hawthornes, even though the Hathorne name that fed the family pride had long since declined from an earlier glory. Hathornes had lived in Salem from the very beginning, the earliest of them, William Hathorne, having settled there by 1636. That earliest Hathorne had risen to prominence as the sternest of magistrates, ordering Quakers to be soundly whipped for their heresies. His son John, another pillar of the community, had participated in Salem's notorious witchcraft trials late in the seventeenth century. But thereafter, such public spirit had eluded the Hathorne progeny, sea captains for the most part down to this present specimen, home from Bowdoin, neither mariner nor magistrate, proud, dreamy, and longing to be a writer.

In fact, both of those earliest, worthy forebears would likely have scorned this distant descendant. "No aim, that I have ever cherished, would they recognize as laudable," Hawthorne himself would observe in introducing the greatest of the novels that he would come to write. "'What is he?' murmurs one gray shadow of my forefathers to the other. 'A writer of story-books! What kind of a business in life,—what mode of glorifying God, or being serviceable to mankind in his day and generation,—may that be? Why, the degenerate fellow might as well have been a fiddler!' . . . And yet, let them scorn me as they will," the author insisted, "strong traits of their nature have intertwined themselves with mine."

Dedication would have been one such trait, and faith, and a deep moral sense, and commitment to a higher calling—in Hawthorne's case, to literature. The business of being a storyteller would require all of this author's time. When circumstances dictated that he do something else as well—work in a customhouse, say—the writing stopped. And Hawthorne must have faith, for through years and years the tangible rewards of storytelling would be meager. And the tales all that while came slowly, after much thought and musing and brooding. Stories, he would instruct an impatient editor, "grow like vegetables, and are not manufactured, like a pine table." Meanwhile, as he awaited such growth, the author would have appeared idle in that very busy age. He would have looked like a man sitting in a room, or walking along a beach, or reading. For Hawthorne did read extensively, and in depth on the Puritan world of his ancestors, but not with obvious industry, not to take notes or fill commonplace books. Instead, he read and absorbed and, as though idle, sat and brooded until the ideas and the stories came.

Surviving notebooks reveal some of what he was musing over during twelve years of isolation in his room in Herbert Street under the eaves. Among much else, Hawthorne was thinking about those who are different from others, alienated, tormented, have secrets, must confess. He brooded on cruelty, suffering, and guilt, on decay and death, on loneliness. "A recluse, like myself, or a prisoner, to measure time by the progress of sunshine through his chamber." "The various guises under which Ruin makes his approaches to his victims: to the merchant, in the guise of a merchant offering speculations; to the young heir, a jolly companion; to the maiden, a sighing, sentimentalist lover." "There is evil in every human heart, which may remain latent, perhaps, through the whole of life; but circumstances may rouse it to activity. To imagine such circumstances. A woman, tempted to be false to her husband, apparently through mere whim,—or a young man to feel an instinctive thirst for blood, and to commit murder." Hawthorne's early notebooks are filled with scores of such suggestive fancies, some startling, some profound, some no more consequential than a passing image ("A gush of violets along a wood-path"), many of them morbid. The morbidity would find its way into the author's published fiction almost as though against his will.

"You are, intellectually speaking, quite a puzzle to me," a friend wrote Hawthorne in later years. "How comes it that with so thoroughly healthy an organization as you have, you have such a taste for the morbid anatomy of the human heart, and such knowledge of it, too? I should fancy from your books that you were burdened with secret sorrow; that you had some blue chamber in your soul, into which you hardly dared to enter yourself; but when I see you, you give me the impression of a man as healthy as Adam was in Paradise." Hawthorne worried about that contradiction himself, and strove to let more sunshine into his writing. Yet it is precisely those dark gleams of insight, so troubling to Victorian gentility, that help account for the author's exalted literary standing these long years later, among us witnesses to horrors that antebellum America could scarcely have conceived of.

From whatever sources, and from such musings as his notebooks partially record, Hawthorne in seclusion wrote his earliest stories, anonymous tales including some of his most disturbing and provocative: "My Kinsman, Major Molineux," "Roger Malvin's Burial," "Young Goodman Brown," "Wakefield," "The Minister's Black Veil." "These stories were published," he noted later, "in Magazines and Annuals, extending over a period of ten or twelve years, and comprising the whole of the writer's young manhood, without making (so far as he has ever been aware) the slightest impression on the public." Amid such neglect Horatio Bridge in Maine had all the while been encouraging his sometimes despondent college friend. Bridge did more. He offered $250 to cover the risk if a publisher would undertake a collection of the writer's stories and sketches. On those secure terms Samuel Goodrich had been willing to move forward, with the result that *Twice-Told Tales* appeared in 1837. "Though not widely successful in their day and generation," Hawthorne would later recall, "they had the effect of making me known in my own immediate vicinity; insomuch that, however reluctantly, I was compelled to come out of my owl's nest and lionize in a small way. Thus I was gradually drawn somewhat into the world, and became pretty much like other people."

In the spring of 1837 Hawthorne's book had appeared, and in that same autumn the author was invited by a neighbor, Elizabeth Peabody, to pay a call on her Salem family. She would remember the call for the rest of her long life, as she treasured a subsequent occasion on a November evening when the handsome author returned. Elizabeth's youngest sister, Sophia, invalid in her room upstairs before, now emerged. "As I said 'My sister Sophia—Mr Hawthorne,' he rose and looked at her—he did not realize how intently, and afterwards, as we went on talking, she would interpose frequently a remark in her low sweet voice. Every time she did so, he looked at her with the same intentness of interest. I was struck with it, and painfully. I thought, what if he should fall in love with her; and I had heard her so often say, nothing would ever tempt her to marry, and inflict upon a husband the care of such a sufferer."

Already strongly attracted to the handsome gentleman herself, Elizabeth may have felt pain as much for her own sake as for her youngest sister's. And yet it does seem extraordinary that one random evening an invalid, twenty-eight at the time and resigned to spinsterhood, should have entered her parlor to discover an eligible, Apollo-like neighbor whose existence had been previously unsuspected. Scarcely less amazing is it that the private, discriminating Hawthorne should have ventured forth in Salem to find five blocks away a cultivated and loving spirit living all the while apparently "in the shadow of a seclusion," he wrote Sophia later, "as deep as my own had been."

In a modest way the visitor's career had been prospering over the few months since he had emerged from his Herbert Street chamber. Cilley down in Washington had been talking him up to an editor friend, so that Hawthorne had heard last April from John Louis O'Sullivan, of the *United States Magazine and Democratic Review,* expressing interest in receiving contributions from him for generous payments. Cilley, meanwhile, was doing more than mentioning Hawthorne to editors. He was looking around for a political appointment for his friend that would provide an income with free time to continue writing. But a fateful duel intervened before Jonathan Cilley was able to find a government post for his college mate. It was left then to Elizabeth Peabody, equally determined to help, to inveigle from the collector of the port back in Massachusetts a position for Hawthorne in the Boston customhouse. Thus in 1839 the author was set to work earning a livelihood from the city wharves, measuring cargoes of coal and salt. Bound to those labors, he would find neither time nor inclination to write more tales. What Hawthorne did write in the years after meeting Elizabeth's youngest sister were love letters. Over a hundred of them have survived.

The earliest of Hawthorne's letters to Sophia Peabody dates from March 6, 1839. In it he assures his Sophie that her words are providing spiritual food to nourish him on the squalid docks of Boston. Hawthorne's spirituality is not to be taken as opposed to materialism—matter versus spirit—but rather as meaning *beyond* matter, as an intensification and heightened consciousness of what behind the changing surfaces of life is real. "All the world hereabouts," he would write, "seems dull and drowsy—a vision, but without any spirituality—and I, likewise an unspiritual shadow, struggle vainly to catch hold of something real. Thou art my reality, and nothing else is real for me, unless thou give it that golden quality by thy touch." Matter without spirit is a corpse, a body without life. The spiritual life reaches *through* matter, through evanescent appearances to the reality behind, beneath, beyond: matter made instinct with spirit—brought to life. So the spirituality that Hawthorne found with his Sophia in no way denied the sexual. "Dearest," he wrote in October 1839, their marriage still three years off, "it will be a yet untasted bliss, when, for the first time, I have you in a domicile of my own, whether it be in a hut or a palace, a splendid suite of rooms or an attic chamber. Then I shall feel as if I had brought my wife home at last. Oh, beloved, if you were here now, I do not think I could possibly let you go till morning—my arms should imprison you—I would not be content, unless you nestled into my very heart."

His beloved was Hawthorne's peace and happiness. She had waked him from a dream into reality. She was his Dove, his holy spirit who had fashioned light out of darkness. "Indeed, we are but shadows," he told her; "we are not endowed with real life, and all that seems most real about us is but the thinnest substance of a dream—till the heart is touched. That touch creates us . . . thereby we are beings of reality, and inheritors of eternity. Now, dearest, dost thou comprehend what thou hast done for me?"

The lovers may have become secretly engaged as early as January 1839, although they were not married until three and a half years later. Much stood in the way of an impoverished storyteller's alliance with an impoverished invalid. But at last from West Street in Boston Sophia was writing ecstatically to a Salem friend in her final days unmarried: "Mr. Hawthorne has been here, looking like the angel of the Apocalypse, so powerful and gentle. It seems as if I were realizing the dreams of the poets in my own person." By that time Emerson had offered the couple his late stepgrandfather's empty residence, which they had resolved to rent. "The agent of Heaven in this Concord plan," Sophia explained to her friend Mary Foote, "was Elizabeth Hoar, a fit minister on such an errand, for minister means angel of God. Her interest has been very great in every detail."

Four days later, on Saturday, July 9, 1842, the Concord plan came to fruition. Nathaniel Hawthorne and Sophia Peabody were joined in wedlock and rode off from Boston to spend their first night together, in the Old Manse that Elizabeth Hoar had filled with flowers.

4

CONCORD IN THE FORTIES

Sophia Peabody had been born in September 1809, five years after and in the same town as her future husband. As an infant she had suffered from teething, for which her father, a dentist, had prescribed a then-fashionable treatment involving mercury, with consequences that appeared to spread through the rest of her life. A major symptom of Sophia's drawn-out invalidism was a crushing headache, capable of being provoked by any sudden noise, however slight. The fall of a fork on a plate, as likely as the boisterous presence of her brothers in the house, could send her to her room to lie abed and eat her white diet of bread and meat and milk. Yet, remarkably, such recurrent struggles with ill health failed to make the girl querulous or self-pitying. On the contrary, Sophia's spirits, as revealed in a vast surviving correspondence of over fifteen hundred letters, seem to have been unquenchably optimistic. Her days as a young person, as all through her later life, were filled with activity and enthusiasm and a steadfast faith.

At ten, she began a rigid system of education under the guidance of her gifted eldest sister, Elizabeth. Sophia learned her lessons well. She grew into a woman of real cultivation, able to read Latin, French, Greek, Hebrew, and some German. In addition, she was more than respectably conversant with geography, science, literature, and history both American and European, besides being an accomplished artist, one whom no less a judge than Washington Allston saw fit to encourage. And she developed into a force. "I never knew," Elizabeth Peabody wrote long after her sister's death, "any human creature who had more sovereign power over everybody—grown and child—that came into her sweet and gracious presence." Not that she was physically prepossessing. Sophia was small of stature—Hawthorne's "little wife"—and hardly beautiful, although beautifully formed, according to one who saw her often. "In person she was small, graceful, active, and beautifully formed. Her face," that expert witness testifies, "was so alive and translucent with lovely expressions that it was hard to determine whether or not it were physically lovely; but I incline to think that a mathematical survey"—a son's voice trying for objectivity—"would have pronounced her features plain; only, no mathematical survey," Julian Hawthorne insists, "could have taken cognizance of her smile."

No more can a surviving engraving or a blurred daguerreotype take cognizance of Sophia's smile. How would it have been to hear her laugh, see her come into a room, watch those lovely expressions play across her face? We can only strive to imagine the source of the pronounced effect that this often ailing little woman had on her family, her husband, her sister Elizabeth, who at another time assured Hawthorne's son grown to adulthood, as Elizabeth herself had grown elderly, that his mother, long dead by then, was the rarest specimen of woman she had ever known.

Sophia began her married life at the edge of a nineteenth-century New England village that was in many ways typical. Not long after their moving to the Manse, her husband was gazing down on that typicality from the bare hill opposite their new home. "The scenery of Concord, as I beheld it from the summit of the hill, has no very marked characteristics," he would note next morning, "but has a great deal of quiet beauty." From up there, what the observer had seen in toy-sized dimensions off at a distance were the spire of yet another New England meetinghouse, rooftops of clapboard homes, a tavern or two, storefronts lining a main street that led to a grassy square surrounded by hotel and jail and graveyard. In the approaching dusk those various generic structures could be seen clustered amid outlying far-stretching farms; for even as late as the early 1840s, such farmland would have largely sustained this and every other village in New England.

Concord, like America itself, remained primarily agricultural; the stores along the Milldam—the commercial part of Concord's main street—were established principally to serve farmers of the vicinity. Concord days, moreover, would still have moved at the more leisurely pace of farmers' time, seasonal activities unfolding with agricultural self-containment, autonomously, more or less independent of the bustling commercial port of Boston three or four hours off to the east. Concord had its own newspaper, for instance—had supported two of them, in fact, one Whig, one Democratic, as late as 1840, in an age when politics invigorated conversations the way professional sports may serve to enliven ours. After 1840 there was the one, the *Concord Freeman,* a four-page weekly that provided abundant agricultural news about such matters as cattle fairs, prices current, and plows and pigs for sale.

Moreover, Concord provided its citizens with a public bathing house, an ornamental tree society, a lyceum where speakers regularly entertained and enlightened the assembled village folk, and an Atheneum, its reading room opening this very month of August 1842. The village boasted a volunteer engine company and a chapter of the Royal Arch Masons. The Female Charitable Society had been doing good work here since 1814. There was a Musical Society, and in a reform-minded age a Temperance Society, a Colonization Society, an Anti-Slavery Society, and Bible and Missionary societies as well. There were three churches in the village, including one to accommodate a Trinitarian congregation that earlier had rebelled against Dr. Ripley's rather too liberal views, as well as the late Dr. Ripley's own church, now in the hands of his less colorful successor. Affiliated with the churches were lodges, clubs, orders, and associations of various aims and high-minded purposes.

Those communal enterprises—along with village balls and suppers and sociables—would have attracted Hawthorne on his hilltop hardly at all. Cherishing his solitude, the author was far more comfortable at the edge of Concord, as now at sunset on a Saturday in summer, standing alone gazing from a height down on the town in its pastoral setting and on the little river flowing beside the Manse—"one of the loveliest features in a scene of great rural beauty"—two or three reflecting miles of river visible over the landscape, "like a strip of sky set into the earth."

In another way the agricultural village lying beside that river was typical. As with other New England settlements of the time,

Concord's people were homogeneous, Anglo-Saxons whose ancestors derived from no more than three or four English counties.
Seven years before the Hawthornes' arrival, one villager had found
occasion to advert to so stunning a demographic: "the agricultural
life favors the permanence of families. Here," the orator of the day
during Concord's elaborate bicentennial festivities had noted, "are
still around me the lineal descendants of the first settlers of this
town. Here is Blood, Flint, Willard, Meriam, Wood, Hosmer . . .
the names of the inhabitants for the first thirty years"—that is,
people recognized in the audience whose ancestors had lived in
these parts as long ago as the 1650s. Two centuries later the present
population of some two thousand remained stable and undiluted.
To be sure, in recent times "the growth of Concord has been slow,"
as the bicentennial speaker, young Ralph Waldo Emerson, had
acknowledged. "Without navigable waters, without mineral riches,
without any considerable mill privileges, the natural increase of her
population is drained by the constant emigration of the youth. Her
sons have settled the region around us, and far from us. Their
wagons have rattled down the remote western hills. And in every
part of this country, and in many foreign parts, they plough the
earth, they traverse the sea, they engage in trade, and in all the
professions."

But that meant that Concord's influence was spreading; towns
in states to the south and west were even taking its name. Indeed,
for all its typicalness, the village was distinctive. One source of
distinction would have been visible these seven years later from the
hilltop where, in gathering dusk, Hawthorne stood gazing. Down
at the village the wooden courthouse rose alongside the green, its
high lantern tower reaching seventy-five feet into the air. Accordingly, in Concord were residing attorneys of note who practiced
before those courts, Squire Samuel Hoar chief among them; and
on court days such luminaries as Rufus Choate and Daniel Webster
would stroll these streets, with food and drink stalls erected around
the green and the gathered crowds filling taverns and gossiping and
gambling and racing horses and arguing politics, as the Middlesex
Hotel opposite the courthouse did a fine business.

The village was distinctive, thus, as a county seat, long having
been both a trading center and the place where people from the
county's farthest precincts brought their grievances to be heard and

settled at law. That distinction, in fact, which dated back to the late seventeenth century, had bestowed on Concord a uniqueness—an attribute that had made this first inland town in English-speaking America different from any other community in the Union. For the central location and good roads in and out that such a village required in order for its courts to function had brought on a pivotal action to which the settlement had responded at the start of the Revolution. Just there, down by the Manse at the river's edge, alongside a colonial bridge since washed away, had occurred the skirmish between redcoats and minutemen that set off a cataclysm creating nothing less than a new kind of nation.

Thus in proud Concord as late as its bicentennial, seven years ago on a morning in early autumn, Ralph Waldo Emerson as orator of the day had been saluting the last human remnants of the fight, ten men now in their decrepitude seated in the front row of the meetinghouse. "The benignant Providence which has prolonged their lives to this hour," the orator Emerson was remarking over the aged heads, "gratifies the strong curiosity of the new generation. The Pilgrims are gone; but we see what manner of persons they were who stood in the worst perils of the Revolution. We hold by the hand the last of the invincible men of old." And for townspeople honoring them, the war in which those old men had fought remained far more vivid than it does for us. For them the heroes of the Revolution—before a civil war had intervened to create and photograph a different set of heroes—still shone in brightest glory, the presence of such as Washington, Franklin, and the Adamses hovering unclouded from scarcely more than a generation in the past.

Concord's additional distinction, of course—what made it unique—was that Nathaniel Hawthorne, a resident these seven years later, was standing on a hilltop looking down at a village where lived Henry Thoreau, currently residing at the home (the substantial clapboard house off to the left) of that same Ralph Waldo Emerson whose presence had attracted others of note to come and live here. The Alcotts were one such family, although at the moment Bronson Alcott was away in England visiting admirers. Lesser talents had been drawn to Concord as well. The poet Ellery Channing, for instance, back East from Cincinnati this past month—July 1842—had knocked at Mr. Emerson's door and would soon be settling with his new wife in the village. So that here in the mid-nineteenth century, what with its autonomy, its rural beauty, its glorious history, and the distinctiveness of its humanity, typical Concord in its uniqueness may have come as near to approximating Utopia on earth as any community in America before or since.

Yet Utopia, flawless from on high, down close has its blemishes. One native would later sourly recall of these same early 1840s, when he had been attending school in the village, that Concord's people (quietly desperate, according to yet another source) "were ignorant, low lived, unambitious save in the money making line, and many large estates were squandered by farmers who neglected their farms, and lounged in the Tavern bar rooms week in and week out." In any case, the agricultural life pursued in New England so long was even then changing. A mill to the west of the village was one sign of such change, as other, massive textile mills furnished far more substantial signs nearby. Nathan Appleton, Boston merchant and now an immensely wealthy industrialist in his mansion on Beacon Hill, was representative of a new breed of American whose initiative was helping to alter the face of rural Massachusetts. In part through Appleton's enterprise, the sleepy village of Waltham had recently been turned into a vast mill complex; and not far off, in what had been no more than an empty field some twenty-five years ago, had arisen all at once another huge mill city, with a population already ten times the size of little Concord.

Those mills at Lowell and Waltham, with their new kind of labor for wages, were transforming America. And still another vast change was on the way. In the issue of the *Concord Freeman* for Friday, July 8, 1842, on the very eve of the Hawthornes' wedding day, had appeared a notice concerning a meeting of the Fitchburg Railroad Company to be held at the Middlesex Hotel in Concord on Wednesday, July 13, at ten in the morning, "to elect directors and other officers and agents of the Company, to adopt by-laws, and transact such other business as may properly come before the meeting." And on the following Friday, with new residents at the Manse settling in, the village newspaper had reported that the meeting to organize the railroad had taken place as scheduled and was well attended. "The Hon. Samuel Hoar of this town presided. . . . Much unanimity of feeling prevailed and all present exhibited a well-tempered zeal in the enterprise which promises well for its success."

So that other momentous change was approaching on its rails, even as Hawthorne a month later, at the end of his interlude on a hilltop at sunset, was starting back down to the Manse. All the while his mind had been elsewhere than on mills and railroads. "May the powers of the upper regions always keep guard over my heart's treasure, whether I am at her side, or afar off!" he would write the next morning. And in the same journal entry, the author reflected on the day just ended: "How sweet it was to draw near my own home, after having lived so long homeless in the world; for no man can know what home is, until, as he approaches it, he feels that a wife will meet him at the threshold. With thoughts like these, I descended the hill, and clambered over the stone-wall, and crossed the road, and passed up our avenue; while the quaint old house put on an aspect of welcome."

5

VISITORS AT THE MANSE

Back in Boston, Sophia's mother had been behaving well through these recent days, considering that she and her youngest daughter had been close for thirty years, considering, too, "how fully we shared each other's thoughts, how soothing in every trial was your bright smile and ready sympathy." After the wedding, with so cherished a companion gone off to Concord, Mrs. Peabody dwelt on a blessing that lightened the burden of her loss. "When I gave you up, my sweetest confidante, my ever lovely and cheering companion," she wrote Sophia just days after the wedding, "I set myself aside and thought only of the repose, the fulness of bliss, that awaited you under the protection and in the possession of the confiding love of so rare a being as Nathaniel Hawthorne."

Of Hawthorne's rarity there can be no doubt—as a literary genius, of course, but also as a person. Most obviously, the man was extraordinarily good-looking; all who knew him agreed on what surviving likenesses confirm. An inch or two under six feet, he was of athletic build and slender at 150 pounds. His voice, which was low, had melody in it, and his dark blue eyes were brilliant and remarkably expressive. "Bayard Taylor used to say that they were the only eyes he had ever known flash fire. Charles Reade, in a letter written in 1876, declared that he had never before seen such eyes as Hawthorne's, in a human head." Others commented to the same effect. To Richard Henry Stoddard, those lightning-like eyes were "unfathomable as night"; Julia Ward Howe called them tumultuous sapphires; Frederika Bremer pronounced them wonderful: "they give, but receive not"; and Elizabeth Peabody corroborated that

Hawthorne's were "wonderful eyes, like mountain lakes seeming to reflect the heavens."

If his physical presence, which included such a sharp bright gaze, was altogether distinctive in its attractiveness, Hawthorne's manner was likewise singular. He was exceptionally reserved, and everyone who knew him remarked on that, too. With a friend alone he might unburden himself conversationally, but in social groups he tended to fall silent. Because the eyes would glow over his beautiful smile, people in his presence often felt charmed to be addressing so focused a listener; he listened "devouringly," as Elizabeth Peabody affirmed. Yet with strangers and half acquaintances the listener declined to do much more than mutely hear their chatter— and thus, knowing his own propensities, would rather stay home than venture out calling. Nor did marriage increase his sociability. During all the time that he and Sophia lived at the Manse on the edge of Concord, "he was not seen," wrote George William Curtis, "probably, by more than a dozen of the villagers," despite regular walks to the post office—although invariably through woods coming and going, not along the public road. The truth was, as Hawthorne admitted: except for Sophia's companionship he was content to be by himself. "I think," he explained to her, "I was always more at ease alone than in any body's company, till I knew thee."

Mary Peabody, Sophia's other sister, was sure that something had to be done about such shyness; Mr. Hawthorne must be forced into visiting, to practice the social graces. She said as much to his wife not once but several times. Sophia finally protested, with barely concealed annoyance. "Of what moment will it be a thousand years hence whether he saw this or that person?" she demanded to know. "Whereas, it is of great account that he should not be constantly disturbed by the presentment of this question. If he had the gift of speech like some others, Mr Emerson & Wm Greene, for instance, it would be different, but he evidently was not born for mixing in general society. His vocation is to observe & not to be observed."

Yet even with that rebuke, Mary would not let the matter drop. She went on harping on her brother-in-law's reclusiveness, his avoidance of public gatherings. By the fall of 1843 Hawthorne's wife had had enough. About this issue of visiting, she wrote her mother, Mary was simply wrong. Mr. Hawthorne could most certainly make himself approach other persons. "But why should he? Why, in the name of common sense & reason should he? Are not there enough persons to pass their days or a portion of them in social intercourse with men & women? Does it not take all sorts of people to make a world—? & why should not each one fulfill his calling? He has not the gift of tongues—he is not a talker like Mr Emerson—He was not born to chat nor converse. Words with him are not 'airy nothings.' . . . Words with him are worlds—suns & systems—& cannot move easily & rapidly—."

Besides, her husband did treat friends graciously, his and hers both, when they visited as guests in Concord. Indeed, although Hawthorne maintained that weeks and weeks would pass in their pastoral setting with him and his wife seeing no one but each other and the maid, we in this later, perhaps less communal America are struck by the number of visitors during their three years at the Manse who did come calling and stayed awhile. His very first full day there, for instance, Sunday, July 10, 1842, Hawthorne had written his sister Louisa to tell her of the wedding: that he and his bride had died yesterday and gone straight to paradise, "as happy as people can be, without making themselves ridiculous." To so cheery a greeting, the groom had appended an invitation: "We intend that you shall be our first guest (unless there should be a chance visitor) and shall beseech the honour and felicity of your presence, sometime in August. New married people, I believe, are not considered fit to be seen, in less time than several weeks."

That hardly sounds like the voice of the glum recluse that Mary Peabody's strictures might have prepared us to hear, all the less so when we learn that as early as the following day, chance visitors did feel comfortable enough to intrude upon this hermit's solitude and found a welcome. Three gentlemen from eastward rode up to the Manse on horseback, one of them a friend of the groom and bride's from Boston, checking on how the newlyweds were settling in. To be sure, the horsemen lingered only a few minutes before riding off toward a distant sightseeing goal in upstate New York. But far from resenting the interruption, Hawthorne himself sat down to write one of the trio early the following month, on August 2:

"Dear Hillard, Concluding that you have by this time returned from your tour, I write to request that Mrs. Hillard and yourself will spend either the coming Sunday, or the next afterwards, at our house." Hawthorne's sister would be a houseguest soon, so "unless you come before her visit, we could not give you a night's lodging until the beginning of September. Pray do not put it off so long; for we are very desirous of seeing you both." The invitation, with nothing perfunctory about it, would appear warm enough to have suited even Mary Peabody's orthodox tastes. The truth is that, despite a lifelong aversion to meeting the demands of social life, Hawthorne was fully capable of cordiality at times and with people of his own choosing.

The George Hillards did make their visit to the Manse, staying two nights, arriving from Boston at twilight Saturday evening, August 13, to spend Sunday in the country. "It was a pleasant sensation," their host noted at its end in recalling the start of so agreeable an interlude, "when the coach rumbled up our avenue, and wheeled round at the door; for then I felt that I was regarded as a man with a wife and a household—a man having a tangible existence and locality in the world—when friends came to avail themselves of our hospitality." At the front door the hosts had welcomed their guests and shown them into the parlor "and soon into the supper-room— and afterwards, in due season, to bed. Then came my dear little wife to her husband's bosom."

This George Hillard, asleep in the room upstairs across the hall, had been Hawthorne's landlord in Boston two or three years earlier, while the bachelor, as he then was, was weighing and gauging for the customhouse. A graduate of Harvard, Hillard had set up a law practice in Boston with young Charles Sumner in 1834. Hawthorne probably met him and Sumner through Elizabeth Peabody, the two attorneys having boarded at the widow Clarke's rooming house in Boston where Elizabeth and her sister Mary, both schoolteachers, were staying. By 1840 Hillard had become Hawthorne's legal adviser. In addition he was a lecturer, reviewer, occasional poet, and recently (only a little more than seven months before this present visit to the Manse) the most warmly received of the various distinguished speakers who had welcomed to America young Charles Dickens at a dinner that a couple of hundred Bostonians had attended in the Englishman's honor at Papanti's Hall on February 1, 1842.

So resounding an accomplishment—Hillard's was the outstanding speech among many on that gala occasion—had been the more striking because of the orator's high-pitched voice and pallid diminutiveness. Yet for all his success as a speaker, writer, lawyer, and friend, George Hillard appeared to be hardly a happy man. He had married in 1835, and a year later the couple had had a child, who died before age three. There would be no more children, and the marriage that had begun with the usual hopes was even now, at the Manse, unraveling into the private discontents that would characterize its later years. A childless, unhappy marriage would taint Hillard's personal life; and as for his professional occupations, literature he valued more than law, so that the legal practice suffered. But all of his own writing—the essays, travel pieces, sketches and speeches and poems—however much others might heap praise on them, failed to satisfy him, leaving him feeling unworthy in the end. A "melancholy shadow of a man" Hawthorne would judge him within a year or two, a man constantly in need of outward triumphs to assuage the inner sense of disappointment—but judged him thus regretfully, for Hawthorne's friendship for Hillard never wavered, any more than did his gratitude for substantial personal kindnesses that lay ahead.

The Sunday morning at the Manse to which this guest of melancholy temperament awakened, a cooling marriage lying beside him, proved to be gray and gloomy; but breakfast downstairs turned out jolly enough. Hawthorne felt sure it was Sophia's sunniness that, despite the weather, made the morning bright and warm. At about nine o'clock, host and friend set out to walk to Walden Pond, stopping by the way at Mr. Emerson's for directions. Emerson lived a couple of miles off, his home (still standing, and visitable) on the northeast edge of the village as the Manse stands on the northwest. Having reached the philosopher's door, the callers were greeted warmly and invited inside. Would Mr. Emerson be good enough to tell them how to get to Walden Pond? But he would do better than that, if they would only wait a few minutes. And to Hawthorne's amusement the host kept his guests indoors for the sake of appearances, "detained . . . till after the people had got into church" from the Sunday streets outside. Only then, and the coast clear, could they venture forth, Hawthorne, Hillard, and Emerson, the last-named "in his own illustrious person" having determined to accompany his visitors on their outing.

Along the way to the pond, two miles off—Walden is what none but New Englanders would call a pond, three-fourths of a mile long and 150 feet deep—the strollers fed on enormous blackberries gathered from beside the path; and with Emerson guiding them, they came in good time through the woods and down to a pebbly beach at the water's edge.

It was beautiful. It looked like "a piece of blue firmament, earthencircled." At the shore the three wayfarers lingered briefly; then Emerson withdrew to return to town. For Hawthorne, at least, left there with Hillard, the trip had proved well worth the effort, even this narrow strand on which they were standing worth a much longer stroll to gaze upon, so different from the weed-filled, oozy edges of the river behind the Manse. In their solitude, with the woods at their back and all around them, the two friends took time to bathe in the pond; "and it does really seem," thought Hawthorne in retrospect, "as if not only my corporeal person, but my moral self, had received a cleansing from that bath. A good deal of mud and river-slime had accumulated on my soul; but those bright waters washed it all away."

Despite overcast weather the outing had been a success, and from its bracing effects the bathers returned to the Manse in time for Sunday dinner. Of the dinner Hawthorne allowed himself to pronounce complacently that he and Sophia had proved the most accomplished of hosts, roles that they were performing for the first time in their own home as husband and wife. Next, the four friends took a siesta. A shower fell during the afternoon, but late in the day the rain ended, allowing all but Sophia to set forth on an expedition to gather trailing clematis, then in blossom. Upon returning home laden with flowers, they discovered Hawthorne's wife entertaining more callers; Elizabeth Hoar had stopped by with her sister and brother-in-law, visiting from Boston. Shortly those three took their leave, and the Hillards and Hawthornes sat up until after ten telling ghost stories, including accounts of the Old Manse itself, of those strange noises in the kitchen that Sophia had heard, and of thumpings and poundings that may have been an old cleric overhead returned to write ghostly sermons from beyond the grave.

Another night's sleep in the upstairs front rooms; and next morning early, at seven o'clock, "our friends left us"—this very Monday morning—"and, at this present moment, being I know not what hour in the forenoon, my little wife is, or ought to be, sleeping off the fatigues of her hospitality. We were both pleased with the visit; and so, I think, were our guests." Pleased enough that on the same day Hawthorne was renewing entreaties that his younger sister—Hillard's age, thirty-four—come stay awhile. "The stage for Concord," he wrote Louisa, "leaves Earle's Coffee house, Hanover-street, every day at four Oclock. There is likewise one which goes early in the morning and another at ten Oclock."

By such means the more amiable of Hawthorne's two shy maiden sisters was persuaded to venture from Salem and visit the Manse.

6

MARGARET FULLER AND HENRY THOREAU

She was due to arrive on August 20 to remain twelve days. And on the same Saturday when Louisa was expected, Margaret Fuller came calling. Miss Fuller was a houseguest at the Emersons' across the village, but there were tensions in the philosopher's home and desk work that his guest had been struggling with; so it was good to get out and away, pleasant, as Fuller herself recorded, to be strolling down the alley of whispering poplars before Hawthorne's Manse—"and everywhere the view is so peaceful."

Peaceful without, if momentarily agitated within. Miss Fuller's unexpected footstep beyond the front door interrupted the newlyweds embracing in their hallway. At the sound, Mr. and Mrs. Hawthorne sprang apart and collected themselves to receive their caller. They were, in fact, delighted to see Margaret Fuller. "'She came in so beautifully,' as Mr. Hawthorne truly said, and he looked full of gleaming welcome," Sophia recorded. The hosts guided their friend to the easiest chair and took her shawl and bonnet and the book she was carrying and prevailed upon her to stay for tea. Margaret "returned the favor by distilling into our ears Sydnean showers of discourse—She was like the moon, radiant & gentle."

The age relished eloquence, whether issuing from lyceum lectures, Websterian oratory, or the parlor talk of practitioners such as Bronson Alcott, whom Emerson would summon as the "prince of conversers" to compensate for what he saw as his own social shortcomings. But if Alcott was the prince, surely Margaret Fuller was the princess of conversationalists. She was brilliant; yet for all her vast learning, Fuller had, as Emerson noted, "an incredible variety of anecdotes, and the readiest wit to give an absurd turn to whatever passed; and the eyes"—it was also conceded that the brilliant, florid Fuller was hardly beautiful—the half-closed, near-sighted eyes, "which were so plain at first, soon swam with fun and drolleries, and the very tides of joy and superabundant life."

Born in May 1810 (and thus eight months younger than Sophia), Margaret Fuller had been reared in Cambridgeport across from Boston, the eldest child of a father who had wanted a brilliant son. The less brilliant sons did follow, but meanwhile the father set to work molding his firstborn; and he did a thorough job of it. Margaret would fill her days, in Cambridgeport and later when the family retired to a farm in Groton, with domestic chores of dress- and bread- and soapmaking, of tending her sick mother and grandmother during her father's frequent absences as a legislator in Washington, of taking care of and diligently instructing her younger brothers and sister, all the while pressing forward with an arduous, paternally guided regimen of self-education.

Study made the autodidact prone to headaches (and surely her friend Sophia Hawthorne would sympathize), as well as to mood swings, nightmares, nosebleeds, and bouts of depression. Yet despite vexatious ailments, Fuller acquired and retained knowledge phenomenally. When her father died, in 1835, Margaret became the family provider. For a while she taught school in Providence, but by the late 1830s she had forsaken teaching to edit the *Dial*, the influential little magazine inspired by Emerson and his circle of poets and thinkers. That demanding work paid her nothing, so to earn a livelihood she conducted for a fee (often in the parlor at 13 West Street, where the Hawthornes would wed) discussions on cultural subjects to enlighten intelligent women whom a patriarchal age denied more formal opportunities for group education. Those celebrated "Conversations," some of which Sophia Peabody attended, were given from 1839 and beyond into the winter of 1844.

Thus Margaret Fuller was already widely known as an intellectual when she came calling in August 1842 at the Manse. Her hostess gave her tea, listened rapturously to her talk, then showed her the rooms upstairs. ("The house within I like," the visitor noted in her journal; "all their things are so expressive of themselves and mix in so gracefully with the old furniture.") "She admired all the house," wrote Sophia delightedly, "& then we returned to the hall & sat & saw the moon rise while she sung of little Waldo, till the dampness sent us back to the parlor."

Little Waldo was Emerson's beloved child, five years old, recently dead of scarlet fever. At the Manse Margaret Fuller reminisced about this favorite little boy, until dampness drove her and Sophia into the warmth of a stove-heated room. The Hawthornes had their guest lie down and rest on the parlor couch; and before long from outside was heard the approach of coach wheels along the avenue, announcing the arrival of Louisa Hawthorne, come to pay her promised visit. Miss Fuller rose to leave. "My husband went home with dear Margaret, while I," wrote Sophia soon after, "welcomed & gave tea to Louisa."

One more of Margaret Fuller's traits was often remarked upon. Not only was this rather plain woman an astonishing intellect and a superb conversationalist; she also had an uncanny ability to inspire trust in those with whom she spoke. As James Freeman Clarke put it, the woman "possessed, in a greater degree than any person I ever knew, the power of so magnetizing others, when she wished, by the power of her mind, that they would lay open to her all the secrets of their nature." Even the taciturn Nathaniel Hawthorne would speak freely to Margaret and about intimate feelings, as on this present walk through summer darkness. "We stopped some time to look at the moon," Fuller recorded. "H said he should be much more willing to die than two months ago, for he had had some real possession in life, but still he never wished to leave this earth: it was beautiful enough. He expressed, as he always does, many fine perceptions. I like to hear the lightest thing he says."

The next day presented the two with an occasion for resuming their talk. Margaret had left her book behind at the Manse, so her host would return it to her. This was on Sunday, Sarah the Irish maid off at Mass in Waltham. In her absence, Sophia for the first time in her married life was preparing midday dinner, of cold meat, boiled corn and squash from the garden, rice in milk, and baked apples from their orchard. Afterward, Hawthorne left his wife and sister resting and set out with Margaret Fuller's book for Emerson's place.

He delivered the book and started for home, his route passing through the woods of Sleepy Hollow. There, to his surprise, he chanced upon Margaret herself, retired to read and meditate in solitude. Joining her, Hawthorne lingered to talk with his friend once more, "about Autumn," she reclining on the grass, he seated beside her, "and about the pleasures of getting lost in the woods . . . and about other matters of high and low philosophy." Freely they chatted together until a rustling among the trees interrupted them, and a voice called out Fuller's name. Emerson emerged, having stumbled in his own rambles upon this secluded spot. "It being now nearly six o'clock, we separated, Mr. Emerson and Margaret towards his house"—and her red room in it, and her inkhorn, and the sixty-page article that she had been writing for the *Dial* on Romaic and Rhine ballads—"and I towards mine," where Sophia was entertaining Hawthorne's sister with tea and a walk to the top of the little hill opposite, to watch the sun set and a full moon rise.

Hawthorne would end this particular Sunday with his customary bath, in "the most beautiful moonlight that ever hallowed this earthly world." That night the river behind the Manse appeared as calm as death, and when the bather entered it, "it seemed like plunging down into the sky. But I had rather be on earth," he wrote, "than even in the seventh Heaven, just now." As for Margaret Fuller, she had not been able to write about those recent hours at all. "What a happy, happy day" was as much as she could manage; "all clear light. I cannot write about it."

Ten days later, at the end of August, another visitor arrived at the Manse from Emerson's direction, this time for dinner. Just turned twenty-five, he was a handyman living at the Emerson home and paying for the privilege by doing such odd jobs as last spring digging and planting the vegetable garden now flourishing beyond the Manse's front windows. "Mr. Thorow dined with us yesterday," Hawthorne noted on the morrow. "He is a singular character—a young man with much of wild original nature still remaining in him: and so far as he is sophisticated, it is in a way and method of his own."

The dinner, with Sophia and the visiting Louisa at the table, occurred on August 31, 1842. Exactly three years before that date, on a rainy Saturday at the very end of August 1839, in a dory loaded with potatoes and melons, this same singular guest and his brother John had pushed off from shore into the Concord River, the two men to spend a couple of weeks in their homemade boat descending the leisurely stream to its merging with the Merrimack, then up that younger, livelier river as far as Hooksett, New Hampshire. Was Henry Thoreau aware that this dinner date at the Hawthornes' coincided with the anniversary of his and John's earlier elated departure? Certainly memories of quiet adventures with his brother through ten happy days along the rivers and into nearby hills abided, not yet fashioned into the book that they would become.

Thoreau's present situation seemed to be, as a sympathetic Hawthorne would put it a short time later, that of one who, in materialistic, utilitarian America, "can find no occupation in life that suits him." He had been born here in Concord in July 1817, into a humble if respectable Huguenot family, had graduated without much distinction from Harvard College in 1837, then had come back to Concord and taught school briefly, ending by setting up a school of his own with his only brother, John. The academy had flourished through three years from the spring of 1838, until John's health had forced him to abandon the classroom. Brother Henry had refused to carry on alone, and the school was closed. But meanwhile the two had undertaken their little adventure together: building a boat and setting off downriver in the summer of 1839.

What Hawthorne knew of his guest these three years later he recorded in his journal. Mr. Thoreau "was educated, I believe, at Cambridge, and formerly kept school in this town; but for two or three years back, he has repudiated all regular modes of getting a living, and seems inclined to lead a sort of Indian life among civilized men—an Indian life, I mean, as respects the absence of any systematic effort for a livelihood. He has been for sometime an inmate of Mr. Emerson's family; and, in requital, he labors in the garden, and performs such other offices as may suit him."

Like Emerson, Thoreau had been recently bereft of a loved one. This past January, hardly two weeks before the death of little Waldo Emerson, Henry's brother, boating companion, and best friend John had been shaving, stropping the razor, when he cut his index finger slightly. A couple of days later his entire left hand began to throb. John went to bed, his jaw stiffening. Dr. Bartlett hurried over, but there was nothing to be done. Friends gathered round, helplessly watching the sufferer in his convulsions, watched into the following afternoon, January 11, 1842, as the patient slipped from delirium into what by then was a merciful death. He was twenty-seven years old.

Soon after his brother's death, Henry suffered his own piercing, monthlong symptoms of lockjaw. "My life, my life—" he cried out in despair in his journal, "why will ye linger?" But he did linger and recover, this Henry David Thoreau who was indeed, as Hawthorne had recognized at once, a singular character. Through a lifetime Thoreau would go his own way. An able craftsman, he could do about anything with his hands. And notably, he was, as Hawthorne had discovered even by this first dinner at the Manse, "a keen and delicate observer of nature—a genuine observer, which, I suspect, is almost as rare a character as even an original poet; and Nature, in return for his love, seems to adopt him as her especial child, and shows him secrets which few others are allowed to witness."

The dory, however, that he and his brother John had built, the vessel in which those two had earlier rowed down the Concord and up the Merrimack to discover nature's quiet wonders farther afield, its owner was ready to part with. Thoreau this very afternoon would sell the boat to his present dinner host, along with a lesson tomorrow in steering. By such means Hawthorne was to acquire the *Musketaquid,* rechristened the *Pond Lily,* aboard which in days ahead he, too, would spend numerous contented hours on the river.

Margaret Fuller was treated to a ride in the boat when she returned to the Manse for a dinner of her own, at the very end of summer, three weeks after Thoreau had dined there and two weeks after Louisa had concluded her visit and gone back to Salem. Wednesday, September 21: "I dined with the Hawthornes," Fuller recorded, "& went with them in their boat up the North Branch. We landed on a foreign shore, but did not find much to reward the discoverer. It was a sallow and sorrowful day, no insincere harbinger of winter."

On the boat ride Hawthorne had spoken of Emerson's wife. Earlier he had been surprised, he said, to meet Lidian at noonday, "said it seemed scarce credible you could meet such a person by the light of sun." Fuller conceded that Mrs. Emerson did look ghostly now, gliding about in her black dress and long black veil. And in her journal this good friend of the Emersons was led to recall a vivid image: "The other eveg I was out with her about nine o clock; it was a night of moon struggling with clouds. She asked me to go to the church-yard, & glided before me through the long wet grass, and knelt & leaned her forehead on the tomb. The moon then burst forth, and cast its light on her as she prayed. It seemed like the ghost of a mother's joys." To this affecting scene the observer added with a dry and altogether characteristic honesty, "I feel that her child is far more to her in imagination than he ever was in reality."

Five days after her boat ride with the Hawthornes, Margaret Fuller left Concord and returned to Boston. There were strains in the Emerson household in any case. Lidian, grieving over her lost child, suffering from dental surgery that had swollen her jaw and made her miserable, enduring a low-grade fever alone in her room, had felt neglected, in part by the failure of her houseguest (busy with writing and expecting to see her hostess downstairs) to step in over the first couple of days to speak with her. Tears had followed that misunderstanding. "I felt embarrassed," Fuller wrote in her journal, "& did not know whether I ought to stay or go." Five weeks of visiting were no doubt long enough. "Farewell, dearest friend," she addressed Lidian's husband in words not for him to see; "there has been dissonance between us . . . yet thanks be to the Parent of Souls, that gave us to be born into the same age and the same country."

The parting was cordial for all that, so that even as the coach was rolling from Concord toward Boston on a Monday morning in late September 1842, Margaret Fuller sat inside with Emerson's wife and mother, who were on their way to visit relatives. "Going down I had a thorough talk with Lidian . . . "

7

HAWTHORNE AND EMERSON TOGETHER

*T*he morning after Margaret Fuller's departure, Emerson and Hawthorne set out on a forty-mile walk, bound for the village to the west where Emerson's father had begun his ministry. The weather the whole way going and coming was gorgeous, as a couple of companions, not yet Giants of American Literature frozen in steel engravings on a textbook page, strolled side by side along nineteenth-century country roads from Concord to Stow and on to Harvard ("according to our best computation, about 20 miles"), then the following morning from the Shaker Village there back east through Littleton and Acton before returning home ("to finish the nineteen miles of our second day before four in the afternoon")— a distance, more precisely then, of thirty-nine miles in all.

The notations above are Emerson's. He tells us in his journal that the Tuesday morning of his and Hawthorne's departure, September 27, was filled with sunshine, so that "it was a luxury to walk in the midst of all this warm & coloured light. The days of September are so rich that it seems natural to walk to the end of one's strength." They passed first Mr. Damon's textile factory in West Concord; but the mills were temporarily idle, the houses beside the river empty. Emerson records those details before characteristically moving on to a cheerful generalization, about the millstream: "Nothing so small but comes to honour & has its shining moment somewhere; & so was it here with our little Assabet or North Branch; it was falling over the rocks into silver, & above was expanded into this tranquil lake. After looking about us a few moments we took the road to Stow."

Flora was everywhere. "Fringed gentians, a thornbush with red fruit, wild apple trees whose fruit hung like berries, and grapevines were the decorations of the path. We scarcely encountered man or boy in our road nor saw any in the fields. This depopulation lasted all day. But the outlines of the landscape were so gentle that it seemed as if we were in a very cultivated country, and elegant persons must be living just over yonder hills." Through the morning and into the afternoon the two strolled on. "Our walk had no incidents. It needed none, for we were in excellent spirits, had much conversation, for we were both old collectors who had never had opportunity before to show each other our cabinets, so that we could have filled with matter much longer days."

Perhaps so. Or perhaps the more fluent Emerson did most of the talking, while Hawthorne listened and smiled. Assuredly, having once returned home, the philosopher sat down and wrote eight pages in his journal recounting the outing, whereas Hawthorne delayed nearly two weeks and then wrote no more than ten or twelve lines about it. They did agree, we learn in those eight pages, "that it needed a little dash of humor or extravagance in the traveller to give occasion to incident in his journey." Adventure happens to those who seek it out, but "Here we sober men easily pleased kept on the outside of the land & did not by so much as a request for a cup of milk creep into any farmhouse." The travelers were keeping to themselves, even as they agreed about the source of incidents—of adventure—on the high road, in the course of this ramble without incident.

Doubtless they found other matters to agree on, either stated or assumed. Both, for example, reveled in nature, which in New England on such early-autumn days as these appears at her most alluring. And both, in common with many of their thoughtful contemporaries (Thoreau and Alcott, for two), would have seen the changing aspects of nature as outward symbols of a deeper, abiding meaning: the spirituality that Hawthorne spoke of, Emerson's World-Soul. The perception is an ancient one, the Platonic understanding that ideas, which seem so insubstantial, are in fact the true, unchanging substance before and behind the altering appearances of things as our senses perceive them: the idea of a tree, of a brook, of a path as the eternal reality behind all the varying and perishing instances of trees, brooks, and paths that nature exhibits and that briefly our eyes may rest upon. Thus both Emerson and

Hawthorne would view a glorious September Tuesday between Concord and Harvard not only literally, as an evanescent manifestation over which the day's sun rose and declined, but also symbolically, as an analogue in hieroglyphics hinting at the ideal perfection beyond. For each traveler, then, nature served both as a palpable joy and as a teacher of insights into universal truths. "What is a farm but a mute gospel?" Emerson had written in *Nature.* "The chaff and the wheat, weeds and plants, blight, rain, insects, sun,—it is a sacred emblem from the first furrow of spring to the last stack which the snow of winter overtakes in the fields."

Hawthorne was thirty-eight and had published one book, *Twice-Told Tales,* at the time of his long walk with Emerson. His companion was thirty-nine and had published not much more: the pamphlet *Nature,* completed in the upstairs study in the Old Manse before the Hawthornes' occupancy; a couple of notable addresses; and a first series of *Essays.* Privately, they didn't care for each other's work. Emerson seldom read fiction; and when Elizabeth Peabody back in 1838 had brought from Salem a sketch, "Footprints on the Seashore," by her new discovery Nathaniel Hawthorne and set it before her Concord friend, Emerson had complained, as he recorded in his journal, "that there was no inside to it. Alcott & he together would make a man." No solid depth he must have meant— and indeed that particular airy specimen would have provided a fragile introduction to Hawthorne's achievement. But later, too— all through his life—Emerson underrated Hawthorne's fiction, found him (they were talking as they strolled today about Dickens and Irving and Landor) a better critic than writer; in this very month he confided to his journal that "N. Hawthorn's reputation as a writer is a very pleasing fact, because his writing is not good for anything, and this is a tribute to the man."

Emerson did value the man Hawthorne highly. "He seems to fascinate Mr. Emerson," Sophia remarked about her husband only days after their present outing. "Whenever he comes to see him, he takes him away, so that no one may interrupt him in his close and dead-set attack upon his ear. Miss Hoar says that persons about Mr. Emerson so generally echo him, that it is refreshing to him to find this perfect individual, all himself and nobody else."

This perfect individual, for his part, found little of interest in Emerson's prose. "Dearest," the bachelor Hawthorne had earlier written his beloved in Boston, "I have never had the good luck to profit much, or indeed any, by attending lectures; so that I think the ticket had better be bestowed on somebody who can listen to Mr Emerson more worthily." For himself, Hawthorne (so his son reported) was increasingly disposed as he grew older to doubt the effectiveness of expressing truth in the abstract. His own versions of truth came in the form of stories with people doing specific things, whereas the general truths of his neighbor Emerson appeared to be spun too much from cloudland to suit even a romancer's taste—vaporous thoughts, as Hawthorne stated rather brusquely, from "an everlasting rejecter of all that is and seeker for he knows not what."

That, of course, was his private opinion; Hawthorne's public utterances about his neighbor were unfailingly gracious: about the "great original Thinker, who had his earthly abode at the opposite extremity of our village," whom the tale-teller at the Manse could admire "as a poet of deep beauty and austere tenderness," while admitting to seeking nothing from his philosophy. "It was good, nevertheless," Hawthorne with retrospective generosity would write of Emerson in his preface to *Mosses from an Old Manse*, "to meet him in the wood-paths, or sometimes in our avenue, with that pure, intellectual gleam diffused about his presence, like the garment of a shining-one; and he so quiet, so simple, so without pretension, encountering each man alive as if expecting to receive more than he could impart."

The two did respect each other, although without ever becoming close. Their natures were so different: the one profoundly optimistic, the other absorbed in humanity's griefs and guilts. As Henry James put it memorably: "Emerson, as a sort of spiritual sun-worshipper, could have attached but a moderate value to Hawthorne's cat-like faculty of seeing in the dark." And then the thoughts of the one were prone to move from specifics to generalizations, to the universal beyond the particular; whereas the other's imagination stayed with earthly matters, fixed on the "very earthliness, which no other sphere or state of existence can renew or compensate. The fragrance of flowers, and of new-mown hay; the genial warmth of sunshine, and the beauty of a sunset among clouds; the comfort and cheerful glow of the fireside," Hawthorne would write wistfully toward the end of "The Hall of Fantasy": "I fear that no other world can show us anything just like this."

Nature delighted them both; yet although the two might start from the same intense love of that nature abundantly in evidence on this shared walk, they ended in different creative realms entirely, the one's generalized and mostly sunlit, the other's particular and much in shadow.

However, this day found both wayfarers in a splendid mood. Sometime after noon they reached Stow, where they dined, then continued their journey toward Harvard. Once they stopped at a tavern, but Emerson found it a cold place, the Temperance Society having emptied the barroom, and Hawthorne required to smoke his cigar on the piazza. Later, back on the highway with a mile yet to go before reaching their destination, the pedestrians were hailed by a friendly elderly stranger in a wagon, who gave them a ride the rest of the way up Oak Hill and on into the village. The Samaritan "knew my name, & my father's name & history"—Reverend William Emerson, Harvard's minister of yore—so he "insisted on doing the honours of his town to us, & of us to his townsmen; for he fairly installed us at the tavern . . . & bespoke the landlord's best attention to our wants."

Those wants would have been for little beyond food and rest, with morning starting early for the wayfarers, at 6:30, and the day ahead promising to be an active one. It would begin before breakfast with a walk of over three miles to the Shaker Village.

Structures of that same Shaker Village survive, secularized as residences in the affluent exurb that is present-day Harvard, Massachusetts. The Shaker burial ground is there as well, its simple stones segregated by sex, as were the generally long-lived existences of the folk whom they commemorate. "Whilst the good Sisters were getting ready our breakfast," Emerson wrote of this visit among living practitioners who now sleep in those quiet rows, "we had a conversation with Seth Blanchard & Cloutman of the Brethren, who gave an honest account by yea & by nay of their faith & practice." The Shakers were, the visitor summarized, "in many ways an interesting Society, but at present have an additional importance as an experiment of Socialism which so falls in with the temper of the times."

The times, indeed, in the early 1840s, were bent on reform: of schools, of prisons, of diet, of drinking habits, of communal life, of medicine, of treatment for the insane. Why New England lay in the path of such impulses is a complex matter, part religious, part national, part philosophical. In religion a New Awakening in the early decades of the nineteenth century had directed attention less on the world to come than on the world here and now, striving to make society better as it rejected the harsher hectorings of Calvinism: less of Original Sin and more of Love Thy Neighbor. American society itself, in which such aspirations were being fostered, was now no longer a colony but an independent nation, and within it was growing a democratic spirit, making for an impatience with earlier Calvinistic doctrines of the elect and the damned, while encouraging a concern with alleviating the plight of society's more vulnerable members: children, prisoners, the insane, blacks, Indians, even, finally, women. The Enlightenment ideals of Jefferson and the other founders of the young republic—"all men are created equal"—contributed to the new democratization and its consequences, and Romanticism as a philosophic movement played a part, too, by extolling the humble while redefining childhood as a value to be cherished.

As for the reforming Shakers, that religious group had abolished sex and private property from their lives. Two hundred of them were in this particular enclave near Harvard village, a "family" following the tenets of the illiterate Englishwoman Ann Lee, who long ago had committed her adherents—eight to start with—to strict celibacy. In 1774 Mother Lee and her United Society of Believers in Christ's Second Appearing had emigrated to America, settling near Albany. After Mother Lee's death her order had expanded, numbering maybe six thousand members in the 1830s, in nineteen communities in and around New England.

Shaker communities awakened considerable interest in that reform-minded era; Hawthorne had written two stories about them, "The Shaker Bridal" and "The Canterbury Pilgrims." In their religious services the celibates courted spiritual release by abandoning themselves to shaking dances that the public was welcome to observe. For the rest, they devised the clothespin, the flat broom, the circular saw; and the Shakers' chaste furniture and distinctive architecture continue to be prized these many years later, when the dancer-farmers of the celibate faith have dwindled to no more than four or five aged sisters. Yet even at their apogee, Emerson had fancied that he might have talked a couple of the brethren out of their beliefs, "if we could have staid twenty four hours: although my powers of persuasion were crippled by a disgraceful barking cold, & Hawthorn inclined to play Jove more than Mercurius," that latter the voluble god of trade. "Cloutman," he went on, "showed us the farm, vineyard, orchard, barn, herb room, pressing room &c."

Emerson found an additional value in the neat industrious settlement "in the heart of the country as a model farm." Neighboring yeomen would see and copy the Shakers' efficient ways. Hawthorne, for his part, took no such cheerful view of what he had elsewhere described as the gravelike "cold and passionless security" of Shaker lives. For now, aloofly Jovian, he would content himself with recording two weeks later that "Mr. Emerson held a theological discussion with two of the Shaker brethren; but the particulars of it have faded from my memory." By then most of the excursion seemed to have faded, including the second day's walk from the Shaker Village on "to Littleton, & thence to Acton, still in the same redundance of splendour," as Emerson had noted at the time. "It was like a day of July, and from Acton we sauntered leisurely homeward."

For Hawthorne, nearly a fortnight afterward trying to recollect, the Shaker Village "and all the other adventures of the tour have now so lost their freshness that I cannot adequately recall them. Wherefore let them rest untold." He had been homesick during the first and only night that he had slept away from his beloved Sophia; that much he did remember. "I recollect nothing so well as the aspect of some fringed gentians, which we saw growing by the roadside"—Emerson too had noted the flowers as they were setting out—"and which were so beautiful that I longed to turn back, and bring them to my little wife. After our arduous journey, we arrived safe home in the afternoon of the second day—the first time that I ever came home in my life; for I never had a home before."

8

FIRST FALL AT THE MANSE

Early in their stay at the Manse, the Hawthornes had endured a long spell of rainy weather, the groom finding his only cheer in the cloudless, beaming demeanor of his bride. Through August days the rain had poured down, "drip-drip-dripping, and splash-splash-splashing, from the eaves, and bubbling and foaming into the tubs which we have set out to receive it." Shingles of the Manse had turned black with the drenching, and an infinitude of raindrops blurred the surface of the nearby river. A mile off, the summit of the hill where the couple had picked whortleberries was covered with mist, "as if the demon of the rain were enthroned there," Hawthorne wrote; "and if we look to the sky, it seems as if all the water that has been poured down upon us, were nothing to what is to come."

Abruptly, a fresh week began with sunlight restored. It looked like a new world. Early on a Monday at the end of August Hawthorne had risen to go fishing—and "how instantaneously did all dreariness and heaviness of the earth's spirit flit away, before one smile of the beneficent sun." He would draw a lesson from the change: "This proves that all gloom is but a dream and a shadow, and that cheerfulness is the real truth. It requires many clouds, long brooding over us, to make us sad; but one gleam of sunshine always suffices to cheer up the landscape." In this present cheer, the early riser was descending alongside his fruitful apple orchard to the river's edge. The mist was so thick that he could barely see the opposite shore, but the sun soon dispersed the early fog, leaving only a smokiness over the surface of the water. "The farmhouses, across the river, made their appearance out of the dusky cloud;—the voices of boys were heard, shouting to the cattle as they drove them to pasture;—a mower whet his scythe, and set to work in a neighboring meadow." And this solitary fisherman all the while stood on the oozy edges of the stream, "beguiling the little fish," catching out of those sluggish waters as many as two dozen bream for that day's consumption.

Day followed day into fall. Hawthorne wrote upstairs while Sophia painted in the breakfast room directly beneath his study. Or she sewed while he worked in his garden, relishing the daily growth of vegetables, leaves up the vine poles becoming blossoms, then beans, the process furnishing a pleasure new to him as he provided food for his family. It was, he imagined, what Adam must have felt in Paradise; "and of merely and exclusively earthly enjoyments, there are few purer and more harmless to be experienced."

Their homegrown bounty helped provide abundance for the couple's first Thanksgiving together, when they made good cheer upon a five-pound turkey, and pudding, and pies, and custards, though only those two were on hand for the feast, with Pigwiggen the cat about the premises. Sophia had cooked the little turkey following directions sentence by sentence in Eliza Leslie's up-to-the-minute *House-Book, or, a Manual of Domestic Economy for Town and Country* (Philadelphia, 1840). This was on a Thursday, November 24, 1842, the weather turning cold by then; into this same Thanksgiving Day fell snow and sleet, enough to end further thought of brisk walks in the woods that had filled earlier bright fall afternoons.

Now, however, there would be skating, as soon as Louisa could send her brother's skates from Salem. After they arrived, Hawthorne got up sometimes at sunrise to skate on the flooded meadows. On one memorable occasion two neighbors joined him at his recreation. "Henry Thoreau is an experienced skater," Sophia reported, "and was figuring dithyrambic dances and Bacchic leaps on the ice—very remarkable, but very ugly, methought. Next him followed Mr. Hawthorne who, wrapped in his cloak, moved like a self-impelled Greek statue, stately and grave. Mr. Emerson closed the line, evidently too weary to hold himself erect, pitching headforemost, half lying on the air." Taking a break, Emerson stepped into the Manse "and said to me that Hawthorne was a tiger, a bear, a lion,—in short, a satyr, and there was no tiring him out; and he might be the death of a man like himself. And then, turning upon me that kindling smile for which he is so memorable, he added, 'Mr. Hawthorne is such an Ajax, who can cope with him!'"

On Christmas Eve that same Ajax sat down to write to Henry Longfellow. In the five years since the Bowdoin classmates had resumed their acquaintance, when *Twice-Told Tales* had appeared, a friendship had developed between them. "I should have responded to your letter sometime since," Hawthorne was apologizing, "but I am very busy with the pen, and hate to ink my fingers more than is necessary. As to coming to dine with you, it is a pleasure which I cannot promise myself at present." But he went on to urge Longfellow to visit the Manse, even now in the midst of winter. To be sure, a guest at such a season would have to warm himself by the glow of the tenants' felicity, "aided by as large a wood-fire as we can pile into the chimney. If you like skating, there is enough of it, over the river, within a stone's throw of our door."

Professor Longfellow would not, however, be lured from the comforts of Cambridge. Perhaps the prospect of spending time with a married couple in felicity held little to tempt that pining lover.

Longfellow and Hawthorne were graduates of the same college, and both had been striving to make their way as writers. So often then the question for writers was this: how—in a utilitarian land of merchants and farmers without much leisure, at a time when the poetry and prose of Scott and Byron and Dickens and other such vastly popular English authors could be pirated for free—does an American author earn a living? Emerson had a bequest from his first wife's estate and gave lectures. Fuller charged fees for the Conversations on cultural matters through which she was currently guiding Boston's female intelligentsia. And in their various ways Alcott, Thoreau, Poe, and most other American authors were having to grapple with making a living while pursuing the artistic calling. In the years after leaving Bowdoin, Hawthorne's friend Henry Longfellow had had to struggle as well.

Longfellow had been born in February 1807 (three years after Hawthorne) in Portland, Maine, his father a lawyer, his grandfather one of Bowdoin's founding overseers. Thus in due time young Harry Longfellow had arrived in Brunswick, as a member with

Hawthorne of the Bowdoin class of 1825. Unlike his Salem class-mate, however, Longfellow had proved to be a splendid, disciplined student, honored at commencement with the distinction of deliv-ering an oration on "Our Native Writers," the speaker himself zeal-ous for authorhood: "my whole soul burns most ardently for it, and every earthly thought centres in it."

But his father had sagely cautioned the graduate that there was no money in literature; Longfellow had better come home to Port-land and study law. And he was preparing to do so when an ex-traordinary opportunity intervened. The enlightened trustees of Bowdoin had recently determined to establish a chair of modern languages, and they asked this eighteen-year-old alumnus, despite his limited knowledge of the subject (only some French), to fill the chair, with the understanding that he would first travel in Europe for two or three years to perfect his linguistic skills. Young Longfellow leapt at the offer, sailing from New York in the spring of 1826 (as Hawthorne sat writing and brooding in his high room in Salem) for three years of roaming through France, Spain, Italy, and Germany, living on a vagabond's budget and learning languages as he went.

At last, in 1829, the traveler returned to take up his responsi-bilities in Brunswick, teaching modern languages to undergradu-ates at Bowdoin, although with little pleasure, "for nobody in this part of the world pretends to speak anything but English—and some might dispute them even that prerogative." The professor's spirits improved in 1831, two years into his tenure off in Maine, with his marriage to Mary Potter of Portland. And his exile would come to a close three years later, when Longfellow was offered a position at Harvard, again contingent upon his traveling abroad to enlarge his knowledge of European cultures.

So again the linguist set sail, now with his wife and friends. But in the course of this second journey, at Rotterdam in November 1835, Mary Longfellow died from complications following a mis-carriage. Eight months later, at the end of July 1836, the grieving widower—"Good God! what a solitary, lonely being I am! Why do I travel? Every hour my heart aches with sadness"—still studying his languages as best he could (in the end he would master eleven of them), had made his way as far as Thun, alongside the Alps. There in his loneliness he sent up his card introducing himself to a Boston family on their own extensive travels through Europe.

The family whom Longfellow was approaching comprised another American widower, Nathan Appleton, then in his mid-fifties, and his two accomplished daughters, enjoying a tour over a couple of leisurely years through England, France, and Italy. By no means were the Appletons traveling, like Longfellow, on a scholar's budget. Expense would have been no object on their tour, for the industrialist—cofounder and investor back home in the flourishing textile mills at Waltham and Lowell—was one of the wealthiest men in America. By this summer of 1836, the Appleton party had wended its way to the beauties of the Swiss lakes, where, near Interlaken, it was to receive the calling card of a fellow New Englander in the vicinity. "I hope the venerable gentleman doesn't pop in on us," eighteen-year-old Fanny Appleton wrote in her journal. But her hopes were to be disappointed; their countryman, age twenty-nine, was soon admitted to the family circle: Professor Henry Longfellow, "a young man after all," as Fanny noted, "or else the son of the poet."

No son, it was the poet himself, although less poet than scholar; Longfellow had written very little poetry since his college days. Of late in his grief he had been disinclined to do much of anything. But now, eight months after his wife's death, the bereaved professor on summer days in Switzerland began once more to feel stirrings of joy, strolling with Fanny Appleton and her sister Mary, riding with the two young women in the Appletons' great traveling carriage to Zurich, watching the girls sketch, translating German poetry with them.

And during nearly a month of such magic he fell deeply in love. The visit ended, and by the close of that year 1836, after eighteen months overseas, the professor found himself back home settled in Cambridge, once more in love although without requital, preparing to assume his new duties at Harvard College. He had located comfortable lodgings in the Craigie House, a grand old home on Brattle Street; and there, some two months into the new year, Professor Longfellow was to receive an unexpected gift from a Bowdoin classmate, Nathaniel Hawthorne's collection of just-published sketches and stories. In the prestigious *North American Review* he proceeded through fourteen generous pages to praise this *Twice-Told Tales* as a work of genius. Hawthorne was delighted. Renewing their acquaintance, the two classmates soon became friends. "I shall see Hawthorne tomorrow," Longfellow wrote a correspondent in October 1838. "He is a strange owl; a very peculiar individual, with a dash of originality about him, very pleasant to behold." And the following year, a weigher and gauger's laborings in the Boston customhouse would furnish additional occasions for those two friends to get together, Hawthorne by then a "grand fellow."

Meanwhile, Longfellow's suit for the affections of Fanny Appleton had been languishing. Back in Boston, the Appletons in their sumptuous parlor on Beacon Street would welcome this friend from their travels overseas: friend of all the family, of Fanny's sister Mary, her brother Tom, friend but no more than friend of Fanny herself. George Hillard had glimpsed the back of Miss Appleton's bonnet "(and there was expression even in that) at church today," as he wrote Longfellow on Christmas Eve 1837, sixteen months after the latter's happiness in Switzerland (and four years and more before Hillard would be the Hawthornes' first visitor at the Manse in Concord). "So," the attorney assured Longfellow, "she is alive and well." A couple of days ago Hillard had called at the Appletons' to lend Mary a book, and "what an atmosphere of beauty and grace and tasteful luxury is diffused over the house. If you are ever its lord," he ventured, "I expect that poetry will ooze out of the pores of your skin. I delight to see you keeping up so stout a heart for the resolve to conquer is half the battle in love as well as war."

The very stoutest of hearts this lover would come to require. Year after year Longfellow was to pursue his passion, Fanny Appleton remaining all the while indifferent to the professor's suit. In late July 1839, three full years after he had first fallen in love, he confided to another friend overseas: "the victory hangs doubtful. The lady says she *will not!* I say she *shall!* It is not *pride,* but the madness of passion. I visit her; sometimes pass an evening alone with her. But not one word is ever spoken on a certain topic. No whining,—no beseeching,—but a steel-like silence." And a year earlier in his journal, inked out at a later date but retrievable: "Thou foolish woman to disdain such love as this!"

In the fall of 1839, Longfellow published *Hyperion,* a book of travels in prose describing the second of his sojourns abroad, to the gratification of an age living long before movies and overnight access across the Atlantic had made Europe a familiar neighbor. Its earliest readers might sit with *Hyperion* by their firesides vicariously journeying with the thinly fictionalized Paul Flemming up the Rhine, lingering with him at Heidelberg, reveling with him in the company of the lovely Mary Ashburton. True, the author's indiscretion in thus making public their private interlude in Switzerland roundly displeased Fanny Appleton, the model for that Mary of the "deep unutterable eyes," of the voice that was "musical and full of soul." But *Hyperion* was a success, attracting much attention, as Longfellow informed his father, and provoking strong reactions. "Some praise, and others condemn in no measured terms; and the book sells with a rapidity far beyond my expectations."

That, no doubt, was partly because the author by then was famous. Although he had written poems in college, afterward Longfellow had found his inspiration flagging, leading him to conclude as far back as 1829, four years after Bowdoin, that he would never write poetry again. And yet there came a day that the professor would always remember: sunshine streaming through the windows in Cambridge while he joyfully paced, in the fall of 1837, in the throes of devising a poem to accompany a bouquet of flowers that he was sending to Fanny. Thereafter, in the coming year he wrote four or five more lyrics, and in October 1838, in the *Knickerbocker* appeared "A Psalm of Life," verses at once enormously popular. Within another year their author published a slim volume of lyrics, *Voices of the Night*, which only confirmed his sudden fame.

Fanny, for all that, did not relent. At his desk, in his classroom, Longfellow labored on, reserved if always cordial and unperturbed in society, but in private tense and often ill. "I am neither in good health nor good spirits," he had written earlier in his journal, "being foolishly inclined to indigestion and the most unpleasant melancholy." Victorian complaints plagued him—neuralgia, dyspepsia, "no sunshine in the soul"—so that he was finally led to request and obtain from Harvard College a leave of absence to repair his health. With that, in the spring of 1842, Professor Longfellow set sail for a third visit to Europe. And by early July (as the Hawthornes in the parlor at 13 West Street, Boston, entered into wedlock), the poet-professor was enduring the rigors of Dr. Schmitz's water cure at

Boppard on the Rhine, from hot blankets emerging to stand under a cold waterfall before submitting to the pummeling of masseurs. Nor was the patient perfectly well yet, had come, in fact, to doubt "that any one can be *perfectly* well who has a brain and heart."

Withal, the water cure would prove beneficial. Late that same fall Longfellow returned home with his health much restored, better than it had been for years; and soon after resettling at Cambridge in November, he would hear from Hawthorne. "I have been look-ing to receive somewhat in the shape of a letter of congratulation from you on the great event of my marriage," his friend chided from the Manse, "but it does not seem to be forthcoming. Perhaps it is the etiquette that I should congratulate on your return from Outre Mer. Be it done accordingly." So during the poet's absence along the Rhine, Hawthorne had married—and was hoping, as he wrote again on Christmas Eve, that the traveler back from his third tour in Europe would venture out to Concord for a visit, to go skating on the river and warm himself by his hosts' hearthfire. Having of-fered such inducements, Hawthorne went on to comment in the candor of friendship: "I never was more surprised than at your writing poems about Slavery. I have not seen them, but have faith in their excellence, though I cannot conjecture what species of excellence it will be. You have never poetized a practical subject, hitherto." It seemed an odd choice for a cosmopolitan linguist, poet of fabled Europe and of such soothing domestic balladry as "The Village Blacksmith"; for the new verses that Longfellow had writ-ten on shipboard returning from Bristol had been published recently as *Poems on Slavery,* a seven-page pamphlet on a topic altogether different from any he had dealt with before—and utterly different from any that his friend Hawthorne would deal with during his idyll at the Manse.

9

HAWTHORNE'S WRITING

*L*ongfellow would remain in Cambridge, never managing to visit Concord during his friend's residence there, not later and certainly not in this coldest winter in twenty years. It might have been just as well. Sophia would remember that her husband had been writing industriously in his stove-warmed study each day through the length of that harsh season, almost without interruption except for the rare call by Henry Thoreau and "a short call now and then from Elizabeth Hoar, who can hardly be called an earthly inhabitant; and Mr. Emerson, whose face pictured the promised land (which we were then enjoying), and intruded no more than a sunset, or a rich warble from a bird."

The new year arrived, the two solitaries in their Concord paradise having "bade farewell to the dear old Year with grateful spirits," so Sophia informed her sister-in-law Louisa, "for it had brought us infinite benefits & felicity, & it died away in a most serene & golden sunset, like a Christian going to rest. The young Year" of 1843 "also was born beneath a golden heaven, as if to signify its bountiful disposition."

Yet bounty was slow in coming, for the fierce winter tarried. Finally the 1843 calendar did say spring, even as cold lingered into late March. "The first month of Spring is already gone," Hawthorne bemoaned with March ending, "and still the snow lies deep on hill and valley; and the river is still frozen from bank to bank." Winter had lasted five months, or by his recalculation as long as seven. It seemed a deplorable span during which to have done without "the smile of Nature, in a single year of human life. Even out of the midst of happiness, I have sometimes sighed and groaned," he confessed, "for I love the sunshine and the green woods, and the sparkling blue water; and it seems as if the picture of our inward bliss should be set in a beautiful frame of outward nature." Yet, remarkably, through all that same gray and cold, this enamored husband was convinced that his wife had not once wished for summer. For "she is sunshine, and delicate Spring and delightful Summer, in her own person; else the winter would have been dreary indeed."

So long a chill did bring the one benefit. Through those same bleak months Hawthorne, after a considerable hiatus, had begun to write again, diligently, up to four hours a day.

The results of his efforts appeared in a number of magazines. Between January and March 1843, *Sargent's New Monthly Magazine* and young James Russell Lowell's *Pioneer* each published a couple of the author's recently written pieces; but John L. O'Sullivan's *United States Magazine and Democratic Review* attracted the bulk of his work. O'Sullivan was the same editor whom Congressman Cilley had urged, back in the spring of 1837, to get in touch with Hawthorne, only then emerging from his twelve years of seclusion. The editor had done so, assuring the solicited author that "compensation to good writers will be on so liberal a scale as to command the best and most polished exertions of their minds." From that time until the end of his stay at the Manse in 1845, Hawthorne would write some thirty articles—sketches, stories, essays—and of those, no fewer than twenty-two appeared in O'Sullivan's *United States Magazine and Democratic Review*.

This present part of the author's achievement, written before the end of March 1843, comprised nine pieces. Among them, "The Old Apple-Dealer" represents a continuation of the kind of sketch that had appeared in *Twice-Told Tales*—not stories but, rather, unplotted verbal impressions that we who prefer the tales may value less highly than did Hawthorne's contemporaries. Indeed, we may fail to appreciate the novelty of what the author was managing through such specimens that contained matter no more consequential than, say, an adult's stroll about town with a five-year-old, or a sightseer's view from the top of a steeple, or ruminations of the town pump rendered in its own voice. An observer's imagination at play, scarcely more than that: but at play on objects that other writers had neglected. As an English reviewer of *Twice-Told Tales* in this very year 1843 would remark, Hawthorne's sketches were somehow able to make the commonest things suggestive: "The pump in the middle of a little town, recalls the days when the spring welled brightly out in the wilderness, and 'the Indian sagamores drank of it'; a walk with a child through the range of shop-window sights, enables the thoughtful man to draw aside the veils which hide our deepest associations and our saddest thoughts."

So with this more recent "Old Apple-Dealer," worked up at the Manse from Hawthorne's notebook observations of a Salem peddler. The humblest of subjects to write about—"an old man who carries on a little trade of gingerbread and apples, at the depôt of one of our rail-roads"—but observed with tender scrupulosity. The world around the fellow's baskets is full of momentum; travelers swarm from the cars. "And in the midst of this terrible activity, there sits the old man of gingerbread, so subdued, so hopeless, so without a stake in life, and yet not positively miserable—there he sits, the forlorn old creature, one chill and sombre day after another, gathering scanty coppers for his cakes, apples and candy." But why does the image settle so firmly in memory? "I have him now. He and the steam-fiend are each other's antipodes; the latter is the type of all that go-ahead" in a young thriving nation; the former "doomed never to share in the world's exulting progress."

An apple dealer's dismal posture might evoke Hawthorne's own earlier isolation in Salem, as it contrasts with his and Sophia's blissful solitude at the Manse. Yet even so tarnished a specimen as this fellow in his shabby overcoat appears to glow when rendered through the author's glorious style. Everything that Hawthorne's prose style touches glows. What his writing does is move matter in the direction of the spiritual and true, language transmuting appearances about us, elevating them, spiritualizing them, taking "the actual circumstances of life" and distilling from them their timeless essence—in sketches, but even more so in tales. Two such are represented in the work achieved over these recent months. One is "Egotism, or The Bosom Serpent." The other is "The Birthmark."

As with the earlier stories in *Twice-Told Tales,* these two are anything but documents of contemporary life. Rather, they are life rarefied, made dreamlike and universal, seen through a magical mist. "The Birthmark," for instance, is set in "the latter part of the last century," at a distance from the commonplace present. Like "The Old Apple-Dealer," the tale derives from notebook entries, although in this case not from an observation but from an idea: "A person to be in the possession of something as perfect as mortal man has a right to demand; he tries to make it better, and ruins it entirely."

The idea comes first, then; so that the writer's task emerges as an effort to dramatize an insight. Consequently, the characters in "The Birthmark," as in other Hawthorne tales, evolve as types, scarcely individualized. Of the three types here that represent attitudes in a moral dilemma, Aylmer is the man of science, almost godlike in his brilliance. The begrimed Aminadab is his assistant, "a man of low stature, but bulky frame, with shaggy hair hanging about his visage." And Georgiana is the beautiful woman whom the scientist has persuaded to become his wife. Yet for all her beauty the wife appears flawed, by a birthmark on her cheek in the shape of a tiny hand. Aylmer has the knowledge to remove the blemish and make Georgiana perfect. With her consent—finally at her urging—he sets to work to render her a "living specimen of ideal loveliness." In the laboratory the scientist and his assistant labor feverishly, concocting a potion that the beloved in turn quaffs with eagerness, "like water from a heavenly fountain." Thereupon she lies down to rest, while her delighted husband watches. The stigma on her cheek is fading as a rainbow fades. Yet as the last tint of the birthmark vanishes from the pallid face, "the parting breath of the now perfect woman passed into the atmosphere, and her soul, lingering a moment near her husband, took its heavenward flight." The scientist has condemned his lovely wife to "put off this birthmark of mortality by relinquishing mortality itself."

Yet such a summary provides only the crudest indication of the care and subtlety with which Hawthorne has developed the various meanings of his story. Aminadab is earthy matter; Aylmer is spirit, intellect. But additional interpretations suggest themselves. The story may be concerned with the reform impulse in society striving to eradicate human imperfections. Or perhaps it is about original sin, or abortion, or idealism and carnality. Or is it about the artist's doomed effort to create eternal beauty, working necessarily with flawed, impermanent matter all the while? Is Aylmer a monster of pride and egotism or (as his dying wife describes him) one who has aimed loftily, done nobly? "Do not repent," she pleads with her final breath, "that, with so high and pure a feeling, you have rejected the best that earth could offer." And in that regard, in Hawthorne's notebooks occurs a second suggestive entry: "A person to be the death of his beloved in trying to raise her to more than mortal perfection; yet this should be a comfort to him for having aimed so highly and holily."

On such complex thoughts was a husband in a near-perfect marriage dwelling during the first year of his stay at the Manse. In addition, the author had been undertaking something new. Neither sketches nor tales, these were satirical essays on aspects of contemporary life. Four of the nine specimens published through the early months of 1843 are in that more current mode, of which "The New Adam and Eve" is representative.

Of course an authorial imagination remains at play. Suppose that Doomsday has swept away all of humankind. And suppose a new Adam and Eve have been created, their hearts and minds fully formed, but the two entirely unaware of their predecessors. They gaze about them at a Boston emptied of humanity. What an un-Edenic place it seems, marked with "wear and tear, and unrenewed decay, which distinguish the works of man from the growth of nature!" What can such ugliness signify to anyone outside the social and historical awareness that gives meaning to pavements, brick, and lampposts? Moreover, the desolation: "In a forest, solitude would be life; in the city, it is death."

Yet this is our present world. The couple wander through it, entering in turn a dry-goods store with its puzzlements of corsets and silver gauze, then a snugly secular metropolitan church, a court of justice (but centuries will be needed to teach these two what crime is), a legislative hall, a prison and its baffling gallows, and a mansion in Beacon Street, much like Nathan Appleton's. At an abandoned dining table, they "turn with disgust from fish, fowl, and flesh, which, to their pure nostrils, steam with a loathsome odor of death and corruption." Instead the two settle for a red-cheeked apple and for cool water in place of the hock and claret. Refreshed, they then visit a commercial bank with its rubbishy piles of money; and even as the couple begin to grasp the bewildering aspects of their situation, "how will they explain the magnificence of one habitation, as compared with the squalid misery of another? Through what medium can the idea of servitude enter their minds? When will they comprehend the great and miserable fact,—the evidences of which appeal to their senses everywhere,—that one portion of earth's lost inhabitants was rolling in luxury, while the multitude was toiling for scanty food? A wretched change, indeed, must be wrought in their own hearts, ere they can conceive the primal decree of Love to have been so completely abrogated, that a brother should ever want what his brother had. . . ."

"The New Adam and Eve" appeared in O'Sullivan's *Democratic Review* in February; "Egotism, or The Bosom Serpent" appeared in March, "The Procession of Life" in April, and "The Celestial Railroad" in May. "The Old Apple-Dealer" had been published in *Sargent's New Monthly Magazine* in January and "The Antique Ring" in February. "The Hall of Fantasy" had appeared in the *Pioneer* in February and "The Birthmark" in March. But for all that productivity—and despite O'Sullivan's earlier assurances of compensation on a liberal scale—Hawthorne had received not a penny for his recent efforts. As the author lamented to his notebook here in March 1843, "the Magazine people do not pay their debts." To be sure, it was a miserable time economically, in the long, lingering wake of the Panic of 1837, with periodical publication the chanciest of enterprises at best. Already, after only three issues, Lowell's *Pioneer* had folded; apparently no money ever arrived from that source. And Epes Sargent, his own magazine defunct after six months, would get around to sending his contributor no more than a measly ten dollars as payment, and not for another three years yet. Even O'Sullivan of the abundant promises failed to forward what was due, "so that we taste," Hawthorne in his paradise was noting, "some of the inconveniences of poverty, and the mortification—only temporary, however—of owing money, with empty pockets. It is an annoyance, not a trouble," the writer in possession of apple orchard, vegetable garden, and fish-full river ended philosophically.

In part, he had been applying himself to writing under the supposition that he was about to become a father. But in early February, Sophia out walking had slipped on the ice; afterward, she had miscarried. In April, in the sober aftermath, Hawthorne alongside his wife was undertaking a bit more writing in the study. A visitor to the Manse will thrill to the words being written at that moment, still visible upstairs. Just here those two were standing, just in this spot as daylight of a Monday faded! With her ring Sophia has scratched on the windowpane: "Man's accidents are God's purposes. Sophia A. Hawthorne, 1843." The Reverend Dr. Ripley's heirs when they reclaim their house will not be pleased, but to this hour you may see the writing there, still feel the Hawthornes in the room before this window. Sophia has given the ring to her husband, who is adding, "Nath. Hawthorne. This is his study. 1843." She writes: "The smallest twig leans clear against the sky." Then he: "Composed by my wife and written with her diamond." Now he is done, and Sophia Amelia Hawthorne reclaims her ring to conclude: "Inscribed by my husband at sunset. April 3rd, 1843. In the gold light. S. A. H."

TWO MORE WEDDINGS

*F*our days later, at around eleven on Friday morning, a wagon arrived at the Manse to take Sophia to the stage house. Hawthorne helped his wife into the wagon and stood on the doorstep watching until she was out of sight. Then, in her new absence, he busied myself with sawing and splitting wood, "there being an inward inquietness, which demanded active exercise." Early that afternoon the husband in his empty house ate a solitary dinner, before lying down with the current issue of the *Dial* to read and rest. But he was unable to nap. Taking up his journal with the intention of keeping a record for his wife's benefit, he was interrupted by a visit from Henry Thoreau. Together the two men chatted about the *Dial*, and Mr. Alcott, and "other kindred or concatenated subjects," including "the spiritual advantages of change of place," because Thoreau, calling this afternoon to return a book, had announced that he would be going to Staten Island to serve as a private tutor in Emerson's brother's family.

Hawthorne had earlier interested himself professionally in this caller, who still seemed unable to take hold and settle down. Maybe Thoreau should concentrate on writing. Last fall, sending "The Old Apple-Dealer" to the editor Epes Sargent in New York, the author had spoken about his neighbor. "There is a gentleman in this town," Hawthorne had explained, "by the name of Thoreau, a graduate of Cambridge, and a fine scholar, especially in old English literature— but withal a wild, irregular, Indian-like sort of fellow, who can find no occupation in life that suits him. He writes; and sometimes— often, for aught I know—very well indeed." Sargent should give the man a try. He "has stuff in him to make a reputation of; and I wish that you might find it consistent with your interest to aid him in attaining that object."

Now here was Thoreau following up: he was going to Staten Island not only to tutor Judge Emerson's son Willie, age seven, but also to investigate with New York publishers the possibility of pursuing a literary career. On his young friend's account Hawthorne welcomed the change. Thoreau's health had not been good lately; the move might be of benefit, while perhaps furnishing him with a consequential role in the world. But as for Hawthorne's own preference: "I should like to have him remain here; he being one of the few persons, I think, with whom to hold intercourse is like hearing the wind among the boughs of a forest-tree; and with all this wild freedom, there is high and classic cultivation in him too."

He liked Thoreau, in short, perhaps better than any of the other village denizens; so that in his solitude Hawthorne could not have minded four days later when his neighbor returned before leaving Concord to take a last ride in the *Musketaquid* rechristened *Pond Lily*. The two men accordingly emptied water from the boat and set forth on their voyage, on a Tuesday afternoon in the spring of 1843, gliding upriver toward the Assabet. "We rowed to the foot of the hill which borders the north-branch, and there landed, and climbed the moist and snowy hillside, for the sake of the prospect." The view from up there had flooded enough to resemble an arm of the sea. Then, having descended, the boatmen were once more riverborne, memorably, Salem native in his thirty-ninth year, Concord native not yet twenty-six, two friends alive and breathing the same air as they boarded a capacious cake of ice that was floating downriver, to be carried by the floe "directly to our own landing-place, with the boat towing behind."

Sophia had gone to Boston to be with her sister Mary, who had sent forth astonishing news. At age thirty-six, Mary Peabody was suddenly about to wed. For a decade this third Peabody sister had secretly been in love with Horace Mann, without once daring to hope that fortune would finally make her his wife. Mary was the pretty one of the three sisters—and the quiet one, unlike the younger, ebullient Sophia, who had married Mr. Hawthorne, or the plumper, more demonstrative woman whom the older, unkempt and unmarried Elizabeth Peabody had become. Yet for all her quiet ways, Mary Peabody possessed a fierce determination. Since soon after meeting him in Boston in 1832, at Mrs. Clarke's boardinghouse, she had loved Mr. Mann; and here, more than ten years later, she would at last become the handsome, high-minded widower's bride.

Sophia had hurried into Boston accordingly, to the Peabody bookstore and residence at 13 West Street—site of her own nuptials nine months earlier—in order to share in the family's new joy, to help with plans and admire any gifts (the flower painting, the inlaid card cases, the pearl feathered penholder from Elizabeth Hoar) that may already have begun arriving for this second wedding, scheduled for May Day, hardly three weeks off.

All during her absence, Sophia's husband back at the Manse eagerly awaited her return. Through five days and four nights Hawthorne fretted. Once Emerson stopped by, "with a sunbeam in his face; and we had as good a talk as I ever remember experiencing with him." Of course Sophia would want to know all that was said. Emerson "seemed fullest," her husband dutifully, drily recorded, "of Margaret Fuller, who, he says, has risen perceptibly into a higher state, since their last meeting. He apotheosized her as the greatest woman, I believe, of ancient or modern times, and the one figure in the world worth considering." Thus went Saturday's ironic entry, concluding in the gathering dusk with a heartfelt utterance: "I would like to see my wife!" For the rest, Hawthorne in his solitude spoke to no one ("Come home soon, little Dove, or thy husband will have forgotten the use of speech"), heard only the dinner bell or the distant slam of a door as the maid Molly went about her chores elsewhere in the house. And each night the abandoned husband would flail about in the vastitude of the couple's bed, longing for his "sweetest little bedfellow, (that ought to be always, but is not now)." In the mornings he worked at writing, once having "caught an idea by the tail, which I intend to hold fast, though it struggles to get free"—an idea not yet ready to be put on paper, however; so he returned to the *Dial*, to a good article that Margaret Fuller had written on Canova, to a less good article by Charles Lane on Alcott's works. And the husband attended to his journal, faithfully, to the very end of his desolation, "and thus the record is brought down to the present moment; ten minutes past six" on Tuesday, April 11, 1843. "To-night—to-night—yes, within an hour—this Eden, which is no Eden to a solitary Adam, will regain its Eve."

Like most other Americans of the age, Horace Mann had been born on a farm, in 1796, in the village of Franklin, well south of Boston toward the Rhode Island line. The settlement had been dominated by a hellfire minister and debased by a dreadful, altogether typical district school. In his childhood Horace had suffered through both school and church, the Puritan doctrines of the one determining the methodology of the other. Children had evil in them. Their wills must be broken. They must be drilled in their duty and caned if they strayed from it. They must be made to memorize and recite aloud, older and younger ones all gathered together in the close single room of the schoolhouse. Mary Peabody, like her older sister a teacher, would in late life recall such classrooms as she had known them in the 1820s and '30s: benches without backs, long rote spelling lessons in a space crowded and ill-ventilated, spans of idleness during which the "little darlings had to sit up straight and not speak or fidget."

Mann in his youth had attended such a school as that, in Franklin with a brutal and ignorant master, although irregularly and for no more than eight or ten weeks a year. Even so, he had hated the school, as he hated the Calvinism of the local church, whose parson, Nathaniel Emmons, had seen fit to preach to the village a timely sermon condemning to hell the unready soul of Horace's admired older brother Stephen, drowned at eighteen while profaning the Sabbath at Uncas Pond nearby. Finally, tardily at twenty, Horace Mann had escaped farm chores in such a stultifying atmosphere and fled to the haven of Brown University, thirty miles off in Providence. There this gifted young man achieved a sterling academic record, graduating in three years, with high honors, in 1819.

He went on to become a successful lawyer in Dedham, Massachusetts, as well as a politician of promise in the Massachusetts legislature, where he set to work on behalf of the insane. For in an era of reform, Mann proved to be a reformer to the bone, full of faith in humanity's perfectibility as he supported the cause of temperance, waged unrelenting war against tobacco, and confidently awaited the betterment of society that the swift-rolling railroads and the well-managed textile mills appeared to be portending.

The joy of Horace Mann's life was his marriage in 1830 to Charlotte Messer; her death two years later—on August 1, 1832, of consumption, childless, at twenty-three—was his great sorrow. Longfellow would grieve over the death of his first wife in Rotterdam; and Emerson, too, was shattered by the lovely Ellen Tucker's death at nineteen. But those gentlemen, after due mourning, managed to get on with their lives, whereas Horace Mann's grief at Charlotte's death appeared beyond consolation. Each anniversary of her demise destroyed the afflicted widower all over again. There seemed nothing to live for; he would rather be dead himself. Elizabeth and Mary Peabody, in Mrs. Clarke's rooming house, where Mann had come to board, had sought zealously to assuage the pain of this most interesting mourner; yet nothing they could say appeared to help. Year after year Mann struggled on with a savorless life, regularly cast into despondency as another August 1 would approach, would arrive, would leave in its wake agonizing memories of the sufferer's lost love.

Thus, despite his worldly success in law office and legislative hall, and despite the Peabody sisters' persistent ministrations of sympathy, Mann's days felt pointless. The law hardly interested him; all that he might do with these remaining months and years was try to help others. And in 1837, a new act of the legislature, moving to reform the public schools of the state, provided him with a fresh opportunity to do so. He abandoned his private practice and resigned his position as president of the Massachusetts senate in order to serve as the ill-paid secretary of the newly formed board of education.

For Horace Mann believed passionately in education, convinced, as he wrote, that "schools will be found to be the way that God has chosen for the reformation of the world." Not such schools as then existed, which the wealthy with their children in private academies avoided. Public schools for everyone was the way. Yet to achieve his mission the secretary had little power beyond that of persuasion. Accordingly, Mann set out in the late 1830s to crisscross the state by horseback, stage, canal, and railroad, visiting each county and township repeatedly, lecturing for nights on end, often writing as many as twenty letters a day. And he instituted normal schools to train teachers to help achieve his all but holy vision of cultivating an informed, public-minded citizenry as America's bed-rock strength. The secretary extolled a vision of the public good, of public morality replacing Puritan sin and guilt, of an educated, enlightened populace capable at last of eradicating such hereto-fore intractable social evils as poverty, violence, war, and disease.

His vision found no place for local district schools. Instead there would be one school system throughout the state, with sepa-rate classrooms for students at different levels of instruction. No more one-room schools, and no more flogging by brute incompe-tents, and no more rote learning. And no more dependency by the poor and dispossessed on the fitful philanthropy of the wealthy; to pay for all these reforms property would be taxed. It was, after all, a public good that the public should support: this institutionalizing of nonsectarian, republican virtue, free of par-tisan politics and divisive ethnic loyalties. Attendance would be compulsory, and not for six weeks or two months but for half the year, with adequately trained teachers teaching an enriched cur-riculum, not simply drilling what fearful pupils were being made to memorize.

Of course the old guard protested. Yet what is remarkable is the success that Mann achieved over twelve years, from 1837 to 1849, during which he inaugurated his immense changes. By the end of that brief period Massachusetts public education had been trans-formed, and in ways that other states across America were fast adopting.

Early on, in the spring of 1838, the indefatigable Elizabeth Peabody had approached Horace Mann on behalf of a "first rate genius" just then emerging from "a life of extraordinary seclusion." The state's schoolchildren, she felt, should be reading (to the genius's pecuniary advantage) *Twice-Told Tales*. But the secretary of the board of education, while acknowledging the book to be beauti-fully written, had pronounced it lacking in moral seriousness; "some-thing nearer home to duty & business" would be needed to benefit the young. And this was the judgmental Whig, foe of tobacco and all things evil, who these five years later was about to wed the sister-in-law of that same book's author.

Perhaps Hawthorne, a good Democrat fond of cigars and brandy, felt less fretful than his wife when May Day arrived with the rain pouring down. As a result, Sophia was unable to venture over impassable roads from Concord to Boston to witness Mary Peabody's nuptials. In her absence, the bridal couple stood together, as the Hawthornes not a year earlier had come together, in the front parlor at 13 West Street: Horace Mann and Mary Peabody, with Dr. and Mrs. Peabody and sister Elizabeth, along with the Reverend James Freeman Clarke who had officiated at Sophia and Nathaniel's wedding. No other guests, none of Mann's friends had been able to push through the morning's inclemencies to attend, although for one absentee Elizabeth described the occasion: the garnishes of geranium leaves, Mary's beautiful grass-cloth gown and about her head Mr. Mann's gift of a gold band, the groom himself "so full of joy & tenderness."

But they must hurry; already they had delayed too long, awaiting guests who never appeared. The vows were uttered, and with the rain finally ended, the wedding party repaired to the Boston waterfront. At the Cunard piers, at 2:07 that Monday afternoon, May 1, 1843, the gangway of the steamer *Britannia* was raised; the paddlewheels port and starboard began to turn, and the great chugging vessel moved out to sea, carrying aboard two sets of newlyweds—the Manns and their friends the Howes—along with, still and forever Mann's lifelong companion, the unfaded memory of his first wife, Charlotte Messer.

The *Britannia* carrying the Manns overseas was the same vessel that a year earlier had brought Charles Dickens, not quite thirty years old, to a triumphant American reception starting in Boston in January 1842. Festivities on the earlier occasion had included the public dinner of forty dishes where George Hillard had delivered the most admired of the numerous addresses, as well as such private celebrations as when Dickens had stolen away and sat down to breakfast across the river from Boston, in Cambridge, at his new friend Henry Longfellow's lodgings in the Craigie House. That spring Longfellow had set out for Europe and the water cure along the Rhine, and while in Germany he and the phenomenally popular Dickens had continued to exchange warm greetings: "How stands it about your visit do you say? Thus: your bed is waiting to be slept in; the door is gaping hospitably to receive you. I am ready to spring towards it with open arms at the first indication of a Longfellow knock or ring."

Over these late years this widower, this Bowdoin classmate and friend of Hawthorne's, had become ever more celebrated as a man of letters himself, the author of a couple of prose travel books as well as of two popular collections of verse. In November 1842, the poet, having by then partaken of the Rhine water cure and a fortnight of Dickens's zestful entertainment in London, had returned to America with his health much restored. Was Longfellow recovered as well from fruitless pinings for Fanny Appleton? As for that, he was all too aware that "crowds are about her; and flatterers enough; and all the splendor of fashion, and suitors manifold." By this time seven years had passed since those enchanted days in Switzerland when he had first known Fanny and her delightful sister Mary, the latter long since well-married. Time kept slipping away, the poet-professor now in his mid-thirties, his beloved a woman of twenty-five, still apparently indifferent to his longings, still unyielding.

Earlier this spring, Sophia Hawthorne had hurried to Boston to be with her sister Mary, returning to her overjoyed husband on the evening of April 11, 1843. In Cambridge two days later, the Andrews Nortons held a dinner party at Shady Hill. Longfellow attended and there, to his surprise, discovered among the guests Fanny Appleton. Between the two a conversation occurred, brief but fraught with significance. They had found themselves together in a window seat, for a moment out of earshot of the others. Fanny was saying that her brother Tom would be leaving for Europe in a couple of days; she expected to be lonely with him gone. "You must come," she added, "and comfort me, Mr. Longfellow."

After all these years so small a hint sufficed. Longfellow did at once recommence his visits to Beacon Street; and on May 10, with Mr. and Mrs. Horace Mann ten days at sea aboard the *Britannia*, Fanny in Boston sat down and wrote a brief note. Her suitor across the Charles would receive it in ecstasy. "The Tenth of May! Day to be recorded with sunbeams! Day of light and love! The day of our engagement; when in the bright morning . . . I received Fanny's note, and walked to town, amid the blossoms and sunshine and song of birds, with my heart full of gladness and my eyes full of tears!"

"How it was gradually brought about," Miss Appleton would soon be writing an aunt, "you shall hear by and bye, or rather what is there to tell but the old tale that true love is very apt to win its reward." And to her brother Tom, who had feared that Fanny was too aloof ever to find a mate, she marveled that she had not seen Henry's true worth long ago, "but we have both come to the comforting conclusion that it is best as it is, that our characters have been ripened to appreciate it and receive it with fuller gratitude than if the past experience had been spared us." Yet Fanny did thank God that in the same long interval she had not, out of a craving for love, been misled into feeling an affection for someone else, "which would have caused a great famine somewhere in my heart."

The wedding occurred promptly, on Thursday, July 13, 1843, two months after Fanny's note of surrender. The contrast with the Manns' wedding directly across Boston Common a couple of months earlier—and with the Hawthornes' almost exactly a year before—was considerable. In the Appleton mansion at 39 Beacon Street the guest list had been limited to intimate friends, yet some fifty were on hand, all in brilliant formal attire. The bride wore a floor-length lace veil with orange blossoms in her hair; a table gleamed with wedding gifts. "Oh, it was a beautiful scene," the groom's sister Anne exclaimed. "My darling brother never looked one half so handsome in all his life before, and Fanny was in all respects the perfection of all brides." After the ceremony (both having said "'I do' in the most audible manner"), guests enjoyed a supper before the bride and groom withdrew, on their way to Cambridge under a full moon. They were bound for the handsome Craigie House in Brattle Street, where Longfellow had lodged in rented rooms these recent years. As a wedding gift, Nathan Appleton had purchased the entire mansion and presented it to his daughter and son-in-law. "Everybody is delighted with this engagement," the fortunate bridegroom had earlier assured his sister, the same who would be in such joyful attendance at the wedding; "and," he had added, "I more than everybody. Life was too lonely—and sad;— with little to soothe and calm me. Now the Future opens its long closed gates into pleasant fields and lands of quiet."

II

RURAL UTOPIAS

*T*he Longfellows dated their engagement from the springtime note that Fanny Appleton had written nine weeks before the couple's summertime wedding in mid-July 1843. Between those milestones of engagement and wedding, elsewhere on a drizzly cold June 1, Bronson Alcott sat at the reins of a loaded wagon carrying his wife, four daughters, and household belongings out of Concord toward a New Eden in the opposite direction from Cambridge. The wagon lumbering west over country roads was headed toward Harvard village, the goal toward which Emerson and Hawthorne had walked companionably the previous September. Bound westward in their turn, the Alcotts and a sharp-faced gentleman trudging alongside were forsaking in part the very world of Nathan Appleton into which Longfellow was about to marry. And as Longfellow after the wedding would fancy himself passing through metaphorical gates into a future of pleasant fields and lands of quiet, so the Alcotts with their sharp-faced friend Charles Lane would seem to have found at the end of their wagon ride just such a literal future in that other direction. Emerson visiting, during the month of the Longfellow nuptials, at a remote farmhouse outside Harvard on land that Lane had purchased to share with the Alcotts, would encounter peace. "The sun & the evening sky do not look calmer than Alcott & his family at Fruitlands," the visitor noted of that July day. "They seemed to have arrived at the fact, to have got rid of the show, & so to be serene."

Emerson thought very highly of Bronson Alcott in any case. After three days spent, for example, with the ceaselessly fluent

Alcott in 1857, "I could see plainly," he wrote, "that I conversed with the most extraordinary man and the highest genius of the time." Or this from Emerson, somewhat earlier: "As pure intellect I have never seen his equal"—the more remarkable for Alcott's having developed his intellect all but unaided.

Born on a Connecticut hilltop farm at the very end of a century, in November 1799, Amos Bronson Alcott took as his teacher nature: "from her, in the still communings of my solitudes, I learned divine wisdom even when a child." As for formal education, no Bowdoin awaited this farm boy, no Brown or Harvard. Alcott as a lad had left Connecticut to become a humble itinerant peddler, trudging for four years from door to door in faraway Virginia and the Carolinas. When at last he did return home, at twenty-three, it was to teach—scarcely less humble an occupation—in the dismal village schools of the 1820s.

But the peddler had ideas of his own about teaching. Children were innately good, and the teacher's task was to develop that goodness. There were to be physical exercises at school, and nature study outdoors, and learning games, and individual desks for pupils, and the honor system; and when Connecticut parents objected to such innovations, Alcott moved, in 1828, to what he hoped would prove more receptive surroundings in Boston. There, in a school of his own, he continued to put his theories into practice: "I ask and ask till I get something fit and worthy. I am not thinking, generally, of any particular answer." Rather, what this innovator sought for his pupils was "to assist you by my questions in finding the answer, by the free exercise of your own minds. All truth is within. My business is to lead you to find it in your own Souls."

At King's Chapel in Boston in the spring of 1830, Bronson Alcott married Abigail May, who had followed him up from Connecticut to help with his work. Elizabeth Peabody began assisting at his Temple School on Boston's Tremont Street; Margaret Fuller would be helping too. Emerson, hearing of Alcott's efforts with five- and six-year-olds, came to see, June 15, 1836, and left impressed. In the classroom pupils and teacher had been talking together about the Gospel of Saint John. "I felt strongly," their visitor recorded, "as I watched the gradual dawn of thought upon the minds of all, that to truth is no age or season." Very soon the wizard who could draw such insights from the young was visiting his new admirer in

Concord. "Evermore," wrote Emerson, "he toils to solve the problem: Whence is the world? The point at which he prefers to begin is the mystery of the Birth of a Child."

And that would be Alcott's undoing. The teacher (and, by then, marveling father of three) had spoken with his charges of spiritual birth. "You have seen the rose opening from the seed with the assistance of the atmosphere. This is the birth of the rose. It typifies the bringing forth of the spirit by pain and labor and patience." Similarly, a mother about to give birth "gives up her body to God, and He works upon it in a mysterious way and, with her aid, brings forth the child's Spirit in a little Body of its own; and when it has come she is blissful." Elizabeth Peabody had tried to alert Alcott to the danger of adverting to such matters. "Why," she cautioned him, "did prophets and apostles veil this subject in fables and emblems if there was not a reason for avoiding physiological inquiries &c? This is worth thinking of." But the visionary would not be deterred, and thus he doomed his school. Horace Mann wanted nothing professionally to do with such a radical. "The Secretary of Education," according to Alcott later, "deemed it unsafe to introduce me to the teachers, and . . . I was informed . . . that I could not aid the cause of popular culture." When, in 1839, the same subverter of values made bold to admit into his classes an African-American child, his career in education was done for, reduced as he was to only five pupils by then: that little girl, his own daughters, and the children of a longtime friend.

Emerson took notice, inviting the Alcott family (deeply in debt, as usual) to move to Concord. In the spring of 1840, Bronson settled into a cottage half a mile west of the village center, along with his wife and their three daughters—of whom the middle one, Louisa, was then seven years old. A fourth daughter would be born that summer, to this brilliant though maladroit husband and father whose career as a teacher was finished, never to be resumed.

Yet the prophet was at least mildly honored overseas. Not far from London, a group of Englishmen had been putting the American educator's theories into practice, even changing the name of their experimental school to Alcott House. Impoverished though he was, their patron should go see; the ever generous Emerson would pay his passage. Accordingly, on May 8, 1842 (the day before, Hawthorne and his intended had first visited Concord together to consider leasing the empty homestead of the late Reverend Dr. Ripley), Bronson Alcott bade farewell to his wife and four daughters and sailed for England. Returning to America in October, he brought with him Englishmen associated with the school at Ham Common, in particular Charles Lane, more determined than even Alcott himself to live on acorns and save the world by forsaking it.

Back in Concord on November 10, Alcott at Emerson's invitation met with friends who shared some of his social goals. Hawthorne attended the meeting, although with views different from those of the others present. The congregants were learning that Alcott and Lane meant to establish a "consociate family" and lead a self-sustaining life, exploiting nothing and no one in this exploitative nineteenth-century America. Cloth from Appleton's textile mills, for instance, was spun from slave-picked cotton. Members of the consociate family would wear no cotton—or leather, or wool either, sheared from unwilling sheep. They would clothe themselves only in linen, fabricated as it is from fibers of the blue-flowering flax plant. "I would abstain from the fruits of oppression and blood," Alcott explained in his journal, "and am seeking means of entire independence"—a course that, if others followed it, would redeem the earth from the curse of man's cupidity. Always the idealist had been striving "to apprehend the real in the seeming," to get past "the showy terrestrial to find the heavenly things." Now, more and more, heaven appeared to lie on the far side of abstention and self-denial.

With his life's savings Charles Lane purchased the Wyman farm on the face of a hill near Harvard, leasing an isolated, dilapidated house and barn that stood on the property. "Fruitlands" they called the place, and onto those ninety acres Alcott with his family was directing his wagon full of household belongings on June 1, 1843. In their new solitude the small company of ten consociates—five adults, five children—set about eating only what was pure and bloodless; no animal substances would pollute their table. They would drink water only, nothing ardent such as coffee or tea. To maintain cheerfulness their bathwater would be unwarmed, their garments simple. No artificial light would prolong dark hours or cost them the brightness of morning. Days at Fruitlands would be orderly, with a focus on the reality that lies behind the simulacra assaulting the senses. Meanwhile, from their neighbors the Shakers these pure folk would learn what they could of husbandry and dedication. The children would be appropriately schooled, and the adults would converse together on such matters as Life's Highest Aim.

So Emerson, visiting in July, found the idealists, old and young apparently in the bosom of peace far from the voluptuaries of Beacon Street and the spiritually maimed in the clattering Lowell mills. The consociates were "busily engaged in manual operations in the field, house, wood yard, etc. Planting, ploughing, sowing, cleaning fruit trees, gardening, chopping, sawing, fitting up, etc., etc." Only think: "ninety acres," they exulted, "every one of which may, in a short time, and without much outlay, be brought into a state fit for spade culture; and much of it very good land." As for farming that land, these laborers, exploiting no beasts of burden, were themselves turning the soil with mattock and hoe and tending their fields in the bottoms.

Emerson over from Concord discovered much to admire during his visit at Fruitlands, although in setting down his impressions of the one summer day, he did remark, "I will not prejudge them successful. They look well in July. We will see them in December."

The solitary Hawthorne may have appeared misplaced among the communitarian reformers who had earlier gathered at Emerson's house to learn about Alcott's plans for Fruitlands. Yet the tenant at the Manse had once been involved himself, improbably, in a not dissimilar experiment. Two years before, in mid-April 1841, while he was still unmarried, Hawthorne had voluntarily left comfortable bachelor quarters to settle at Brook Farm, a collective home nine miles south of Boston. There the author had led a life odd indeed, especially for someone of his reserved and skeptical temperament.

In his new role this charter member of the Brook Farm community had risen early, sounding the horn that woke the others at four-thirty every morning to milk the cows and do the other abundant chores of an agricultural day. Hawthorne had eaten with his fellows at a common table before sleeping a well-earned sleep in a room in the Hive near where all those others were sleeping. Moreover, in that collective world the erstwhile customhouse weigher and gauger had appeared to be thriving, at least early on. "This is one of the most beautiful places I ever saw in my life," he wrote his sister Louisa. "Our house stands apart from the main road; so that we are not troubled even with passengers looking at us. Once in a while, we have a transcendental visitor, such as Mr. Alcott; but generally we pass whole days without seeing a single face, save those of the brethren."

The brethren and sisters for their part—hardly more than fifteen in the spring of 1841—had come to Brook Farm for purposes somewhat different from Hawthorne's. They intended, like Alcott two years later at Fruitlands, to help save the world by setting a good example. Instead of fragmenting people in joyless factory-like toil, these denizens of a better society would minister organically to the whole person. They meant to promote "industry without drudgery, and true equality without its vulgarity." Accordingly, class was abolished at the farm; everyone ate together and worked together, all the while hoping that labor would expand thought as they applied thought to labor.

Such high goals had been only tangentially Hawthorne's when he joined Brook Farm, but he had pitched in with a will nonetheless. In his cowhide boots, blue frock, and wide-brimmed hat, he had been out early cutting straw, chopping hay, feeding the cattle, spreading manure, planting potatoes, bringing in wood for the fires, in the late summer gathering squash and apples and thrashing the crop of rye. One who got to know him then (and remained a friend afterward) recorded a first impression of the unlikely farmer as "a very handsome finely formed man, but very silent & diffident or reserved, however I have become somewhat acquainted with him in the course of our hoeing, shovelling & milking together and find something very pleasing in him." Apparently others did too, electing Nathaniel Hawthorne finally and despite his reticence to the high office of treasurer of their association.

He had joined them, in truth, less to reform the world than because the idea had seemed eminently practical. After emerging finally from his Salem owl's nest, Hawthorne in 1839 and '40 had been laboring in the Boston customhouse, in order to make money enough to marry Sophia Peabody. Brook Farm might let the two marry sooner. "Think that I am gone before, to prepare a home for my Dove," he wrote his intended day after arriving at the farm, in a snowstorm on April 12, 1841. He had hoped for a dual outcome:

to find a place where he and Sophia could live together, and to set up a schedule where physical and intellectual labor might coexist, so that he could work half a day in the fields and spend the rest fruitfully writing.

Yet it never happened. Within a very few weeks, by June 1, Hawthorne was noting privately that this new life had proved even less hospitable to authorship than was the Boston customhouse. "I have not the sense of perfect seclusion, which has always been essential to my power of producing anything," he confided to Sophia at summer's end. There was all that farmwork. "Oh, belovedest," he was led to exclaim, "labor is the curse of the world, and nobody can meddle with it without becoming proportionately brutified. Dost thou think it a praiseworthy matter, that I have spent five golden months in providing food for cows and horses?" And to an editor pestering for a tale he would explain that there could be no writing with this crop of blisters on his hands, and anyway, who can "expect pretty stories from a man who feeds pigs"?—or milks cows, or shovels manure.

So he had left Brook Farm. He had come there in the spring of 1841, worked hard as a laborer through the summer, and would leave in the fall. "Thou and I must form other plans for ourselves," he had been obliged to warn Sophia, "for I can see few or no signs that Providence purposes to give us a home here." Providence was to withhold a home from them a while longer. In November Hawthorne had withdrawn from Brook Farm, and the following February: "I wonder, I wonder, I wonder," he was writing his lover, "where on earth we are to set up our Tabernacle. God knows;—but I want to know too." In May they had visited the late Dr. Ripley's place in Concord together, and in July they married and moved there. Settled at last in the Manse, this new husband wrote three months later resigning as an associate of the Brook Farm Institute. That was in October 1842. Thereupon was returned to the shareholder $475.95 of his investment, with a promissory note to pay on demand the balance of $524.05 plus interest. Hawthorne's brush with communal living was ended.

Even so, that same fall, on November 11, he had been invited to Mr. Emerson's, along with others associated with the Brook Farm venture, to hear of Bronson Alcott's plans for establishing a more abstemious Eden elsewhere. On the first of June following, the Alcott family had departed from Concord in a wagon bound for Fruitlands, near Harvard village. At the Manse, meantime, Hawthorne—with a winter of diligent writing behind him—could exult all the while that his Eve had returned to her Adam, in a Concord paradise that the two were creating on their own.

12

SEEKING A LIVELIHOOD

From the first, Hawthorne had loved the Manse. "I live in an old parsonage," he explained to a New York correspondent after a year in residence, "the most quiet place, I believe, in the whole world, with woods close at hand, and a river at the bottom of my orchard, and an old battlefield right under my window. Everybody that comes here falls asleep, there is such an unearthly quiet; but for my own part, I feel as if, for the first time in my life, I was awake. I have found a reality, though it looks very much like some of my old dreams." He and, more remarkably, his wife were enjoying splendid health: six months into their stay, Mr. Hawthorne "is in the glory of health," Sophia reported, "& so am I." So much so that they tirelessly explored the surrounding woods, ran races along the avenue out front, slid down a snowy hillside in Sleepy Hollow, "or I danced before my husband to the measures of the great music-box," their maid exclaiming that "it did her heart good to see us as joyful as two children."

The bliss may have surprised them both, far deeper and more pervasive than either had ever experienced. Like his wife during this first year together, Hawthorne was "continually learning to be happy"—testimony offered seven months after their having settled in Concord—and we "should consider ourselves perfectly so now," he wrote, "only that we find ourselves making advances all the time." They tried to record their feelings in pages of a journal jointly kept; but "what is there to write about at all? Happiness," the husband was persuaded early on, "has no succession of events, because it is a part of eternity; and we have been living in eternity, ever since we came to this old Manse." Sophia felt every bit as elated. "We wandered down to our sweet, sleepy river," she recorded of a typical interlude, "and it was so silent all around us and so solitary, that we seemed the only persons living. We sat beneath our stately trees, and felt as if we were the rightful inheritors of the old abbey." All about them in that still moment was loveliness. "But the bloom and fragrance of nature had become secondary to us, though we were lovers of it. In my husband's face and eyes I saw a fairer world, of which the other was a faint copy."

As the seasons advanced, through late summer and fall into winter, Hawthorne in evenings read aloud to his wife, including all of *Paradise Lost*. Sophia adored hearing him read, loved the rich expressive melody of his voice. They took to dining later than midday and forgoing an afternoon tea ceremony, which would have broken up precious hours reading together after time spent at separate occupations. "We have passed the happiest winter," she wrote a Salem friend sometime later, "the long evenings lifted out of the common sphere by the magic of Shakespeare. Mr. Hawthorne read aloud to me all the Plays. And you must know how he reads, before you can have any idea what it was." In the study upstairs a hanging astral lamp had cast warm hues night after night over the yellow walls, the cozy furniture, the woodstove, an opened book, and two figures seated in hours aglow with pleasure.

Yet in time Hawthorne wondered about the isolation, only those two and the servant Molly Bryan. "My wife," he wrote, "is, in the strictest sense, my sole companion; and I need no other—there is no vacancy in my mind, any more than in my heart. In truth, I have spent so many years in total seclusion from all human society, that it is no wonder if I now feel all my desires satisfied by this sole intercourse. But my Dove has come to me from the midst of many friends, and a large circle of acquaintance; yet she lives from day-to-day in this solitude, seeing nobody but myself and our Molly . . . ; yet she is always cheerful, and far more than cheerful. Thank God that I suffice for her boundless heart!"

Sophia's cheerfulness, like her good health, abided. With the arrival of the first spring after their summer wedding, "I myself," she exulted, "am Spring with all its birds, its rivers, its buds, singing, rushing, blooming in his arms. I feel new as the earth which is just born again. I rejoice that I am, because I am his, wholly, unreservedly his. Therefore is my life beautiful & gracious. Therefore is the world pleasant as roses."

The anniversary of their wedding day came round, and in the notebook where both of them wrote, knowing the other would read, Hawthorne paused over the blank page for July 9, 1843. "Dearest love," he set down, "I know not what to say, and yet cannot be satisfied without marking with a word or two this holiest anniversary of our life. But life now heaves and swells beneath me like a brimfull ocean; and the endeavor to comprise any portion of it in words, is like trying to dip up the ocean in a goblet. We never were so happy as now—never such wide capacity for happiness, yet overflowing with all that the day and every moment brings to us." This "birthday of our married life" was, he thought, like a cape of land "which we have now doubled, and find a more infinite ocean of love stretching out before us. God bless us and keep us; for there is something more awful in happiness than in sorrow—the latter being earthly and finite, the former composed of the texture and substance of eternity, so that spirits still embodied may well tremble at it."

Sophia's feelings were more simply expressed. Two years and longer—fully two and a half years beyond that moment when they had first stepped down from the carriage and opened the door of the Manse into their new married life, she wrote to her husband: "I bless God for such a destiny as mine; you satisfy me beyond all things."

Their paradise harbored a serpent, of course, as paradises do. By the spring of 1843, the thirty-eight-year-old Hawthorne was nationally, even internationally, celebrated as one of America's outstanding authors. Orestes Brownson in the *Boston Quarterly Review* had already enrolled himself "among those, who regard Mr. Hawthorne as fitted to stand at the head of American Literature." Other critics united in praising the author's style on the one hand and his originality on the other. From New York, Evert Duyckinck submitted categorically that "Of the American writers destined to live, he is the most original, the one least indebted to foreign models or literary precedents of any kind." And from Philadelphia, a reviewer in the pages of *Graham's Magazine* had written last April, in 1842: "The style of Mr. Hawthorne is purity itself. His *tone* is singularly effective—wild, plaintive, thoughtful, and in full accordance with his themes." But more: "His *originality* both of incident and of reflection is very remarkable; and this trait alone would ensure him at least *our* warmest regard and commendation. . . . Upon the whole," this reviewer concluded, "we look upon him as one of the few men of indisputable genius to whom our country has as yet given birth. As such, it will be our delight to do him honor."

Those are the words of Edgar Allan Poe, America's most penetrating (and sharpest-tongued) literary critic, a poet and tale writer besides. Indeed, between the two of them independently, one in the North and one farther south, Hawthorne and Poe in the 1830s had invented a new literary genre. If the former appeared less aware of the originality of his achievement, the more analytical Edgar Poe knew exactly what they had been about; so that in reviewing *Twice-Told Tales* that critic not only extolled this new way of writing over all other kinds of imaginative prose but also identified its defining characteristics: brevity, coherence, unity of effect. Here was something different from any such earlier examples of the brief fictional narrative as anecdote, parable, legend, fable, or fairy tale. Hawthorne's brand of tale—and Poe's—departed from such predecessors by being consciously crafted from the very first word, every element artfully chosen to convey a mood and inform an overriding purpose, the beginning cognizant of the end and tending toward it: in brief, what we now call a short story.

But about that serpent in the Hawthornes' garden: its name was Poverty. "Had my husband been dealt justly by in the matter of his emoluments," Sophia would write her mother, "there would not have been even this shadow upon the blessedness of our condition." The trouble was that nobody paid what he owed. "It is impossible," the storyteller was complaining to his friend Horatio Bridge this spring, "for any individual to be just and honest, and true to his engagements, when it is a settled principle of the community to be always behindhand. I find no difference in anybody, in this respect; all do wrong alike. O'Sullivan is just as certain to disappoint me in money matters, as any pitiful little scoundrel among the booksellers. On my part, I am compelled to disappoint those who put faith in my engagements; and so it goes round. The devil take such a system." But how singular a system it was: "nobody's scribblings seem to be more acceptable to the public than mine; and yet I shall find it a tough match to gain a respectable support by my pen."

Part of the reason lay in the parlous economy, hard times spread through six grievous years after the Panic of 1837, so that only now, in 1843, had the first faint light of a dawning prosperity begun to glimmer, although still at some distance from the Manse. Meanwhile, Hawthorne and Poe had alike been scrambling in their different worlds to earn a livelihood. Poe in Philadelphia had been angling to secure a government post through the professed interest of President Tyler's son Rob. Something in the customhouse would do fine; accordingly, Poe was much exercised during these same months with obtaining the secure income that such light duties promised. But the dream failed to materialize. As a New York weekly reported in March: "the Custom House is beset with an army of eager applicants for the office, and name after name is diligently sought after to append to petitions and recommendations. All this indicates the hardness of the times. Thousands of men are ready and anxious to take a public office now, who, in ordinary times, would rather trust to their own independent exertions for a living." In an America without pensions, social security, or other such financial recourse, thousands had been seeking that kind of help. Edgar Poe would be among the very many who failed to obtain it.

Hawthorne in Concord was lined up among those thousands, hoping just now, like all those others, for some sort of governmental post to relieve his and Sophia's indigence. At the end of March 1843 the tenant at the Manse was summarizing in his notebook a winter's worth of authorship. "I might have written more," he concluded, "if it had seemed worth while; but I was content to earn only so much gold as might suffice for our immediate wants, having prospects of official station and emolument, which would do away the necessity of writing for bread." True, like the gold, nothing in the official line had come through yet, but "we are well content to wait; because an office would inevitably remove us from our present happy home—at least from an outward home; for there is an inner one that will accompany us wherever we go."

In June, the need for a regular income became more pressing when Sophia revealed that she was pregnant again. A further consequence of his wife's news was that Hawthorne's sister Louisa must return for a visit to the Manse at an early date, before her sister-in-law's confinement. Pick the month: July, August, September. And tell us, Sophia wrote to Salem in mid-June, whether Mr. Hawthorne's mother and other sister might come with Louisa to Concord. But neither Ebe nor Madame Hathorne, then or ever, would dislodge herself from Salem to make the thirty-mile journey to the Manse. Sophia professed disappointment "that our dear mother will not be persuaded to come at all. I am sure she *would not* be ill here. But I can entirely sympathise with her shrinking from such a journey, with her delicate nerves & disuse of travelling. When the rail-road is finished I shall teaze her again, & wish she would endeavour meanwhile to accustom her thoughts to the idea of coming."

The railroad was all this while edging closer to Concord village. This same summer of 1843 Emerson would write Henry Thoreau, absent tutoring on Staten Island, of local news: of the Alcotts experimenting with Eden at Fruitlands and of Irish laborers in nearby woods, surveyors in their midst waving red flags, peering through theodolites, and calling out their feet and inches. Soon, by Walden Pond, Hawthorne would see for himself immigrants living humbly in shanties, "Irish people who are at work upon the rail-road." Strolling past, he was to hear the shouting and laughter of children, playing about "like the sunbeams that come down through the branches. Women are washing beneath the trees, and long lines of whitened clothes are extended from tree to tree, fluttering and gambolling in the breeze."

By that time, his mother and older sister not coming to him, Hawthorne had gone to them in Salem in late August and, passing through Boston on the way, had met up with Longfellow at George Hillard's law offices at 4 Court Street. These six weeks after the wedding in the Appleton mansion, Fanny's new husband had bloomed and grown more solid and substantial, as his friend reported back to Sophia; the poet seemed no more aware of troubles than was a sunflower—which lovely blossom, according to Hawthorne, Longfellow appeared somehow to resemble. John O'Sullivan, editor of the *Democratic Review,* was along on that outing, engaged all the while in trying to find some governmental appointment that would suit an impoverished author. Something in the Salem post office perhaps. Or how would Hawthorne take to a posting in China, in Pekin? Or Marseilles, or—Bridge's suggestion—maybe he could supplant Longfellow's good friend Greene as consul at Rome? But nothing was working out just yet, while summer turned into fall, and Hawthorne back at the Manse late in September, at harvest-time, presided over his orchard fast ripening, and saw apples and thumping big pears bestrew the grass. "Well; we are rich in blessings, though poor in money," he concluded; "and I see my little wife rounding apace, and anticipate the greatest blessing that is yet to come."

On a day in November further delightful news reached the Manse. "Beloved Mary," Sophia wrote excitedly on Tuesday, November 7, "Yesterday noon my dear husband came home from the village but a few seconds it seemed even to me after he left me, shining with glad tidings. They were that the Steamer had arrived with you in it!" After a boisterous passage from England, the *Britannia* had docked at last in Boston; and Mr. and Mrs. Horace Mann, gone since May 1, had been able to step on native soil once more. They must come visit in Concord. Mr. Mann must come and lecture at the lyceum here, "as soon as he possibly can." Squire Hoar told Emerson that "he had never heard such eloquence from human lips as from Mr Mann's." So do come, Sophia urged, and tell her beforehand of any particularities about Mr. Mann's diet, so that she might have what he liked ready for the visitor.

Another absentee returned home that November; Henry Thoreau was back from Staten Island. "Methinks," the tutor down there had written his mother in the course of half a year away from everything he loved, "I should be content to sit at the back-door in Concord, under the poplar-tree, henceforth forever." Now Thoreau was home again and, after a brief return to New York in December to gather up his few belongings, would settle down in the village to stay, nevermore dreaming of living anywhere else on earth.

Friends through the passing seasons continued all this while soliciting the well-placed on Hawthorne's behalf, former senator Frank Pierce having no more luck than the others as yet; so that at winter's return and the end of another year looming, the author remained without prospects of an official station. On Christmas Day, Sophia was nevertheless glorying in her and her husband's paradisiacal dinner of preserved quince, apples, dates, bread, cheese, and milk. It was a different age from ours, this wife the same month complaining that her bathwater wasn't properly cold! "My water this morning," she wrote her mother, "was deadly cold instead of livingly cold, and I knew the Imp"—her maid?—"must have taken it from some already drawn, instead of right from the well." That same morning, after she and Hawthorne had breakfasted, "as I could not walk out on account of the snow, I concluded to house-wife. My husband shoveled paths (heaps of snow being trifles to his might), and sawed and split wood, and brought me water from the well."

Water more to Sophia's liking, livingly cold, with the coldest of seasons ahead. If last winter had been the most frigid in two de-cades, the early weeks of 1844 were to be appallingly worse. "In the papers it is said that there has not been so cold a January for a hundred years!"

13

UNA

*A*mong sufferers through that grim winter were Edenites at a little distance to the west, exposed on their snowswept hillside at Fruitlands. Six months earlier, a consociate family's venture toward Utopia near Harvard village had begun with exalted expectations. Through June days, Bronson Alcott and Charles Lane, clad in their linen tunics, had laid plans to build cottages on their acres, lead water down to the cottages from springs in outcroppings above, convert pastures below into gardens, fashion paths through surrounding woods as repose for naturalists and poets, clean the brook on the property to connect their boat landing to the Nashua River. "Such are the designs which Mr. Alcott and I have just sketched, as, resting from planting, we walked around this reserve," around a Fruitlands filled with summertime promise.

Their greatest need back then had been for more female help, as Lane had written to Henry Thoreau down on Staten Island: "Far too much labor devolves on Mrs. Alcott. If you should light on any such assistance, it would be charitable to give it a direction this way." The occasional visitor did arrive to help with the cooking and the farming, yet as weeks advanced toward fall the mood of those Edenites had grown intermittently cloudy. Thursday, September 14: "I had a music lesson with Miss P. I hate her, she is so fussy." This is the ten-year-old, writing in her diary about a visiting Miss Page. But despite outbursts of petulance, despite the ironing and the dishes to wash, little Louisa Alcott was finding intervals to relish in her new Eden. "I ran in the wind and played be a horse, and had a lovely time in the woods with Anna and Lizzie. We were fairies, and made gowns and paper wings. I 'flied' the highest of all." On other days the child read Plutarch or *The Vicar of Wakefield* or *Oliver Twist,* dressed her dolly, wrote poems, went berry picking, and, when fall came, gathered leaves and husked corn in the barn by lamplight: "It was good fun."

But autumn brought tensions as well, among unwarmed baths outdoors on the hoarfrost in dawn's gray light, at midday among the Socratic lessons concerning God's Noblest Work and the Meaning of Man, among the evening suppers of bread and fruit and water. October 8, her mother's birthday: "I wish I was rich, I was good," the ten-year-old grumbled at the end of it, "and we were all a happy family this day." They were not rich; they were very poor—and increasingly unhappy. Seed had been planted late in the planting season. Crops substituting for forbidden manure had been too often plowed under, so that not enough had been harvested against approaching winter. Lane and Alcott were too frequently away seeking recruits, while the fields at Fruitlands went untended. But mostly the tensions at home arose out of spiritual matters. According to Charles Lane, "Mrs. Alcott has no spontaneous inclination towards a larger family than her own natural one, of spiritual ties she knows nothing, though to keep all together she does and would go through a good deal of exterior and interior toil." Which means that to keep together her own as distinct from a larger consociate family Mrs. Alcott would work very hard—but how could converts be lured to an Eden so exclusionary?

There were carnal aspects to Lane's complaint; he was much attracted to the celibacy of the Shaker life nearby. Abba Alcott, meanwhile, persisted in adoring her husband, and the physicality of that adoration interfered with achieving Lane's high, pure goals. In short, the flesh-and-blood family at Fruitlands had got in the way of the spiritual, consociate family, with Lane pulling at Bronson Alcott from one direction and Abba tugging from another.

Mrs. Alcott had the advantage. The enterprise was in debt: "The crops, I believe, will not discharge all the obligations they were expected to liquidate," as Lane was driven to admit, and Abba's friends the Lovejoys had offered a place to live nearby. "Thereupon ensued endless discussions, doubts, and anticipations concerning our destiny. These still hang over us. But in the midst of them Mrs. Alcott gives notice that she concedes to the wishes of her friends and shall withdraw to a house which they will provide for herself and her four children. As she will take all the furniture with her, this proceeding necessarily leaves me"—the Englishman—"alone and naked in a new world."

Lane would end by moving in with the Shakers; and on a bleak winter day—as Louisa May Alcott grown to maturity recalled— "with their few possessions piled on an ox-sled, the rosy children perched atop, and the parents trudging arm in arm behind, the exiles left their Eden." On that freezing mid-January day in 1844, the six Alcotts, with only thirty-two dollars remaining to them, retreated finally to Still River to live out the winter in three rooms of the Lovejoy farm. "Yesterday," Abba wrote on January 11, "having ate our last bit and burnt our last chip, we sent for Mr. Lovejoy to come and get us out—which he did." And she added, "All Mr. Lane's efforts have been to disunite us. But Mr. Alcott's conjugal and paternal instincts were too strong for him."

Yet the struggle had exacted a terrible price, for by then Bronson Alcott was a broken man. In a Samaritan's home the disillusioned idealist took to his bed, faced the wall with his back to his family, and would not eat, would hardly move, as days of that dreadful cold winter crawled by.

In February Horace Mann, the reformer of the state's education system, came to Concord for a visit and to lecture at the village lyceum as his sister-in-law had urged him to. The Hawthornes made sure that a sleigh was waiting at the depot to bring Mary's husband to the Manse, because their guest must not be allowed to walk so far in the cold. And he must be fed his special diet, or as close to his diet as Sophia could manage on limited resources. No Dyspepsia Bread was to be found in all of Concord; but there were Graham crackers and gingerbread, currant jelly, always baked apples and milk, and boiled syrup to mix into Mr. Mann's hot water. Nor would he be permitted to sleep in the chilly guest room. Instead, Sophia converted her husband's stove-warmed study into a bedroom to receive their visitor during the brief visit. As for the lecture, neither host was able to attend. With the baby expected soon, Sophia spent all of her evenings at home; "and Mr. Hawthorne would not leave me to hear Paul preach at this time." So Horace Mann, his lecture delivered and his crotchets indulged, hurried on

to complete this present set of engagements on behalf of education reform, journeying from Concord into New Hampshire, then
returning as expeditiously as possible to his own wife, Mary, at their
boardinghouse in Boston. For Mary Peabody Mann was about to
have a baby as well. Horace Mann, Jr., would be born on February 24, 1844.

A week later, Sunday morning the 3rd of March, the Hawthornes'
child arrived at the Manse—entered the world headfirst "after being
ten awful hours in getting across the threshold. I have not yet seen
the baby," Hawthorne wrote his sister Louisa the morning of the
birth, "and am almost afraid to look at it. . . . Dr. Bartlett has the
audacity to say that it looks like him, and has *red* hair."

Some people were displeased when the parents named their
baby Una. From Salem, Louisa was not long in conveying family
feelings about the choice of that name, of the beautiful, allegori-
cal figure of the One True Faith, heroine in Book I of Spenser's
Faerie Queene. "Dear L.," her brother responded tartly on the 15th,
"I did not impart your letter (which I received yesterday) to Sophia,
on account of your strictures on the name. Almost everybody has
had something to say about it; but only yourselves have found out
that it does not sound prettily!" Nothing could be done in any case;
the name was sticking like tar and feathers, so "there seems no use
in any further criticism, especially from you, whom Sophia has been
anxious to please in the whole concoction of this baby." Thus, with
this present letter undeliverable, his sister must write another at
once, "as like the last as you please, except about the name."

Hillard, too, had protested the affixing to an earthbound baby
of a name so allegorically sublime: "If your little girl could pass her
life in playing upon a green lawn with a snow white lamb . . . but,"
wrote the counselor, "imagine Sophia saying, 'Una, my love, I am
ashamed to see you with so dirty a face,' or, 'Una, my dear, you
should not sit down to dinner without your apron.' Think of all this,
before you finally decide." Their mutual friend did dilute his reservation by reporting genially on the Longfellows, both at present
well and happy, "and you will be glad to learn that there is a bud of
unexpanded joy in store for them which will one day ripen and
expand into such another perfect flower of bliss as now blooms upon
your hearth. God bless the poets, and keep up their line to the end

of time; for you are a poet," the lawyer was assuring his friend and Concord writer of tales, "and a true one, though not wearing the garb of verse."

The expectant Longfellows must have appeared all but carefree amid the opulences of the Craigie House, even as fatherhood was bringing to the tenant at the Old Manse more to fret about than his daughter's given name. In responding to Hillard, Hawthorne alluded to deeper disquiet. A baby's birth "ought not to come too early in a man's life," he was opining, "not till he has fully enjoyed his youth—for methinks the spirit never can be thoroughly gay and careless again, after this great event." The new father in Concord was harassed by doubts about his professional future. "It will never do for me to continue merely a writer of stories for the magazines— the most unprofitable business in the world." Formerly, as he assured Hillard, rather than write for bread he would have sooner starved; yet this baby had changed everything. Now Hawthorne required a regular income, or "poor little Una would have to take refuge in the alms-house—which, here in Concord, is a most gloomy old mansion. Her 'angel face' would hardly make a sunshine there."

The problem rose at every turn. To his sister, too, the author had lamented his lack of funds. "It has troubled me greatly," he had added in that recent tart letter to Louisa, "not to be able to send you any money this winter; but my great extra expenses, and the delay of payments which I had every right to expect, have prevented me. The moment I have more than enough for my own immediate use, I shall send it to you. I must," he had gone on, "within no long time, make some arrangements to establish a more regular income. If any Democratic candidate be elected President, all will go well enough" for this loyal Democrat in quest of patronage. "I shall be certain of the Post Office, or of something as good. If otherwise"—if the Whigs currently in power should manage to hold on come November—"I shall connect myself permanently with some paper or magazine, which it will not be difficult to do; and, I think, without removing from Concord, as the rail-road will soon be opened," providing swift, ready access to Boston.

In any event, Hawthorne would be obliged to come out of his cloudland and let his life be woven, as he said, "into the sombre texture of humanity." There was no getting around it. "I have business on earth now," he told Hillard, "and must look about me for the means of doing it." Tale writing would no longer serve. Even if it paid, even if editors met their obligations and the demand for stories was ever so brisk, "I could not spend more than a third of my time in this sort of composition. It requires a continual freshness of mind; else a deterioration in the article will quickly be perceptible." No, if Hawthorne meant to make a living by his pen, it would have to be by drudgery: by translating, or grinding out schoolbooks, or scribbling forth newspaper articles. If, however, the Democrats won in November—that talisman ever gleaming— "I shall again favor Uncle Sam with my services, though, I hope, in some less disagreeable situation than formerly," when before his marriage he had been weighing and gauging for the Boston customhouse.

As for Sophia all this while, in the midst of their poverty the new mother appeared possessed of joy unqualified. Her baby was proving to be incomparable: all health and beauty and goodness, growing beautifully, so that within a couple of months the infant weighed "14 lbs & more & talks & laughs also." Such a marvel was taken into Boston to be admired by the mother's family. Mrs. Peabody and everyone else duly raved about Una, as Sophia on her return to Concord assured her sister-in-law. Louisa would delight to know that complete strangers had testified to the infant's perfection. "She was called 'a piece of statuary'—'a Picture'—'an Ideal child'—'a Queen,' 'a born-lady' 'a Princess'—'Morning glory'"—each separate compliment treasured—"'Morning star,' 'a Dove' & more sweet names than I can account." The child's blessed tranquillity had been remarked upon as well, and her shining looks and "her sweet smiles enchanted the world—as they do us continually. A sculptor wanted to take a cast of her, he thought her form so perfect."

The father of such a paragon had gone into Boston, too, in late May, in part to dine with Longfellow across the river and meet his friend's new wife. Mrs. Longfellow would have been looking forward to the occasion eagerly. A month earlier Fanny had read in the latest *Graham's* a "capital" new story, "Earth's Holocaust," by her husband's Bowdoin classmate; and the dinner, on the 25th, would allow her to become acquainted with its author. As befitted the hostess's condition (the birth of her first child was scarcely more than two weeks away), only a small group would be present, including her convivial, adored brother Tom, as well as George Hillard, good friend to both Hawthorne and Longfellow.

From an afternoon among the comforts of Craigie House survives perhaps the most graphic first impression of the Salem author that a perceptive observer ever furnished. Afterward, privately, Fanny took time to remark, as everyone did, on her guest's good looks, on his "fine manly head." But what struck her more forcefully about Hawthorne was what others invariably noted as well, if with less vividness: he "is the most shy and silent of men. The freest conversation did not thaw forth more than a monosyllable and we discussed art glibly enough." Even then, even there with friends amid agreeable talk, Hawthorne had kept silent. "I really pity a person under this spell of reserve," wrote cultured, kindhearted Fanny; "he must long to utter his thoughts and feels a magic ban upon so doing, as Dante's poor sinners could not weep through their frozen lids."

For his part, her reticent guest had lived through a different afternoon, unaware, it would seem, that his monosyllabic ways were stirring wonder. Soon, complacently, he would report from the Manse to the absent Sophia: "We had a very pleasant dinner at Longfellow's; and I liked Mrs. Longlady (as thou naughtily nicknamest her) quite much. The dinner was late; and we sate long."

14

WOMEN IN THE NINETEENTH CENTURY

*E*arth's Holocaust," Hawthorne's "capital story" in *Graham's Magazine* that Fanny Longfellow had relished, is less a story than another sketch, like "The New Adam and Eve," reflecting on contemporary issues. To be sure, the setting of this latest sketch represents itself as "Once upon a time," a time when the earth has grown "so overburthened with an accumulation of worn-out trumpery" that a great bonfire has been proposed on the western prairies to reform the world by ridding it of excess. From all directions accordingly are arriving travelers, "women holding up their aprons, men on horseback, wheelbarrows, lumbering baggage-wagons, and other vehicles great and small, and from far and near, laden with articles that were judged fit for nothing but to be burnt."

First are thrown into the flames, to get them started, "yesterday's newspapers, last month's magazines, and last year's withered leaves," all worthless in an age fixed on the future. Next to go is rubbish from the Herald's Office, all that blazonry, "crests and devices of illustrious families; pedigrees," medals, Orders of the Garter; at the sight of such baubles melting, "the multitude of plebeian spectators set up a joyous shout, and clapt their hands with an emphasis that made the welkin echo." Here come crowns and scepters and purple robes of kings: toss those in, while temperance advocates are lugging to the flames "all the hogsheads and barrels of liquor in the world," exulting as spirits from the pothouse explode into a blaze that reaches to the clouds.

Some few may fear that life will be gloomier now. "How are old friends to sit together by the fireside, without a cheerful glass

between them? A plague upon your reformation!" But the deliri-
ous mob jeers at such qualms, as Virginia planters arrive with their
mountains of tobacco to burn, and milliners bring their ribbons and
lace, lovers their perfumed letters, parsons their old sermons, armies
of the earth their swords and muskets, drums beating all the while
and trumpets sounding the prelude to eternal, universal peace.

"Onward, onward." Burn the gallows, the reformers shout; into
the flames with every implement of death and torture. And the fire
licks higher, and some throw in their marriage certificates, others
cry out to burn the coffers of the rich, burn property deeds, burn
statute books and legislative acts that promulgate their arbitrary
laws. Meanwhile, a modern philosopher is urging the multitude
to "get rid of the weight of dead men's thought": set afire old pamphlets, old books, commentaries, lexicographies, the works of
Voltaire, Shelley—burn them all. And miters and crosiers and all
such popish emblems. For "the Titan of innovation—angel or
fiend, double in his nature, and capable of deeds befitting both characters—at first shaking down only the old and rotten shapes of
things, had now, as it appeared, laid his terrible hand upon the main
pillars, which supported the whole edifice of our moral and spiritual state," so that even the Bible is finally cast into the flames, as
"Man's age-long endeavor for perfection" culminates in that ulti-
mate temerity, futile—as all this frenzy of reform around the bonfire must be—because within the human breast still beats the heart:

"The Heart—the Heart—there was the little, yet boundless
sphere, wherein existed the original wrong, of which the crime and
misery of this outward world were merely types. Purify that inner
sphere," the sketch concludes, "and the many shapes of evil that
haunt the outward, and which now seem almost our only realities,
will turn to shadowy phantoms, and vanish of their own accord"—a
betterment to be looked for only when the human heart is cleansed.

"Yet, no doubt"—here, by contrast, is the voice of one of those
reformers whom Hawthorne knew personally and would be seeing
again at the Manse this very summer—"a new manifestation is at
hand, a new hour in the day of Man." Margaret Fuller at the time
was expanding to pamphlet length an essay that she had published
in the *Dial* the year before. Finishing the little book in the fall of
this present 1844, she would entitle it *Woman in the Nineteenth*

Century, a work like nothing that had ever been written in America. It called for a new life for women in a New World, in an American society that had already hurled upon the fires of history nobility's medals and crests, here where all were created equal. In our class-less democracy man-made distinctions no longer signified, only those that God Himself had instituted. Of those, two natural dif-ferences among human beings abided. One was of sex. Men and women *by nature* differed, and Margaret Fuller conceded as much. Men were energy, power, intellect; women were harmony, beauty, love. But those faculties "have not been given pure to either, but only in preponderance. There are also," Fuller insisted, "exceptions in great number." She knew of families, for instance, where "some little girls like to saw wood, others to use carpenters' tools." In short, all men partake—more or less, to some extent—of the feminine nature, as all women in part have masculine traits about them.

Let a woman develop what traits she possesses. Let her develop her intellect, and not to benefit men but for herself. As for that, this reformer would have every arbitrary barrier removed, not just the barrier to female education. "We would have every path laid open to woman as freely as to man." This is the place, now is the time: "The world, at large, is readier to let woman learn and mani-fest the capacities of her nature than it ever was before; and here"— in a new land—"is a less encumbered field and freer air than any where else." Especially now, women must "rouse their latent pow-ers" by undertaking many more kinds of occupations than have been allowed them in the past. And "if you ask me what offices they may fill; I reply—any. I do not care what case you put; let them be sea-captains, if you will. I do not doubt there are women well fitted for such an office, and, if so, I should be glad to see them in it."

With such bold notions simmering in her mind, at a time when women could neither own property nor divorce nor attend uni-versities nor vote nor enter the professions, Margaret Fuller came again this summer to quiet Concord. Tuesday, July 9, 1844 (the Hawthornes' second wedding anniversary): "to Concord with Almira. Find Sarah, and the happy pair. The little Una is a most beautiful child." At the Manse Fuller was standing with Hawthorne, half of that happy pair, gazing at Una as the baby "lay in her basket-cradle outdoors, looking up and smiling to the whispering trees." Emerson stopped by. "He staid some time and then I went with him through

Sleepy Hollow to see Ellen and her little one whom they call Greta. It was a scene of distress."

In part to support her luckless sister Ellen (another new mother, married miserably to the poet Ellery Channing) Margaret had returned to Concord. But while she visited over several weeks, she was often at the Manse. July 14: "I staid with Una while H. & Sophia took a walk & then S. went to Ellen. Then I went to the river bank and lay there watching the clouds till dinner time." Afterward: "Walked with H. to a distant hill." The next day, "while Sophia was gone to Greta, I staid with Una & her father. We had most pleasant communion. He is mild, deep and large." On the 17th: "H. came down about six and we went out on the river & staid till after sunset. We talked a great deal this time. I love him much, & love to be with him in this sweet tender homely scene. But I should like too, to be with him on the bold ocean shore."

And what did a proponent of radical aspirations for her sex make of Hawthorne's wife in a new calling, of that mother of a firstborn who appeared the very model of conventional Victorian womanhood? For instance: "If I could help my husband in his labors," Sophia reported from the Manse, "I feel that that would be the chief employ of my life. But all I can do for him *externally* is to mend his shirts & socks—spiritually, it is another thing." Thus was Mrs. Hawthorne submerging herself in her wifely role, and as a new mother was similarly, selflessly employed.

In fact, taking care of her infant Una had been proving full-time work for this former semi-invalid. Beset with mountains of sewing, Sophia was serving as nursery maid, nursing mother, and housekeeper as well. Yet she wanted no help from her husband: "I cannot bear to have him tend baby, though he does it so beautifully, because his time is gold & because I only want him to have the felicity of her & not a particle of trouble." This loving wife intended to create for Mr. Hawthorne—by no means an uncommon aspiration of the age—the sanctum of domesticity that her era so valued, the refuge from heartless competitiveness in the outside world that a dreamy writer of tales must soon reenter. For if beyond the front door of the Manse lay the go-ahead public amorality of the workplace, within, in the privacy of a serene hearthside, abided values of the spirit, closer to heaven. "Home, I think, is the great arena for women," Sophia had already explained to her mother, "and there, I am sure, she can wield a power which no king or conqueror can cope with." That expression of opinion had been provoked, in fact, by Margaret Fuller's essay in the *Dial* that *Woman in the Nineteenth Century* was expanding. "Had there never been false and profane marriages," the earlier essay had led Sophia to reflect, "there would not only be no commotion about woman's rights, but it would be Heaven here at once. Even before I was married, however, I could never feel the slightest interest in this movement. It then seemed to me that each woman could make her own sphere quietly."

Which was what this wife and mother had been striving to do in Concord: keep pure an individual marriage from within, the way her husband would have us first purify the human heart before setting out to reform the world. And in this instance Sophia's more radical friend Margaret Fuller would have concurred. Even after the one half of humanity had achieved its proper place in the world, "a large proportion of women," Fuller would write in her manifesto, "would give themselves to the same employments as now. . . . Mothers will delight to make the nest soft and warm. Nature would take care of that. . . . The difference," the advocate for her sex affirmed, "would be that *all* need not be constrained to employments for which *some* are unfit." As for Sophia's doting on her baby—why, she had every right to. Fuller doted on little Una as well, treasured in memory sweet images of the remarkable child. "Never was lovelier or nobler little creature! Next to little Waldo," she wrote, "I love her better than any child I ever saw," the off-spring of a "holy and equal marriage. She will have a good chance for freedom and happiness in the quiet wisdom of her father, the obedient goodness of her mother."

In August, at the end of her summertime visit, Fuller had spent a last day at the Manse before returning to Boston. "O it is sad that I shall see Una no more in this stage of her beauty. When I *do* see her again she will be quite another child." And she added in summary: "I feel more like a sister to H. or rather more that he might be a brother to me than ever with any man before. Yet with him it is though sweet, not deep kindred, at least, not deep yet."

As it happened, Margaret Fuller did return several times in weeks ahead for brief visits to her sister Ellen's, excursions more easily managed now that the railroad had come at last to Concord. In light of consequences that were to follow, the local newspaper greeted the arrival of this revolutionary mode of transport calmly enough. Inside on page 2 of the *Freeman* for June 14, 1844, appears no more than a small notice: "*The Railroad.* A train of cars have come up nearly every day since our last. We hear that the road will be open for travel next week, and that four trains will be run every day." And on the 21st, another modest mention, again inside the weekly: "The cars commenced running between this place and Charlestown, on Monday last. They make four trips per day, in each direction." The twenty-mile ride, which cost fifty cents, took an hour, as compared with four hours for seventy-five cents by stagecoach. "Every thing bids fair to work well, and we doubt not of the realization of the most sanguine hopes of those who have projected and carried through the enterprise."

To be sure, some few were unhappy with the change. Earlier, proprietors of canals had drawn up remonstrances, in vain, as in vain had teamsters, tavernkeepers, and stagecoach drivers leagued together to post along the turnpike their desperate messages of "No Monopoly," of "Free Trade and Teamsters' Rights." The railroad's westward advance was unstoppable; too many stood to gain by it. And how magical the adventure must have seemed to those first riders, who only a brief sixty minutes before had been boarding at the Concord depot, now debarking at Warren's Bridge in Charlestown, no more than a short omnibus ride from downtown Boston. Before, you left the village at six A.M. for a bumpy journey to reach the city late in the morning—and with this far smoother, faster ride costing much less! So Mr. Emerson will be able to get to his lecture halls easily, and Mr. Hawthorne might even take a job in Boston while keeping his home at the Manse. There would be no slowing ineluctable progress—with all its convenience, its hopes to fulfill and money to be made. July 12, 1844: "*Fitchburg Railroad stock* is in demand at an advance of seven per cent, and no sellers at that. It increases in favor with the public, as the receipts on the road between this place and Boston, are already much greater than were anticipated."

Of course Concord henceforth would never be the same. Yet the age would revel in its railroads as the very emblem of the times— had grown obsessed with its Fire Titan that promised to harmonize art and nature, joining to the city's refinement the purity and virtue of the countryside. Such progress seemed, in fact, no less than part of the divine plan, whereby Yankee shrewdness was helping ease humanity's physical labor in order to free the mind of man on its grand advance toward perfection.

A mere year or two after this present date Henry Thoreau in the woods around Walden Pond, lifting his head at the sound of a passing train, would picture on board "the cattle of a thousand hills." The air would seem filled with "the bleating of calves and sheep, and the hustling of oxen, as if a pastoral valley were going by." And Thoreau would know that aboard the cattle train were drovers and shepherds "on a level with their droves now, their vocation gone, but still clinging to their useless sticks as their badge of office." So, mused a rustic philosopher alone in his woods, "is your pastoral life whirled past and away."

Village readers of the time would seem to have been less interested in the railroad's arrival close by than in a political contest far off at the Democratic National Convention, news of which had appeared prominently and at length on page 1 of the *Concord Freeman* on Friday, June 7, 1844. Filed a week earlier, the account reported breathlessly from Baltimore on May 29 that the "convention have this moment, at ½ past two o'clock, unanimously nominated for the presidential candidate of the democracy, JAMES K. POLK, of Tennessee, on the ninth ballot." Such an outcome had seemed inexplicable. "Yesterday the convention appeared to contain elements of discord utterly irreconcilable, and our enemies were exulting in our family quarrel." A seventh ballot last night had shown Van Buren with 99 votes, Cass with 123, Johnson with 21, Buchanan with 22, and Secretary of State Calhoun with 1. So where had Polk's name come from this morning? Whigs of the opposing camp would reasonably demand to know: Who *is* James Polk? This earliest dark-horse compromise had formerly been a member of the House of Representatives—for four years Speaker of the House—and had then served a two-year term as governor of Tennessee before being twice defeated for reelection to the same office. That was Mr. Polk. The Whigs, whose own convention in Baltimore had transpired in perfect harmony three weeks earlier, had nominated as *their* candidate Senator Henry Clay. So how were the likes of Mr. Polk to prevail against such a towering figure as Harry of the West, the silver-tongued orator and statesman in retirement—against Henry Clay of Kentucky, the most popular politician in America?

Many years later an old man of distinguished lineage and profound thought would reconsider this present season, when he had been six years old. *The Education of Henry Adams,* printed privately in 1907, at one point casts a long glance backward and settles upon this same 1844, this very spring and summer, when the just invented telegraph had sped "from Baltimore to Washington the news that Henry Clay and James K. Polk were nominated for the Presidency," at a moment when the Boston and Albany Railroad had just opened, when the first Cunard steamer had appeared in Boston Harbor. In retrospect, an elderly Henry Adams—deep student of American history—would conclude that just here, in May 1844, was when "the old universe was thrown into the ash-heap and a new one created," a new world "ready for use."

15

THE NATION BEYOND CONCORD

One means of classifying humanity that Hawthorne's era regarded as God-bestowed was by gender: men naturally differed from (were stronger than, more intelligent than) women. The other classification deriving from nature was by race. On this second matter, the nineteenth century with its certainties seems to us odious; yet in deploring ancestral blindness, we might ponder our own fallibilities. Who can know how we, a century and a half removed from Hawthorne's age, will appear to posterity at the end of an equal time span further on, say in the middle of the twenty-second century? From as distant a vantage point as 2150, will our patriotism—Old Glory aloft inspiring hatred of the homeland's enemies—seem a treason against humanity? Will our feeding on pigs and cows have come to appear scarcely less benighted than our indifference to widespread hunger? For posterity, will our blithe spoliation of the planet rank as a crime abhorrent as any among the blackest charged against our predecessors?

That said, if the nineteenth century's certainties about women dismay us, this matter of race seems appalling. Americans were so sure: that Caucasians—and specifically Anglo-Saxons—were by nature superior to any other of the races on earth, superior to the proud uncivilizable red race, to the cunning cowardly yellow race, to the obsequious childlike black race, lowliest of them all. For dominant Caucasians such a view of race was clear-eyed science, grounded in disinterested observation and the measurement of skulls to determine brain capacity; so that even the brightest among them (Hume, Franklin, Jefferson, Agassiz, Lincoln) accepted such prejudices as proven fact. Hawthorne certainly did, when he thought about race at all—although that tale-teller's concerns lay less with sociological issues than with psychology, with matters of the individual soul and heart.

Treating racial bigotry as science, antebellum America could accordingly behave in ways that astound our own raised consciousness. For example: the sovereign state of South Carolina had, in 1835, passed a law declaring that any black person who entered the state would be warned to leave; if he did not, or afterward returned, he would be sold into slavery. Moreover, even if a free black entered a South Carolina port as a crewman on board ship, he would be seized at once, put in jail—the vessel's captain required to pay expenses—and kept there until the ship departed. If the captain should fail to come up with the money, or if the crewman once gone should ever return to South Carolina, this free black, too, would be sold into slavery from the public auction block.

That was the law, which applied only to free citizens of the United States who happened to be African American. Those included blacks aboard merchant vessels from Massachusetts calling at Charleston to load cargoes of cotton for the textile mills of Waltham and Lowell. The sight of such seamen laboring in freedom might have threatened the public peace by encouraging slave revolts; on such unspecified fears was the law predicated. But to northerners it was a flagrantly unconstitutional law, this putting in jail people innocent of any wrongdoing. Thus, eight years into the tenure of the act, the Massachusetts legislature authorized the governor of that state to appoint an agent to gather "accurate information respecting the number and names of citizens of Massachusetts, who have heretofore been or may be during the period of his engagement, imprisoned without the allegation of any crime." The agent was to proceed to Charleston empowered to bring suit against South Carolina on such plaintiffs' behalf. Governor Briggs thereupon chose as his commissioner for those purposes a gentleman of exceptional probity: Samuel Hoar, judge of the circuit court, leading citizen of Concord, and conscience of the community.

Squire Hoar, at the time a most distinguished sixty-six, tall and slender, Dantesque in appearance, dutifully set sail with his daughter Elizabeth, Emerson's beloved friend and good friend of Sophia Hawthorne and Margaret Fuller, to reach Charleston on a Thursday morning at the end of November 1844. Upon arriving, the agent for Massachusetts promptly submitted his commission to Governor Hammond ("I do not know that your Excellency will consider it proper in any way to notice this subject, yet propriety seemed to require the communication") and settled into his hotel room to await the town's courtesies.

The mayor of Charleston happened to be away and would not return until Monday; but over the weekend, South Carolina's governor inland at Columbia called his legislature into special session. As soon as he did, commotion erupted in the capitol, wrath and tumult; while back on the streets of Charleston mobs started to gather. That was on Saturday, and by Monday the local sheriff was hurrying to Squire Hoar to offer advice: "It is considered a great insult on South Carolina by Massachusetts to send an agent here on such business. This city is highly incensed; you are in great danger, and you had better leave the city as soon as possible." Threats were heard of lynching this most distinguished representative of the Commonwealth of Massachusetts, although the sheriff meant—at the risk of his life, he said—to defend elderly Judge Hoar. But Judge Hoar must leave the city at once.

The agent couldn't do that. He was here on lawful business, his commission in order. When his duty had been performed, he would depart. Dr. Whittredge, the head of the medical profession in Charleston, arrived "agitated and distressed." The danger had become both real and imminent. People had gathered on the piazza outside: "nothing seemed wanting but for some one to say 'Now is your time' to bring on the attack." So the anxious Dr. Whittredge had come with a carriage to whisk the Hoars twenty miles out into the country to his own plantation, to safety.

But where would the agent go from there? He couldn't come back to Charleston and would be ashamed to return to Massachusetts having fled from his duty. The legislature meanwhile was hastily passing a series of fiery resolves: "*Resolved,* That the right to exclude from their territories seditious persons, or others whose presence may be dangerous to their peace, is essential to every independent State. . . . *Resolved,* That the emissary sent by the State of Massachusetts to the State of South Carolina, with the avowed purpose of interfering with her institutions, and disturbing her peace, is to be regarded in the character he has assumed, and to be treated accordingly." In Charleston Mr. Rose, the president of a local bank, had appeared at the hotel with two members of the bar. At any moment the mob in the streets might force its way inside; officials had been doing their best to maintain order out there, assuring incensed citizens that soon Judge Hoar would be gone. He *must* leave; the frantic state of affairs now made it his duty to go.

But the emissary was an old man and his life was not worth much, he said, so that "he had rather the boys should troll his old head like a football in their streets" than that he should cower in fear of fulfilling his mission. And only after officials had declared their intention to remove him by force, carry the visitor bodily out of the hotel and down to the wharves, did the commissioner and his daughter at last capitulate. By then it had seemed to Hoar only a question of "whether I should walk to a carriage or be dragged to it." Since no benefit would be served "to any State, cause, or person in choosing the latter," the agent finally agreed to depart. And in that way on Friday afternoon, December 6, 1844, more than a week after their arrival, Judge Samuel Hoar and his daughter Elizabeth were accompanied by local dignitaries from the hotel outside to a carriage that would speed them through Charleston streets toward a ship in the harbor standing ready to cast off for Boston.

At a meeting in Concord after Squire Hoar's return from the South, Waldo Emerson, seething at so gross an insult to an old friend, assured his fellow villagers that the southern state in question would henceforth be infamous. Not that New England should retaliate for such boorish behavior as that displayed by degraded South Carolinians. "Ours," he insisted, "is not a brutal people, but intellectual & mild." And his notes indicate that he reminded his listeners that New England was no jail, either: "we keep open house we have taken out the bolt & taken off the latch & taken the doors off the hinges. Does S.C. warn us out & turn us out, and then come hither to visit us? She shall find no bar. We are not afraid of visiters. We do not ring curfews nor give passes nor keep armed patroles." In the interest of future profits, some Boston merchants would willingly overlook the present outrage; but mill owners and their class will hereafter be unable, said Emerson, to "receive Southern gentlemen at their tables, without a consciousness of shame."

One such mill owner was Nathan Appleton, who years earlier, as a young tutor in Virginia, had viewed the ugliness of slavery up close. Appleton in his Beacon Hill mansion felt no sympathy for the South's peculiar institution, any more than he approved of his own state's officious meddling in the internal affairs of another sovereign state of the Union. Of course Appleton's views were hardly impartial, dependent as were his immensely lucrative textile mills on cotton shipped from southern ports. In the interest of trade, he and his associates did receive gentlemen of the South at their dinner tables, leaving Appleton's daughter Fanny and her poet husband across the river in Cambridge free all the while, with such close friends as attorney Charles Sumner, to entertain more radical opinions. Earlier, Professor Longfellow had even chosen to poeticize on slavery (to Hawthorne's surprise), ominously describing "a poor, blind Samson in this land" who, "Shorn of his strength and bound in bonds of steel," might yet raise his hand one day and shatter "the pillars of this Commonweal,"

> Till the vast Temple of our liberties
> A shapeless mass of wreck and rubbish lies.

Precisely that nightmare vision of slaves rising up in revolt—a specter that was forever darkening southern days—had provoked South Carolina's recent inhospitalities, even as life in the North was advancing through sunny prosperity and peace, even as a visitor to free, peaceful Concord village this same January 1845 was reporting pleasantly to her absent friend Margaret Fuller of having heard from Elizabeth Hoar's own lips the exciting story of the Charleston adventure, "almost as good as a crime for her, only she had the womanly part to play: of ignorance & security, but it is something to have a father in danger,—for those who have filial hearts."

Margaret Fuller was in New York by that time, far from the Old Manse and Miss Hoar's Main Street home and Emerson's house off the Lexington Road. She was living in Manhattan with the family of Horace Greeley, editor of the *New York Tribune.* Last fall on returning from Concord to Cambridge, Fuller had received a proposal from Greeley, an admirer of her writings, to come work for him. She should come to New York and work on his newspaper, contributing columns of literary criticism and social commentary, and Greeley would publish *Woman in the Nineteenth Century*. Sunday, September 22, 1844, on a subsequent visit to Concord: "went to see Ellen & Greta. A very affecting interview with Ellen. . . . Then some hours with Waldo." Afterward: "Tea at the Hawthornes & walk home with H. Very bright, cold moonlight. Both W. & H. think the N.Y. plan one of great promise, which I did not expect." Fuller's hesitation may have arisen in part from the novelty of this that Mr. Greeley was proposing: a woman to occupy the role of columnist and correspondent. But "if you ask me what offices they may fill," she herself had written, "I reply—any. I do not care what case you put." So in the end Fuller did embrace the opportunity of becoming the earliest American female journalist and—later, again for Greeley—the *Tribune*'s foreign correspondent in England, France, and Italy. For now, at the start of 1845, this pioneer had only just embarked upon her new responsibilities, which would allow her to write of oppressions on which the nation's prosperity depended: oppressions of slaves, of immigrants, of Indians, especially of women. In the *Tribune*'s pages Fuller would examine American culture as well, evaluating works of Hawthorne and Longfellow among others—for all those efforts being paid well enough to support herself, her mother, and her needful younger brothers by means of a career advancement that her friend Hawthorne might well have envied.

In his penury back in New England Hawthorne had been composing, into the fall of 1844 just ended, such profound tales as "The Artist of the Beautiful" and "Rappaccini's Daughter," although hardly augmenting his income by doing so. By December he was again visiting his reclusive family in Salem. From there on the 20th the author sought to reassure his wife, on a visit of her own to 13 West Street, Boston. "Now that I stand a little apart from our Concord life," he wrote her, "the troubles and incommodities look slighter—our happiness more vast and inestimable." It would be a pity, Hawthorne was thinking, "to have our recollection of this first home darkened by such associations;—the home where thou didst first sleep in my arms—where our love assumed human life in the form of our darling-child." Except for worrying that creditors might

interpret their absence from Concord as flight, he could almost relish being briefly away from the Manse and back in his native town.
In Salem he felt temporarily free of the burden of debt, "of providing even for the day's wants. This trouble does not pursue me here;
and even when we go back, I hope not to feel it nearly so much as
before. Polk's election has certainly brightened our prospects."

For last month James Polk of Tennessee, Democrat, had nar-
rowly won the electoral contest against Kentucky's Henry Clay,
Whig. Texas had proved Prince Hal's undoing. Clay on his plantation near Lexington had expected to be running for chief executive
against former president Martin Van Buren, who was opposed to
allowing the Lone Star Republic, then seven years old, into the
Union. Mexico had continued to claim Texas as its own, so annexing the region might bring on war between the United States and
its southern neighbor. Moreover, northerners were balking at acquiring so huge an area, which could be carved into as many as
four states, thereby extending slavery and assuring the South's
dominance in the halls of Congress. Because Van Buren opposed
annexing Texas, Clay of Kentucky (a slaveholder already confident
of the southern vote) reached out to the North in a letter expressing his own opposition to allowing it into the Union.

But that was before last May, when at the Democratic National Convention in Baltimore Van Buren had failed to win the
nomination even after seven ballots. Vastly popular old Andrew
Jackson had entered the fray on behalf of his protégé Polk; so that
suddenly Whig nominee Clay was running not against the New
Yorker Van Buren but against a southerner, Mr. Polk of Tennessee. And all at once Harry of the West was changing his mind:
yes, he would welcome Texas into the Union if so desirable a result could be achieved without war. Northerners grew wary. Votes
were cast, with a third party, the Liberty Party, enfeebling Clay's
strength in the free states, where he lost crucial New York nar-
rowly, while down South fraud in Louisiana allowed Democrats
to claim a victory that hadn't been earned. James Polk would be
going to the White House after all, bringing with him territorial
ambitions that spread far beyond Texas. The South was exultant,
the North downcast—and the defeated Henry Clay, the Old Coon,
the Star of the West, felt sure that his long, distinguished public
service was ended.

In the North, meanwhile, the Democrat Hawthorne hoped that he and his wife and baby might benefit from this turn of events. As for Fanny Appleton Longfellow, before the election she inquired of a sister-in-law in New Orleans, "How do they feel in your part of the world about the annexation of Texas? Here there is great excitement and indignation, and many that have been cowardly about slavery are warmed by the occasion into a clearer expression of abhorrence. Heaven defend us from an act so foolish and wrong!" Now, in the aftermath of Polk's narrow victory, a vast new home for human bondage did enter the Union, moving Fanny during these same early months of 1845 glumly to confess to another friend, "Since Texas was annexed my patriotism has almost died a natural death."

16

LEAVING THE OLD MANSE

Woman in the Nineteenth Century, which Horace Greeley published in February 1845, derived from Conversations on morality and culture that Margaret Fuller had conducted a few years earlier for the benefit of the inquiring ladies of Boston. Back then Greeley's wife had attended some of those gatherings, as had Sophia Peabody. Often the groups had met in Sophia's sister Elizabeth's bookstore parlor (the site of the Hawthornes' future wedding); and sometimes the eldest Miss Peabody had transcribed what went on, as, for example, with the Eighteenth Conversation, in 1840. The topic on that occasion had been, unsurprisingly, "Woman," and in its course a question was raised about the first duty of man, which would seem to be to support his dependents. Squire Samuel Hoar's wife is likely the "Mrs. H." who interjected that "she knew of a man reputed to be of the highest genius, who to indulge this"—his superior mind—"neglected & was very indifferent to the comforts of his family, who lived on charity that it was hard for his wife to receive from conscientious feelings—& who having borrowed of every body who would lend, till he was deeply in debt, yet remained insensible to debts as such, & made something of a parade of his serenity & spiritual elevation above all such things." In response Miss Fuller had drawn a distinction between indifference to wealth (a good trait) and to debt (bad), even as many in her audience were surely recognizing Bronson Alcott as the unnamed example being deplored.

The exchange had occurred after the failure of Alcott's Temple School in Boston had led to his family's removal at about that time, in March 1840, to Concord, where lived the observant Mrs. Hoar. From Concord, Alcott had traveled alone to England, to see the school near London named in his honor, and had returned with Charles Lane determined to establish Utopia in Massachusetts. But the resulting experiment at Fruitlands had ended disastrously, deep in the frigid depths of January 1844, leaving the Alcotts huddled together in a farmer's unused rooms at nearby Still River, Bronson himself taken to bed immobilized in despair.

The dejected idealist did finally arise, although he was forever changed. Through that spring and summer Alcott lingered with his family at Still River, working in the garden there. "I have now abrogated all claims to moral and spiritual teaching," he wrote his brother-in-law. "I place myself in peaceful relations to the soil, as a husbandman intent on aiding its increase." The husbandman managed a visit to Concord, where Emerson observed that "after all his efforts on that most incorrigible of materials, man," Alcott seemed to be discovering "a real comfort in working on that most corrigible and docile of all pupils, Nature." Even so, "Very sad indeed it was," the Concord sage concluded, "to see this halfgod driven to the wall, reproaching men, & hesitating whether he should not reproach the gods."

In the autumn the Alcott family moved back to Concord. Mrs. Alcott had come into a little money, acquired from her father's estate these four years after his death. With that—and with further help from the ever-supportive Emerson—the family was able to purchase, early in 1845, the Cogswell place on the Lexington Road, a dilapidated old farmhouse the earliest inhabitant of which had been mustermaster of the Concord Minutemen before the Revolution. Thereupon the new home owner Bronson Alcott (quondam teacher, erstwhile reformer) set to work amid his dilapidations carpentering and planting trees over the bleak hillside adjacent and tending vegetables in the field across the road—at the start of a long future that would contain for him little so noble or notable as had filled the years that were past.

The Alcotts moved into the Cogswell house on April 1, a day or two after a neighbor of theirs had set out to change his own life drastically. "Near the end of March, 1845," Henry Thoreau would later recall, "I borrowed an axe and went down to the woods by Walden

Pond, nearest to where I intended to build my house, and began to cut down some tall arrowy white pines, still in their youth, for timber." By mid-April this solitary builder had framed his one-room hut back some yards from the pond and was ready to raise it. For siding boards he had bought a shanty belonging to an Irish laborer on the railroad; and on July 4, the accommodation erected under its snug, peaked roof, Thoreau moved in to search alone for what living was all about. "Most of the luxuries, and many of the so called comforts of life," he had come to feel, "are not only not indispensable, but positive hinderances to the elevation of mankind." Thoreau meant to live a life without those hindrances, through—as it happened—the next two years, two months, and two days. And at the end of it he would explain, "I went to the woods because I wished to live deliberately, to front only the essential facts of life, and see if I could not learn what it had to teach, and not, when I came to die, discover that I had not lived. I did not wish," he goes on in his crystalline prose, "to live what was not life, living is so dear; nor did I wish to practise resignation, unless it was quite necessary. I wanted to live deep and suck out all the marrow of life . . ."

So he had withdrawn into the woods, in part to encounter life's essence, but in part to write a book—about his earlier trip with his brother John down the Concord and up a way on the Merrimack River. And he would have a word to say, at the end of his experiment, concerning the business of making a living, the problem that Mrs. Hoar in Margaret Fuller's Eighteenth Conversation had adverted to, the problem that Alcott through a lifetime blithely ignored to his family's distress, the problem that Hawthorne even now had been grappling anxiously with at the Manse. For his part, Thoreau by his pond would feel the burden of earning a livelihood very lightly. The bean grower tending his garden at Walden calculated that over the first eight months of his life in the woods he spent a mere twenty-seven cents a week on food, for "pray what more can a reasonable man desire, in peaceful times, in ordinary noons, than a sufficient number of ears of green sweet-corn boiled."

Moreover, in the woods to which he had withdrawn on Independence Day (his friend Hawthorne's forty-first birthday), Henry Thoreau would be out of earshot of contemporary American bluster, as articulated, for instance, by another friend of Hawthorne's—

and the godfather of little Una—John Louis O'Sullivan, editor of the *United States Magazine and Democratic Review*. In the July-August 1845 issue of that periodical, O'Sullivan was writing that America, and more precisely the Anglo-Saxon race, had the "manifest destiny to overspread the continent allotted by Providence for the free development of our yearly multiplying millions." *Manifest Destiny*—O'Sullivan's phrase would ring through the coming decades and in modified form resounds globally now: we Americans in a New World were obviously destined to spread superior Caucasian values and institutions ever westward over this entire vast continent that God had blessed and bestowed upon us.

But in the onrush of that destiny none others in the world need fear. Just this past spring, in Washington on March 4, our eleventh president, James Knox Polk, had spoken reassuringly during his inaugural address. The Republic of Texas, the chief executive had reminded his hopeful listeners, was entering the Union "to form a part of our Confederacy and enjoy with us the blessings of liberty secured and guaranteed by our Constitution." The matter concerned foreign powers not at all; it was purely an internal affair, "belonging exclusively to the United States and Texas." Meanwhile, sovereignties beyond our borders could rest assured: "The world has nothing to fear from military ambition in our Government." We, Polk explained, are a democracy, our chief magistrate and legislators serving at the pleasure of the people; and as long as that situation prevails, "our Government can not be otherwise than pacific. Foreign powers should therefore look on the annexation of Texas to the United States not as the conquest of a nation seeking to extend her dominions by arms and violence" but rather as a peaceful acquisition of territory that adds another member to the Union, "thereby diminishing the chances of war and opening to them"—in foreign lands—"new and ever-increasing markets for their products."

Texas had been providentially acquired; and at the same time—just as Americans had earlier moved over the border into that Mexican province, preparing the way—now, by 1845, some seven hundred Americans far to the west were already naturalized citizens in possession of land grants in Mexico's distant province of California, even as elsewhere, in regions of the Oregon Territory jointly occupied by Great Britain and the United States, Americans in ever increasing numbers had begun asserting claims into Canada as far north as the fifty-fourth parallel of latitude. Moreover, despite all his bland reassurances, the Tennessee expansionist James Knox Polk very much coveted Oregon and California.

Convivial Frank Pierce, Hawthorne's Bowdoin college mate, was a good friend of Mr. Polk's. Indeed, the new president would ask Pierce, who had resigned from the United States Senate two years earlier, to serve in the federal cabinet as attorney general. But Mrs. Pierce's poor health at home, far from Washington, put such service regrettably beyond her husband's reach; he would have to remain in the other Concord, New Hampshire's capital city, as district attorney of his native state and reigning power in the local Democratic Party.

A couple of months after Polk's inauguration, former senator Pierce did venture from home and called on his college friend Hawthorne in the Concord of a neighboring commonwealth. On Friday, May 9, 1845, Sophia in the Manse looked out to behold, coming down the avenue from the public road, two gentlemen, only one of whom she could identify: Horatio Bridge, purser in the navy and close friend of her husband's since their years at Bowdoin. "I immediately recognized the fine, elastic figure of the 'Admiral.' When he saw me, he took off his hat and waved it in the air, in a sort of playful triumph," she would recall with pleasure, "and his white teeth shone out in a smile. I raised the sash, and he introduced 'Mr. Pierce.'" Sophia had never met her husband's other closest college friend, but she saw at once that he was possessed of delicacy and refinement. Hawthorne all this while was in the shed hewing at his woodpile. "Mr. Bridge caught a glimpse of him, and began a sort of waltz towards him. Mr. Pierce followed; and when they reappeared, Mr. Pierce's arm was encircling my husband's old blue frock." It was a picture for a devoted wife to treasure. "How his friends do love him! Mr. Bridge was perfectly wild with spirits. He danced and gesticulated and opened his round eyes like an owl. He kissed Una so vehemently that she drew back"—that one-year-old—"in majestic displeasure, for she is very fastidious about giving or receiving kisses. They all went away soon to spend the evening and talk of business." But Sophia's first impression of this new acquaintance was of "loveliness and truth of character and natural refinement. My husband says Mr. Pierce's affection for and reliance upon him are perhaps greater than any other person's. He called him 'Nathaniel,' and spoke to him and looked at him with peculiar tenderness." And from the three gentlemen's ensuing business talk, Sophia could assure her mother that the Hawthornes had been able to derive a solid hope.

Those delinquent tenants were in need of something more than hope, and promptly. Their landlord, Reverend Samuel Ripley, grown restive over in Waltham, had expressed a desire to move back to Concord next spring to live in the Manse. To pay that creditor meanwhile, Bridge would lend his beleaguered classmate a hundred dollars; but as Hawthorne himself implied, not only a landlord but "the butcher, the baker, the tailor, the doctor, and the tax gatherer" all were waiting to be satisfied. "Our friend O'Sullivan," he had written a month before, "is moving Heaven and Earth to get me an office": perhaps as consul at Genoa or Gibraltar, or maybe as clerk at the Smithsonian Institution, due to open next year. Yet for the moment neither O'Sullivan nor Bridge nor the influential Frank Pierce had found anything suitable. In late May, to ease their situation, the Hawthornes would temporarily take in a boarder; and when their maid left in early June, Sophia did not replace her. Later, over the summer, with Alcott nearby tending his meadow and Thoreau settling in by Walden Pond, Bridge would entertain Hawthorne, Sophia, and Una for two weeks in his quarters at the Portsmouth Navy Yard, in part to let the guests meet political friends (Senator and Mrs. Atherton of New Hampshire, Senator Fairfield of Maine) who might lend a hand in establishing the author comfortably at the public till.

The summer passed, and still nothing had been worked out. Abruptly the Ripleys, who had talked of reclaiming the Manse next spring, moved their date of occupancy to the present. Could the Hawthornes vacate the premises by September 1?

Retreat was turning into a rout for "the best writer of the day," as Fuller was soon to describe her friend in the *New York Tribune*. No, not by September 1; the family would need a month to make other arrangements. They could be gone from Concord no earlier than October. Sophia's sister Mary passed on a rumor that the Reverend Mr. Ripley wasn't planning to move from Waltham until next spring anyway; did he simply want the lodgers out of his house?

Hawthorne in desperation meanwhile, in order to pay his debts, instructed attorney Hillard to sue Brook Farm (to no avail) to recover the $524.05 balance of that earlier investment in a now-faltering West Roxbury Utopia. Sophia for her part was writing her mother, as September arrived and the end of their time at the Manse drew near: "The three years we have spent here will always be to me a blessed memory, because here all my dreams became realities. I have got gradually weaned from it, however, by the perplexities that have vexed my husband the last year, and made the place painful to him." Their financial troubles would have been easier to bear if Hawthorne had been at fault, but the couple's embarrassments came about "only through too great a trust in the honor and truth of others." What was owed her husband for his writings and his shares in the Brook Farm enterprise would pay all outstanding debts thrice over, Sophia insisted, yet here they were, reduced to pursuing a most dreary plan. She would have to take the baby and move in with her Peabody family in Boston—what else could she do?—while apart from his wife and daughter, Mr. Hawthorne would live in Salem with his mother and sisters until friends could secure him a place in public service.

Soon, however, Sophia came up with a better idea. She approached her sister-in-law. Could wife and baby perhaps rent from Mr. Manning, who owned the Salem house, a room "beneath your parlor for our sleeping apartment, & pay you the price of my board at table"? Louisa responded that Mr. Manning was making difficulties; he wanted too much for his empty room. Hawthorne in turn would be reduced to appealing again to his friend Bridge in late September: "I rather think you did not receive a letter from me a few days since, in which, horrible to say, I requested to borrow $150. Very probably you may not be able to lend it—in which case it cannot be helped; but I shall find myself in a devilish ugly predicament, as we are to be ejected from this house on Thursday of next week."

Devilish ugly in truth is the whole ignominious episode, this humiliation of a supremely gifted author whose stories had been accepted readily, published forthwith, and then not paid for. Bridge as soon as he returned home did send $150, and O'Sullivan came through at last with $100, so that Hawthorne in the end was "enabled to leave Concord with flying colors, although I found," he reported, "only ten dollars in my pocket on reaching Salem." It had all come down to this, then. Here in Salem, his wife and baby finally in rented quarters elsewhere in the house, Nathaniel Hawthorne, whom knowledgeable opinion already judged fit to stand at the head of American literature, was in October 1845 "again established in the old chamber where I wasted so many years of my life," discharged from paradise to take up his pen in his mother and sisters' home, back in the familiar, dismal room under the eaves on Herbert Street.

THE FIFTIES

We Are Politicians Now

Hawthorne in 1850, by Cephas Thompson (oil on canvas), courtesy
The Grolier Club of New York. Gift of Stephen A. Wakeman, 1913.

17

THE WAYSIDE

The Hawthornes were ejected from the Manse in the autumn of 1845. By then, elsewhere in Concord village, the Alcott family were settled at last in a home of their own. Living that fall in the old Cogswell farmhouse, across Concord a couple of miles southeast of the Manse, were Bronson and Abba Alcott and their daughters: Anna, fourteen, Louisa, twelve, Elizabeth, nine, and little May, aged four. After life in cramped quarters in a succession of rented rooms, the family was to remain at what they called "Hillside" over the next three years; and here they were to experience days that one of the children would later mold into an imperishable interval to be recounted in *Little Women*. From the pages of that famous novel Bronson for the most part is spectrally absent, but Abba Alcott appears very much as a presence, transmuted therein into the wise and loving Marmee, maternal guide to four lastingly appealing children: Meg, Jo, Beth, and Amy. And in those same pages generations of readers have come to feel at home in the March household and in a New England village in the latter half of the 1840s, within Hillside and around Concord as Louisa May Alcott, participant in events at those places at that time, was later to immortalize them.

The years at Hillside proved the longest span until then that the Alcott family had stayed in a single home. During his time there Bronson, if still and always indifferent to family income, had been by no means idle. Early in 1845 he had set about promptly enlarging and beautifying the tumbledown Cogswell place. On either end of the house he attached half of Cogswell's bisected wheelwright shop to create a new bathhouse, woodhouse, and study. He added pillared piazzas along the fronts of the new wings, and paths and a stone wall out back. He constructed another set of stairs inside and a gabled dormer window over the entrance. He installed a pump. Elsewhere on the property Alcott erected fences, a beehouse, a conservatory. He graded terraces into the hill behind. He dug up trees from the surrounding woods and replanted them to adorn that same bare hillside. And in the eight acres of Emerson's meadow across the road he planted an orchard of peach and apple trees and tended a garden of melons, rhubarb, cucumbers, potatoes, and beans.

In his disillusionment, the man had grown averse to institutions of all kinds—church, state, private—as well as to any remunerations that institutions might offer; he even deplored the corruption implicit in Abba's efforts to invest a portion of her father's small bequest for the family's benefit. Yet although this individualist refused to lift a finger to earn institutional money, he could hardly be charged with sloth. His labors at Hillside were unending. Even so, all Bronson's prodigious toil around house, hill, orchard, and garden would serve his wife and children only a bit beyond fair weather. In winter's depths the Alcotts suffered for lack of funds. Food, coal, and clothing grew scarce. They borrowed. They took in boarders. And within a couple of years the house about them was already starting to sink back into disrepair.

This was the dark reality out of which, somehow, *Little Women* would weave its hearty charm. Abba wanted to move, was sick of Concord anyway. In the fall of 1847, over two years into their Hillside adventure and the children's idyll ending, the oldest girl, Anna, went off to teach at a school in New Hampshire. Louisa, the second child, had been instructing the Emerson offspring nearby, but that hardly supplemented the meager three hundred dollars a year that the family was forced to subsist on. They determined to move to Boston. They would sell Hillside; and in the city the older girls could teach, Bronson would be able to conduct Fuller-like Conversations for a fee, and Abba would look for work as well. Thus in November 1848 they set out once more from Concord to take up residence in Boston, on Dedham Street.

Pleased to be near her friends in the city, Mrs. Alcott was able to find a position as an agent of charitable societies. Bronson for his part rented a room on West Street in which to conduct his

Conversations. But the Alcott ventures faltered. Over the next seven years the family would move six times, all the while growing poorer as they eked out their wretched existence. Early on, smallpox laid them low. Bronson's Conversations hardly prospered. Their house for sale in Concord remained on the market. The older Alcott children taught in their school, while Abba set up an employment office for domestics, taxing work for which she earned sometimes no more than five cents a day. "My life," she would write her brother Samuel May, "is one of daily protest against the oppression and abuses of Society. I find selfishness, meanness . . . among people who fill high places in church and State. The whole system of Servitude in new England is almost as false as slavery in the South." The dreariness of their Boston years edged on into a new decade; and in 1850 that same brother was driven in his exasperation to admit, "I am unable to advise Mr. Alcott"—whom he liked and admired—"and yet it does seem to me, as well as to everybody else, that he might find something to do, for which he would receive something toward the support of his family." For all that, the paterfamilias continued serenely as before, eschewing institutions of all kinds as he mused and scribbled orphic prose in his interminable journals.

Finally, one bit of luck did come to the family. They had been away from Concord for over three years when a gentleman in the market for a home expressed interest in buying Hillside. In February 1852, Nathaniel Hawthorne returned to the village to look over the old Cogswell farmhouse that Bronson earlier had enlarged and renovated. The prospective purchaser viewed the hill behind with its woods and terraces and crumbling bowers, and he considered the field across the road, the forsaken orchard and vegetable garden. Two days later Hawthorne settled on buying the place, including the meadow opposite. Accordingly, in April he delivered to trustees for the Alcott family half the purchase price of fifteen hundred dollars, the balance of which was to be paid within a year. And in June the new owners moved in.

Mrs. Hawthorne came first, with two of her three children, in order (as she said) to civilize the vacant house in advance of her husband's arrival. She came to guide workmen in putting down carpets and setting up furniture, bringing with her Una, now eight years old, and their youngest, Rose, little Rosebud, thirteen months. The middle child, the five-year-old Julian about to turn six, stayed behind with his father. From West Newton, the Boston suburb where the family had been living, Hawthorne had written a friend to explain, "I have bought a house in Concord, deeming it better to do so, on the whole, than to spend the money in going to Italy, although I do not yet give up that long-cherished idea." His artistically gifted wife would surely have relished such a European interlude in which to view the old masters, but an author's income hardly allowed for both, a new home and a voyage abroad as well. As for Italy, "It is best, perhaps," Hawthorne had concluded, "to keep it by way of a second youth, wherewith to gladden my late declining age."

So the family—its numbers now complete: father, mother, three children—were moving back to Concord, to the site of earlier happiness. This newly purchased home on the other side of the village from the Manse was the first that Hawthorne had ever owned (and, as it turned out, it would be the last). The author had forsaken dreams of travel in order to return to Concord to write; for, as he had informed his friend Bridge a year ago, his situation was different now. Readers had begun buying his scribblings, and paying for them, and "as long as people will buy, I shall keep at work; and I find that my facility of labor increases with the demand for it." So he stood ready to wield his pen with vigor—and by the way, as he had gone on to announce in his letter to Bridge last June, "Mrs. Hawthorne published a little work, two months ago, which still lies in sheets; but, I assure you, it makes some noise in the world, both by day and night. In plain English, we have another little red-headed daughter—a very bright, strong, and healthy imp, but, at present, with no pretensions to beauty."

That was Rose, by now a toddler on hand as her mother and older sister set about putting in order the vacant house on the Lexington Road. Hawthorne had already renamed the place: instead of Hillside, he would call it "The Wayside"; so that "at four o'clock," as Sophia related about this June afternoon of their moving in, "I was driven to The Wayside. The cartman had tumbled all the wet mattresses in a heap in the farthest corner of the barn, and I had them all pulled out to dry. It was very hot weather. A good deal was accomplished, when the man and woman who were working for me went to supper, and left me and Una in quiet possession of our home."

Father and son arrived on Saturday, the 5th, with much still to be done. To his friend William Ticknor, Hawthorne was soon writing from the Wayside, on the 8th, of finding himself "surrounded with a host of carpenters, masons, &c:—each presenting a long bill." But unlike in earlier days in Concord, these more prosperous times had furnished money with which to pay the bills; and Ticknor, Hawthorne's friend and publisher, whom he had not even known at the Manse, would see that the bills were paid. For in the interval the author had found something considerably more profitable to write than tales. So his situation was changed. He and his wife had grown older (Hawthorne was about to turn forty-eight, and Sophia was forty-two; it had been a decade precisely since the summer of their wedding, seven years since their leaving Concord in haste and humiliation), and his family had grown, from one child to three. But he had a competency now, and work to do with his pen that should support the larger family in reasonable comfort.

So the Hawthornes were settling down for good, back here in a village where the children could thrive under Sophia's loving attentions and where their father could produce more of what an eager public appeared ready to purchase. For in truth, there had been wandering enough since that earlier inglorious departure from Concord and return to Salem. Since his wedding ten years ago, Hawthorne had lived in seven different dwellings. Now, arriving at the Wayside in early June, he felt he was finally done with moving about. The family would make their home here, as he forthwith wrote to his sister Louisa, inviting her, exactly as he had written her from the Manse a decade earlier, on the first full day of his and Sophia's wedded life, to come see them:

"Dear L.," he wrote on June 18, 1852, "We wish you very much to come immediately. Our house is not yet in order; but we can make you comfortable, and if you do not come now, something may intervene to prevent your coming this summer. We like the house and the place very much, and begin, at last, to feel that we have a home. We shall expect you on Monday, and from that time till we actually see you." He ended with words to convey his family's heartfelt wish for this aunt's, this sister's company: "The children long to see you. Baby trots about all day, and keeps us continually on the trot after her." And one last thought before sending off the letter: "P.S. Arrange matters for a good long visit."

18

RETURN TO CONCORD

Seven years had intervened between this letter to Louisa and the dismal hour when Nathaniel Hawthorne, driven from the Manse with only ten dollars in his pocket, had retreated with his wife and year-old daughter to live with Louisa, her sister, and their mother in Salem. In those surroundings of his bachelorhood on Herbert Street, awaiting news of a hoped-for political appointment, Hawthorne had settled into a drearily familiar room up under the eaves to write. But the writing had not gone well. "I have not now," he complained, "the quiet which has always been my portion aforetime; and therefore nothing prospers with me."

Another year had opened: 1846. And in coming days the author's situation brightened. An essay with which he had been struggling had finally appeared on the page: "The Old Manse," a richly textured introduction to the rural Concord world where he had written many of the tales in a new collection of his work, to be published in June of that year. *Mosses from an Old Manse* hardly rewarded the author financially, but it was warmly greeted by reviewers, who in chorus (perhaps unlike us later readers) judged the collection an advance over the earlier, much-praised *Twice-Told Tales*. In the same summer month of fruition, Sophia had given birth to the Hawthornes' second child, a boy, Julian. And by then, at last, the author's coveted political appointment had come through, as surveyor of the Salem customhouse. Hawthorne would serve in the customhouse at the head of Derby Wharf three years and longer, putting in mornings of not overly demanding work and having his afternoons free.

Yet during those years he wrote very little, no more than three or four pieces. To be sure, America's cultural climate was hardly yet hospitable to literary effort, as a friend of his had been deploring at the time: "In truth it must be spoken and recorded—this is a dreadful country for a poet to live in." Thus Henry Longfellow complained in his journal in June 1846. "Many poetic souls there are here, and many lovers of song; but life and its ways and ends are prosaic in this country to the last degree." Yet it was more than that. Hawthorne confessed to Longfellow in November 1847, in a letter expressing his admiration for his friend's just published *Evangeline*, "I am trying to resume my pen, but the influences of my situation and customary associates are so anti-literary, that I know not whether I shall succeed. Whenever I sit alone, or walk alone, I find myself dreaming about stories, as of old; but these forenoons in the Custom House undo all that the afternoons and evenings have done. I should be happier if I could write."

Fate was arranging the means for him to do so. From the start, the Democrat Polk had declared himself a one-term president, and at the end of his single term, a Whig would succeed to the chief magistrate's office. In March 1849 Zachary Taylor was inaugurated, and Hawthorne the Democrat learned that he was to lose his place at the customhouse. The political firing was made official in early June. The day he was informed of it, the 8th, the indignant author wrote his attorney and Whig friend in Boston:

"Dear Hillard, I am turned out of office!" The stark sentence he let stand alone as a paragraph, resuming on the next line down: "There is no use in lamentation. It now remains to consider what I shall do next." He was ready to take any kind of job whatever: "If you could do anything in the way of procuring me some stated literary employment, in connection with a newspaper, or as corrector of the press in some printing-establishment, &c, it could not come at a better time." Hawthorne's situation had become desperate. "Do not think anything too humble to be mentioned to me."

George Hillard had set out to do what he could, as would others, on behalf of the gentle Democrat who three years earlier had received his appointment apolitically, as a reward for contributions to American letters. Yet Salem Whigs had been justifying the firing by accusing Hawthorne of "corruption, iniquity and fraud"! The experience was teaching one victim of the spoils system to loathe politicians, as newspapers all over the country took up the Salem scandal. But maybe the wretched politicians had done Hawthorne a favor. "I have come to feel that it is not good for me to be here," he wrote Hillard from Salem. "I am in a lower moral state than I have been;—a duller intellectual one. So let me go; and, under God's providence, I shall arrive at something better."

Meanwhile, he would have to scratch about for other work, while Sophia painted lampshades for sale, and hand screens for the fireside. Moreover, in the grim weeks immediately ahead Hawthorne was forced to endure what he would denominate "the darkest hour I ever lived." At the end of July his mother died; and afterward, the author was stricken with what Sophia termed brain fever. Finally he did resume writing, although hardly before late summer, out of work, angry, humiliated, grief-stricken, wondering how he and his family would live once his wife's small savings from the household budget were spent. "He writes immensely," Sophia reported near the end of September 1849. "I am almost frightened about it. But he is well now and looks shining."

Hawthorne's friends all this while were interesting themselves in a dismissed surveyor's welfare. They hit upon the idea of getting some money together. Thus in mid-January 1850, a letter arrived for the former customhouse official, still unemployed: "It occurred to me and some other of your friends," George Hillard wrote therein with admirable delicacy, "that, in consideration of the events of the last year, you might at this time be in need of a little pecuniary aid. I have therefore collected, from some of those who admire your genius and respect your character, the enclosed sum of money, which I send you with my warmest wishes for your health and happiness. I know the sensitive edge of your temperament; but do not speak or think of obligation. It is only paying, in a very imperfect measure, the debt we owe you for what you have done for American Literature. Could you know the readiness with which every one to whom I applied contributed to this little offering, and could you have heard the warm expressions with which some accompanied their gift, you would have felt that the bread you had cast upon the waters had indeed come back to you."

The gesture continues to stir the heart these long years afterward, as does Hawthorne's response to such unexpected kindness. Nothing else he ever wrote more clearly gives the measure of the man. He had read Hillard's letter in the post office entry, "and it drew" he said, "—what my troubles never have—the water to my eyes; so that I was glad of the sharply cold west wind that blew into them as I came homeward, and gave them an excuse for being red and bleared." The tears, however, had been both sweet and bitter. It was sweet to be remembered by friends who thought him worthy of support. "And it is bitter, nevertheless, to need their support. It is something else besides pride that teaches me that ill-success in life is really and justly a matter of shame. I am ashamed of it, and I ought to be." Failure, this dependent on monetary aid insisted with Puritan grimness, is the fault of the man who fails. "I should apply this truth in judging of other men; and it behoves me not to shun its point or edge in taking it home to my own heart." Even so, "the money, dear Hillard, will smooth my path for a long time to come. The only way in which a man can retain his self-respect, while availing himself of the generosity of his friends, is, by making it an incitement to his utmost exertions, so that he may not need their help again. I shall look upon it so," Hawthorne resolutely concluded, "nor will shun any drudgery that my hand shall find to do, if thereby I may win bread."

All this while, in the midst of the newspaper battles between Whig and Democrat over Hawthorne's celebrated case, another Whig, Longfellow's Boston editor, had been aware of the Salem author's difficulties. James T. Fields had hardly known Hawthorne except through his writings, but he had admired and wanted to help him. Toward the end of 1849 the editor had accordingly come up to Salem.

He had been in his early thirties then, this James T. Fields, partner at Mr. Ticknor's Old Corner Book Store in Boston. Earlier, Ticknor had been publishing books of a sort from his store: sermons, etiquette books, juveniles, pamphlets; but it was Fields who had moved the firm toward literature, so that by midcentury, in times much improved economically, Ticknor & Fields could boast of publishing Longfellow, Whittier, Holmes, and Lowell, among many others. And now this innovative editor, thoroughly conversant with the market, adept at publicizing books as was no one else at the time, uniquely certain that good literature could be made to pay, had come to Salem to see Hawthorne. On a chilly day he found the author hovering over the stove in his sitting room. Fields entering into conversation had raised the subject of literary prospects. Surely Hawthorne had written something during these several years in Salem that was ready for publication. The author shook his head in denial; but as Fields was leaving he did offer him, doubtfully, a manuscript that was, he said, "either very good or very bad,—I don't know which."

On the train down to Boston Fields looked over what had been handed him. Soon he was reading it "all aglow with admiration," reading the "marvellous story" that begins with bearded men in steeple-crowned hats gathered with their womenfolk around a wooden edifice: earlier Bostonians assembled before their Puritan jail, the spike-studded door of which opens to expose a grim-faced beadle leading forth a young woman who carries at her breast a baby squinting in unfamiliar sunlight. The baby's form half hides on the woman's somber gown a piece of fine red cloth, fantastically embroidered, gold-threaded, in the shape of the letter *A*.

The Scarlet Letter, which Ticknor & Fields published in that same spring of 1850, would launch its author on the far more lucrative career that enabled him two years later, in June 1852, to move his family back to Concord, to a home of their own at last, at the Wayside. Not that a single wonderful novel had made this author and new property owner rich. By no means. From its publication in 1850 throughout the remainder of his life, *The Scarlet Letter* would earn Hawthorne the hardly princely sum of fifteen hundred dollars—and that over fourteen years. Yet in contrast to his earlier efforts, the novel did prove a grand success. The initial printing of twenty-five hundred copies had sold out in the first ten days, and within six months two additional American editions found ready purchasers. Moreover, *The Scarlet Letter* was a triumph in England as well; it was selling better there, the actress Fanny Kemble reported, than any novel since the enormously popular *Jane Eyre* three years earlier—although to her father, Sophia found occasion quite legitimately to complain of the botheration that, from those vast overseas sales in an era before copyrights, "the author should not have even *one* penny a volume."

Meanwhile, friends had been urging Hawthorne to move to the western part of the state, into the Berkshire hills; and in May 1850, soon after *The Scarlet Letter* had issued from the press, he and his family did so, to a little red cottage in Lenox—or just on the Lenox line. There the author would remain a year and a half, initially reveling in the brisk clear mountain winter, the lake that stretched beneath his windows, the quiet in which his mind and pen could function undistracted. As for Whigs and Democrats, "I am getting," he declared, "damnably out of the beaten track, as regards politics; and I doubt whether I can claim fellowship with any party whatever." He was no politician anyhow; he was a writer, now with a resourceful editor to encourage him, a readership here and abroad waiting to read what next he wrote, a family to support (baby Rose would be born in Lenox May 20, 1851), and ideas clamoring to be set down. By far the most productive creative period of Hawthorne's life had got under way.

He wrote no more tales, however, now or ever. One that he had on hand, "Feathertop," was to be his last; henceforth he would write only long romances—novels—and at Lenox was already at work on a new one, to be set not in a distant, Puritan past but in the present, in that Salem from which he had recently fled. It took five months to write, this new work, and was done early in 1851: *The House of the Seven Gables.* This, too, proved a success: "it has sold finely, and seems to have pleased a good many people better than the others"—that is, than his first novel and the volumes of tales. And already Hawthorne was thinking of a third novel he might attempt: "When I write another romance, I shall take the Community for a subject, and shall give some of my experiences and observations at Brook Farm." Even now, writing a friend in the summer of 1851, he could report having in addition completed a retelling of myths for children, *A Wonder Book,* which the faithful Ticknor and Fields were putting to press.

Yet Hawthorne off there in Lenox had all the while been growing discontented. His and Sophia's health suffered in the mountain climate; they both had colds. In summer he felt excessively listless. He missed the sea, the smell of wharves, the feel of pavement underfoot. For various reasons, the author wanted out of Lenox, and in the autumn of 1851 an opportunity arose.

Upon returning eight years earlier from their working honeymoon visiting schools, prisons, and orphanages in Europe, Mr. and Mrs. Horace Mann had moved into a boardinghouse in Boston while the reformer resumed his work as secretary of the Massachusetts Board of Education. Early in 1844, Mary Mann's first child had been born. Before long Boston was proving too expensive for the family; so that by the summer of 1846 Horace Mann had built a modest house ten miles west of the city in the hamlet of West Newton. Not two years later, he resigned from his long-held position as secretary in order to become Whig member from the Eighth District in the House of Representatives in Washington. Thus, the legislator and his family would be away in Washington through the winter and spring of 1852, during the current term of Congress. In their absence, the Hawthornes were welcome to rent their little house in West Newton, which, despite its humbleness, did offer the not inconsiderable inducements of a study, a sunny nursery, and a bathing room.

Late in 1851, accordingly, the Hawthornes had loaded a wagon at the red cottage in Lenox and made their way to the railroad station and from there back east across the state and down via the Boston & Worcester Railroad to West Newton, to that hamlet twenty minutes outside the city. And there, during his half year residence in the Manns' house, the now productive Hawthorne succeeded in writing his third novel, about Brook Farm.

Moreover, toward the end of winter, in February 1852, he ventured from West Newton for a visit back to Concord, to look over the dilapidated Alcott house for sale. And he bought the house, and moved there early in June, Sophia and the two girls arriving first on the premises. Painters, paperers, carpenters, and upholsterers had worked magical changes. Hawthorne duly appearing at the Wayside with five-year-old Julian "was delighted with it, not having seen it since his first visit in snow-time, when it seemed fit only for a menagerie of cattle." At the sound of her husband's carriage that Saturday morning, Mrs. Hawthorne hurried out to the piazza with the baby. "When Julian passed, he was at the open window of the carriage; and baby saw him and screamed for joy; and Julian shouted to see me; and the echoes were fairly roused by the ecstasy of meeting, all round."

There was history about this home. It stood, as its new owner noted, "within ten or fifteen yards of the old Boston road (along which the British marched and retreated)" on—for the regulars— the horrific April day that had started the Revolution. Between road and house nearby rose a fence, "and some trees and shrubbery of Mr Alcott's setting out. Whereupon, I have called it 'The Wayside'—which I think a better name, and more morally suggestive than that which, as Mr Alcott has since told me, he bestowed on it—'The Hillside.'"

Indeed, the hill behind the house had particularly attracted the purchaser's notice last February, and to that hill in years ahead Hawthorne's steps would return again and again, as would his thoughts when absent from the Wayside. Among elms and white pines and oaks were locust trees fragrantly blooming during these same early June days of 1852, "the whole forming rather a thicket than a wood. Nevertheless, there is some very good shade to be found there. I spend delectable hours there," the satisfied home owner would soon be reporting, "in the hottest part of the day, stretched out at my lazy length, with a book in my hand, or some unwritten book in my thoughts. There is almost always a breeze stirring along the side or brow of the hill." And when in his new outdoor study he chose, as he often did, to climb to the brow, Hawthorne atop his very own crest of ground seventy feet above road level could enjoy a fine view, south and west over the roof-tops of the Wayside and beyond to "extensive level surfaces, and gentle hilly outlines, covered with wood, that characterize the scenery of Concord."

19

CONCORD IN THE FIFTIES

*T*en summers earlier, Hawthorne had gazed from a hill opposite the Manse upon Concord's roofs, spires, and storefronts
off to the left. Now from his hill behind the Wayside he was looking upon the village to his right. An observer's angle of vision had
changed, along with much else in the interval. To be sure, much
remained the same. Like the Manse, the Wayside below him, with
its long history, stood as it had since before the Revolution. That
far back, General Gage's spies out from Boston had reported in their
cryptographic schoolboy French that "Il-y-a sept toneaux de poudre
a feu deposités chez un certain nommé Whitney, pres de l'entre
du Vilage de Concord"—seven tons of gunpowder stored in a house
near the entrance of Concord owned by one Whitney; that is, by
Samuel Whitney, mustermaster of the village Minutemen living in
the 1770s here at the Wayside, which survives to the present day.

Gazing in 1852 out over roofs of the ancient house and its wings
that Alcott had added, a new owner would have seen from his height
a settlement of stores and dwellings beyond that appeared hardly
changed from the village he had left in penury and discouragement
seven years before. The population of Concord was much the same
now as then, two thousand people more or less; and into these early
1850s the composition of that population was remaining for the
moment homogeneous: mostly white, mostly descendants of English
come over two centuries earlier from Kent and East Anglia. Irish
laborers building the railroad in the 1840s had moved on beyond
Concord as tracks had edged westward, leaving Hunts, Buttricks,
Flints, and Hosmers to till their farms as they and their ancestors

had done in these parts for generations. Nor did rural Concord furnish sufficient industry to attract a coastal population; nor had people in Boston yet accustomed themselves to spending a couple of hours a day in transit on the railroad in order that they might work in the city while enjoying benefits that arise from dwelling in a drowsy country village.

So Concord among its low hills was about the same size and much the same in appearance and composition as an observer would have remembered, although even from Hawthorne's high vantage point one change was obvious. The clapboard courthouse with its spire seventy-five feet in the air had disappeared, burned to the ground in 1849 by an arsonous defendant under indictment, bent on destroying evidence within its wood walls. Some in Middlesex County had not wanted to replace the building. Why hold court sessions in a village so far out of the way? For many litigants now, their business would be conducted more conveniently in bustling Lowell. Yet in the end the courthouse in Concord was rebuilt, if less imposingly, even while forces of change indicated that the town's long days as the county seat were numbered.

If, in the early 1850s, you had gone down from the hill behind the Wayside into the streets of Concord and entered houses, you might have observed other indications of change. Parlors exhibited more trappings of gentility than earlier: furnishings shopped for in the city, more pianos, books, elegant magazines. In these now prosperous times more Concordians had journeyed to Europe; more of their children were going to college. And this increase in sophistication and social grace seemed to some in a reform-minded age a confirmation of progress, that the world was becoming increasingly cultured, increasingly gracious and civilized. All the while, material life appeared to be gaining in comfort. During these seven years, from 1845 when Hawthorne and his family had fled the Old Manse to their present arrival at the Wayside, Singer had invented his sewing machine, Hoe had invented his rotary printing press, Cyrus McCormick had built a Chicago factory to sell his harvester, and—momentously—ether had come into use in American medical practice. The earliest woman in the Western world, in fact, to bear a child (her third, and first daughter) under ether's miraculous oblivion had been Fanny Longfellow, in April 1847: "I am very sorry you all thought me so rash and naughty in trying the ether. Henry's faith gave me courage, and I had heard such a thing had succeeded abroad." The pioneer had felt proud to lead the way toward less suffering for womankind. "This is certainly," she wrote, "the greatest blessing of this age."

For humanity in pain, Mrs. Longfellow was incontestably right; yet day by day, among Concordians more or less pain-free, the railroad may have seemed an even greater blessing, and assuredly the greater instrument for change. The very days were changed now. Inhabitants of the early fifties were coming to live by clocks and pocket watches, Waltham nearby a clock-making town for the nation. Trains ran on schedule, as did textile mills in Waltham and Lowell, so that, for many, the farmers' more casual approximations of time by the sun had grown obsolete. "The startings and arrivals of the cars are now the epochs in the village day," one Concord resident recorded of this new era. "They go and come with such regularity and precision, and their whistle can be heard so far, that the farmers set their clocks by them, and thus one well-conducted institution regulates a whole country."

Moreover, that same railroad was linking Concord ever more closely to Boston, replacing the village's earlier autonomy with the dependencies of a suburb. No need for stagecoach operators any longer, and little use for teamsters in their wagons hauling goods along the highways. The railroad moved people and freight with unrivaled efficiency, bringing Boston so close that shops and taverns in the village saw custom decline. At the same time, markets everywhere were expanding, labor specializing, farmers taking to furnishing the coastal city with milk, fruits, and vegetables; and those who didn't, who went on planting as in olden days, could watch their livelihoods dwindle.

During the early fifties, Concord's one newspaper would cease publication, the village thereafter—at least for a considerable while—reduced to reading of local events in pages of the Lowell *Journal*. Assuredly, the opening years of a new decade were in many ways different from when Hawthorne had lived at the Manse. Back then—as another instance—in September 1845, the very month of his and his wife's anguished packing to leave their debt-ridden paradise and move to Salem, had occurred overseas yet one more event destined to wreak vast changes upon the future now arrived. In Ireland had appeared a mysterious rotting blight on the lowly potato, destroying half of that year's crop. Heavy rains through the following winter had allowed the fungus to thrive and spread, so that the potato crop planted in the horrific year 1846 had decomposed all over Ireland into a mass of black putridity. And emigrants had fled the disaster.

True, from the beginning immigrant vessels had been arriving at America's shores. Some years earlier the bachelor Hawthorne had witnessed one such arrival, in 1839, when the brig *Tiberius* had brought from England as many as seventy girls, "some pale and delicate-looking, others rugged and coarse," as the weigher and gauger at the Boston customhouse had observed, before going on to record: "The scene of landing them in boats, at the wharf-stairs, to the considerable display of their legs;—whence they are carried off to the Worcester railroad in hacks and omnibuses. Their farewells to the men—Good-bye, John, etc.—with wavings of handkerchiefs as long as they were in sight." Immigrants to America had been enacting such intimate leave-takings from the beginning, but never in the numbers that would pour from Ireland aboard coffin ships through this heartrending interlude in the late 1840s. By the start of the fifties, roughly 140,000 people were living in Boston, of whom 46,000 were Irish—and the numbers of Irish would triple over the next five years, while the native-born population rose a mere fraction of that, no more than 15 percent.

Even as far back as 1839, the English girls whom Hawthorne had seen debark from the *Tiberius* had been bound for labor in textile mills, those mills having thus early betrayed their founders' utopian dreams. The philanthropist Nathan Appleton and his colleagues had meant to build in fields alongside the Merrimack River a humane city to reproach the squalor of English mill towns. In these new mills of Lowell, daughters of Yankee farmers were to work for a couple of profitable years before marrying, fed well all the while, housed well amid schools and parks, with respectably chaperoned hours of leisure at church and lecture hall to nourish their spiritual and mental needs, all at wages far higher than girls could earn anywhere else. But Appleton was living away in his mansion on Beacon Hill. At Lowell and at Waltham, on site at the mills were supervisors of cramped vision in charge of enterprises the very success of which had engendered fierce competition. More machines were being installed and run longer hours. Some accompanying abuse of the hands who worked those machines arose from ignorance of health practices that we take for granted: windows nailed shut to maintain humidity for the sake of the yarn, lint left thick in the unventilated air, girls on their feet all day through six days of the week, their work time extended in summer to match the conventional fourteen hours of farmwork (although labor amid the horrendous racket of the looms could by no means compare in humaneness with labor on farms). And all the while, machines in the mills were sped up and overseers paid bonuses to get more output, always more output from their harried help.

So Yankee farm girls had abandoned the textile mills, their places taken by low-paid immigrant workers from England and Ireland and Canada. And withal, the mills thrived into the late forties, into the fifties, spinning and weaving southern cotton into cloth to increase the already vast fortunes of mill owners. More cloth, more cotton from which to weave the cloth, more slaves in the South to pick the cotton: and the fates of New England and the slaveholding South were being thus ever more tightly intertwined.

In the interval between 1845 and the return of the Hawthornes to Concord in 1852 had occurred one further, enormous change affecting both village and nation. In the course of those seven years America's gaze had turned westward. President Polk, taking office in March 1845, had hailed the annexation of Texas in his inaugural address, moving promptly thereafter to acquire in addition, first, Oregon. His diplomats negotiating with Britain had succeeded in drawing a northern boundary along the forty-ninth parallel of latitude to the Pacific, thus incorporating much of the broad Northwest into a swelling nation. Next, Polk had carried America into war against Mexico, to the revulsion of such northerners (among many others) as Representative Abraham Lincoln, as well as Henry Thoreau and the Whig Horace Mann. Still serving as secretary of the Massachusetts Board of Education, Mann did not allow himself "to mingle at all in the political contests of the day," yet his private views in letters to friends were unequivocal. He could only decry a republic that on the one hand affected to uphold peace and freedom, churlishly refusing on the other hand to help the starving Irish through the horrors of their potato famine while mustering fifty thousand troops and appropriating $10 million in pursuit of an act of naked aggression, the outcome of which must surely lead to a further, blightlike spread of slavery.

Polk's generals had waged and won their war against Mexico nevertheless, and the victors in February 1848 had imposed a crushing peace on our southern neighbor. More than half of Mexico's territory was ceded to the United States, and in that way the president acquired the California that he coveted—a prize richer than even Polk had bargained for. For scarcely days before the signing of the treaty that ended the war, a California laborer at work in late January 1848, at the millrace of a sawmill at Sutter's Fort, had uttered a cry that would sound all over the world: "Boys, I believe I have found a gold mine!" Word of James Marshall's discovery reached New York in August, to be generally dismissed as hyperbole. Not until President Polk's annual message to Congress in December did beckoning wealth come clearly into focus nationwide: "The accounts of the abundance of gold in that territory," according to the president, "are of such an extraordinary character as would scarcely command belief were they not corroborated by the authentic reports of officers in the public service." Thereupon newspapers all over the East took up the cry, and soon a new kind of notice was filling columns of the *New York Herald*: of ships bound for the Isthmus, of associations recruiting members to make the overland journey West, of such items abruptly for sale as digging tools, scales, tents, washing machines, blankets, canned goods, coffee grinders.

Good times appeared at hand. The California Gold Rush would pour a vast infusion of wealth into the American economy, abetted by imperial England's investments in railroads in the New World. Much English money had been frightened away from investment in Europe in any case, following upon revolutionary turmoil there in 1848. That money was coming here instead, along with, incidentally, hordes of emigrating Germans, fleeing repression at home. But there was money in abundance now in these United States, and prosperity; and the hard economic days at the Manse, with literary magazines folding and authors left unpaid, seemed far in the past. By 1852, the new owner of the Wayside could turn carpenters' bills over to his publisher to settle, and the obliging Mr. Ticknor stood ready, moreover, to publish whatever Mr. Hawthorne might write in the months ahead.

Good times—except for one major matter. All the new western territory that President Polk's initiatives had bestowed on the nation, thereby fulfilling America's manifest destiny across the vast breadth of a continent, had brought with it controversy violent enough to threaten the very Union. Into those new lands the North had determined that slavery would not advance; the South was equally intent on seeing its peculiar (and legal) institution extended into shared territories jointly won, jointly possessed. In the crisis, it was left to Mr. Polk's presidential adversary from 1844, the defeated Henry Clay, Star of the West, with his long career presumed to be over and done, to come forth and guide the nation through to a compromise. In 1849, Clay had emerged from retirement to reenter the Senate. The following year saw him crafting a series of resolutions as the final political act of a life of distinguished public service, so that in his frail age Senator Clay would live to witness his resolutions become law as the Compromise of 1850. By their terms, the new, rich state of California entered the Union as free soil, whereas the ample territories of Utah and New Mexico were to allow or forbid slavery as their inhabitants (on soil hardly hospitable to the institution in any case) might later determine.

Within two more years, by 1852—with the Hawthornes newly installed in their Concord home—the honorable Rutherford B. Hayes of Ohio felt moved to pronounce confidently, "Politics is no longer the topic of this country." By then, Representative Hayes felt certain that the nation's important questions had all been settled, and government had ceased to figure prominently in the lives of its citizens. "Its duties and powers no longer reach to the happiness of the people. The people's progress, progress of every sort, no longer depends on government." Prosperity was permitting Americans to provide for themselves and get on with their lives unaided, in times that seemed glitteringly new.

Indeed, Hayes's pronouncement followed hard upon demises signaling (yet again) an earlier time's passing. In June the Hawthornes moved back to Concord; and very soon, in what appears to have been its final issue, the village newspaper was informing readers of the death of the Great Compromiser, Henry Clay, "at Washington on Tuesday last, June 29th, in the seventy-sixth year of his age." Three months before, John C. Calhoun had died; Daniel Webster would be gone in the fall—senatorial giants removed all at once and forever from a political scene that the trio had dominated for so long. Senator Clay's end had come quietly, the Kentucky statesman having been shaved within his final hour and his mind remaining clear to the very last. The *Freeman* article recapitulated the Star of the West's lengthy, glorious career, then shared with its readers the last spoken thought that the Great Pacificator's silver tongue had been heard to utter: "a request," as it turns out, "to his son to fix his shirt collar."

20

TWO NOVELS

*P*oliticians who remained on the scene appeared hardly of the stature of Calhoun, Clay, and Webster. Among survivors were leaders of the Democracy with names such as Butler, Lane, Dickinson, and Dodge. Adherents of that lackluster foursome, along with supporters of other aspirants to the Democratic nomination for the presidency, had convened in Baltimore on the first day of June 1852; and two days later—with Sophia Hawthorne at the Wayside civilizing the place in advance of her husband's arrival—balloting had begun. Eight readings of the roll call of states unfurled at the raucous session without definitive result. At day's end, Cass could count 113 votes toward nomination; Buchanan, 88; Douglas, 34; Marcy, 26; Lane, 13; Houston, 9; Dodge, 3; Butler, 1; and Dickinson, 1. Thereafter through Friday the balloting at the convention dragged on, and on into Saturday. Over forty times the roll of all the states was called, and still none of the candidates had managed to amass enough votes to win. Saturday morning—with Hawthorne and his young son in Concord at the carriage window, wife and baby greeting them ecstatically from the piazza of the Wayside—weary politicians in Baltimore were embarking on the calling of yet more rolls. "Nothing of the kind ever before took place," a reporter noted. "It is without precedent in the history of our national conventions . . . that so many ballotings should be had before a candidate could be selected."

But Hawthorne would have cared little about all that. In Salem the author had had his fill of politics, was returning to Concord to ply his pen in order to earn enough to support his family. It was

June, to be sure, and this particular storyteller normally didn't write in summertime—relaxed, rather, and mused, and waited for cooler days of autumn to resume what he called his scribbling. But a year ago, uniquely in June out in the Berkshire hills, the father of three had composed his fiction for young people, A *Wonder Book for Girls and Boys,* retelling such ancient myths as The Gorgon's Head and The Golden Touch. Nothing Hawthorne had ever written had brought him more pleasure in the composition than his uncharacteristically cloudless *Wonder Book.* He planned to get started on a sequel to that, having already, only days before, finished (and dated from Concord) the preface to his most recent novel, *The Blithedale Romance,* written during the months in West Newton.

The *Blithedale Romance* is a book-length fiction arising out of its author's recollections of his earlier days at Brook Farm. Some commentators in our time have handled the novel very roughly, this only work by Hawthorne written in the first person, wherein he seeks to transpose the world close around him into fiction. *The Scarlet Letter,* his first novel, written a couple of years earlier, had ventured back two centuries to colonial Boston to find its setting. The second novel, finished over a year ago, was set, to be sure, in the present, but in a present much circumscribed, in Salem within the walls of a decrepit seven-gabled mansion over which hovered dolefully, relentlessly, a past that would not be buried. *Blithedale,* by contrast, is Hawthorne's attempt to re-create in fiction a generally familiar episode no more than a decade removed from the here and now. Many readers would have known of the author's involvement in hopeful, utopian beginnings at Brook Farm in 1841, as well as of his early withdrawal, of debts over time that had accrued to the enterprise, and of the collapse in 1847 of West Roxbury's venture toward the Ideal. By then a general prosperity had weakened the lure of communal life in any case, as the rising strength of the slaveholding South was driving reform impulses in a direction different from any that might be striving to reconcile high-minded living and manual labor.

It was in part the swelling materialism of a prosperous Gold Rush age against which Hawthorne was reacting in *The Blithedale Romance.* In such a world spirituality was not easily found. Hence the appeal of the atypical Brook Farm experiment, "a little removed from the highway of ordinary travel," as he wrote in his preface to the novel. Brook Farm, as the author tells us there, was "certainly, the most romantic episode of his own life—essentially a day-dream, and yet a fact—and thus offering an available foothold between fiction and reality."

That was where this particular creator chose to reside, in the Faery Land (as he termed it) between reality and fiction, actual and imaginary, material and spiritual, fact and ideal. Only there could the truths that he sought shine forth recognizably, while unobscured by the dully ephemeral. In common parlance his longer works are termed novels; yet because they unfold in such a distinct locale, he himself preferred to call them by another name: *romance*.

Romance in this sense he had defined in the preface to *The House of the Seven Gables*. There he had observed that novels— those of Dickens, say—presume "to aim at a very minute fidelity, not merely to the possible, but to the probable and ordinary course of man's experience." In novels, surface appearances matter: how different people speak, dress, eat, travel, live. The romance writer, by contrast, makes no attempt to reproduce such surfaces. Instead, he strives to present only the "truth of the human heart," by mellowing the lights and deepening the shadows of scenes in order to evoke a world that transcends the quotidian commonplace, an enchanted world, mysterious and remote, bathed as may be in gloomy dusk or silvery moonlight.

This very year Sophia's mother, speaking of her son-in-law, would set down her high opinion in terms that help further distinguish the romance from the novel. Hawthorne, Mrs. Peabody wrote her daughter in August, "is one of the few who can not only look at things, but into and through them. The world has great claims on one who can do so much towards raising the mind from stupid materialism to translucent wonder." Precisely. As Hawthorne conceived it, the romance attempts to look less *at*, than *into* and *through*, with the result that reality becomes transmuted into something still familiar yet wondrously strange. In *The Blithedale Romance*, for example, components of Brook Farm have been invested with symbolic values that disclose meanings below the surface; the brawny Hollingsworth happens by trade to be a blacksmith, he who in his earnest rigor hammers thought, as he says, out of iron after heating the iron in his heart. Similar correspondences are developed carefully throughout, with little effort made meanwhile—any more here than elsewhere in Hawthorne's fiction—to capture peculiarities of speech or idiosyncrasies of manner. The author's notebooks may abound in such particularizing effects, but not his fiction. Characters in his fiction accordingly emerge (as we saw in "The Birthmark") less as unique individuals than as representative types: here, of the brilliant, beautiful feminist chafing in the confines of Victorian propriety; of the inflexible reformer monomaniacally intent on his mission; of the pale figure of conventional, vulnerable womanhood—Zenobia, Hollingsworth, and Priscilla, those three interacting in their Arcadian setting under the observation of the ineffectual artist (passive spectator as artists may be), the minor poet Coverdale, who out of boredom and mild curiosity has drifted from Boston to Blithedale, where he will narrate this story that he scarcely comprehends.

A number of other characters appear—rather more, indeed, than are usual in Hawthorne's romances, which aim not at range but at depth. Consider deeply: what are the consequences of fanaticism on a human psyche? To explore such an issue hardly takes multitudes, but rather a single individual and his few associates closely scrutinized. Observing, for instance, the fanatical blacksmith at Blithedale with his plan to redeem hardened criminals, one "grew drearily conscious that Hollingsworth had a closer friend than ever you could be. And this friend was the cold, spectral monster which he had himself conjured up, and on which he was wasting all the warmth of his heart." The man had become enslaved to his theory of how to reform the world, having taught "his benevolence to pour its warm tide exclusively through one channel; so that there was nothing to spare for other great manifestations of love to man, nor scarcely for the nutriment of individual attachments, unless they could minister, in some way, to the terrible egotism which he mistook for an angel of God."

This new romance, then, is in part about social reform, and appropriately so given its setting in a utopian community in the early 1840s. But Hawthorne, typically, is concerned with the effects of reform less on society than on the individual. For always his themes are psychological: what pride, or isolation, or guilt, or egoism may do to the individual human heart. And in *The Blithedale Romance,* such issues as these that the novel ponders appear as profound as any he ever considered, among pages containing, as invariably with this writer, passages of stunning beauty.

Yet as narrative the work seems lacking, at least for the modern reader. Its subtleties have provided academics of our time with much to weigh and analyze, but readers in quest of the deepest rewards that the writings of Hawthorne offer have found them elsewhere, in *The Scarlet Letter*, in *The House of the Seven Gables*, and in the finest of the shorter tales. Even in its own day *The Blithedale Romance* was less uniformly welcomed than its two great predecessors. Sales were disappointing, and from the start a few critics voiced reservations. Not that such reservations were widespread. The respected E. P. Whipple, for example, would pronounce in *Graham's* that "'The Blithedale Romance,' just published, seems to us the most perfect in execution of any of Hawthorne's works, and as a work of art, hardly equalled by anything else which the country has produced"; while overseas, in England, the *Athenaeum* proclaimed that "Mr. Hawthorne's third tale, in our judgment, puts the seal on the reputation of its author as the highest, deepest, and finest imaginative writer whom America has yet produced."

A glance at another book-length fiction about reform, published this same spring of 1852, may further illustrate differences between the conventional novel and what Hawthorne meant by romance. That other book was the creation of "a little, feeble, timid-looking woman," as Fanny Longfellow described her; or as its author herself would trenchantly volunteer, of a "mother to seven children— six of whom are now living," a woman, consequently, the greater part of whose "time & strength has been spent in the necessary but unpoetic duties of the family." True, Harriet Beecher Stowe, Connecticut born and reared, had found time to write stories as far back as the 1830s. But there was much in a wife and mother's life to keep Mrs. Stowe, now moved to Ohio, occupied otherwise than with writing; and, moreover, by the early 1850s she had suffered through miscarriages, a brother's suicide, the death of a beloved child, penury, and the baleful effects of poisonous blue pills administered over a protracted period as medicine. "To begin, then," she would attempt to sketch out her life to this point, "I am a little bit of a woman—somewhat more than 40—about as thin & dry as

a pinch of snuff never very much to look at in my best days—&
looking like a used-up article now. I was married when I was 25
years old to a man rich in Greek & Hebrew, Latin & Arabic, & alas!
rich in nothing else."

That would be Calvin Stowe, Bowdoin class of 1824, who in
Hawthorne's senior year there had served as librarian of the little
college out on the Maine frontier. Destined to become the most
knowledgeable biblical scholar in the country, Stowe had moved
on from Bowdoin to the Lane Theological Seminary in Cincinnati,
and there had married a daughter of Lyman Beecher, president of
the institution. By 1850, the scholar was being summoned back East
to fill a professorship at his alma mater; and it was in Brunswick,
at Bowdoin, that his wife, Harriet, felt impelled to forsake the folksy
subject matter of her earlier literary work and undertake a composition out of passion—for the first time full-length and national in
scope—that would address the issue of slavery.

What had inflamed Mrs. Stowe to do so was the passage that
year of the Fugitive Slave Act. Senator Clay's compromise resolutions of 1850, to settle controversies connected with new western
territories acquired from Mexico, had seemed to grant much to the
North. But if a compromise is to work, both sides must benefit,
and what the South got from the bargain—aside from reaffirming
the principle that slavery might enter the territories—was a new
Fugitive Slave Law, which required that slaves escaped to the North
be returned to their owners. And this new law, unlike a similar one
on the books since 1793, was to be rigorously enforced.

Harriet Beecher Stowe (although by no means she only) was
incensed with this effort by the South to make slave catchers of
unoffending people up North, incensed with "this miserable wicked
fugitive slave business—Why I have felt almost choked sometimes
with pent up wrath that does no good." But perhaps she might wring
some good out of her wrath after all. When, in the aftermath of
the Compromise, she heard humane Christian people up North
conclude that their duty was to return human beings to slavery,
"she could only think," the author later explained, "these men and
Christians cannot know what slavery is." Mrs. Stowe resolved to
tell a story that would show them the institution fairly. And when
she was done, when under inspiration she had finished her story
and, after seeing it published, could look back and appraise it, she

found *Uncle Tom's Cabin* to be successful in portraying the best aspects of slavery no doubt; "but, oh! who shall say what yet remains untold in that valley and shadow of death, that lies the other side?"

Appearing in book form in March 1852, a few weeks before *The Blithedale Romance*, Stowe's powerful presentation of slavery's assault on the human spirit proved an enormous commercial success. "How she is shaking the world with her Uncle Tom's Cabin!" wrote a marveling Longfellow. "At one step she has reached the top of the stair-case up which the rest of us climb on our knees year after year." Ten thousand copies of the novel were sold in the first week, an extraordinary three hundred thousand by the end of the first year. Nothing like that had ever happened before. In three months this mother of six had earned with her first full-length fiction ten thousand dollars, "the largest sum of money," newspaper readers were instructed, "ever received by any author, either American or European, from the sale of a single work in so short a period of time."

Hawthorne with his writings, for all his critical success, would never come anywhere close to money like that. True, the American reading public had grown since the thirties and early forties, many lured into the habit by Dickens, by the Brontës and Thackeray; but the new public was of a decidedly feminine cast, in quest of pathos and sentiment, less drawn than an earlier readership to the Gothic tales of Scott, Poe, and Nathaniel Hawthorne. Stowe's domestic emphasis gratified the new feminine audience.

Yet in other ways her novel differs from Hawthorne's, even as both in their almost simultaneous appearance treat of reform. *Uncle Tom's Cabin* is sociological in its purposes, and as such introduces a large cast of characters spread over a spacious geography. *The Blithedale Romance*, by contrast, with its psychological concerns, ventures no farther afield than nine or ten miles, from a rural Arcadian community to urban Boston and back; and the characters number no more than six or seven. Stowe's outward-looking novel is thus broad and horizontal; Hawthorne's looks inward, and is vertical and deep. The former is filled with the contrasting dialect voices of slaves and southern planters, of oafs, knaves, and highborn ladies; whereas *Blithedale* makes little effort to exploit local color, so that one character speaks no more differently from an-

other than Cinderella does from Prince Charming; it is *what* the
characters say in Hawthorne that matters, not their individual ways
of saying it. And *Uncle Tom's Cabin*, for all its grimness in pictur-
ing an atrocity of human degradation, is at its core an optimistic
work, moving confidently forward with a sense that reform can bring
about amelioration and that human beings can change; whereas
The Blithedale Romance, free and lovely as are its rural enterprises,
remains nevertheless—as typically with Hawthorne—more pessi-
mistic than otherwise, bearing throughout evidences of a Puritan-
ism by no means certain that a depraved humanity can become
much better than it is. And even if it could be reformed, "the good
of others, like our own happiness," the author would insist to his
sister-in-law Elizabeth Peabody, "is not to be attained by direct
effort, but incidentally. All history and observation confirm this. I
am really too humble to think of doing good!" Stowe felt otherwise;
and in the end, each of us will determine individually which of the
two, with their many differences, speaks more pertinently to our
own philanthropic, war-ravaged times, times hardly more replete
with compassion than with cruelty and injustice.

As for the Fugitive Slave Act, Democratic politicians assembled in
early June 1852 in Baltimore had determined, like good people both
South and North, to ignore altogether whatever contentions such
controversial legislation had raised. The act was now the law of the
land; and the Compromise of 1850, of which it was a part, had been
accepted as uttering the final word on the slavery question. Accordingly, Democrats in convention, like their Whig counterparts a
couple of weeks later, crafted a presidential platform that accepted
all parts of the Compromise without demur.

And the Democratic politicos had finally finished balloting. On
Saturday morning, June 5, the delegates had resumed by calling
the roll of states a thirty-fourth time, although with no better luck
in selecting their presidential nominee than during the preceding
two days. Then, on the very next roll call, Virginia put forth the
name of a candidate who had not even been considered earlier, but
who nevertheless began to pick up strength in succeeding ballots,
so that by the forty-sixth he was, amazingly, over the top. On the
forty-ninth ballot a party stampede made the dark-horse choice all
but unanimous.

Back at the Wayside, Hawthorne was to learn nothing about such lively happenings until Wednesday, not for four days yet. When he did, he must have shared some of the surprise felt all over the nation, even if in writing the victor the following day he professed otherwise. For the Democrats had chosen former senator Franklin Pierce of New Hampshire to carry their party banner; so that "Dear Pierce," the author found himself explaining to his good friend and Bowdoin college mate on June 9, "I came to Concord on Saturday; and, residing at some distance from the Post Office, I did not hear of your nomination till yesterday. It was not unexpected to me; nor, I think, will it surprise any-one who has looked attentively at your position and character, and the tendency of all your fortunes."

21

HAWTHORNE AND SLAVERY

*A*s his friend was implying, Pierce's fortunes had tended to
be agreeable, although before this late spring of 1852, most
Americans would have hardly been paying attention. As a young
senator in Washington Franklin Pierce had made no mark, and in
any case he had been away from the federal capital since leaving
the Senate voluntarily in 1842, a decade ago. Since then he had
practiced law in Concord, New Hampshire, had served in the
Mexican War, and had led his home state's Democratic Party. But
all of that had made the politician something less than a national
figure, as Hawthorne's letter of congratulations implicitly acknowledged. Or more precisely: "I hardly know whether to congratulate
you," the well-wisher had gone on to write; "for it would be absurd
to suppose that the great office to which you are destined will ever
afford you one happy or comfortable moment—and yet it is an end
worthy of all ambition, as the highest success that the whole world
offers to a statesman." Meanwhile, the author had been wondering: Pierce was by no means so well known as other Democrats
denied the nomination, as James Buchanan or Stephen Douglas
or Lewis Cass or the Texan Sam Houston. "It has occurred to me,"
Hawthorne now ventured, "that you might have some thoughts of
getting me to write the necessary biography," with the purpose of
making the candidate better known. "Whatever service I can do you,
I need not say, would be at your command." But Pierce should realize that others would manage such a job more effectively. "It needs
long thought with me, in order to produce anything good, and, after

all, my style and qualities, as a writer, are certainly not those of the broadest popularity, such as are requisite for a task of this kind."

Be that as may, Pierce wanted the crucial document written by his Bowdoin friend, wanted Hawthorne to write an account of the nominee's life that would let the whole nation know the merits of this dark-horse Democrat. Accordingly he came for a visit to the Wayside on July 5, even before the house was fit to receive such distinction, and, as his host had promised, was treated as simply as if he "were a mere country lawyer." Matters were there arranged: the author would put aside his fictions and get to work in the heat of summer, under a tight deadline, producing this factual campaign biography for a friend. But at once a problem arose. As the reluctant biographer was explaining at the start, he had become sensible "of a very difficult and delicate part of my task, in your connection with the great subject of variance between the North and South"; that is, in Pierce's record on the issue of slavery.

We would prefer that those we admire be admirable in every way. A brief year earlier, Nathaniel Hawthorne had written to a friend this appalling sentence: "I have not, as you suggest, the slightest sympathy for the slaves; or, at least, not half as much as for the laboring whites, who, I believe, as a general thing, are ten times worse off than the Southern negros." How is such callousness to be accounted for? The assertion—and Hawthorne privately issued others in a similar vein—must detract from the stature of a man in so many respects worthy of our grateful admiration. But how can we even explain, from such a source, an utterance so unfeeling?

We must put ourselves backward in time, of course. For those in the North, the South's peculiar institution would have seemed a far-off abstraction. Distances were greater then. One's state and region figured far more prominently then than now; so that for most New Englanders the South appeared alien terrain. Moreover, everybody North or South, or nearly everybody, accepted the institution as a regional peculiarity, present from long before the beginning of the Republic, as much a given fact as different dialects are, as hills and rivers are, as are the poor. Indeed, the great majority of Hawthorne's contemporaries shared his prejudices. To us, the overt racism of those times astonishes; but then, as has been noted, all of white America—abolitionists included—regarded blacks as inferior. *Knew* them to be inferior, like children. Like other people's nineteenth-century children, whom one chastised as need be, loved on occasion, and from whom one expected little beyond service and obedience. All the while, northerners at their considerable distance clung for conscience's sake to assurances that slaveholders, except for the random brute or fool, would sooner abuse a good workhorse than mistreat property worth money on the auction block.

Besides, slavery had biblical sanction. It had constitutional sanction. And most emphatically it had economic sanction, woven as the institution was into the very fabric of American affluence. Cotton is king; you dare not make war on it! Too many jobs, too many fortunes North and South depended on the fruits of slave labor, and not just in New England textile mills. Rice, sugar, hemp, tobacco all flourished because of slavery; Americans of the time could no more imagine life as they knew it going forward without slave labor than we can imagine life without meat and poultry counters at supermarkets, and the style of living that those counters furnish us, and the jobs they provide—and the slaughterhouses out of sight that sustain them.

The bloody slaughterhouses we put out of mind. Maybe rue them as a necessary evil, but we don't dwell on them any more than antebellum Americans dwelt on slavery. Look away: that is what people do and did with disagreeable subject matter; and those who insist on ranting about such things are ill-mannered and badly bred—are vegans, are troublemakers who would take away jobs, are abolitionists who would threaten the Union.

What did Hawthorne know about slavery anyway? He had never seen a slave in his life, and the blacks that he did see were porters and dockhands and house servants and the numerous poor about the streets of Boston. And with all his imagination, all his sense of history, all his faculty for looking beneath the surface of things, he never saw beneath that surface to the human potential that ill-clothed subservience disfigured. So few whites did, for all their talk of freedom. Their word *free* we may misunderstand in any case, as in *free soil*: territories were to be kept free of slavery because its presence undermined white labor. In a world with such attitudes as commonplaces, Hawthorne had spent his mostly solitary life in New England brooding on history two hundred years old and on matters of the human heart. What did he, whose broad tastes in reading never ran to abolitionist tracts, know about the institution of slavery? He regretted it, as all good people did. And looked away, feeling assured, like many others in a Union progressing toward the light, that Providence in its wisdom would remove that scourge of bondage by means not yet discernible, and in its own good time.

Even so, we could wish in this matter that he had been more like his neighbor Emerson. Both had started from similar presumptions. They both were certain that meaningful reform could never be imposed from without. As Hawthorne had insisted in "Earth's Holocaust," reform must grow from within: if society is to become better, each individual must make the effort to reform his own heart. In that regard, the example of Puritan New England would have appeared instructive. From their city on a hill, the earliest followers of a severe faith had exhibited living virtues—of purity, simplicity, duty, devotion—that arose from inner conviction; only after internal fires had burned low did elders of the community impose a dead virtue on the Bay Colony from without, enforced by a code that featured public humiliations such as pillories and brandings and the wearing of penal initials. Emerson would have agreed with the author of *The Scarlet Letter* about the futility of attempting to reform humanity by such external means. Society's abundant problems, both of them felt, were but symptoms of moral deficiencies that would be cured only when the individual's diseased morality was cured.

Both Hawthorne and Emerson were private people anyhow, both upholders of the middle way and uncomfortable with public controversy, with politicians, with extremism in any form. For Emerson early on, abolitionists with their shrill argumentativeness were "an altogether odious set of people, whom one would be sure to shun as the worst of bores & canters." But for all his scholarly love of serenity and solitude, the Concord sage was also a good citizen; so that when the ladies of the local Female Anti-Slavery Society had asked him to address their annual meeting in Concord, he had consented to do so. The occasion, on August 1, 1844, had been to mark the anniversary of the abolition of slavery in the West Indies a decade earlier (a far easier manumission, by the way, than abolishing slavery in the United States would be, the former managed with a single vote in Parliament affecting far-off islands overseas).

Emerson would prepare his lecture carefully, immersing himself in the subject to be considered. One wishes that Hawthorne had sometime, somewhere, done something of the sort. But Hawthorne was no scholar, or lecturer either. His business was elsewhere; and about such matters Emerson himself, with his faith in pursuing one's own aims, had raised the question in his journals: "Does not he do more to abolish Slavery who works all day steadily in his garden, than he who goes to the abolition meeting & makes a speech?"

Hawthorne had been literally tending his summertime garden at the Manse those several years ago, while his neighbor Emerson had been studying slavery. But as the date for the Female Anti-Slavery Society lecture approached, churches in the village declined to host the event out of deference to conservative opinion. Whereupon Hawthorne at the edge of Concord offered the grounds of the Manse as a site for the lecture; but on the appointed day it rained. The address, which a reclusive storyteller would not have attended, was given finally in the courthouse. The sexton of the First Parish Church had refused even to ring the bell to summon an audience forth to hear Mr. Emerson, leading Henry Thoreau defiantly to pull the bell cord himself; so the audience came—and was enlightened by the speaker's vivid, fiercely condemnatory account of West Indian slavery in all its horror, including details of "the whip applied to old men, to tender women; and, undeniably, though I shrink to say so, pregnant women set in the treadmill for refusing to work," of "men's backs flayed with cowhides, and 'hot rum poured on, superinduced with brine or pickle, rubbed in with a cornhusk, in the scorching heat of the sun,'" and of "a planter throwing his negro into a copper of boiling cane-juice."

An awareness of such barbarities that far back, in 1844, had pushed the gentle Emerson forcefully in the direction of abolition. Hawthorne should have attended the lecture and let himself be moved by it. For all this while Emerson was edging ever closer to the abolitionist position, having abandoned the commonly shared conviction that blacks were too primitive to feel physical suffering as whites do, too mentally limited to think as whites think. Preparing for his antislavery lecture he had gratefully come upon evidence that black Sunday school children in the West Indies had been performing altogether on a level with their white counterparts. Such reassurances had moved the retiring scholar farther along the road to abolition, a position that he would embrace outright upon learning in 1850 of the passage—"I will not obey it, by God"—of the Fugitive Slave Act.

That piece of legislation translates inhumanity into bloodless legalese by a process both repugnant and fascinating to observe. Thus the talk in the act is of "a person held to service or labor" and "the person or persons to whom such service or labor may be due." The talk is of "the duty of all marshals and deputy marshals to obey and execute all warrants and precepts issued under the provisions of this act, when to them directed." The better for them to execute their duties, the act empowers said marshals to sweep barrooms and chophouses, as it were, for whatever thugs or drifters might be bribed into forming a posse comitatus to help in pursuing and reclaiming fugitives from service or labor; "and all good citizens are hereby commanded to aid and assist in the prompt and efficient execution of this law, whenever their services may be required, as aforesaid, for that purpose."

Through such abstractions were the concrete obscenities of slavery advanced. The law itself—that "filthy enactment," as Emerson called it—was on its face an outrage, and all the more so for its evidencing the growing strength of the planter oligarchy. In those states where slavery had existed when the Constitution was ratified, northerners had heretofore been willing to tolerate the peculiar institution, to let it exist within its limits and hope in time to see it pass away. But of late the limits had been expanding, into Texas, perhaps into territories won in the Mexican War, now certainly into the North itself, slave catchers with their warrants and bands of deputies roaming through city streets and into the Yankee countryside.

Emerson was appalled, and Mrs. Stowe was so affronted that in one prolonged burst of indignation she wrote *Uncle Tom's Cabin*. Even Hawthorne, the dreamy Hawthorne, had finally had enough. In the same letter to his Salem friend Zack Burchmore that contains the distasteful sentence about lacking the slightest sympathy for slaves, the author had gone on to write, in sentences immediately following: "Still, whenever I am absolutely cornered, I shall go for New England rather than the South;—and this Fugitive Law cornered me. Of course, I knew what I was doing when I signed that Free-Soil document, and bade farewell to all ideas of foreign consulships, or other official stations." The document that Hawthorne alludes to has not survived. But given the perilous nature of a writer's income even in prosperous times, that this writer, Democrat, husband, and father of three would put his name to something so Rubiconian showed both conviction and courage—and perhaps goes a little way toward mitigating the stony sentence that had preceded these two just quoted.

22

DEATH BY WATER

*H*awthorne's sister Louisa wondered whether he should be writing the biography anyway. In mid-June she had ridden the train from Salem to Boston, where she had encountered a couple of her brother's friends in the depot at her destination. David Roberts had delayed her to talk about the glorious diplomatic opportunities that awaited Hawthorne if his collegemate Pierce should win the presidency. "I remember being Minister to Russia was one of them," Louisa was passing along on July 1. "I," she continued, "not by any means thinking office the most direct path to glory for you, very coolly told him I hoped you would have nothing to do with it. I believe he thought I was very ridiculous." But clearly this younger sister was of the opinion that Nathaniel had better spend his time garnering rewards from future romances than by undertaking the hackwork of an ephemeral campaign biography, for whatever reason.

Three years earlier, Louisa's mother had died in the Mall Street house in Salem where all the Hawthornes had been living. Afterward, the son had moved with his wife and children to the little red cottage out in Lenox, and the two daughters, Elizabeth and Louisa, had sought other living arrangements. Ebe, the older, had found quarters on the north shore of Salem Bay near Beverly; and in that rented room she remained for the rest of her long life, existing "in perfect contentment," as her nephew would testify, "for more than thirty years, a life the solitude of which would have killed most women in as many days." Louisa had moved in with favorite relatives in Salem. Neither sister visited their brother in Lenox; but Louisa had come to stay briefly with the Hawthornes at West Newton. And from the Wayside in Concord in June, Hawthorne had written promptly to extend another invitation to his younger sister. This time, he urged, arrange matters for a longer stay; in fact, he and Sophia were hoping that they might persuade the amiable Louisa, the children's adoring aunt, to move to the Wayside permanently.

She was to arrive at the start of July, but instead came the letter telling of her encounter with David Roberts in the Boston depot. The letter conveyed news as well of illness at home in Salem; Mrs. Manning was ill, so that Louisa must be there to help out. A week later, after the crisis had passed, a different relative furnished reason for another postponement ("We wish you very much to come immediately," Hawthorne had written in June, fearing that if Louisa put off her visit, "something may intervene to prevent your coming this summer"). Her uncle John Dike was proposing a trip with his niece to Saratoga Springs in upper New York State, farther than Louisa had ever ventured before. There he would take the waters for his health, then they would travel down to New York City, before returning to New England in time for Louisa to begin her visit at the Wayside in late July.

In the interval the Hawthornes entertained other visitors, among them William Pike, who had worked with the author in both the Boston and the Salem customhouses. Pike spent a summer weekend with his hosts, then left them Monday to return to Salem. But on Friday, abruptly, Pike was back.

Sophia, upstairs at her dressing table before breakfast, looked out and saw the coach from the train station drawing to a stop on the road below. It was not yet seven. "I was astonished to see Mr. Pike get out"—and at once she suspected bad news. "I called from the window, 'Welcome, Mr. Pike!' He glanced up, but did not see me nor smile. I said, 'Go to the western piazza, for the front door is locked.'" Sophia continued fixing her hair. That done, she went downstairs, but Mr. Pike was not to be found. Had she seen a ghost? She approached the piazza with her husband; and there on the far side of the door stood Pike, making no effort to enter. "Mr. Hawthorne opened the door with the strange feeling that he should grasp a hand of air. I was by his side. Mr. Pike, without a smile, deeply flushed, seemed even then not in his former body."

Well might their visitor hesitate, bearing news from Salem of the most dreadful kind. "Your sister Louisa is dead!" he managed finally to tell them.

"I thought," writes Sophia of the terrible instant, "he meant that *his own* sister was dead, for she also is called Louisa. 'What! Louisa?' I asked."

And the story came out. At midmonth Hawthorne's younger sister and her uncle John had set forth on their planned vacation together, spending two weeks among the therapeutic waters of Saratoga Springs before boarding the *Henry Clay* for the journey down the Hudson to Manhattan. But almost at their destination on the second day aboard—three days ago it was, Tuesday, July 27, 1852—the steamboat on which they were traveling had exploded amidships. At the moment the travelers had been apart; elderly Uncle John would be saved with many of the other passengers, but Louisa, in terror of the spreading flames, had leapt into the river and drowned.

On the piazza Pike relayed to the Hawthornes what few details he knew. Sophia urged him to come inside. Soon after, her husband left the room and shut himself in his study. The others gathered around the breakfast table, but no one could eat. After a while, Sophia went to tell Una upstairs the sad news and, while doing so, broke into tears. She returned with her daughter to the breakfast table. Mr. Pike stood up. Unless there was something else he might do for them, he must get back. Sophia all the while was being visited with "the terrible contemplation of Louisa's last agony and fright"—until suddenly, all at once, she envisioned her sister-in-law "supremely happy with her mother in another world. For she was always inconsolable for her mother, and never could be really happy away from her." The two would be together now: Sophia shared that consolation with her children. Through his own tears young Julian rose and rushed off to tell the comforting thought to his father.

But Hawthorne was no longer in his study. He had taken his grief to the hill behind the Wayside, where he remained throughout the day. No one approached him there; and when he came down and entered the house at last, he uttered not a word about his sister's death.

As for six-year-old Julian, for the rest of his life he would remember that morning, "with its bright sunshine and its gloom and
terror; Mr. Hawthorne standing erect at one side of the room, with
his hands behind him, in his customary attitude, but with an expression of darkness and suffering on his face such as his children
had never seen there before. Mr. Pike sat at the breakfast-table;
but no one could eat anything, and no one spoke. After a while
Mr. Hawthorne went out, and was seen no more that day. It was a
blow that struck him to the heart; but he could never relieve himself with words. Louisa's body was recovered a few days later."

A vivid imagination would have forced the author to picture his
sister's recovered corpse with excruciating clarity. About drowning, he had written in *The Blithedale Romance,* "Of all modes of
death, methinks it is the ugliest." Experience as well as imagination had molded that opinion; for here in Concord, on a July evening
seven years before, the author had stared intently, up close, at the
horrors of a different death by drowning.

The episode had occurred on the evening of his third wedding
anniversary, in 1845, three months before Hawthorne and his wife
and baby daughter had left the Manse for good. On that July night
Ellery Channing had knocked on their door between nine and ten.
A local girl was missing—"a Miss Hunt, about nineteen years old;
a girl of education and refinement, but depressed and miserable
for want of sympathy." A search party had formed to look for her.
Soon Hawthorne had cast off his boat and was scrambling aboard,
taking the paddle to steer while Channing sat at the oars. Downriver, below the bridge, lights were visible on the shoreline. The
dory drifted alongside dim figures on shore holding lanterns at the
spot where the girl's bonnet and shoes had been found. While voices
called out advice as to where to search, Channing wielded a hay
rake, bringing up from the river bottom water weeds that looked in
the starlight like clothing. Two others boarded the rowboat to help,
one seated beside Hawthorne plying a pole through the lantern-lit
surface into the stream. Abruptly, "What's this?" the boy with the
pole cried; and then there was heaving up, and light garments
emerging dimly in the gloom, and a portion of the body breaking
the surface. Hawthorne steered toward the bank, "all the while

looking at this dead girl, whose limbs were swaying in the water, close at the boat's side."

What most appalled him was the corpse's rigidity. When those on shore stepped into the stream to help carry the body to land, its arms did not droop over the shoulders lifting it, nor could the sodden dress hide the stiffness of the legs beneath. The corpse's hands were clenched, its inflexible posture in "the very image of a death-agony"; and when a living foot was placed on a stiffened arm to compose the body, the dead arm returned to its rigid posture as soon as the foot was removed. Blood streamed from the corpse's nose, and although a couple of the men fetched water from the river and tried to wash clean the purplish face, the blood "flowed and flowed and continued to flow." An old-timer said that that was always the case, a purging that would go on until the burial, and that the body would swell and be unrecognizable by morning.

The thought had passed through Hawthorne's mind that the dead girl's stiff posture might be emblematic of an inflexible judgment pronounced upon her despairing act. "Ah, poor child!" one helping to draw the corpse from the river had cried out. In life religious, of high morality, melancholy by temperament, Martha Hunt had been managing a district school of some sixty difficult scholars. "I suppose," thought Hawthorne at the time, "one friend would have saved her; but she died for want of sympathy—a severe penalty for having cultivated and refined herself out of the sphere of her natural connections."

Such reflections as those, awakened before midnight on July 9, 1845, in Concord beneath an oak tree at the water's edge, were being revisited seven years later, in the spring of 1852, as the author at West Newton was bringing to its climax his *Blithedale Romance*. In the pages of that novel, the poet Coverdale, the farmer Silas Foster, and the blacksmith Hollingsworth are searching the river bottom at Blithedale. The poet is at the helm, the yeoman wielding a hay rake, Hollingsworth probing with a pole. Suddenly the pole strikes an object. "Hold on! You have her!" The blacksmith heaves amain, "and up came a white swash on the surface of the river. It was the flow of a woman's garments. A little higher, and we saw her dark hair, streaming down the current. Black River of Death, thou hadst yielded up thy victim! Zenobia was found!" In art, as in life, two in the boat were grappling with the body while a third, the artist, steered for shore; and, again, once ashore that terrible rigidity! For years both Coverdale and Hawthorne would live with the moon-bathed memory: "It seemed . . . it seemed as if her body must keep the same position in the coffin, and that her skeleton would keep it in the grave, and that when Zenobia rose, at the Day of Judgment, it would be in just the same attitude as now!"

"These characters . . . are entirely fictitious," their creator insisted in the preface to *The Blithedale Romance.* All of them "might have been looked for, at BROOK FARM, but, by some accident, never made their appearance there." Even so, the earliest readers of Hawthorne's new romance, and many since then—despite the author's efforts within the narrative to discourage such an identification—have found in the figure of the intellectually brilliant feminist Zenobia a fictional counterpart to Margaret Fuller, author of *Woman in the Nineteenth Century.*

Perhaps the identification is misapplied. Hawthorne had learned to think less well of Fuller than in days at the Manse, when in 1842 the two had talked at length alone one drowsy afternoon at Sleepy Hollow, had ventured on the river together and spoken freely and intimately on long walks homeward in moonlight of summer nights, then and again in 1844. Since that time Fuller had gone on to complete her seminal work on women's rights, had moved to New York and written over two hundred literary and cultural columns for Horace Greeley's *Tribune,* and had, in the late summer of 1846, set sail for England, in part as a foreign correspondent for Greeley's newspaper. Thus, after leaving New England the intellectual had become increasingly active in public affairs, her columns in the *Tribune* dealing not only with literature but with such social ills as the plight of slaves, the condition of prisons, the lot of the poor in slums, the exploitation of immigrants, and, as always, the oppression of working women. Arriving in Italy by early 1847, Fuller would be inspired by democratic uprisings that broke out all over Europe the following year; those revolutions reached her personally when the Republic of Rome was proclaimed in February 1849. Thereafter, her columns to the *Tribune* implored American readers to support so deserving a triumph of republicanism.

"My life at Rome is thus far all I hoped," Margaret wrote her mother during those exciting times. "I have not been so well since

I was a child, nor so happy ever, as during the last six weeks." Part of the journalist's happiness arose from having fallen in love—this woman in her late thirties—with a handsome, ill-educated, impoverished Italian count eleven years younger than she. "His love for me has been unswerving and most tender," she would write of Giovanni Angelo, marchese d'Ossoli. By Ossoli she had a child in September 1848; the preceding spring the count in his late twenties may have overcome his church's prohibition and married his Protestant lover. Both were involved in giving aid to the Roman republic—he resisting in the siege of Rome, she tending the wounded—so that when French troops entered the city in the summer of 1849 to reestablish tyranny in the pope's name, Margaret, her husband, and their baby were forced to flee. They made their way to Florence, and in the spring of 1850 the poet Browning saw them off at Leghorn aboard a ship bound for America.

But what would those three do with themselves back there? Gossip had preceded the little family. "The greatest piece of news," Fanny Longfellow had written her brother in October 1849, "is Margaret Fuller's marriage to an Italian marquis, poor as herself— a secret marriage of a year's standing, and a baby is actually alive to confirm it!" In the *Tribune* earlier, Fuller had been severe on Fanny's husband, judging him to be a poet "artificial and imitative," cultivated but shallow, lacking force. Mrs. Longfellow had not forgotten: "Think of the dry, forlorn old maid changed into a Marguerita Marchesa d'Ossoli!"

And what would the marchesa do back in democratic America, with her baby and her young, ill-lettered Italian count who had no money and spoke the scantiest English? She had forebodings about the *Elizabeth* on which the three were sailing in any case; and indeed, the vessel was but a short way out at sea before the captain came down with smallpox. He died at Gibraltar, so that the inexperienced first mate Mr. Bangs had to assume command. Angelino, Fuller's child, also took sick in the course of the five-week voyage westward, but the two-year-old recovered; and all went well thereafter till approaching Long Island, east of New York City.

It was the early morning of July 19, 1850, 3:30 A.M. in heavy seas, when the *Elizabeth* bearing its ponderous cargo of Carrara marble slammed into a hidden sandbar and stuck there. Subsequent waves battered the vessel against the bar and hurled the cargo through the ship's sides. Dawn disclosed to passengers and crew Fire Island no more than a hundred yards off, but the vessel was breaking up; and although it was in sight of land and help, the wind was too fierce, the waves too high for spectators ashore to launch a boat or even fire a lifeline out. Some on the doomed ship chose to swim, and a few even made it through the raging surf to the beach; but when Charles Sumner's brother Horace leapt from the *Elizabeth* into the swirling water, it was only to drown in full view of the others on board.

No more than a handful made it to safety, eight people remaining on deck at the last as the winds howled and the long morning stretched into afternoon. The storm gave no sign of abating. At three, the *Elizabeth* began coming apart, the last survivors huddling around the mast. Abruptly a mountainous wave swept Ossoli from the vessel, and another behind it took Angelino, his mother, and all the others over the side. The baby's body washed ashore soon after, but neither Ossoli's nor Margaret's was ever found.

From Concord Henry Thoreau came down, at Emerson's urging, to comb the beach at Fire Island for what he could recover; but by then there was nothing left beyond a bit of clothing and a few letters. After the initial shock, seeking comfort in the midst of grief, one of Fuller's friends would wonder whether such an end, horrible as it was, might not have been for the best: "a fit & good conclusion to the life. Her life was romantic & exceptional," Mrs. Barlow submitted. "So let her death be; it sets the seal on her marriage, avoids all questions of Society, all of employment, poverty, & old age, and besides was undoubtedly predetermined when the world was created."

People made their peace with so violent a loss in whatever ways they could. At the time, Hawthorne was living in Lenox, in the red cottage. No mention of his feelings survives, although by then his respect for Margaret was hardly what it once had been. He had come to regard her as intellectually pretentious, with a mind unextraordinary despite its vast learning. Still, she continued to figure in his thoughts. Death by water: her fate would have recalled poor Martha Hunt's, nineteen-year-old schoolteacher in Concord whose rigid body he had helped recover from the dark bottom of the river on which he and Margaret Fuller had taken boat rides in happier times. Soon he would begin writing his new romance with the climactic suicide of its brilliant, flawed feminist heroine. Martha Hunt had drowned in July 1845; Margaret Fuller in July 1850. Now, in July 1852, with *The Blithedale Romance* just published on the 14th of the month, and even as Hawthorne was settling down to the less congenial task of writing a friend's campaign biography, had come this latest dreadful news—so inescapably vivid in its contemplation—of yet one more terrible death by drowning.

23

CREATING A LIFE

I have been delayed by the necessity of going to Salem," Hawthorne wrote Pierce from the Wayside on August 6. His sister Louisa's funeral was the unmentioned cause that had kept the author from moving forward with the candidate's biography. Earlier, William Pike in Salem had sent along particulars concerning the funeral, but his letter had reached Concord late, so that the ceremony was over before Hawthorne had arrived at the scene. Sophia thought it might have been for the best, given her husband's sensibilities. Afterward, after the burial in the Manning plot in the Howard Street cemetery, Hawthorne had gone with his surviving sister, Elizabeth, back to her rented room near Beverly before returning to the Wayside. As a remembrance, he brought eight-year-old Una the brooch that her aunt Louisa had been wearing at the time of her drowning. And all the while progress on the task for his friend the presidential candidate had been set aside, although the author was able to write Pierce on his return that he hoped to send along perhaps half of the biography within a week or two.

Writing it was proving to be no easy undertaking. Hawthorne seldom, if he could help it, wrote in the summertime, yet in his grief and in the heat of this August he had to push ahead—on material not congenial to his particular gifts anyway: composing a factual account of a career unfolding in the real world, far from romance, with little about it of the wondrous or enchanting. From the start Franklin Pierce's life had been prosaic, for the most part the account of a fun-loving child and mediocre student who became a congenial, gregarious politician and military officer before settling in to practice law in a New England town of no great pretensions. Democrats in the past had been able to boast of leaders: Old Hickory, victor at New Orleans, Indian fighter who had defied France and the United States Bank and the Nullifiers; and Young Hickory, Andrew Jackson's Tennessee protégé Polk, who by standing up to Britain and Mexico had vastly extended the size of the nation. Now they were trying to make of Frank Pierce of New Hampshire another Young Hickory, of the Granite Hills: "We Polked You in '44; We Shall Pierce You in '52." But how were such modest accomplishments as Pierce's to be molded into something resembling those of his predecessors?

Put another way, Hawthorne's challenging task regarding Pierce became, in his own words, to account for "how it has happened that, with such extraordinary opportunities for eminent distinction, civil and military, as he has enjoyed, this crisis should have found him so obscure as he certainly was, in a national point of view" at the time of his nomination. And one discovery very early would dismay the biographer: "My heart absolutely sank, at the dearth of available material." The paucity of letters and articles about his friend was requiring Hawthorne to launch forth telling the thin story with no more than the scantiest ballast of documentation.

Franklin Pierce had been born in November 1804 in a log cabin on New Hampshire's Contoocook River—a romantic enough start, although Pierce's father was by no means as inconsequential as the cabin might have indicated. Earlier, when news of the Concord Fight had arrived in 1775, the senior Pierce had abandoned his plow and rushed off to join the colonials, and in the course of the Revolution had served at Bunker Hill, at Saratoga, and through the rigors of Valley Forge. A true patriot, Benjamin Pierce had gone on to fill two terms as governor of New Hampshire; so his son had been born into an esteemed family. Nor did the infant have to spend much time in the log cabin; the Pierces had moved early on to a spacious home in Hillsborough, where Franklin would live out his high-spirited childhood. In due course the boy went off to Bowdoin and by his junior year was at the very bottom of his class, although he did settle down at last and end his college career with a respectable rank scholastically. Thereafter, helped by his father's broad popularity, young Pierce was elected to the New Hampshire state legislature at age twenty-four, was chosen speaker at twenty-six, was elected to the federal House of Representatives at twenty-eight, and entered the United States Senate at thirty-two, taking his seat as its youngest member.

Yet his record in the Senate was undistinguished, much of it spent conferring on military affairs and veterans' pensions. Earlier, Pierce had married the daughter of a former president of Bowdoin College, a deeply religious woman, not strong physically and unhappy with the demands of political life. Yielding to Jane Pierce's wishes, her husband had resigned from the Senate in early 1842 and returned to New Hampshire, where he pursued a lucrative law practice in the state capital while serving as chairman of the Democratic Party and United States district attorney. With the outbreak of the Mexican War, Pierce enlisted as a private, rose to the rank of brigadier general, and was injured in an accident on horseback at the battle of Contreras and from a knee sprain at Churubusco. He resigned from the army in 1848.

For an aspirant to the presidency, the story had its weaknesses. That other politician from New Hampshire's granite hills, Daniel Webster, now in the last weeks of his life, had been a font of erudition, but no one was making any such claims for Franklin Pierce. Moreover, Pierce had had trouble with alcohol. This was a hard-drinking age, yet among indulgent politicians in the Washington boardinghouses the senator from New Hampshire had earned a reputation for holding his liquor very poorly. So Pierce, his Whig opponents charged, fell far short of being a leader, having distinguished himself—they joked—principally as the hero of many a well-fought bottle.

As for strengths in his candidacy, one was a gift from those Whig opponents. Their nominee was General Winfield Scott, chosen after fifty-three ballots by a party in even greater disarray than the Democrats. Old Fuss and Feathers was a brilliant general but a dreadful, pompous politician. The ineptness of the Whig campaign would prove a considerable help to Pierce, and another of the dark-horse Democrat's strengths lay in his anonymity. Cass, Buchanan, and Douglas, whom he had defeated for the Democratic nomination, were national figures with enemies nationwide. Pierce of New Hampshire was so little known that he had few enemies outside his native region. But that he was hardly known was precisely why the nominee was lucky to have enlisted a writer with a national reputation to tell his story. And no other writer even close to Hawthorne's literary standing would have agreed to undertake such a task; for the politician from New England had been consistently sympathetic to the southern slave power's interests. That was part of his strength, of course—that as a compromise candidate he could garner votes in states both South and North. But abolitionists loathed the "paltry Franklin Pierce," as Emerson called him; and in the aftermath of the Fugitive Slave Law and of *Uncle Tom's Cabin,* the numbers in the North favoring the abolitionist cause were growing massively. Among those numbers, not only Stowe herself but Emerson, Thoreau, Lowell, Whittier, Longfellow, Holmes, and many lesser literary figures would all have scorned to associate their names with this doughface Young Hickory of the Granite Hills.

One of Hawthorne's principal tasks, then, would be to justify as best he could Pierce's pro-southern stand on slavery. But the biography also set out to tell of the candidate's childhood, his college years, his rise as a public servant, his retirement from the Senate, his return to Concord, New Hampshire, to practice law, and finally his response to the call of his country as a leader of men during the Mexican War. Through it all, the sparse record showed the nominee to be a diligent party politician; but little in Pierce's story could be made inspiring, and certainly nothing about it would place him alongside such contemporary political giants as Webster, Calhoun, Benton, and Clay.

Hawthorne did get the job done, finishing the slender volume of 138 pages in two months. He did it in part by quoting other people's writing through more than a third of the text. He quoted from speeches of no great distinction that Pierce had made in Congress, at length from a journal that the general had kept during his service in Mexico, and from letters of New Hampshire lawyers testifying to attorney Pierce's skills in the courtroom: his faultless demeanor at the bar, his courtesy in and out of the courthouse, his kindly heart. And it was doubtless true that the handsome Pierce was charming, courteous, and kindly; but those seemed perhaps ancillary qualifications for one aspiring to be president of the United States.

The biographer wrote at some length of the candidate's worthy father. His description of Benjamin Pierce made that Revolutionary patriot sound like the better nominee; but the aged hero had died some years before, so that the extensive attention the biography paid to him could be justified only as indicating virtues that Franklin may have inherited and values among which he had been reared. Hawthorne dwelt as well on his friend's childhood in all its mischievously high-spirited normality, on the boy's light curly hair and his sweet expression, the cheerful aspect of his face, which "made a kind of sunshine, both as regarded its radiance and its warmth." This is the romancer at work, telling us how Pierce would forgo recess to help a slower scholar with his lessons. The young man's life as it unfolded had furnished other signs of worth, as when he had taken hold at Bowdoin and through sheer will raised himself from the bottom of the class to a respectable standing. Similarly, the young lawyer had dismally lost the first case he tried; but undaunted, he had met defeat with resolve, vowing to try a thousand cases and if need be lose them all in order to learn his craft. Learn it he did, turning each weakness into a strength. The *Life of Franklin Pierce* assures us that as a legislator Pierce was painstaking and eloquent, as a general brave and compassionate. From such stuff did the loyal Hawthorne strive to fashion out of his friend a hero in the grand Jacksonian style.

But the author was serving up thin gruel, even while sweetening it as best he could. And there was the matter of Pierce's stand on slavery. Here Hawthorne need not stretch for his effects, because biographer and subject were of one mind when it came to that vexed issue. "I am ashamed," Elizabeth Peabody's brother-in-law would exclaim to her in years ahead, "what wretched things men perpetrate under the notion of doing good!" Hawthorne, heir to Puritan convictions about evil, felt sure that only Providence could solve the South's peculiar curse. He and Pierce both deplored slavery; but more than they hated slavery, both of them loved the democratic idea that the American Union exemplified. Their attitude was not uncommon then. Here is Francis Parkman, for one— before composing histories that rank among the glories of American culture and with *The Oregon Trail* a year behind him—writing a friend in 1850: "For my part, I would see every slave knocked on the head before I would see the Union go to pieces and would include in the sacrifice as many abolitionists as could be conveniently brought together." Do nothing to threaten the Union, which shone like a beacon for such oppressed peoples of the earth as those brave democrats all over Europe who had recently risen up against tyranny. The American Union, which abolitionist ardor did seem to menace, could never have been formed in the first place without compromises wisely made by the Founding Fathers in regard to the South and its property in slaves. Thus slavery was intrinsic to the Union. Let God remove it in His own good time; and meanwhile, as Hawthorne's *Life* assures us, Franklin Pierce with his practical sagacity would take the Union as he found it, working to evolve good in the world as it exists, while acknowledging, as he had done from the start of his political career, the rights pledged to the South by the Constitution.

As for the Fugitive Slave Law, Pierce held the opinion that it must be obeyed—"for the sake of the slave!" The decisive exclamation point is Sophia Hawthorne's. Of course she and General Pierce both knew that the act legislated an abominable wrong; but, as Hawthorne's wife explained to her mother, it must be tolerated and obeyed for the present, having been provoked by the unceasing agitation of the abolitionists, who were forever stirring up discord. If the North defied the Fugitive Slave Law and disavowed the Compromise of 1850, the South would secede; and, as Sophia wrote, "it certainly seems that the severance of the Union would be the worst thing for the slave."

Such logic could be entertained at a time when waging war to thwart secession lay beyond most people's imaginings: blacks would be better off in the Union than in a southern nation no part of which was free. This had been Pierce's view from the start of his political career, in less contentious times; nor, wrote Hawthorne in the *Life*, had the statesman wavered when such a view became controversial, out of principle accepting "the obloquy that sometimes threatened to pursue the Northern man who dared to love that great and sacred reality—his whole, united, native country—better than the mistiness of a philanthropic theory."

By late August 1852 the *Life of Franklin Pierce*, with its tenuous justifications, was finished and put in the hands of Hawthorne's publisher. Already Ticknor and Fields had begun advertising this forthcoming work by the author of *The Scarlet Letter* and *The House of the Seven Gables*. But their notices appeared tepid for the purposes. "I think you must blaze away a little harder in your advertisement," Hawthorne chided his friend Ticknor, and went on to tell him how: put the author's name in a more prominent position; use larger type, capitals, boldface. "Go it strong, at any rate. We are politicians now; and you must not expect to conduct yourself like a gentlemanly publisher."

For while writing the life, the biographer had come to respect his subject more highly, so that by this time he was backing Pierce's candidacy to the full. Hawthorne's friend Bridge might have marveled once, in 1836, at their Bowdoin college mate's rapid rise in politics: "With no very remarkable talents, he at the age of thirty-four fills one of the highest stations in the nation," as a United States senator. Hawthorne had shared that estimate of Pierce's mediocrity then, but now he was judging his political friend more favorably. True, scores of people in government were brighter; but "Frank has the directing mind," he would explain to Bridge, "and will move them about like pawns on a chess-board, and turn all their abilities to better purpose than they themselves could. Such is my idea of him, after many an hour of reflection on his character, while making the best of his poor little biography. He is deep, deep, deep. But what luck withal! Nothing can ruin him."

Sophia reading the biography that Hawthorne had written would appreciate it more than her husband finally did. To her it appeared "as serene & peaceful as a dream by a green river, & such another lily of testimony to the character of a Presidential candidate, was, I suspect, never before thrown upon the fierce arena of political warfare." But what finally impressed her most about the volume, as she wrote her mother in September, was the truth in every line of it. Of course Mr. Hawthorne was incapable of uttering falsehood, even to help a friend gain the White House. And regarding certain rumors that may have come Mrs. Peabody's way, another fact should be clear about Sophia's husband: "As no instrument could wrench out of him a word he did not know to be veracious in spirit & letter—so also no fear of whatsoever the world may attribute to him as motive would weigh a feather in his estimation. He does the thing he finds right, & lets the consequences fly."

24

DAYS AT THE WAYSIDE

*T*he rumors to which Sophia was alluding concerned rewards that Franklin Pierce as chief executive might bestow on his biographer. Earlier this summer David Roberts, chatting with Hawthorne's sister Louisa in a Boston train station, had spoken of just such opportunities opening up. But Sophia was categorical: Mr. Hawthorne had agreed to write the biography for no reason other than that he had felt unable to refuse such a favor to an old friend, even knowing all the while that people would accuse him of low motives. That hadn't influenced him; "provided his conscience is clear, he never cares a *sou* what people say," his wife insisted. "He knew he never should ask for an office, and not one word on the subject has ever passed between General Pierce and Mr. Hawthorne."

On the same subject Hawthorne confirmed to his and Pierce's friend Bridge that, before starting the biography, he had resolved to accept nothing from the candidate. Yet by summer's end, with the *Life of Franklin Pierce* delivered to the printer, its author may have been harboring second thoughts. From his Old Manse days and his days in Salem he knew what it is to be miserably poor. Now there were a wife and three children to consider, and an opportunity arising that would never come again. In November, if the Whig party were thrown out of office, thirty thousand Democratic place seekers would be importuning the new administration in Washington for the seven hundred posts available. And here stood Hawthorne, uniquely positioned to step to the very head of the line, where, in exchange for four years of service to the nation, he might secure financial comfort for his family for the rest of their lives, at the same time providing himself with the means of writing fiction untroubled by any further economic worries. Accordingly, about the earlier vow to take nothing from Pierce for writing his *Life*, "to say the truth," Hawthorne told Bridge when the task was behind him, "I doubt whether it would not be rather folly than heroism to adhere to this purpose, in case he should offer me anything particularly good. We shall see."

Through these same busy weeks, the Whig candidate, General Scott, had been demonstrating his incompetence by inditing indiscreet and widely reprinted letters on current national affairs. As for that, with the principal controversy over slavery agreed upon as settled by the Compromise of 1850, the contest was proving to be less about issues than abuse. On both sides it grew ugly. Pierce's followers portrayed Scott as a papist, a martinet, and a fussy, argumentative gambler; the Democrat was condemned as a coward and a do-nothing drunkard. But in those days before candidates traveled about delivering stump speeches, Pierce's handlers had been shrewd enough to keep their man quiet. Unlike the Whig, the Democratic candidate had avoided saying or writing anything damaging during the requisite months, leaving to others the task of appealing to everybody and promising something for all. Moreover, the politicians of national stature whom Pierce's dark-horse candidacy had defeated at Baltimore came forth to support the nominee. The party united so successfully, in fact, that the Whigs never had a chance. The hapless, disorganized Whigs were doomed, as General Scott went down to a crushing defeat in November 1852, carrying Henry Clay's party with him once and for all. Franklin Pierce had won the electoral votes of all but four states, 254 to only 42 for Winfield Scott; and thus the Democrat, one of Hawthorne's oldest friends, would be moving in March to the White House.

On Friday, October 1, 1852, Sophia had set out with her family—all but Rosebud—on a walk from the Wayside. The day was still, the sky overcast. The four Hawthornes had gone through the woods north and west a couple of miles until they came to Peter's Path and the hill (bare then, in our day thoroughly wooded) that rises opposite the Old Manse. There Sophia left the others and descended alone to the public road and the tree-lined avenue beyond familiar gateposts.

For the first time in seven years she was returning to their earlier home in Concord. "As I stood there and mused," she wrote, "the silence was profound. Not a human being was visible in the beloved old house, or around it. Wachusett was a pale blue outline on the horizon. The river gleamed like glass here and there in the plain, slumbering and shining and reflecting the beauty on its banks." Of course the wife and mother was led to compare her life at the Manse, as a bride in months immediately after her wedding, to life now, at the Wayside a decade later. She concluded that although indescribable happiness had forever consecrated for her everything about this spot, yet, amazingly, her later years were providing even more happiness than she had felt then, "for I am ten years happier in time, and an uncounted degree happier in kind. I know my husband ten years better, and I have not arrived at the end; for he is still an enchanting mystery, beyond the region I have discovered and made my own."

From the start of her new life at the Wayside, on the other side of the village, Sophia had loved being back in Concord. Her first day here, when she and Una had come ahead to see that the furniture was put where it belonged, with the chores of the day done the two had set forth late on the warm June afternoon to walk to the village. Along the way they had encountered Emerson and Thoreau. Imagine the good fortune of living where, your first day back and out for a stroll west on the Lexington Road, you see ahead of you Thoreau and Emerson walking together. "Mr. Emerson was most cordial, and his beautiful smile added to the wonderful beauty of the sunset. He turned back and walked with us." How delightful had been such a welcome! The Emerson home was not far from the Wayside, and Mrs. Emerson soon came calling with her three children, and her husband invited the Hawthorne children to a picnic and had his young son Edward share his pony with six-year-old Julian. All but breathlessly Sophia relayed such pleasures to her mother in West Newton: "Mr. Emerson took Julian to walk in the woods, the other afternoon. I have no time to think what to say, for there is a dear little mob around me. Baby looks fairest of fair to-day. She walks miles about the house."

About *their* house, which the Hawthornes owned. As its new name suggested, the Wayside was where they intended to linger, at the side of the road over which they had wandered long enough. "I am beginning to take root here," her husband would soon be writing his friend Longfellow, "and feel myself, for the first time in my life, really at home." Home was where Una and Julian could have Mr. Emerson's children for playmates. And in the village was Mr. Thoreau, who had a wonderful way with the young. Coming to make a survey of the Wayside property, Thoreau took a liking to Julian, whom he proceeded to invite along on nature hikes, calling the youngster's attention to the beauty of a dragonfly, to the shadows that a waterskate casts into the depths of a stream, to the closed buds of water lilies opening their whiteness at first light of morning.

Five years earlier, in the fall of 1847, Henry Thoreau had ended his experiment of getting at the meaning of life beside Walden Pond, leaving the woods for as good a reason as he had gone in. "Perhaps," he explained, "it seemed to me that I had several more lives to live, and could not spare any more time for that one." So he had come back to the village, where he had been residing with his family ever since, picking up the little that he needed to exist on by doing odd jobs around town, all the while spending four or five hours a day roaming about in neighboring woodlands.

That would have looked not at all like a successful life as the world measures success, all the less so because of the fate of the book that Thoreau had written while living at Walden. *A Week on the Concord and Merrimack Rivers* had been published finally only at the author's expense; and of the thousand copies printed, the great majority had gone unsold, to be delivered at last to the Thoreaus' attic to augment Henry's library up there of, as he said, nearly a thousand volumes now, over seven hundred of which he had written himself. As for the other manuscript that he had been working on at the pond—an account of his life in the woods—he had not been able to find a publisher for *Walden* (six times revised so far) on any terms. So this Harvard graduate day laborer in his mid-thirties would have appeared by now pretty much a professional failure, as his interests moved away from speculations and philosophical reflections in the direction of simple observations of the unfolding seasons; for instance, of the earliest crocus or robin sighted in springtime or, this very autumn, on October 20, of

"Canada snapdragon, tansy, white goldenrod, blue-stemmed ditto. Aster undulatus, autumnal dandelion, tall buttercup, yarrow, mayweed."

Julian's older sister was only now starting to read. Her mother had designed it that way. Absorbed in home-schooling, Sophia had consciously been striving to cultivate Una's best nature by reading to her from a carefully chosen regimen of the finest literature. Now, having reached age eight, her daughter was at last being allowed to read on her own, with an eye to fact and detail. "They never will be arbitrary facts," however, Sophia insisted. Rather, the facts would support the quest for beauty, showing the way from a sometimes sordid material world to a world of eternal spirit—for Una and her brother Julian as well. "But it is a year with him before I shall make him study really," Sophia explained before going on to report of Rosebud, not yet two, to her pedagogical and ever-interested mother. "Darling baby is an exemplary student. All day she goes about with some book under her arm, and whenever she sees a very inviting little chair, or corner, or spot on the carpet, down she sits & opens her book & devoutly reads & turns over the leaves."

The domestic scene is appealing: three children being nurtured by gifted parents who shelter them from ugliness in the sanctuary of a home full of love. Yet so much love as Sophia bestowed on her husband and children must at times have seemed overpowering, stultifying. "Appalling" is the word Julian uses on one occasion: "it was almost appalling," he would write in retrospect, "to be the object of such limitless devotion and affection." Even so, the children loved their mother, dearly, and adored their famous father. Page after page of Julian's writing—he would become a writer, too, and a far more prolific one than his sire—reflects tributes to Hawthorne as a parent, the most wonderful on earth, a judgment that Una and Rose in mature remembrance of their father corroborated. "He was capable of being the very gayest person I ever saw," Una recollected in adulthood. "He was like a boy. Never was such a playmate as he in all the world."

It was a time when the home was growing holy, as changes that recent years had brought to Concord and the nation threatened its earlier cohesion. The railroad, the mills, the great West, a new market economy, an increasingly specialized agriculture, a population increasingly heterogeneous were all tearing at the home as the autonomous center of life. The loom at the hearth had fallen silent; daughters went off to the mills, to the cities; sons went off to the West. And feeling those centrifugal forces, Sophia and her contemporaries responded by exalting the sanctity of the home ever higher. Yet—and Sophia felt this strongly—such an Edenic refuge had to be re-created day by day, in an unceasing effort, with love, praise, sympathy, vigilance. Home she would strive to make into heaven on earth—or move it as close as she could to heaven—with her three children as angels whose spirits she devoted her waking hours to keeping pure.

Of course there were strains. Brother and sisters would quarrel and scold, and Sophia would suffer with her headaches, lying on the sofa with a newspaper over her face to ward off the horrid blackflies. In that less aseptic world, matter battled ceaselessly with spirit; but there was much laughter, too. Come, said Una on one occasion when playing with her brother: "we are two boys—you are James Jones." And then she proceeded, to her mother's utter amazement, to talk just like a yokel, reproducing the uncouth diction and accent and manner to perfection. "Where she ever heard—how she ever knew—I cannot imagine. Julian came near dying of laughter to see & hear her." But the scene confirms that for all Sophia's attentiveness, the walls of the Wayside were porous. Sooner or later the world outside would force its way in.

How she loved those children though! Her letters are crammed with their excellences: their extraordinary beauty, their rare sensibilities, their instinctual wisdom. Ellery Channing visiting the Hawthornes a year or two earlier, at Lenox, had seen them differently. "The children brought up in the worst way for visitors, by themselves, never having been to school, have of course nothing but bad manners," reported the irascible Channing, who cared little for children in any case. "They break in when not required & are not in fact either handsome or attractive." Photographs of the three make them out to be handsome enough; and certainly to their mother they were more than handsome—were beautiful, were peerless, as was her husband peerless. Sophia could still marvel, nearly a decade into their marriage, over the ease with which Hawthorne, on matters both great and small, did "the highest, wisest, loveliest thing" invariably, instinctively, spontaneously. "I never knew such loftiness, so simply borne. I have never known him to stoop from it in the most trivial household matter, any more than in a larger or more public one." With a gratitude that defied question or doubt, she went on exulting in the happiness of a life shared with a husband like that, among three such children as theirs.

The biography of Pierce behind him, Hawthorne had set about in the autumn writing his myths as retold for the young, a congenial labor that would trade upon the success of his earlier *Wonder Book for Girls and Boys.* The new volume, *Tanglewood Tales,* he would finish the following spring, of 1853. Much besides had been keeping the author and friend of a president-elect busy during these same months at the Wayside. As always, people sent him their literary creations to read and comment on. Visitors came calling, and correspondents wrote, expecting replies. Some made demands on Hawthorne's time for political reasons, requesting from him autographs of General Pierce or asking that he interest himself with the president-elect on behalf of distant acquaintances. And would Mr. Hawthorne come lecture at Holliston? Would he come speak before the Rochester Athenaeum? ("I heartily wish it were in my power to comply with your request . . . but having never appeared before a public audience . . . I am convinced that it is now too late in life for me to succeed in that line"). In short, the busy fall had drawn a would-be recluse out of his sought-after retirement in Concord village; and before year's end in 1852, he would have realized that any hopes of writing another romance must be deferred.

His present residence at the Wayside would be ending. Soon after the new administration assumed office in Washington, Hawthorne was to set out for Liverpool as United States consul: a noble gift on General Pierce's part, as Sophia explained excitedly to her father, for the consulate there "is second in dignity only to the Embassy in London, and is more sought for than any other, and is *nearly* the most lucrative, and General Pierce might have made great political capital out of it if that were his way. But he acts from the highest and not lowest motives, and would make any sacrifice to the right." And what could be more right than that a celebrated author, old friend, biographer, and beloved husband should be well rewarded? Consequently, the Hawthornes were to pack soon and leave Concord, having eight months earlier, on their arrival at the Wayside, never anticipated such a change in the direction of all their lives.

25

TO WASHINGTON

Early in 1853, Sophia's mother died. Her youngest daughter found consolation for the loss in the certainty of an afterlife, the same certainty that had sustained her six months earlier at the time of her sister-in-law Louisa's death. Both losses were intense. As for her mother, Sophia's feelings throughout her life had approached the worshipful. This good daughter had thought to write Mrs. Peabody from Lenox a couple of years earlier: "I trust you realize the blessing you have been to us, in the way of high principle and sentiment, and lofty purity of heart, and elegance of taste,—to say nothing of a motherly tenderness which has never been surpassed in God's universe, and seldom equalled. To me especially this unspeakable tenderness has been a guard-angelic." Now the guardian angel had fled, and yet Sophia was at peace. "If there is anything immortal in life," she had written at the time of Louisa's death, "it is the home relations, and heaven would be no heaven without them. God never has knit my soul with my husband's soul for such a paltry moment as this human life! I have not loved my mother for one short day! My children do not thrill my heart-strings with less than an eternal melody. We know that God cannot trifle! This is all more real to me than what my human eye rests on. I heard one of the truly second-sighted say once, that in a trance he saw the spiritual world; and while gazing enraptured on its green pastures, a spirit whispered to him, 'Out of this greenness your earthly pastures are green.'"

Death, which in the course of nature had come for an elderly, much-loved woman, hovered as well over life triumphant, over even the greenest of earthly pastures. Since his election to the presidency in early November, General Franklin Pierce had, for the convenience of the location, been spending time at the home of wealthy friends in Boston. Of course there was much to do in preparing for his new duties, dealing from the first with importunate office seekers and with aspiring cabinet members who might hope to work together while representing different regions and widely differing views of the party and nation. The president-elect made time in December to deliver a eulogy at a memorial service for Daniel Webster, and at the first of the new year 1853 he attended the funeral of the elder Amos Lawrence, brother and father of textile magnates. Then on January 6, Pierce and his wife and son boarded an express train in Andover, Massachusetts, where Mrs. Pierce's sister lived, in order to return to Concord, New Hampshire, to begin final preparations for the move to Washington.

The train, consisting of the locomotive and a single spacious car, was no more than a mile out of the station—one sees again the passengers in their seats, hears the rhythmic clatter of wheels over the rural landscape—when suddenly a jolt, a grinding, a pitching sideways, as a front axle shatters and the car is dragged a distance before overturning and tumbling down an embankment to the rocky bottom. In that violent interval, General and Mrs. Pierce are hurled about and bruised, while eleven-year-old Bennie lies mangled amid the wreckage in view of them. When the car comes to rest at last, the boy's parents have been badly shaken up, and other passengers have suffered broken limbs, one a crushed foot; but only the boy is dead, only Bennie Pierce, their sole child and adored son, is dead.

Why had God come for that cherished life? There had to be a reason. Mrs. Pierce, a devoutly religious woman, utterly devastated, settled in time on an awful explanation: their beloved Bennie had been taken from them in order that General Pierce might devote his full attention, undistracted, to the heavy duties awaiting him in Washington. Pierce himself, filled with a sense of his own shortcomings, blamed the catastrophe on such personal failings as his lack of spiritual grace. In any event, everything that lay ahead—the inaugural ceremonies, the disposal of patronage, grappling with matters of public policy, dealing with the temperaments of cabinet and Congress, presiding at state functions—all of it appeared suddenly unbearable to contemplate, empty of meaning. After Bennie's funeral in Andover, twelve of his schoolmates carried the rosewood coffin down the principal street of New Hampshire's capital before committing it to the family tomb. Mrs. Pierce was inconsolable. Detesting the role of politician's wife in the best of times, she would become virtually a recluse during the dark months ahead, spending hours alone writing letters to her dead son.

Somehow the sorrowing president-elect did make his way back into public life, reaching Washington in late February to deliver his inaugural address on March 4, with snowflakes falling. At the inaugural ceremonies, the new chief executive, up from a log cabin and never defeated in an electoral bid, broke precedent in several ways. At forty-eight, he was the youngest thus far to assume the leadership of the nation. And on that cold, blustery morning the new president had removed his overcoat and, to the amazement of the crowds before the east portico of the Capitol, delivered his inaugural address without text or notes, entirely from memory, an innovation that impressed those in attendance very favorably. They were well inclined toward their new chief executive in any case, full of sympathy for his and his wife's bereavement. "It is a relief," he began his address by saying, "to feel that no heart but my own can know the personal regret and bitter sorrow over which I have been borne to a position so suitable for others rather than desirable for myself." And with that single allusion to his private grief, the president went on to speak of public issues both foreign and domestic that he meant to address in the four challenging years ahead.

In foreign affairs, Pierce explained, his administration would take a bold line in acquiring new territory for the nation. World peace itself urged that new lands—by which the president would have been understood to mean Cuba—should come under the American flag. However, any such additions would be made "through no grasping spirit, but with a view to obvious national interest and security, and in a manner entirely consistent with the strictest observance of national faith"—whatever those last rolling phrases might mean. Moreover, a foreign policy thus motivated would be "entirely consistent with the tranquility and interests of the rest of mankind."

Pierce had a politician's knack for uttering grandiosities. In domestic affairs the unavoidable issue was slavery; and on that matter, the fourteenth president offered a program for peace. The federal government will confine itself to exercising powers clearly granted by the Constitution. That is, this administration will not interfere with the South's peculiar institution. What it will do is preserve the Union. "With the Union," President Pierce declared feelingly, "my best and dearest earthly hopes are entwined." He explained his views more specifically. "I believe that involuntary servitude as it exists in different states of this Confederacy, is recognized by the constitution. I believe that it stands like any other admitted right, and that the states where it exists are entitled to efficient remedies to enforce the constitutional provisions. I hold that the laws of 1850, commonly called the 'compromise measures,' are strictly constitutional and to be unhesitatingly carried into effect." But the president fervently hoped that those same compromise measures had laid the issue of slavery to rest at last, that the abolitionists were now done with their agitation, "and that no sectional or ambitious or fanatical excitement may again threaten the durability of our institutions or obscure the light of our prosperity."

A fresh face—in Pierce's case a young, attractive one—often receives the benefit of the doubt. And in those prosperous times onlookers attending at the Capitol on March 4, 1853, would have found that the new president's inaugural address had articulated a policy—of external adventurism to unite the nation and distract it from its internal tensions—that seemed to reach out a hand to everyone. Radicals welcomed Pierce's expansionist ambitions, and conservatives were reassured by the president's resolve to preserve the Union and abide by the Constitution. The general feeling, here at the very start of his administration, was that this Young Hickory down from New Hampshire had proved up to the mark. He could do it: Pierce seemed the man to hold together America's brawling factions, while extending its boundaries outward in directions sure to increase the nation's security and prosperity.

Yet for all the newfound optimism in the capital, the White House itself had become a sorrowful place. The inaugural ball had been canceled. Social functions—a formal dinner for outgoing President Fillmore, the unavoidable receptions—were held to a minimum and ended early. "Everything in that mansion seems cold and cheerless," one visitor recorded. "I have seen hundreds of log cabins which seemed to contain more happiness." Mrs. Pierce, when she finally reached Washington, kept to her room. Only rarely did the clouds of grief in those early days lift a little, as, for example, when the president's old friend Nathaniel Hawthorne came calling.

Hawthorne had not intended to undertake such a visit. In February the author had written from the Wayside to an acquaintance, "I do not think of going to Washington myself; Pierce having now got into that condition of life when it behoves respectable men to avoid his society." Hanging around an old friend risen to such heights might look like trolling for favors. But by this time Hawthorne would have known of his own pending appointment as consul; as far back as mid-December he had mentioned offhand to his editor Fields that he would be going abroad soon. So a substantial favor had already been granted the author; and with *Tanglewood Tales* done by mid-March and pilgrimage weather arriving, Hawthorne was changing his mind. By March 28, the Senate had confirmed his appointment as consul to Liverpool, to take effect on August 1; and he was writing his publisher about a notion that they had talked over earlier. "I feel rather inclined," he wrote Ticknor, "to follow out our idea of going to Washington in two or three weeks. My best dress-coat is rather shabby (befitting an author much more than a man of consular rank); so, when you next smoke a cigar with our friend Driscoll, I wish you would tell him to put another suit on the stocks for me—a black dress-coat and pantaloons; and he may select the cloth. I shall want them before we go to Washington."

Cornelius Driscoll was a Court Street tailor, and William Ticknor was the partner of James T. Fields, who had come to Salem and pried from an out-of-work author the manuscript of *The Scarlet Letter*. An affable, gregarious salesman with a genius for finding creative talent, promoting it, and winning its loyalty, Fields was the highly successful literary part of the publishing enterprise, whereas Ticknor was its business part. Together Ticknor and Fields had been making a very good thing out of Hawthorne over the last three years, while the author was prospering as well, having in that time published three full-length romances and reissued earlier volumes of tales in addition to a new collection (*The Snow-Image*) of his unpublished tales from old magazines. Moreover, Hawthorne had completed two volumes of myths for children and a successful campaign biography. In short, he had found his publishing house at last, and would remain with Ticknor & Fields for the rest of his life.

Forty-two years old at this time—eight years older than Fields, six years younger than Hawthorne—Ticknor was less flamboyant than his partner, and less literary. Yet he appealed to Hawthorne and would grow, in fact, as close in the years ahead as any other friend the author had. William Ticknor, according to his daughter, "supplied just that which Hawthorne felt he lacked and understood precisely what was needed before the other asked for it." Moreover, the publisher took care at once of the author's various needs: for instance, paying carpenters and masons at work at the Wayside, or sending out from Boston a half dozen bottles of claret, or ordering a suit of clothes to be sewn for a trip to Washington.

The two did make their trip together. "My husband," Sophia noted from the Wayside on April 14, 1853, "went off in a dark rain this morning on his way to Washington"—via Boston, where Ticknor joined him, and on from there to New York, which they reached after midnight at the end of a long day's traveling. And Hawthorne would be kept busy on the way. This close friend of the president's had been busy in any case in recent weeks, with callers to deal with and letters to write; so that his correspondence of early 1853 abruptly resumes the political tone that had enveloped it during final days at the Salem customhouse: "Mr. Warren Thomas," he had found himself writing, "is an applicant for one of the offices in your gift . . ." Or: "Mr. Merrill Pettingill having informed me that he is an applicant for a place . . ." Now in New York over several days, Hawthorne would be preoccupied with callers and engagements, so much so that not until before breakfast on Sunday morning, three days after his arrival, was he able at last to find a moment to write Sophia: "I really could not put pen to paper until now." He wished he would be let alone. "To-day, I am to dine with a college-professor of mathematics, to meet Miss Lynch!! Why did I ever leave thee, my own dearest wife? Now, thou seest, I am to be lynched." He and Ticknor would likely be setting out from New York tomorrow, hoping to reach Washington by way of Philadelphia on Wednesday, the 20th. "I am homesick for thee. The children, too, seem very good and beautiful at this distance. I hope Una will be very kind and sweet. As for Julian, let Ellen make him a pandowdy.

Does Rosebud still remember me? It seems an age since I left home. No words can tell how I love thee."

Once arrived in Washington, the publisher Ticknor was soon writing his own wife: "Hawthorne is quite a lion here. Much attention is shown, and yet it annoys him very much. He is to take tea with the President to-night. We shall hardly leave here before Monday." Again, there was a great deal to attend to. The popular writer Donald Grant Mitchell was angling for the consulship of Venice, and Hawthorne helped him gain that prize. As one happy consequence, Mitchell (who wrote under the pen name of Ik Marvel) left a verbal portrait of the novelist as he appeared at the time, the two of them fellow guests at Willard's Hotel. "Mr. Hawthorne was then nearing fifty—strong, erect, broad-shouldered, alert—his abundant hair touched with gray, his features all cast in Greek mould and his fine eyes full of searchingness, and yet of kindliness; his voice deep, with a weighty resounding quality, as if hearing echoes of things unspoken; no arrogance, no assurance even, but rather there hung about his manner and his speech a cloud of self-distrust, of *mal-aise*, as if he were on the defensive in respect of his own quietudes, and determined to rest there. Withal, it was a winning shyness; and when—somewhat later—his jolly friend Ticknor tapped him on the shoulder, and told him how some lad wanted to be presented, there was something almost painful in the abashed manner with which the famous author awaited a school-boy's homage."

For all the talk of Hawthorne's shyness, he proved effective in making and keeping friends and in looking after theirs and his and his family's interests. A dozen letters awaited his attention at Willard's when he arrived for this first visit to Washington; and in the course of forthcoming conversations with figures in the new administration, Hawthorne was able to put in a word on behalf of Concord's postmaster and of an upholsterer from Salem hoping to re-cover furniture at the White House. At the same time he managed to extend the range of his own consular duties overseas to include the town of Manchester, thereby increasing his annual salary by a substantial three thousand dollars. The grieving Mrs. Pierce even consented to accompany her aunt and Mr. Hawthorne in delightful weather to Mount Vernon. "The President has asked me to remain in the city a few days longer, for particular reasons," he wrote Sophia on the day after that outing, "but I think I shall be free to leave by Saturday. It is very queer how much I have done for other people and myself since my arrival here. . . . Ticknor stands by me manfully, and will not quit me until we see Boston again."

On the journey down to the capital, he had been wondering why he had ever left home, and away from home Hawthorne continued to miss his family acutely. Yet it was always a pleasure for him to see new places, even if in doing so he longed for his wife's company "beyond all possibility of telling. I feel as if," he wrote her in the course of these three weeks away, "I had just begun to know that there is nothing else for me but thou. The children, too, I know how to love, at last. Kiss them all for me." And again, in a final surviving note before setting out for the Wayside: "How I long to be in thy arms is impossible to tell. Tell the children I love them all."

26

DEPARTURE FOR EUROPE

During her husband's absence, Sophia kept busy at the Wayside caring for her three children. Hawthorne had left for Washington on April 14. At Concord five mornings later occurred the anniversary of the day seventy-eight years before that had started the Revolution. This present 19th of April began ritually with a thunder of cannon and clanging of bells to wake the townspeople at the daybreak hour that the British regulars had arrived in the village. "I read the history of the day to the children," Sophia recorded. "What made the morning beautiful and springlike to me was a letter which Julian brought from my husband." Surrounding days provided other pleasures. The weather had grown warmer, allowing for raking, planting, and pruning in the garden and orchard across the way. Weekly, Sophia's little flock of neighborhood pupils gathered at the Wayside for Sunday school lessons, and during the week for lessons in reading, geography, and drawing that she had volunteered to give them. Julian played with his pet turtle or set off on walks in the woods or on a longer stroll, at Mr. Emerson's invitation, to Walden Pond, from where the boy returned bearing cowslips, violets, and anemones for his mother. In late afternoons Sophia might retire to Hawthorne's cherished hillcrest behind the Wayside. "The peach-trees are all in bloom," she wrote of one such occasion, "and the cherry-trees also. I looked about, as I sat down in our pine grove, and tried to bear my husband's absence but it is desolation without him." And in the next breath: "This is the sweetest place—I really cannot bear to leave it." This home of theirs, in this village: Sophia could hardly imagine leaving her Wayside, even with the adventure lying ahead to anticipate.

Between Hawthorne's return from Washington in early May, however, and the family's departure for England in July, so much remained to be done as to leave little time for pining. The family was planning to live abroad for five years, having decided to spend the last of those years in Italy, that earlier dream to be realized after the completion of the consul's term in office. So in addition to packing and making arrangements for the disposal of the house (Sophia's pharmacist brother would rent it), final visits must be paid and callers entertained who were not to be seen again for a very long time.

One task to attend to was Hawthorne's own, a self-imposed, solitary task—dealt with sometime during these same final months. A note in his journal alludes to it under the date of June 1853. "I burned great heaps of old letters and other papers, a little while ago, preparatory to going to England. Among them were hundreds of Sophia's maiden letters—." Sophia's letters, hundreds of them! which had called forth responses such as this, from August 1839, during their courtship, before Brook Farm, before the wedding and the Manse and Salem and Lenox: "Your letter, my beloved wife, was duly received into your husband's heart, yesterday. I found it impossible to keep it all day long, with unbroken seal, in my pocket; and so I opened and read it on board of a salt vessel, where I was at work, amid all sorts of bustle, and gabble of Irishmen . . ." Or this, from June 1840, still two years before their wedding: "Belovedest, what a letter! Never was so much beauty poured out of any heart before . . ." Or this, from April 1843: "Dearest wife, I had not expected a letter; and thou canst not imagine what a comfort it was to me in my loneliness and sombreness . . ." Or this, from July 1848, six full years into their marriage: "Unspeakably belovedest, thy letter has just been handed me, and I snatch a moment from much press of business to say a word to thee. It has made my heart heave like the sea, it is so tender and sweet. Ah, thou hast my whole soul. There is no thinking how much I love and desire thee; and how blessed thy love makes me." Treasures occasioning such gratitude, with hundreds of others and all their balm, their tenderness, to be destroyed in one immolation—"the world has no more such; and now," wrote Hawthorne in his journal, "they are all ashes. What a trustful guardian of secret matters fire is! What should we do without Fire and Death?" Long before—two years and even longer before their Boston wedding—he had assured Sophia: "Nothing like our story was ever written—or ever will be—for we shall not feel inclined to make the public our confidant; but if it could be told, methinks it would be such as the angels might take delight to hear." Half of that love story remains by great good fortune, through an adoring wife's preservation of Hawthorne's letters, along with no more than four of Sophia's that have somehow survived after all the rest were consigned to the guardian flames and are gone.

Longfellow gave a farewell dinner party for his friend on June 14. Emerson was there, in the big house in Cambridge with its wines and servants, as well as Lowell, Longfellow's brother Sam, Charles Eliot Norton, and Arthur Hugh Clough on a visit from England. And "very pleasant it was," Fanny Longfellow reported afterward to her absent brother Tom. "The new Consul looks quite radiant for him, and feels no doubt the cares of life lightened for some time. He is to give us in the autumn another volume of his charming mythological tales, the old gold in a new mould." In that report the governing phrase is *for him:* for the reticent Hawthorne, appearing all but radiant, with his *Tanglewood Tales* at the publisher's and a prestigious public office promising financial security. The radiance was to last three thousand miles across the ocean. "In the early years of our stay in England," Rose Hawthorne Lathrop, using the identical word, remembered of her father, "his personality was most radiant. His face was sunny, his aspect that of shining elegance. There was the perpetual gleam of a glad smile on his mouth and in his eyes." How different was the author's life from any that could have been predicted a year before, on his coming to the Wayside! To view ahead so bright a prospect as distinguished public service and money enough at last! As for that, at Longfellow's farewell dinner Hawthorne would have been reminded again, in his host's and James Russell Lowell's company, of what had not for long left his thoughts since the grim, poverty-ridden days in Salem that had followed his dismissal from the customhouse. Accordingly, among early acts after his arrival in Liverpool, the United States consul would set about discharging a debt of four years' standing to those two and other friends who had never thought of their gift as a debt at all: "I know the sensitive edge of your temperament; but do not speak or think of obligation," George Hillard had written unambiguously upon earlier transmitting a substantial check that constituted a grant from Longfellow, Lowell, Hillard, and other such friends of the destitute Salem author. "It is only paying, in a very imperfect measure, the debt we owe you for what you have done for American Literature," the anonymous donors had insisted. At the time a grateful Hawthorne had responded that the gift would incite him to apply himself so as never to need such help again. But more than that. He all the while had been intending to repay the money, and now he could.

"Dear Hillard," the debtor would write from Liverpool in August, "I herewith send you a draft on Ticknor for the sum (with interest included) which was so kindly given me by unknown friends, through you, about four years ago. I have always hoped and intended to do this, from the first moment when I made up my mind to accept the money. It would not be right to speak of this purpose, before it was in my power to accomplish it; but it has never been out of my mind for a single day, nor hardly I think, for a single working hour." He was gratified, the consul wrote, to be able to repay the loan without impoverishing his wife and children. "We are not rich, nor are ever likely to be, but the miserable pinch is over." Meanwhile, his friends' kind act in Salem had done Hawthorne what he revealed now to have been "an unspeakable amount of good, for it came when I most needed to be assured that anybody thought it worth while to keep me from sinking. And it did me even greater good than this, in making me sensible of the necessity of sterner efforts than my former ones, in order to establish for myself a right to live and be comfortable. For it is my creed (and was so, even at that wretched time) that a man has no claim upon his fellow creatures, beyond bread and water, and a grave, unless he can win it by his own strength or skill."

Both skill and strength of purpose—along with considerable luck (the last in the form of James T. Fields and Franklin Pierce)—had managed matters since those Salem days so that by June 1853, as Hawthorne sat radiantly at his friend Longfellow's dinner table shortly before leaving Concord, he might reflect complacently on contrasts between his present departure and an earlier leave-taking from that same village. Then, in October 1845, he and his wife and infant had all but snuck away, owing rent to the landlord of the Manse, owing town taxes (both debts finally paid), as the little family hurried off in humiliation to Salem with no more than ten dollars of borrowed money among them, to take up residence with Hawthorne's mother and sisters. Now, eight years later, their withdrawal from Concord would be of a different order entirely.

"My dear Longfellow, I like so well to come and see you," the consul-designate wrote on June 26 from the Wayside, "that when I made a floating engagement of that kind, yesterday, I quite forgot how many things I have to do, in the course of the present week. Really you must excuse me—and I should be glad to think that you regretted it half so much as I." Two staterooms had been booked aboard the *Niagara,* leaving Boston on July 6, scarcely more than a week away. Thus about this second proposed festivity Longfellow was obliged to write his good friend Charles Sumner (now senator from Massachusetts) that Hawthorne had so much yet to get done at home that "it will be impossible for him to fulfil his promise; and so the dinner vanishes into thin air." There would be packing, and last bills to discharge, and the house to be made ready for leaving, and purchases to attend to, and letters to write— Ticknor and Fields, for one example, must be instructed formally that Hawthorne's sister Ebe be allowed to draw up to two hundred dollars annually from the author's account—and parting visits to be paid in the village, and the children's good-byes, and provision made for Ellen and Mary Hearne, who would accompany the family as servants. Then suddenly a certain July morning was upon them and time run out, a hot Wednesday morning with the Hawthornes all piling into the train to Boston and making their way to the waterfront excitedly to board the Cunard side-wheeler.

Having concocted business of his own to pursue in England, the ever faithful William Ticknor would be on board and sailing with the family; and waving the travelers off from shore was James T. Fields alongside the widower Dr. Peabody. Sophia's last, gratifying view of those two well-wishers was of the lively editor saying something agreeable that made her father smile. And all the while cannon were booming. Having endured a springtime cannonade in Concord paying homage to Revolutionary patriots, Mrs. Hawthorne must now bear with this additional, headache-inducing thunder of summer, not learning until the *Niagara* was well under way that all that martial commotion in the harbor had been saluting her husband, an honor extended to the distinguished author and United States consul departing for Liverpool.

Now the noise in the port and the hurry of recent weeks, as well as their friends at home, had slipped astern. The vessel was steaming into open water. Near the close of the second day, at eleven in the evening, the *Niagara* reached Halifax, where for a long while Hawthorne, his wife, and his publisher stood on deck together, the three voyagers taking in all that they could of a nighttime's strangeness by the light of lamps ashore and a sky full of stars.

THE SIXTIES

Such a Sad Predicament

Hawthorne in 1860, by J. J. E. Mayall (photograph) in the C. E.
Frazier Clark collection, courtesy Peabody Essex Museum,
Salem, Massachusetts.

27

ONCE MORE TO CONCORD

*I*n the summer of 1853, in the course of eleven days aboard the *Niagara* bound for Liverpool, William Ticknor would come to know the Hawthornes as a family; so that upon arriving in England, he was able to offer an informed opinion, privately, of the celebrated author's marital situation. "Mrs. Hawthorne," he concluded in a letter home, "is a very sensible woman. A better wife he could not have." The judgment is worth noting, arising out of a perceptive observer's nearly two weeks in close proximity with Sophia. The publisher would take less time to form his impression of Liverpool: "In Liverpool there is not much to be seen," he decided after disembarking, "except the Docks and their Commercial buildings. I would not have remained twelve hours, but for Hawthorne. He wished me to stay by him as long as possible."

And the ever helpful Ticknor had done so, for three days, before setting off for London. As consul, Hawthorne for his part was to serve in Liverpool from August 1853 to October 1857, throughout and beyond Franklin Pierce's presidency. During that time he performed his many bureaucratic drudgeries to entire satisfaction. And when the four years of public service had ended, he and his family traveled as they had long hoped to do—to Italy, where they remained well beyond the one year anticipated. Yet even afterward they lingered overseas, back in England for yet another year, during which the author completed a new novel, *The Marble Faun*, his first since *The Blithedale Romance* nearly a decade earlier.

Thus, as with the seven-year interval between their leaving the Old Manse in 1845 and their return to live in Concord, another seven years were to pass after 1853 before the Hawthornes would come back to the Wayside, this time for good. Now it was 1860, and summer again, when the *Europa* out of Liverpool delivered the family at last to Boston, at the end of a twelve-day voyage. By then Sophia's kindly, bumbling father, who had waved the Hawthornes off from that same port, had died at the good old age of eighty; her husband had reached a week short of his fifty-sixth birthday; she (to whom Hawthorne had now been married eighteen years) was fifty, Una sixteen, Julian just turned fourteen, and Rose still budlike at nine.

While aboard the steamer Boston bound, Hawthorne had been feeling as though he wanted to sail on forever, of two minds about this homecoming in any case. He would sit in his cloak at the stern of the *Europa* gazing from under his soft felt hat at the wake and the eastern horizon. Earlier he had written his editor Fields, "As regards going home, I alternate between a longing and a dread." For his own sake he would as soon have remained in England, but for the children the author was finally ending his voluntary exile, so that Julian, approaching college age, might prepare himself in American schools to enter Harvard, and in order that Una and Rose, after much moving about, might experience the novel benefits of a fixed and stable home.

Aboard ship on the same crossing of the Atlantic in June 1860, and very nearly as ambivalent about returning to America, were James T. Fields and his young wife, Annie. Those two, who had been relishing twelve months of entertainment and sightseeing in various European capitals, had arranged near the end of their stay to take passage on the *Europa* so as to travel with the Hawthornes. Fields by now enjoyed an international reputation, everybody's friend, and Hawthorne was but one—although doubtless the most illustrious one—of several authors whom this remarkable editor had succeeded during the last decade in elevating into the luster of an American literary pantheon. In fact, part of Fields's business overseas this past year, in addition to showing his young wife the glories of Europe, had been to foster and spread abroad the ever-widening reputation of such homegrown authors, such newly established literary immortals, as Henry Wadsworth Longfellow and Nathaniel Hawthorne.

Another American author, on her third visit to Europe at the time, had been so eager to interest James T. Fields in furthering her own career that she, too, had made travel plans specifically to board the steamer out of Liverpool on which the editor would be sailing. Following upon the extraordinary success of *Uncle Tom's Cabin* eight years earlier, Harriet Beecher Stowe had journeyed in 1853 to England, where her first novel had proved as wildly popular as at home; and there the frail little mother of six had been acclaimed at vast antislavery rallies and introduced at banquets to every English figure deemed worth knowing, including literary lights and assorted statesmen and lords, during an extended reception of such warmth as to encourage her to return to Europe in 1856 and, again, in 1859. Nothing else that Stowe would write during that busy decade or at any time afterward came near the success of her novel about slavery; yet she had been publishing steadily all this while. Now at the end of her forties and the start of a new decade, Stowe was determined to secure as editor for her future writings James T. Fields, and toward that end had arranged to be aboard the *Europa* with four of her children when the vessel sailed from Liverpool on June 16.

During much of the voyage home, Hawthorne would stay out on deck alone or keep to his cabin; but in the twelve-day interval at sea Mrs. Stowe, Mrs. Hawthorne, and young Mrs. Fields became close traveling friends. Indeed, the friendship between Sophia Hawthorne and Annie Fields survived the voyage to flourish into the years immediately following, in the form of extensive, affectionate letters between them and frequent visits by the Hawthorne parents as well as their children at the Fieldses' hospitable quarters on Charles Street in Boston. Aboard ship, meanwhile, Harriet Beecher Stowe did succeed in befriending the distinguished editor as well as his wife, so that by the time the *Europa* put in at Boston on June 28, she had added her name to the imposing list of authors published by Ticknor & Fields.

Once disembarked after their long absence overseas, the Hawthornes proceeded directly to Concord. Sophia had been eager to be in her home again, her own home, among her friends. Yet the American village that came into view in the heat beyond the train windows— its dusty trees, its monotonous white-clapboard, green-shuttered houses—must have disheartened those longtime cosmopolitan residents of Italy and England. Nearly forty years later, Rose Hawthorne

Lathrop would recall her ride as a nine-year-old aboard the railway wagon from the village depot: "When we drove from the station to The Wayside, in arriving from Europe, on a hot summer day, I distinctly remember the ugliness of the un-English landscape and the forlornness of the little cottage which was to be our home." The child taken from America at age two was going to need time to adjust, and so were the others. Their years overseas had changed them all, as the same years had vastly changed the country to which they were returning.

Mary Mann was on hand to greet her sister and brother-in-law. Since the previous autumn Mary had been living at the Wayside with her three children, and only just a few days earlier had moved to a home of her own some blocks away on Sudbury Road. Mrs. Mann was a widow now. Her husband Horace's political career as a representative in Washington had ended when Franklin Pierce and the Democrats triumphed in the election of 1852. That fall Horace Mann of the doomed Whig Party obliged friends by running for governor of Massachusetts on the Free-Soil ticket. Defeated in his bid, he left politics to reenter the field of education, as the first president of a college just opened out west. Thus from 1853 to 1859, the Manns had lived in Yellow Springs, Ohio, in the midst of uncertainties that beset Antioch College through its founding years. Horace Mann, tireless battler against the world's evils—against slavery as well as tobacco, profanity, and ardent drink, against the lottery as well as ballet dancing—now was influencing higher education statewide as he guided a small, coeducational institution toward developing a social conscience in its students, while he taught those same charges theology and moral philosophy. Some of Mann's causes have grown quaint with age, yet his accomplishments over a lifetime remain remarkable, on behalf of the insane and, above all, through education of the young, on whom he continued to the last to exert his influences. But Antioch was underfunded, faculty members fought among themselves, and in 1859 the college had to be sold and reorganized. Burdened with such troubles, Mann delivered a final commencement address—"*Be ashamed to die until you have won some victory for humanity*," he admonished the graduates—then returned home exhausted and, a few weeks later, died himself, at sixty-three, his own victories for humanity as his principal legacy.

Learning of Mary's untimely loss, the Hawthornes from England in the fall of 1859 had made the empty Wayside available to her and her family; and thus the surviving Manns had been living there over the past nine months, before moving just the other day into a home of their own nearby. So Mary could be present to welcome her younger sister back to Concord and to report firsthand on the family after their long absence. "They are all delighted with the Wayside," she assured a friend within days of the Hawthornes' arrival, "except with the old house, which they seem to think will come tumbling down about their ears at any time. Mr. Hawthorne is going to build a tower with three fine rooms in it." Sophia (who "looks perfectly well") had set about directing the unpacking, all the while answering questions and pointing to this and that to be put here and there, while "Una did the hugging & kissing & rejoicing, & poor Mr. Hawthorne looked wretched in the confusion." According to Mary, he always let his wife do exactly as she pleased, so that Sophia got on without any interference; and as soon as she grew tired or thought that anybody else was tired, she would insist that they all sit down and talk and pay no attention to the chaos around them.

Bronson Alcott and his wife came over that first evening, he and his family having three years earlier moved back from Boston to Concord, into a house next to the Wayside at a little remove to the west. Those peripatetics were to live at their Orchard House from that time on, finally having found a permanent home no more than a couple of minutes away from the Hawthornes. So this first evening Alcott, too, would arrive to welcome the travelers and to chat with his new neighbor about plans for Wayside renovations. Then on the following afternoon Emerson held a strawberry party for the homecomers, to which were invited the Alcotts, Thoreau, Frank Sanborn as the schoolmaster new in town, along with several other villagers. And still another party must have been the one soon afterward that a young woman in attendance would recall in late age. "I saw Mr. and Mrs. Hawthorne," the elderly Annie Sawyer Downs recollected years later, "at a summer fete on the Concord river after their return from Europe when praises of *The Marble Faun* were in everybody's mouth. Many old acquaintances present that afternoon remarked the great change which had taken place in the personal appearance of both Mr. and Mrs. Hawthorne. When they left America Mr. Hawthorne's hair was black as night, while

Mrs. Hawthorne's was the tawny red which Titian loved. At the festivity in Concord both their heads were silver white!"

Moreover, the formerly clean-shaven Hawthorne would have been wearing his mustache, grown during the family's stay in Italy. By one account the mustache was there to hide wrinkles around the author's mouth; or (as his son thought) it may have appeared simply because he had grown tired of shaving his upper lip. For whatever reason, after initial, mild reservations Sophia had become accustomed to it, as have we all; for back in America in the coming years the mustachioed author would be often photographed, so that now he is more frequently represented and remembered that way, even though the writings through which his reputation flourishes— *The Scarlet Letter, The House of the Seven Gables,* the wondrous tales—all were the work of a younger Hawthorne clean-shaven.

He of the bushy mustache did write *The Marble Faun,* the romance that, according to Annie Downs, everyone in 1860 was reading. William Dean Howells looking back would confirm the popularity of Hawthorne's new novel: "Everybody was reading it, and more or less bewailing its indefinite close, but yielding him that full honor and praise which a writer can hope for but once in his life." Readers had waited a long while for this new romance; and when at last they held it in their hands, to most of them it appeared worth the delay. The lengthiest of Hawthorne's novels, it was beautifully rendered as a matter of course, and—as the only one set outside New England— filled with magical descriptions of Rome and Tuscany. For such readers as Fanny Longfellow who knew the Eternal City, those descriptions were in themselves enough to make the novel precious; and for those who didn't, *The Marble Faun* would serve as a guidebook on future travels or for vicarious roaming. But more than that, Hawthorne was burrowing yet again, in his own words, "into the depths of our common nature, for the purposes of psychological romance." Thus his distinctive, familiar themes were present, reexamined with characteristic subtlety in a story of innocence at risk in a sinful world, of the human heart in isolation and the evils that rise therefrom, of murder provoked, of secret guilt, and of the long grievous path to expiation.

Reviewers found much to praise in *The Marble Faun.* "The English critics generally (with two or three unimportant exceptions) have been sufficiently favourable," Hawthorne wrote his editor while still abroad, "and the review in the Times awarded the highest praise of all. At home, too, the notices have been very kind, so far as they have come under my eye." Calvin Stowe, professor of sacred literature at Andover Theological Seminary, would soon send the author an additional, laudatory article that his first wife's sister had written: "The Marble Faun: An Allegory, with a Key to its Interpretation." Hawthorne's response to the gesture was deft. "I am perfectly amazed," he wrote his fellow Bowdoin alumnus, "at the success with which the allegory is made out, and am inclined to think that I have never heretofore given my writings credit for all the profound meaning that exists in them. It is delightful to find such an interpreter as this lady—a reader capable of making up for the deficiencies of the author out of her own rich stores." In her article Martha Tyler Gale had, to be sure, gently expressed one reservation—the familiar hope for less gloomy subject matter in any romances forthcoming—and Hawthorne concurred. "I heartily wish," he wrote Professor Stowe, "I could take her advice as regards a larger infusion of cheerfulness into my future productions; but it has often seemed to me that an evil and unhappy spirit gets into my inkstand, and can only be exorcised by pensfulls at a time. In my personal self, I am not a melancholy man." And he adds with model grace, "The article has given me great pleasure. Its depth and delicacy of appreciation are worthy of a better theme. With kind remembrances to Mrs Stowe, and the young people of your family"—thus acknowledging, in closing, the author of *Uncle Tom's Cabin*, whom Hawthorne had come to know aboard the *Europa* from Liverpool.

Now that he was home, he did hope to write a more cheerful novel. But these early days would provide little means to undertake such an effort. Workmen were arriving promptly to enlarge the Wayside, which the family had outgrown; and social claims were pressing. Hawthorne must come with Judge Rockwood Hoar, Elizabeth's brother and the late squire's distinguished son, to Boston this weekend, within a couple of days of his return, to a meeting of the Saturday Club. The club had been founded three years earlier, its members including the most select of New England's cultural elite: Emerson, of course, and Longfellow, Louis Agassiz, Lowell, and a mere handful of others, meeting for a dinner on the last Saturday of each month at Parker's on Tremont Street. Of course the illustrious Hawthorne must join them. And there was a dinner planned early on by Fields and Ticknor: "pray don't let it take the form," the author pleaded, "of a banquet in my honour! You will think me vain for apprehending any such thing." Yet that was precisely the form that the banquet in Boston did take, with Lowell and Longfellow and others on hand to salute their returning friend. Among the guests was former president Franklin Pierce. Soon Hawthorne would visit Pierce in New Hampshire; and when he returned to Concord, he would find letters awaiting answers and visitors to receive at the Wayside and his children to consider and carpenters and masons whose labors around the place would drive him repeatedly to the solitude of his hilltop.

Thus very little writing got done for now. But he was home at last after seven years away, his family all together and his public duties overseas successfully discharged, with some of his earnings as consul saved, even after the year and a half in Italy and the additional year in England. And from the Italian sojourn had come a new romance that was selling well. Moreover, Hawthorne had earlier assured Fields that he was arriving home with his mind full of no fewer than five additional stories well thought out, ready to write, as well as parts of a draft completed for a new novel set in England.

So he had much to be thankful for. Yet very soon, as June was ending, Longfellow would encounter his mustachioed friend in Fields's office in Boston, beyond the green curtain in the back of the Old Corner Book Store on Washington Street. This was on the 30th, two days after the family's return. Hawthorne was tanned from his recent hours on deck, although Fields looked pale still from seasickness, and both of them appeared "bewildered and sad." Back in their native land, both of them, Longfellow noted in his journal that evening, seemed to be going through what he called a "schoolboy's Blue Monday." Were the travelers experiencing no more than the anticlimax of having reached home at last?

28

ALTERING THE WAYSIDE

*I*n my personal self, I am not a melancholy man," Hawthorne was to write Calvin Stowe in days directly ahead; yet at least for the moment he had appeared downcast when Longfellow saw him in Boston just after his return to America. Beyond the letdown of homecoming, any number of reasons might have helped account for the mood. For one, the reaction to *The Marble Faun* had been not altogether to its author's liking. People were complaining about the novel's inconclusive ending. So perplexed was its initial audience, in fact, that soon, reluctantly, Hawthorne had been persuaded to furnish a brief postscript. "There comes to the Author, from many readers of the foregoing pages, a demand for further elucidations respecting the mysteries of the story." What was in the package that Miriam entrusted to Hilda? Where did Hilda go when she disappeared? What was the precise nature of the connection between Miriam and her sinister, relentless pursuer? And was Donatello human after all, or a faun whose flowing locks hid furry ears? Through three or four sly pages of postscript that were to be published in all subsequent editions, Hawthorne professed to address such questions, although in doing so he merely deepened the reader's perplexities.

To be sure, sources of those perplexities are of a sort not found in the best of his fiction. Compared, say, to *The Scarlet Letter*, this present novel appears ill-developed, despite its author's deep thought and taking of pains with it. Its shadowy characters act for reasons not always sufficiently clear, their motives less complex than merely cloudy; and the narrative is obstructed by heavy chunks of description lifted from notebooks that Hawthorne had kept during his travels. Throughout, the settings appear overly intrusive, in a story that for all its length feels unfinished. The author, in short, is off his stride, so that what he attempts to justify as obscurities inevitable in the weaving of a romantic tapestry seem rather of a sketchiness that simply, finally exasperates.

But he had finished the novel and seen it published, and with it had won a good share of favorable reviews. "I have been much gratified," he wrote Ticknor, "by the kind feeling and generous praise contained in the notices you send me. After so long absence and silence, I like to be praised too much." Yet despite the praise, as his son would record years later, he came to regard his Italian novel as a failure. It was always lamentably easy to persuade Hawthorne that what he had written was not good. Fields reports on having very early learned to refrain from expressing even the slightest reservation; in the case of *The House of the Seven Gables*, for instance, the editor had realized that one such word would have led its author to toss the entire manuscript into the fire. Similarly with doubts about this latest work. "'The thing is a failure,' he used to say. He meant, perhaps," according to Julian, "that he had failed in making his audience take his point of view towards the story." But its author intended to try again, now that he was home and had several subjects for romances on his mind and time on his hands to write them. Hawthorne meant to compose something more genial, as he assured Fields, and soon would get started working on his English novel. He felt he had to, in fact, the monetary rewards of the consulship having proved less substantial than predicted; "with a wing of a house to build, and my girls to educate, and Julian to send to Cambridge, I see little prospect of the 'dolce far niente,' as long as there shall be any faculty left in me." Home now, he must resume writing in order to support his family.

Only he couldn't, and that may have contributed to the dejection that Longfellow noticed very early. Workmen would be all over the Wayside, sawing and hammering, building new rooms to accommodate young people grown beyond childhood, as well as a couple of servants' rooms and a lofty studio for the world-famous author. That last, absurdly enough in clapboarded Concord, had been inspired by a medieval stone tower in Italy, at a villa that the family had rented near Florence and thoroughly enjoyed. Hawthorne had loved ascending his Tuscan tower; so a tower back home, roughly twenty feet square, wooden-framed with sash windows and a four-gabled roof, was being built on the Wayside, where to this day it thrusts its disproportionate, architecturally outrageous bulk through the top of the old colonial farmhouse alongside the Lexington Road.

In the midst of the carpentry work constructing his tower, the home owner was to entertain a visitor—one among a number, to be sure, although this particular young man has left an account vivid enough to permit our going along with him on his call. It was the William Dean Howells already mentioned, at the time in his early twenties and newly arrived east from Columbus, Ohio, a news-paperman who nourished high literary ambitions. In decades that lay ahead, Howells would become in his turn a great Boston and New York editor and a distinguished novelist; but for now he was simply a young journalist from Ohio who had written poems and sent them east to the prestigious *Atlantic Monthly*. That magazine's editor, James Russell Lowell, had published some of Howells's poems; and thereupon, the young man had traveled to Boston and introduced himself to Lowell and called on James T. Fields and, to his delight, soon found himself dining in awe with both editors and from them gaining the matchless gift of a letter of introduction to Nathaniel Hawthorne.

Accordingly out to Concord went Howells in August 1860, to stand hesitating beside piles of lumber before the door of the modest Wayside. He gazed at the field across the road and the hill behind. At last he knocked, and a tall boy who must have been Julian came to the door. The visitor was admitted, the boy disappeared, and soon from a back room Hawthorne himself emerged. "He advanced," Howells recalled, "carrying his head with a heavy forward droop, and with a pace for which I decided that the word would be *pondering*. It was the pace of a bulky man of fifty, and his head was that beautiful head we all know from the many pictures of it. But Hawthorne's *look* was different from that of any picture of him that I have seen. It was sombre and brooding, as the look of such a poet should have been."

Their visit turned out to be not much after all, no more than an hour long and with no advice, no brilliant conversational sallies to record. There wasn't much to record in sum. Hawthorne asked if his visitor would like to join him in smoking a cigar on his hillside. Although Howells didn't smoke (and in mock disapproval Lowell's note of introduction had said as much), he went along. The two climbed up behind the house and sat on a log, and Hawthorne smoked. Then they came back down to find tea laid. Would the visitor like to stay for tea? Long stillnesses surrounded the sipping that followed. Would he like to call on Mr. Emerson? Very much. Hawthorne scribbled a note: "I find this young man worthy." Then Howells left. That was it; "there was a great deal of silence in it all, and at times, in spite of his shadowy kindness, I felt my spirits sink," the visitor recollected some forty years later.

The hour had been an awkward one, yet in the course of its long pauses the two had somehow related to each other. "Nothing," Howells concluded, "could have been farther from the behavior of this very great man than any sort of posing, apparently, or a wish to affect me with a sense of his greatness. I saw that he was as much abashed by our encounter as I was; he was visibly shy to the point of discomfort." For all that, the caller would leave profoundly impressed. Nor was it the starstruck bedazzlement of a midwesterner giddy on Olympian heights. That same day young Howells went forth in Concord to call on Thoreau and, though admiring his writings, didn't like the man at all. Afterward he called on Emerson and didn't like him much either. But Hawthorne: "My memory of him is without alloy one of the finest pleasures of my life"—this the judgment at century's end of a major literary figure, wide traveler, sophisticated novelist, for years successful editor himself of the *Atlantic Monthly,* close friend of Mark Twain and Henry James and virtually every other contemporary author of note. Howells knew them all; and yet meeting Hawthorne and spending an awkward, often silent hour in his company remained to the end of a long life one of its highest joys.

What was there in that presence that impressed people so? Hawthorne had looked "sombre and brooding" on this occasion, as he had appeared to be going through a "schoolboy's Blue Monday" when Longfellow saw him earlier in the summer. Yet despite the despondency, and despite the silences, people came away enchanted. Hawthorne's daughter Una would go visiting in Boston some weeks later, at the Fieldses' and elsewhere, and return home exclaiming, "Why mamma, how everybody loves, *adores* him!" And they would seem to do so despite any low spirits persisting.

The lumber that Howells had seen in the yard of the Wayside might help further explain a restless soul's dejection, with all the author's spare money being poured into home renovations. As is often the case, those would continue longer than planned, far into the following spring; so that no earlier than May 1861 was Hawthorne able, rather ill-temperedly, to write his friend Bridge of "making the final disbursements on account of my house—which, of course, has cost me three times the sum calculated upon. I suppose every man, on summing up the cost of a house, feels considerably like a fool; but it is the first time, and will be the last, that I make a fool of myself in this particular way." The final result was satisfactory, to be sure, with enough space for them all and yet no more elaborate than was needed. But, as he concluded to his friend, "the worst of it is, that I must give up all thoughts of drifting about the world any more, and try to make myself at home in one dull spot."

In that same spot, meanwhile, in Concord that summer and fall, another cause for dejection had enveloped the author's homecoming. It concerned Una, Hawthorne's sixteen-year-old daughter.

During their earlier stay in Italy, the family had spent what Julian— in his two-volume biography of his parents—would later conclude had been, on the whole, the happiest interval in Hawthorne's entire life. Then they had been living in a rented villa near Florence, through a bright summer and into October of 1858, during an idyllic interlude at the end of which they had returned to Rome, to ill fortune in dismal weather. "It is extremely spirit-crushing," Hawthorne had noted in his journal early that November, "this remorseless grey, with its icy heart; and the more to depress the whole family, Una has taken what seems to be the Roman fever by sitting down to sketch in the Coliseum." Thereafter the child had endured what her father records as "fits of exceeding discomfort, occasional comatoseness, and even delirium." A local doctor had diagnosed the illness as malaria of a nervous kind; that is, involving the mind. It had grown in severity and length. For six interminable months, into March of 1859, Una had suffered, her life appearing at times in the gravest danger. Twice it was despaired of. Unable to sustain the intensity of his alternating hope and fear, Hawthorne had finally given up, resigning himself to Una's death. He who, ever since leaving America, had been writing copiously in his various notebooks, closed them and for four months wrote not a word. Nor could he express his grief aloud, any more than he had been able to speak of feelings at his sister Louisa's drowning. Still, as the children's companion in the household, Ada Shepard, had written in the course of the crisis, "It is almost the worst trial in all this to see his face."

Sophia for her part never did stop hoping. Faithfully, all but exclusively, she had tended her daughter. "No one shared my nursing, because Una wanted my touch and voice. . . . For days, she only opened her eyes long enough to see if I were there. For thirty days and nights I did not go to bed; or sleep, except in the morning in a chair, while Miss Shepard watched for an hour or so." Finally, at the most critical juncture in the fourteen-year-old's ordeal, the agonizing mother, herself at last on the edge of despair, all at once felt faith surging back. "Why should I doubt the goodness of God?" she asked herself. "Let Him take her, if He sees best. I can give her to Him. I will not fight against Him any more." And with that, with her spirits restored, Sophia had stepped to the bedside and touched her daughter's forehead. It felt cool. The pulse was regular. Una slept soundly, the crisis passed.

Or so it had seemed. In fact the young woman was never fully to recover from the illness that had devastated her and her family over those long, terrible months in Rome. More than a year later, back in Concord in this summer of 1860, Una appeared to be nervous in the extreme, could scarcely abide the solicitude of that mother who had nursed her through her illness. To a young Salem cousin the sixteen-year-old wrote in mid-July from Aunt Mary Mann's house: "My heart ached hard yesterday when I said goodbye to you, because I saw how sorry you felt for me, though I had so far overcome my rebellious feelings by that time as to feel happy enough, except for you." But there was good news, as she went on to share: she had been conferring with her doctor, confidentially, and he had "agreed with me in the most *unqualified* manner in everything I said, & he is going to talk to Papa and tell him his mind, and then I shall be as free as air! Think how happy I must be! Last night I thought I would stay here till Monday, as for many reasons that would be very agreeable & convenient, but last night & this morning tell me that I shall have a brain fever if I do." She had to get away, go to Salem. "I shall certainly go tomorrow by the half past six train, & I may go today. Oh, I long to be there, out of this killing place."

She longed to be anywhere but Concord: with her Manning cousins in Salem, or with her aunt Ebe in Beverly, or at the Fieldses' in Boston—anywhere except at the Wayside. Una spent as much time as she could on Sudbury Road, at her aunt Mary Mann's with her cousin Horace, Jr., trying to get her mind off herself. "From having followed that wise course until now & keeping away from home I have greatly improved but though I appear, & am, perfectly well while I do as I please, (did you ever know such a wilful & headstrong young woman as I am?) there is a certain little group of events & sights & sounds that in a minute by a most wonderful magic make me faint & sick & all over shooting pains, but as I avoid these unmentionables whenever I can I keep very jolly, as the English say." Such jollity was obviously forced; and indeed in days ahead Una would grow irrational, exhibiting behavior so violent that she had to be strapped down. In desperation, her parents were driven to submit her to electric shock treatments. Fortunately, according to Henry James, Sr., within two days the galvanic doses had cured the girl "of one of the most fearful attacks of *dementia* ever suffered," transforming Hawthorne's eldest child "from a condition of fury dangerous to every body and everything about her to a state of tranquil rationality like health itself."

Her father's private correspondence confirms the gossip. "I am most happy to give you good news of Una," Hawthorne was able to reassure his intimate friend Pierce in early October 1860. "All the violent symptoms were allayed by the first application of electricity, and within two days she was in such a condition as to require no further restraint. Since then, there has been no relapse, and now, for many days, she has seemed entirely well, in mind, and better as to her bodily health than since we left Rome." But through all those tormented months the poor girl had been ailing, and by no means was she cured yet. Even at year's end Hawthorne, still troubled, would confide to a close friend in England: "Una has been very much out of health since our return. The dregs of that miserable Roman fever are still in her blood; and we sometimes feel very much discouraged about her."

Through griefs such as those had her parents' hair turned white.

29

CONCORD IN THE SIXTIES

*T*he author himself was not well, a fact that would have contributed its part to Hawthorne's no longer radiant spirits on
his moving back to the Wayside. For his children had remembered
him as radiant in England, as often hilarious in his play with them;
and Julian afterward would suggest that the family's summer residence in Florence as late as 1858 had constituted perhaps the happiest period of all. That late joy had come, however, just weeks
before their return to Rome and Una's prolonged illness, from which
anguish her father seems never to have fully recovered. Back in Concord during the summer and autumn of 1860, he appeared less vigorous than formerly, and continued thus; so that Sophia would
wistfully recall, in December 1863, her husband's earlier zest, his
astounding vitality and good health from the Manse days onward,
when he had known nothing of colds, indigestion, or other enfeeble-
ments: "It is long since he had it,—four or five years, I think." The
remark puts the date of the change at 1859 or '58, in pestilential
Rome. "I am amazed," Sophia would add in her later retrospect,
"that such a fortress as his digestion should give way. But his brain
has been battering it for a long time,—his brain and his heart."

Heart and brain both had had to bear a daughter's drawn-out,
near-fatal illness; and both brain and heart, having struggled to
create *The Marble Faun,* had been required to absorb the public's
ill-comprehending reception of that late novel. Back home in Concord, not feeling well, Hawthorne was grieving over Una's relapse,
even as he worried continually about money: about the cost of
educating his children and of making necessary renovations to the

Wayside, which latter were keeping him all the while from the income to be earned at his writing desk. And meantime in Concord, the author's heart and brain both were aware, to their continual distress, of how much the village and the nation had changed during the family's seven years of absence overseas.

In the earlier, happier summer of 1853, as cannon in Boston Harbor boomed a salute to the United States consul departing for Liverpool, Franklin Pierce's Democratic administration had appeared firmly in control of the government in Washington, with a cabinet assembled that would seem to exemplify the various factions of a nation brought together in harmony, and with the Compromise of 1850 having settled the divisive issue of slavery once and for all.

Yet in its unfolding, Pierce's presidency had proved an all but unmitigated disaster. Scarcely a year into his term, in the spring of 1854, slave catchers in Boston had pounced upon one Anthony Burns, a runaway from Virginia. Such incidents had happened earlier in the port city, but this particular consequence of the Fugitive Slave Law was following upon the vast, educative popularity of *Uncle Tom's Cabin,* and it occurred precisely on the day that Congress passed the Kansas-Nebraska Act. Pierce endorsing that legislation was, he felt sure, signing into law a great accomplishment of his presidency; by its terms, which in effect repealed any earlier compromises, settlers themselves would decide whether or not to admit slavery into new states formed from the western territories. This meant, so the president assumed, that all that huge region would end up free soil anyway; slavery could not root itself in the prairies, mountains, and deserts of the West. Most northerners, however, read the new legislation differently, as opening to the South's loathed institution regions that had previously been off-limits. The slave power appeared on the march again, the foul stain of plantation labor about to spread westward at the very moment when, here in Boston, Anthony Burns had been snatched from his innocent toils in a clothing store and identified as a fugitive slave.

Burns was hied off to the courthouse. A crowd of protesters gathered at Faneuil Hall, famed patriot meeting place of colonial times, and there plotted loudly to rescue the runaway. Bronson

Alcott was deeply involved in the effort to spirit Burns north to Canada and freedom, even as Longfellow in Cambridge watched with feelings that multitudes of his fellow citizens shared. May 27, 1854: "Last night there was a meeting in Faneuil Hall, and afterward an attempt at rescue, which, I am sorry to say, failed. I am sick and sorrowful with this infamous business." The marshal in Boston kept Washington informed by wire: two military companies were guarding the courthouse; an effort to rescue the fugitive had been foiled; "Everything is now quiet." President Pierce responded: "Your conduct is approved. The law must be executed." But Boston's Mayor Smith was wondering about calling out more troops if needed. Back came Pierce's reply: "Incur any expense deemed necessary by the Marshal and yourself, for city military or otherwise, to insure the execution of this law." On such high authority Anthony Burns was to be harrowed back into slavery.

A company of marines, another of infantry up from Newport, and Boston's own National Lancers on horseback would lead the fugitive at quickstep down State Street to the piers. It was 2:30 in the afternoon. "The windows of every office and place of business were full, the shops shut." The procession, two thousand soldiers in all, hurried along, militia units with drawn bayonets forcing a way through the crowds, as bricks flew and voices yelled out, "Kidnapper! Slave Catcher! Shame! Shame!" At enormous cost the authorities were succeeding in putting Anthony Burns aboard a cutter that President Pierce had sent expressly for the purpose of getting one black man back to Norfolk, a rendition that would cost dearly not only in taxpayer money but also in the widespread outrage it provoked in the North; mill owners with southern sympathies were abruptly changing their minds, coming to regard the slave power's aggressiveness as intolerable in a free society. The South for its part was wondering how much longer it could remain in a Union that flouted the rights of property—that refused, indeed, to abide by the Constitution and the laws of the land. And soon, in the wake of the Kansas-Nebraska Act, the field of conflict would shift from New England to Kansas, as emigrants South and North made their way to the territory alongside slaveholding Missouri in order to be on hand, settled and ready to cast their votes for or against slavery when Kansas should enter the Union.

Through the remainder of Pierce's administration Kansas would bleed. The president's policies—the steps he took and declined to take in the strife-torn territory, the governors whom he appointed and relieved there—seemed clearly to show his bias for the slave-holding faction. That wasn't how Pierce saw it; all he meant to do was maintain the Union. He would oppose troublemaking abolitionists while upholding the Constitution. But on this issue of slavery the nation was coming apart; and the affable president, persuaded by whoever last spoke to him, leaving nobody satisfied in seeking to appease everyone, hardly knew what to do about it.

In May 1856, Charles Sumner of Massachusetts, abolitionist, Hillard's former law partner, Longfellow's close friend and for two decades personally known to Hawthorne, at his desk in the Senate after delivering a fiery antislavery oration was so severely beaten by an irate, cane-wielding southerner that he was unable to resume his Senate seat for three years. Not only New England but the North as a whole was appalled, as southerners gleefully furnished Congressman Brooks with elaborate new canes to replace the one he had broken over the Yankee's head and shoulders. That same month saw old John Brown and his sons out in Kansas drag from their cabins along the Pottawatomie River five pro-slavery settlers who were thereafter hacked to death with broadswords, the mutilated bodies left for the settlers' families, their wives and children, to recover. In an atmosphere thus poisoned both south and north, President Pierce's hopes for a second term in office had withered away. For their candidate in 1856 the Democrats turned instead to an old political warhorse who had spent these recent contentious years far off, unspotted across the Atlantic in Westminster as American ambassador to the Court of St. James.

Hawthorne, the consul at Liverpool all this while, had official dealings with Ambassador Buchanan and liked him as much as he cared for any politician. But since his abrupt dismissal from the Salem customhouse, Consul Hawthorne had little time for politicians of whatever sort; nor were his prejudices about their cant, their hypocrisy, their backstabbing in any way mollified by the treatment meted out to his friend the well-intentioned Frank Pierce, who near the end of a single term in the White House was being reviled mercilessly on every hand. "I must confess," the consul wrote from England in the election year 1856, "I am in no hurry to return

to America. To say the truth, it looks like an infernally disagreeable country, from this side of the water." Politicians and shrill
reformers, people telling other people what to do: Hawthorne cared
for none of them—cared, he said, for no party anymore, hated them
all, "free soilers, pro-slavery men, and whatever else—all alike."

But in the year that followed, after the Democrat Buchanan
had succeeded Pierce in the White House, Hawthorne in England
would learn to his dismay that if not politics, at any rate reform
would be moving right next door to him back home, the abolitionist Bronson Alcott having somehow got together nine hundred
dollars to purchase property adjacent to the Wayside. To the serviceable Ticknor he wrote from overseas: "I understand that Mr. Alcott
(of whom I bought the Wayside) has bought a piece of land adjacent to mine, and two old houses on it. I remember the situation
as a very pretty one. . . . If he should swamp himself by his expenditures on this place, I should be very glad to take it off his
hands. . . . You would oblige me by having an eye to this."

As it happened, when Hawthorne did return to Concord at last,
Alcott was permanently established at his Orchard House next
door. Indeed, that visionary neighbor would appear at the Wayside promptly on the Hawthornes' first evening back, ready to help
with renovations; "I shall delight to assist him," the kindly if
exasperating Alcott wrote in his journal, "and build for him in my
rustic way, restoring his arbours if he wishes." But Hawthorne
wished, perhaps more than ever before, only to be left alone, back
home where his views on a number of matters were at odds with
those of his vegetarian neighbor and of his fellow villagers in general. Nor would Alcott be long in discovering (this, too, recorded
in his journal) that the elusive Hawthorne, returned to live among
them, had dug "his moats wide and deep, his drawbridges all up
on all sides, and he secure within from invasion."

When, in weeks ahead, Professor Agassiz invited the recluse
behind his drawbridges to join fellow members of the Saturday Club
in Boston at a dinner honoring Nathaniel Banks, the outgoing governor of Massachusetts, Hawthorne chose not to attend. "Beyond
a general dislike to official people," he responded bluntly to the
invitation, "I have no objection to the Governor, and I care very
little about his politics"—which were lately those of a Republican,
the man having espoused five different parties during twenty years

in Congress. Hawthorne all the while had remained a Democrat. "But," he pressed on, "(speaking frankly, as brethren of the Saturday Club ought, among themselves,) I doubt whether my political virtue would be rigid enough to keep me away, if I anticipated any great pleasure in being present; so, as I don't think it will be half so delightful as our customary dinners, I decide not to come. Truly Yours."

He meant to keep his distance from politicians as well as from any such reformers as were abundant in reform-minded Concord. Charitable associations, antislavery fairs, lyceum lectures, philanthropic teas, dances for society's improvement—all such activities enjoyed long histories in this village where fervent apostles seemed to predominate. The character of Hollingsworth in *The Blithedale Romance* furnished Hawthorne's commentary on the perils of such zeal, even as an extreme specimen of zealotry—Concord-connected—had lately appeared in real life, in the figure of the fanatic John Brown, veteran of skirmishes in Kansas that had culminated in midnight massacres along the Pottawatomie River. Old Brown had afterward made his way east to raise money with which to free slaves from bondage—had come to this very village, in fact, on two occasions while Hawthorne was still abroad, and both times, in 1857 and 1859, had enjoyed a warm welcome. The Thoreau family, Lidian Emerson, the Alcotts, the Hoars, the Whitings, Mary Merrick Brooks, Mary Mann and her older sister and frequent visitor Elizabeth Peabody were all active abolitionists; so that, uplifted by John Brown's biblical zeal in a lofty cause, the villagers had been able to exonerate the old man of any personal involvement in still vaguely reported Kansas wrongdoings on the basis of his few cryptic answers to gentle queries. Emerson, Thoreau, Alcott, and other prominent townspeople thereupon had offered Brown their wholehearted moral support; and the village schoolmaster, young Frank Sanborn, secretary of the Massachusetts Free-Soil Association, had even gone so far as secretly to join a small group of easterners supporting Brown in concrete ways, with weapons and money.

Brown had taken the money and the pikes and rifles and had led his sons and followers to the number of seventeen on a forlorn escapade, in mid-October 1859, to seize the United States arsenal at Harpers Ferry in the mountains of Virginia. The ill-planned venture, meant to lead freed slaves armed into the surrounding hills, was doomed from the start. Not a single slave answered Brown's summons, while the South rose up in fury. The captain's followers were slaughtered or captured and their leader seized. In Charlestown, lying wounded on a cot in the courtroom, Brown was tried for murder, treason, and—abiding southern horror—incitement of a slave insurrection. Despite a self-defense of inspired, prophetic eloquence, the old man was found guilty and sentenced forthwith to hang.

Longfellow saw the day of Brown's execution, December 2, 1859, as a great day in our history, "the date of a new Revolution,—quite as much needed as the old one." Many in the North felt that way. In tiny Concord on the day of the old man's hanging, church bells tolled at the hour of execution; Louisa May Alcott, in her mid-twenties, wrote in her journal about "St. John the Just"; and both Emerson and Thoreau spoke passionately at services marking the solemn interval, Thoreau drawing a comparison that others would echo: "Some eighteen hundred years ago Christ was crucified," he told his listeners; "this morning, perchance, Captain Brown was hung. These are the two ends of a chain which is not without its links. He is not Old Brown any longer; he is an Angel of Light."

Not to the South, he wasn't; old Brown was a madman, a meddling fanatic, as satanically far from angelhood as the black pit of hell lies from the glories of heaven. Some up North would have concurred in the South's harsh opinion of Brown, although in Concord sentiment ran strongly in the old captain's favor, as a Gideon selflessly pursuing the noblest of aims. Meanwhile, searching the Maryland farmhouse where Brown's pitiful forces had gathered before launching their raid, authorities had come upon letters incriminating several northern supporters—a clergyman, a businessman, a wealthy philanthropist—and one of the names they had found was Frank Sanborn's. The Concord schoolmaster was ordered to come bear witness before a committee of Congress called to investigate the affair. This was in early 1860, after the hanging and not long before the Hawthornes returned to the village. Doubting his personal safety down South, Sanborn had chosen to forgo the journey to Washington. Whereupon a scene had erupted on Concord's quiet Sudbury Road.

At nine on a Tuesday evening, April 3, 1860, the schoolmaster had answered a knock at his door. Two men stood in the darkness out front. As one started reading aloud from a warrant, Sanborn shouted to his sister, "Run to Col. Whiting!" Screaming, Sarah slipped past the men, past two others outside and yet a fifth coming up in a carriage. Her screams were rousing neighbors as the deputies handcuffed her brother and began dragging him out to the yard. Sanborn stood six feet four inches tall—the physical stature of a certain Illinois politician of the time—and with his long legs and his youth, at twenty-eight, he was struggling with his abductors, bracing himself against the side of the carriage. Church bells had started ringing, and the street came alive with villagers, thirty or forty of them, finally a hundred. Emerson was there, and Attorney Keyes, who hurried away to Judge Hoar's nearby to secure a writ of habeas corpus. Keyes returned, and the writ was hastily served. When the abductors protested, some in the crowd began mauling them; stones were battering their carriage. Before long, Sanborn went free, as the carriage clattered off from the village with the five intruders huddling inside.

Thus, raucously, were Concord's views on old Brown and the slavery issue proclaimed. Very soon that same John S. Keyes would be departing for Chicago as a member of the Massachusetts delegation attending the Republican National Convention in May. The new political party, which combined the defunct Whigs with Free-Soilers and Nativists and disgruntled Democrats, had offered their first presidential candidate in 1856, against Buchanan; Republican nominee John Charles Frémont had polled as many as 114 of the 288 votes cast that year in Concord. Such a show of support had boded well for the future, now arrived as Attorney Keyes rode forth to participate in the mere formality of nominating Senator William H. Seward of New York as the Republicans' choice for president.

Only it worked out differently. Delegates in Chicago ended on the third ballot choosing for their nominee a former Whig and disciple of Henry Clay, a local railroad lawyer with little education and no administrative experience, a long-ago, one-term member of the House of Representatives who was by now the party's favorite son in Illinois, Abraham Lincoln.

30

SECESSION

*H*alf a decade earlier, in 1855, New Hampshire–born Frank Sanborn, age twenty-three and just out of Harvard, had moved to Concord at Emerson's urging to set up a school in the village. During the five years since, Sanborn had come to be friends with the absent Hawthorne's friends and acquaintances: Thoreau, Ellery Channing, Alcott, Emerson himself. With Hawthorne's writings, too, Sanborn was thoroughly familiar; so when in the summer of 1860 the two did finally meet, at the strawberry party at Emerson's on the Hawthornes' second afternoon back from their long European sojourn, it was as though Sanborn were encountering someone he already knew. One thing, however, the schoolmaster was not prepared for, as he noted years later, and that was the author's "remarkable personal beauty," even after such beauty had passed its mid-fifties in discouraging times and been partially concealed under a droopy mustache. "His portrait by Thompson I had seen, but it does not convey the charm of the features; his other portraits were not then much known. Of all the Concord and Cambridge authors," according to this witness who would end by knowing each one personally, Hawthorne "was by far the most distinguished in feature and in the impression he produced"— far handsomer, Sanborn insisted, than was Byron in the best of his portraits, handsomer by far than was Webster, and with none of that statesman's marring arrogance.

Sanborn himself was of the reforming bent for which the author newly returned to the Wayside would hardly have felt an affinity. Three months earlier, after townspeople had helped him escape from would-be abductors, the schoolmaster had spent successive nights of the following week in different houses in the village so as to foil any further efforts to spirit him off to Washington. One of those nights he had hidden in the garret at the Wayside, guest of the abolitionist Mary Mann. And by week's end, with Elizabeth Hoar and Mrs. Samuel Ripley agreeing to mind his school in his absence, Sanborn had hurried away to Canada until matters at home could calm down.

By June he was back in Concord, in good time to meet the Hawthornes. A major reason for those travelers' having returned from Europe at all had been to get fourteen-year-old Julian, home-schooled until then, into a more formal academic setting that would prepare him properly to enter Harvard College. Sanborn's school, successor to the Thoreau brothers' Concord Academy, was the obvious choice for such purposes. "My Dear Hawthorne," Ellery Channing was writing in early September, two months after the author's return, "In numbering over the things that had been added to the town, t'other day, I left out the first and best,—which is the School for boys and girls, under the charge of Mr. Sanborn." In the early 1840s, during the Manse years, this Channing had often gone boating on the river with Hawthorne; a poet married to Margaret Fuller's sister, he had since continued to guide his life by Emersonian values, trusting himself rather too much perhaps, neglecting his family, and after his wife's death wandering in the woods with Thoreau, never quite taking hold. Now he was writing Hawthorne a recommendation for Sanborn's academy, new to the village. "I have never heard of a school before," Channing attested, "where there was so much to please and so little to offend. . . . Our schooldays are *the* days of our life; it is then we learn all we ever know; and without these mimic contests, these services, sports and petty grievances, what were all our after days?"

He had a purpose in saying this: "If you were as intimate with Mr. Sanborn as I have the good fortune to be, I think nothing would give you so much satisfaction as to have such nice girls as yours seem to be, directly under his charge." The poet may have been remembering the impression that Una and Julian had made on him when he had visited Lenox ten years earlier. ("The children brought up in the worst way for visitors, by themselves, never having been to school, have of course nothing but bad manners.") Now he was urging a father and friend to change course in rearing such off-spring. "Nothing seems to me more unfortunate, in this land of activity," Channing wrote, "than to bring up children in seclusion, without the invaluable discipline that a good school presents. Forgive me for dwelling a little on this, out of regard to Mr. Sanborn, who deserves to be sustained."

As it turned out, Julian would indeed attend Sanborn's school starting that September, and in so doing would join a notable group of twenty or thirty scholars in the front rooms of the schoolmaster's home on Sudbury Road, next door to the Manns'. Two of the martyred John Brown's daughters were in the school, as well as Emerson's children, the two youngest sons of Henry James, Sr., Judge Hoar's children, and Mary Mann's. Hawthorne's son would join that co-educational group even though his mother had doubts, about boys and girls at so critical an age studying together and about the wisdom of attempting to mix study and pleasure as Mr. Sanborn was doing; Mrs. Hawthorne's own youthful intellectual pursuits had been rigorous and unrelieved, whereas Julian would be varying his classroom work with occasional picnics, dramatic presentations, weekend dances, and school-sponsored woodland walks.

In such extracurricular pleasures Una and Rose were allowed sometimes to participate, but they were forbidden the coeducational classrooms. The one girl was still very young, the other delicate. Una, when she could, would benefit from tutoring with the polymath Mrs. Sarah Ripley at the Old Manse, and nine-year-old Rose would continue pursuing her lessons at home. Thus, as a nation was going tensely about the business of electing a new president from among sectional candidates of four political parties, this first autumn of the Hawthornes' return to America unfolded: with Julian at last enrolled in school, with noisy construction adding a tower to the Wayside, and with worries about Una's health persisting. Early in the fall, for instance, for two weeks in September Hawthorne would take his oldest child for a recuperative visit with Horatio Bridge at the Portsmouth Navy Yard. A note that school-master Sanborn wrote a friend a couple of days after their return conveys the abiding distress: Una "is now sick with a brain fever and quite delerious. She came home from Portsmouth with her father on Saturday and had been a little strange while there. Her friends feel very anxious about her, for she has never fully recovered from her fever at Rome." Much later Sanborn would recall having around this time been summoned next door to Mary Mann's to help subdue the poor girl, deranged and violent. Yet gradually Una's condition did improve, until in the coming months she was able to visit Boston and Beverly and partake of whatever consolations her brother's school and a quiet New England village might offer, through seasons full of personal stress and national crisis.

Abraham Lincoln of the sectional Republican Party won the presidential election in November 1860 with no more than 40 percent of the popular vote. Immediately South Carolina moved to secede from the Union. Hawthorne would have ignored it all if he could; America would be a fine place to live "if Presidential elections and all other political turmoil could be done away with," he had written Ticknor from England earlier in the year, "and if I could but be deprived of my political rights, and left to my individual freedom. The sweetest thing connected with a foreign residence is, that you have no rights and no duties, and can live your own life without interference of any kind. I shall never again be so free as I have been in England and Italy." Now back in the United States, in Concord and feeling less free, the author was again, on December 7, in touch with Ticknor, nearby in Boston in the wake of Lincoln's election. "The study table is all right," he reported, "and I am writing this note at it, in my study." The author was at last in his new, lofty, comfortable sky parlor, even though the rest of the tower remained to be finished. And he ended his note on the dismal perplexity of the moment: "Is there going to be a general smash?"

Three days earlier, President James Buchanan had sent his final annual message to Congress. In it the Pennsylvania dough-face, with three months of his term yet to serve, had squarely assigned blame for the national crisis: "The long-continued and intemperate interference of the Northern people with the question of slavery in the Southern States has at length produced its natural effects." Northern agitators in the American confederation had violated their neighbors' sovereignty; abolitionists should have left the slave states alone. Even so, the president went on, "Secession is neither more nor less than revolution." What he was proposing for dealing with the crisis was a constitutional amendment guaranteeing slavery in the South—hardly an expeditious remedy—along with a resolve to defend the national forts wherever threatened. So feeble a program for settling civic differences had ended by leaving no one satisfied. Southerners resented the president's chiding them for having responded the only way they could to insufferable grievances, whereas northerners were irate that Buchanan blamed *them* for the South's bellicose stance, at the verge of secession.

All the while massive economic and political issues were gathering. Southerners owed northern manufacturers huge sums, close to $300 million, for manufactured goods that an agrarian society had purchased and not yet paid for; was all that indebtedness to be repudiated? (Indeed it would be.) Were northern mills and factories to be denied the immensely lucrative products of slavery, no less crucial to the antebellum economy than is the oil industry to ours? And was the federal Union, unique in the world and not yet a century old, really about to be dissolved? Some thought that last not so fearful a prospect—the regionalist Hawthorne for one, as he explained by letter to an English friend in mid-December: "What do you think is going to become of us?—of our Republic, I mean. For my part, I am ready for anything that may happen, knowing that, if the worst comes to the worst, New England will still have her rocks and ice, and be pretty much the same sort of place as heretofore."

What do you think will become of us? The president-elect out in distant Illinois was keeping his own counsel, but press and public speculated frantically through these late days of 1860. Some felt sure that fire-eating South Carolina was bluffing, talking loudly as it had for three decades—ever since Nullification—and would give in now as it had before. If not, so be it. "I hope the North will stand firm, and not bate one jot of its manhood," Longfellow wrote amid the clamor that followed immediately upon Lincoln's election. "Secession of the North from freedom would be tenfold worse than secession of the South from the Union." Stand firm, many urged, and concede nothing further to keep the Union intact. Others, for the sake of that precious Union, wished to go on conciliating; abide by the Constitution, by the laws of the federal legislature, by the Supreme Court's Dred Scott decision that had recently confirmed slaves to be property and thus transportable into all of the national territories. Still others, unable to tolerate that lands at present restricted to free white labor should be invaded by the coerced and unpaid labor of blacks, felt nevertheless willing to leave unmolested any state where slavery currently existed, even to the extent of amending the Constitution to guarantee such states protection in perpetuity for their peculiar domestic arrangements. And some people wanted simply to let the erring sisters go in peace. Neighbors cannot be conquered and forced to live contentedly alongside their conquerors. Let the malcontents secede. Without the slave states, "I should not wonder," Hawthorne was soon writing another close English friend, "if we become a better and a nobler people than ever heretofore. As to the South, I never loved it. We do not belong together; the Union is unnatural, a scheme of man, not an ordinance of God; and as long as it continues, no American of either section will ever feel a genuine thrill of patriotism, such as you Englishmen feel at every breath you draw."

He wrote thus on December 17. Three days later South Carolina did vote to secede from the Union. In January, on the 9th, Mississippi followed, Florida on the 10th, Alabama on the 11th, Georgia and Louisiana before the month was out. Still the ineffectual sitting president, sixty-nine-year-old James Buchanan, mumbled and blustered, and the president-elect in Springfield declined to utter a word to address the crisis. "I could say nothing," Lincoln had remarked early on, "which I have not already said, and which is in print and accessible to the public." In early February the six seceded states met in Montgomery, Alabama, and chose former president Pierce's secretary of war and close friend Jefferson Davis to lead their new Confederacy. They would draft a constitution, issue their own currency, fly a flag of their own. On February 23, Texas seceded and joined the nation that was assuming form and substance.

By then, President-elect Lincoln had started on his leisurely way east from Springfield via Indianapolis, Cincinnati, Columbus, Pittsburgh, Cleveland, Buffalo, Syracuse, Albany, New York City, Philadelphia, Harrisburg, and—having uttered noncommittal generalities all along the route—surreptitiously through Baltimore at the end of February into the southern city of Washington, D.C. On March 4, 1861, the rawboned Illinoisan was standing bespectacled in new black clothes before his fellow citizens North and South, ten thousand of them gathered around the east portico of the Capitol, where citizens had gathered sixteen years earlier at the inauguration of James K. Polk, where they had gathered eight years earlier to witness the inauguration of Franklin Pierce. To the eleventh and the fourteenth presidents, Chief Justice Roger Taney had administered the oath of office; now, once more and for a final time, the cadaverous Taney sat ready to perform that public duty when the sixteenth president was finished with his remarks. In a high-pitched, practiced voice that carried far, Abraham Lincoln spoke to the attentive multitude:

"Fellow citizens of the United States, In compliance with a custom as old as the government itself, I appear before you to address you briefly, and to take, in your presence, the oath prescribed by the Constitution." Above all, the speaker intended to make clear, as he had done repeatedly in the past, that the South had nothing to fear from the accession of a Republican administration. "I have no purpose, directly or indirectly," he said in an accent out of the Midwest unfamiliar to many of his listeners, "to interfere with the institution of slavery in the States where it exists. I believe I have no lawful right to do so, and I have no inclination to do so." Yet again, in the hearing of this audience, the incoming president would reiterate that sentiment, which was written into the Republican platform and in "nearly all the published speeches of him who now addresses you." The property of the South was in no danger. The Fugitive Slave Law would be enforced.

But—and for the first time in this hour of "great and peculiar difficulty" President Lincoln was asserting the policy that he meant to follow—"the Union of these States is perpetual." That is, there would be war if the South persisted. Even if the Union is no more than an association of states, "one party to the contract that made it cannot rescind the contract lawfully without the consent of all parties to the contract." The Illinois lawyer was reasoning with his audience, about a Union that predated the Constitution, that extended back as far as the Declaration of Independence of 1776 and the Articles of Association of 1774. The Union predates the Constitution. No state, therefore, "can lawfully get out of the Union." Accordingly, resolves and ordinances proclaiming secession are legally void. This president would take care that the laws of the Union were faithfully executed; that was his simple duty, enjoined by the Constitution, and he would meet that duty.

The address was nearing its end. "My countrymen, one and all, think calmly and *well,* upon this whole subject. Nothing valuable can be lost by taking time. . . . In *your* hands, my dissatisfied fellow countrymen, and not in *mine,* is the momentous issue of civil war. The government will not assail *you.* You can have no conflict, without being yourselves the aggressors. *You* have no oath registered in Heaven to destroy the government, while *I* shall have the most solemn one to 'preserve, protect and defend' it. . . ."

A month later, and despite the anguished eloquence with which the new president concluded his inaugural address ("I am loth to close," he had said. "We are not enemies, but friends"), Virginia seceded from the United States. ("We must not be enemies.") Arkansas followed a month after that. ("Though passion may have strained, it must not break our bonds of affection.") Then North Carolina. ("The mystic chords of memory, stretching from every battle-field, and patriot grave, to every living heart and hearthstone, all over this broad land, will yet swell the chorus of the Union, when again touched, as surely they will be, by the better angels of our nature.") Then finally, in a tortured June of 1861, Tennessee, the last of the eleven, broke away.

31

PATRIOTIC AMERICANS

*A*ll this while, Hawthorne had been striving to come to terms with being home again. "I meet Longfellow and all the other prominent literary people at the monthly dinner of the Saturday Club," he had written back to Liverpool, to a close English friend who would have known some of those people from travels in America. The club was "an excellent institution," Hawthorne had explained, "with the privilege of first-rate society, and no duties but to eat one's dinner; and it is one of its great advantages, that you can take a guest there, and make him acquainted with all our northern notabilities at one fell swoop." Of the notabilities, "Longfellow has grown younger in appearance," the homecomer felt, "but seems not to dress quite so smartly as of yore," the earlier Longfellow having been something of a dandy. "Emerson is unchanged in aspect—at least, he looks so, at a distance, but, on close inspection, you perceive that a little hoar-frost has gathered on him. He has become earthlier during these past seven years; for he puffs cigars like a true Yankee, and drinks wine like an Englishman."

One other report this dear English friend would have been expecting. "As for me," Hawthorne had written Henry Bright last December, "I spend a monotonous life, seldom quitting my own hill-side, and trying earnestly to take root here. I find, however, that I staid abroad a little too long, and as a consequence, have lost my home feelings for the present, if not forever. Already, I begin to think of paying another visit to England, though whether this idle notion is ever executed will depend, in the first place, on my writing a new Romance, and, secondly, on the contingency of my being able to get a good price for the London copyright."

Only in December 1860, six months after returning to America, did the author have a place, finally, in which to write such a letter, in the sky parlor of his tower ready for use at last, with a walnut desk set up and an inkstand in easy reach. Even so, as the nation was in upheaval, so the Wayside remained distractingly topsy-turvy. "Ah me, we shall have order at some future day I dare to say," Hawthorne's wife wrote Annie Fields in January. "But now there is but one nook where we can take refuge from the Fury of Hubbab." That was a tiny library downstairs twelve feet by twelve, although without any books yet, "as we have spent all we can on the house building." As late as May 1861, "Painters, paperhangers and gardeners still molest us," Sophia wrote, "and I have to look three ways at once. But we verge to a conclusion, and begin to bud and bloom on the lawn and hillsides." Finally, on June 5—as the last of the southern states was leaving the Union—Una was able to inform her aunt Elizabeth Peabody that "Our house is now entirely finished, & we are furnishing it at our leisure, & doing as much to our grounds and garden as Papa can afford, which is not a great deal."

Hawthorne must settle down to his writing to augment the family income. "I spend two or three hours a day in my sky-parlor," he had reported to his publisher Ticknor early in 1861, "and duly spread a quire of paper on my desk; but no very important result has followed, thus far." As always, this author needed uninterrupted quiet in which to create his fictions; and just now neither the house nor the nation offered much quiet. The nation coming asunder certainly did not. In mid-April insurrectionary military forces under the command of the Louisiana general P. G. T. Beauregard bombarded a federal fort in the harbor of Charleston, South Carolina. The flag of the Union had been fired upon. At the start of a new week, Bronson Alcott in Concord noted the shocking event with red letters in his journal. Monday, April 15: "News comes of Gen'l. Anderson's Surrender of Fort Sumter, and of Pres. Lincoln's call for 75,000 Volunteers," soldiers to serve three months putting down the southern uprising.

Promptly the North rallied to the president's summons. In Concord April 19, just four days later and on the very anniversary of the skirmish against the redcoats at the North Bridge in 1775, sixty-four members of the local militia were mustering in the Town Hall. In afteryears Emerson's son would recall that particular spring morning, in fine weather with flags flying, volunteers in their absurd uniforms of red-trimmed blue coats, indigo pants, beaver hats, and bearskins gathered where young Edward as a schoolboy had joined the crowds of townspeople watching from the gallery. Lieutenant Prescott formed his men and marched them around the hall. He dressed them and gave the command "Order arms!" From the center of the hall Judge Hoar spoke to the men, reminding them of the country's and the federal capital's danger, of their duty to Concord, of the example set them by their forefathers. A sum that would amount to $5,000 was being raised to be given to the soldiers and their families. "At noon," Edward Emerson recalled years later, "the company, in their old-time Napoleonic uniform, were arrayed under the flag-staff, cut that morning in Walden Woods, the flag was run up, saluted by the cannon, while the young women sang the 'Star Spangled Banner,' Mr. Reynolds made a solemn prayer, and mid cheers and tears, accompanied by all Concord, her soldiers marched to the train." Citizens collected there too, at the "old homely depot," cheering, crying. "We watched the cars," the Reverend Mr. Reynolds remembered, "until they disappeared behind Walden woods, then walked silently home."

War had come to a broken nation; within a month it would reach the very doors of the Wayside. A worker helping with renovations there had been among the first of those Concord volunteers to leave the village, and in May Mrs. Hawthorne heard from him. The recruit sent "his best regards, and a request that I would write to him! He was one of my High Contracting Powers in building our Tower. I have spent this morning partly in writing to this hero, who left a sweet little family of six children and a gentle wife at the first call to arms. He never dreamed, in his simplicity, of being heroic in his act." No more did the many others. Fred Stowe, for one, Harriet Beecher Stowe's son, had dropped out of medical school as soon as he heard the president's call for volunteers and had enlisted at once in the Union army. Stowe's mother had been in the midst of writing not one but two novels, the first appearing as a serial in the *Independent,* the second in the *Atlantic.* But she had to break off. "Who could write stories," she protested, "that had a son to send to battle, with Washington beleaguered, and the whole country shaken as with an earthquake?"

Who could write with the country shaken? The problem was Hawthorne's as well, immobilized before sheets of paper in his Concord tower. Bronson Alcott did record the occasional sighting of his neighbor as he dodged among the trees on his hill behind the Wayside; and given the author's penchant for solitude, it was as well perhaps that neighbor Alcott had at last found public labor to his liking, having two years earlier been appointed superintendent of schools in Concord. That congenial duty kept the educator occupied visiting classrooms in the village and outlying districts, although he still made time for sociable calls next door. Generally, Bronson had to content himself with seeing Mrs. Hawthorne (whom he had known for a quarter century, since well before her marriage) and helping her with landscape renovations. But on a May day he found himself on their shared hillcrest actually chatting with Sophia's elusive husband. The sad gist of their conversation the educator set down in his journal: "He says he can think of nothing but the state of the country. He wishes to go to the seaside and recruit for a month or more; says he likes Concord as well as any place to live in, but remembers London with pride and could spend his life there delightfully. Wonders if some means cannot be devised to bring us oftener together, and seems to feel the want of more society than he has here. He says he sees nobody."

The man was not well, despite whatever protestations he offered to the contrary. Writing his friend Bridge toward the end of this same month, Hawthorne claimed to have been heartened by the current crisis. "The war, strange to say, has had a beneficial effect upon my spirits, which were flagging woefully before it broke out." He had found it "delightful," he said, to share in the general outpouring of patriotic sentiment; it had made him feel young again. He insisted that he approved of the war as much as any man, despite being unable to figure out just what the North was fighting for. "If we pummel the South ever so hard, they will love us none the better for it; and even if we subjugate them, our next step should be to cut them adrift." But maybe the war was all about ending slavery. If so, "we should see the expediency of preparing our black brethren for future citizenship by allowing them to fight for their own liberties." All the while, instead of romances, such immediately pressing matters as these were filling the author's mind. Whatever the outcome of the crisis, he was telling Bridge, the North should rejoice "that the old Union is smashed. We never were one people, and never really had a country since the Constitution was formed."

Any such rejoicing, however, in those early days before South and North met in the fields alongside Bull Run, was dampened in Hawthorne's case by frustrations awaiting him at his writing table, by frustrations there and by a deepening apathy that his wife had been observing of late with puzzlement and distress.

During this May of 1861, Hawthorne's friend Longfellow ventured over from Cambridge to Boston and the Old Corner Book Store. "Nothing alive but the military," the poet noted. "Bookselling dead. Ticknor's looks dark and dreary." Another visit to Washington Street ten days later found conditions unimproved. "The 'Corner' looks gloomy enough. Ticknor looks grim and Fields is fierce. Business is at a standstill. So much for war and books."

As with Stowe and Hawthorne, Longfellow was finding it hard to get on with his writing: "When the times have such a gunpowder flavor, all literature loses its taste." By this date, to be sure, the poet had already succeeded in creating an imposing body of work. In 1854, a year after the Hawthornes had sailed for Liverpool, Professor Longfellow had ended a quarter century of teaching in order to devote himself fully to verse. He had started *The Song of Hiawatha* within months of his final lecture; that enormously popular poem had appeared in 1855. Three years later had appeared *The Courtship of Miles Standish*. More recently Longfellow had published "Paul Revere's Ride," addressing his country's current political predicament by evoking an earlier, Revolutionary crisis when Americans had responded to duty's call. Other verse had emerged from his pen in the fifties to burnish an already shining reputation. Harvard awarded the poet an honorary degree in 1859. And there was ample money to accompany all this growing success: Longfellow's income from his writing was unprecedented for a poet in America, and his wife, Fanny, possessed a share of the enormous wealth that her textile magnate father, Nathan Appleton, had accumulated.

However reluctantly she may have behaved before their marriage, Fanny had proved the perfect spouse through the many years that had followed a Beacon Hill wedding in 1843. The Longfellows' marriage was every bit the equal of the Hawthornes'; if it is less well documented, that is because Fanny and her Henry were so seldom apart. For a rare written specimen of their feelings for each other, this of Fanny's from within the Craigie House early on must serve: "Henry took his sunset row on the river. Sat at the window and followed the flashing of his oars with my eyes and heart. He rowed round one bend of the river, then another, now under the shadow of the woods and now in the golden sunlight. Longed to be with him and grew impatient for wings he looked so far away. How completely my life is bound up in his love—how broken and incomplete when he is absent a moment; what infinite peace and fullness when he is present. And he loves me to the uttermost desire of my heart."

The two remained bound up in each other through all the years that followed. During those years Longfellow suffered intermittently from poor eyesight; then the cultured Fanny would read aloud to him and transcribe for him, delighting to do so. As much as she could, she relieved her husband of the irksome task of letter writing. She entertained the frequent visitors of this amiable, world-famous poet, and always with grace and sensitivity. The couple had six children, one of whom died in her second year (till then about the only real grief burdening so fortunate a pair); the other children thrived into adulthood. In their grand Cambridge home the Longfellow family lived happily, sociably, and productively year after year, vacationing in summertime at their cottage near Lynn, at Nahant, on the seashore north of Boston.

Through the gathering national crisis of the fifties, Longfellow and his wife had privately deplored the contaminations of slavery. The planter oligarchy's growing strength dismayed them, the presence of slave catchers directly across the river from Cambridge disgusted them, the brutal assault in the United States Senate on their dear friend Sumner outraged them, and Abraham Lincoln's election to the presidency filled both of them with intense satisfaction. In Longfellow's private words, that last event promised no less than "the redemption of the country." Publicly, to be sure, it had never been—nor would ever be—the poet's way to champion causes; his calling dealt in the ideal. As a poet he looked elsewhere than at current events to find subjects for his verse, which strove to evoke the timeless. As he understood it, that was what poetry ought to do.

Nevertheless, this contentious present did trouble the Long-fellows deeply, into the summer of 1861. Now, because feeble old Nathan Appleton, past eighty, was in steep decline in his Beacon Hill mansion across the river in Boston, the family had postponed their usual sojourn to the cooler weather of the seashore. The Fourth of July was very hot. The parents took Alice to Boston so that their ten-year-old might for the first time see the balloons go up and the fireworks explode. "The immense, well-behaved crowd is a fine part of the show," Fanny noted, "but when the patriotic emblems appeared there was more enthusiasm than usual, of course"—although it saddened her to realize that now an entire portion of the country would be indifferent to a holiday that the North invested with such meaning. Three days later Mrs. Long-fellow was writing one of her other children, absent from home, that "Dear Grandpapa is very feeble, but much the same as when you left. We wish he could get down to Lynn, thinking the sea air might strengthen him a little."

That was on July 7, still hot, so that daughter Annie was droopy, her mother wrote, "and Edie has to get her hair in a net to free her neck from its weight. . . ."

The daughters were at home with their mother two days later, July 9, on what by chance was the Hawthornes' wedding anniversary. The windows in the house were open. Longfellow had retired across the hall to lie down for a nap, while Fanny sat with the children sealing locks of their hair in little packages. A Victorian genre scene: Domestic Love and Innocence. Since that untroubled moment on the edge of horror, a century and a half has passed, yet the instant after still has power to appall.

Suddenly, shattering the quiet from across the hallway come piercing screams that bring Longfellow upright in terror on his couch. At the parlor entry a human being aflame, a beloved wife engulfed in fire, is running screaming toward her husband. He seizes a rug and springs at her, clutching her, trying to wrap the rug around her. Horrible, horrible moment: Fanny breaks away, runs from him back toward the hall. At the entry the helpless woman all afire turns and rushes again toward Longfellow's arms. He embraces the flames. His wife's gauzy summer dress, lit by hot wax or a fallen match, has been utterly consumed. Her husband's grasp spares Fanny's face, but his own face and hands are scorched, as his wife's body burns black. The flames are finally extinguished, and the victim is carried to her bedroom. A doctor administers ether to ease her agony. Through the night the poor woman is in and out of consciousness, in the morning asks for coffee, dies in mid-morning, soon after ten.

They brought the tidings across the river to Fanny's father. "She has gone but a little while before me" was as much as the old man could manage in response. On the day of her funeral—it was the Longfellows' wedding anniversary—old Nathan Appleton rose in the Beacon Hill mansion where his daughter had been married eighteen years before, had himself dressed in full mourning, and sat in his armchair attentive through the hour in which the distant funeral was taking place. Later that day he requested and was given a minute account of Fanny's death and burial. He heard it all with composure. By the following morning Nathan Appleton was dead, and three days later he was buried in Mount Auburn Cemetery, where lay his daughter's remains.

Sedated with laudanum for the pain and grief, Longfellow had been unable to attend his wife's obsequies. Although the burns were healing two weeks later, his face was still swollen, "and he cannot yet shave"—would never be able to shave again, so that from that time forward the formerly beardless poet wore the white beard with which he is most often depicted.

On the 14th, from Concord, Hawthorne had written to Fields: "How does Longfellow bear this terrible misfortune? How are his own injuries? Do write, and tell me all about him. I cannot at all reconcile this calamity to my sense of fitness. One would think that there ought to have been no deep sorrow in the life of a man like him; and now comes this blackest of shadows, which no sunshine hereafter can penetrate! I shall be afraid ever to meet him again; he cannot again be the man that I have known."

Like Hawthorne, the poet's many other friends were stupefied by news of such a horrific loss. Sumner could not find it in himself to leave Washington. "You are entirely right," another of their circle assured the senator, "not to leave a post of public duty for any private sorrow. I do not, however, wonder at your feeling. You loved our dear friend now gone and she always spoke and thought of you as one singularly near and dear." The correspondent, Cornelius Felton, was able to report that by now "Longfellow is in a calm state of mind. I sat by him Wednesday evening an hour or two."

But as Hawthorne had said—and of course it was true—the bereaved would never be the same again. To Fanny's sister Mary, one of two blithesome young women in Switzerland a quarter century before, when an American poet and student of languages had met them both and fallen in love for a lifetime, to Mary he would write tenderly of her sister, a month after so dreadful a fate had overtaken them all: "I never looked at her without a thrill of pleasure; she never came into a room where I was without my heart beating quicker, nor went out without my feeling that something of the light went with her."

32

IN THE SKY PARLOR

Even before Fanny Longfellow's horrible death, Hawthorne had felt in low enough spirits that, two months earlier, he had spoken to his neighbor Alcott of needing to recruit at the seashore. Salt air and sea breezes had always served as restoratives for this ship captain's son and native of Salem port. Yet, for all of Sophia's urging, her husband would not make the effort and go. Through the heat of summer he continued to languish at the Wayside, withdrawing to his hilltop to find what comfort he could up there. Then came news of the catastrophe befalling the Longfellows in Cambridge, domestic horror irreconcilable with any sense of the fitness of things. And soon afterward arrived word of yet another catastrophe, this on a national scale.

On Wednesday, July 17, accompanied by carriages bearing congressmen and lighthearted ladies with picnic hampers south to witness the crushing of rebellion, thirty thousand raw federal troops had at last set forth from camp outside Washington to march twenty-some miles over the dusty road to meet the secessionist enemy. But at Bull Run on July 21, the North was to learn disastrously of the Confederacy's military mettle, as the first major encounter of two great armies ended in a humiliating, rain-soaked rout of Union forces. Among the troops fleeing in disarray were the volunteers of Company G, Fifth Massachusetts, the men from Concord village. Like many others up North, Hawthorne in the new reality was left clinging to a single feeble consolation: "if it puts all of us into the same grim and bloody humour that it does me," he wrote shortly after the battle, "the South had better have suffered ten defeats than won this victory."

By then, fortuitously, a means had emerged that would pry the author away from Concord. "I am to start, in two or three days," he was writing in that same letter of July 23, "on an excursion with Julian, who has something the matter with him and seems to need sea-air and change." If so, they both were in need of it, father and son; so that both together would set out four days later by train for Pride's Crossing, on Boston's North Shore, near where Hawthorne's sister Ebe had been living these many years. Sophia was relieved to wave her son and husband off on their way to such healthful surroundings. "Of all the trials this is the heaviest to me," she wrote Hawthorne revealingly as soon as he was gone from the Wayside, "to see you so apathetic, so indifferent, so hopeless, so unstrung." Ever since hot weather had arrived, what this wife had wanted most was to have her husband away in the sea air, unencumbered with work or worry, with nobody around to bother him. "I saw no way," she wrote him gratefully, "until this plan of taking Julian occurred to you."

If Julian was ill when they left, the seashore appears to have done the boy a world of good, and promptly. From "West Beach (or Somewhere else)" on the 28th, Hawthorne was writing back to Dear Onion, his pet name for Una, to report, in terms that betray the despondency that Sophia had regretted, "We arrived duly, yesterday afternoon, and find it a tolerably comfortable place. Indeed, Julian seems to like it exceedingly, and I am not much more discontented than with many other spots in this weary world." Father and son were staying in a little house belonging to a couple attentive yet unobtrusive, by a railroad with woods close at hand and the sea a few minutes beyond. Soon they would be rambling off to see Aunt Lizzy, Hawthorne's reclusive sister, in her Beverly room not far away. With reassurances that "Julian is redundantly well," the father ended this account to the rest of his family left back in the heat of the Wayside.

The vacationers stayed near the seashore through a couple of weeks, although in Hawthorne's case without deriving the full benefits that Sophia had hoped for. Even here the weather proved hot— "The sea itself seemed to reflect heat; as though it were made of hot molten metal"—and all the while Hawthorne was wearing his Victorian broadcloth. Julian for his part did fine: went fishing, ate vastly, and lamented the thought of ever going home. But not his father: "Dear Bab," father wrote daughter Rose, age ten, a week and more into the adventure, "I am very homesick, and have come to the conclusion that when a person has a comfortable home of his own, and a good little Bab of his own, and a good great Onion, and a best mamma, he had better stay with them than roam abroad. Thank Heaven, we shall return on Saturday."

Off in exile the author had been brooding over his partly written romance, perhaps determining to lay aside that English subject and start afresh in September's more temperate weather. What Hawthorne had been working on was a story about an American roaming in England in search of the estate of his British ancestors. A portion of the plot he had sketched in Italy in the spring of 1858, before a more pressing Italian theme had led him to take up *The Marble Faun* instead. Then Una had fallen dreadfully ill, and after her recovery the family had gone back to England, where the author had completed his Italian romance. So not until a couple of years later, in Concord, had he been able to resume the English subject, whenever carpentry work at the Wayside, or Una's relapse with its attendant grief, or the grievous national crisis allowed him to. But the writing had not gone well, even though he had struggled with the project manfully morning after morning in his sky tower, trying to fashion various unruly elements of character, plot, theme, and symbol into the coherent entity that constitutes a finished novel.

Precise dating of his various undated attempts to create fiction up there must remain conjectural, but the matter of an American coming to England to reclaim his heritage had clearly been occupying Hawthorne's pen during the months before the vacation with Julian in the summer of 1861. By then, in fact, a great many pages of it had been written. The romance was to reveal significant contrasts between old England's aristocracy and the democracy of new America, a matter that four years and yet another year of dwelling among the English had allowed the author to muse on deeply. But he was aspiring to write a novel, not an essay on contrasting cultures; so there must be characters, scenes, a story. Young Middleton, the American claimant, is to be discovered searching through England for the estate of his ancestors, much as Hawthorne had earlier attempted in vain to locate traces of his own forebears in English church records and graveyards. A pretty young English-woman comes into the story, and a villain with Italian connections. Middleton is entertained at a manor house over which hangs a mysterious sorrow. A bloody footprint stains its threshold; genera-tions of wear and scrubbing have failed to efface the print. A leg-end relates the enduring stain to brothers quarreling two centuries earlier, the younger of them having won the love of the other's betrothed before fleeing with her to the New World. In a bed-chamber in the manor house, where that emigrant's descendant Middleton is being entertained these two centuries later, is a cabi-net in which, in a hidden recess, are found ancient documents of great moment. What will they say? Murder is to be attempted; and an age-old secret that the American possesses—or discovers—will have power to transform the story. What exactly is the secret? And will the American claim his inheritance at last, or forsake it and return with the Englishwoman to the fresher air of the New World?

Sketchiness of this sort risks making any such undertaking sound absurd; the wonder is that, in reading the manuscripts that survive from Hawthorne's labors over such material, so much of what he wrote in his sky parlor appears auspicious. Indeed, a num-ber of narrative passages manage the true Hawthornean magic. "A traveller, with a knapsack on his shoulders, comes out of the duski-ness of vague unchronicled time, throwing his shadow before him in the morning sunshine, along a well trodden, though solitary path. . . ." Thus opens one effort to launch the story, and with that bright, haunting, archetypal image set in motion, the Gothic para-phernalia stir once more to life, and we find ourselves reading the following pages with a growing pleasure.

Yet Hawthorne was dissatisfied. Repeatedly in the course of its progress he interrupts his narrative with authorial recapitulations of what the story has accomplished so far, as well as notations to himself—often perplexed, sometimes exasperated, finally desper-ate—of problems that loom ahead. "I don't in the least see my way," the author will blurt out dejectedly. Or: "A certain property shall attend him wherever he goes; a bloody footstep. Pshaw! He shall have the fatality of causing death, bloodshed, wherever he goes; and this shall symbolize the strife which benevolence inevitably provokes, because it disturbs everything around it. Make this out. 'Twon't do. Oh, Heavens!" Or, about one troublesome character: "This wretched man!—A crossing sweeper?—a boot-black?—He comes of a race that is degenerated in a certain way. . . . How? It should be from some cause that had existed in the family for hundreds of years. It can't be. Some irremediable misfortune has got possession of this poor devil. . . . 'Twon't do." Yet again: "Well; all that nonsense might be easily enough arranged; but what is his lordship, and what is he to do? He is a member of a secret society in Italy, who have a hold upon him, which they strenuously assert; and he thereby becomes most miserable. 'Twon't do. He has a secret ulcer. Pish. What does he do? He makes a soup for Etherege out of the bones of his long dead ancestors, spiced with the embalming out of the bowels of one of them; and he himself partakes. Very well. Oh, Heavens! I have not the least notion how to get on. I never was in such a sad predicament before."

Defeated, pathetically so, the author in his disordered frame of mind finally sets aside the massive effort (the fragments print to 487 pages, as the posthumously designated "American Claimant Manuscripts" that constitutes volume 12 in the definitive *Centenary Edition of the Works of Nathaniel Hawthorne*). Nor would he ever come back to the subject. Returning home after his stay with Julian at the seashore, he planned to start over again. During September of 1861, James T. Fields journeyed out from Boston to Concord to meet with the author, and the two walked together on the hill above the Wayside, Fields listening encouragingly as Hawthorne related his newest literary project. Soon the editor would be writing eagerly, "I wish very much to begin your new story (about the house) in our *January* number" of the *Atlantic*. "Now dip your pen steadily and briskly to that end. When shall I have the first instalment?"

It would be a story about the house—about this Wayside. In rough draft the new story opens with what seems studied good cheer on a day in early spring: "as that sweet genial time of year and atmosphere calls out tender greenness from the ground, beautiful flowers, or leaves that look beautiful because so long unseen under the snow and decay, so the pleasant air and warmth had called out three young people, who sat on a sunny hill side, enjoying the warm day and one another. For they were all friends." The two men and the young woman dwelt as neighbors alongside the Lexington Road here in Concord, "along a ridge that rose abrupt behind them, its brow covered with wood"—the very ridge that Hawthorne had later come to know intimately, along the comforting crest of which he had been spending so many daytime hours.

He would write about Concord in a moment of peril. But the author's mind kept wandering from his romance back to the more immediate peril of civil war in progress. In October he would respond to his friend Bridge, who was aiding the war effort in Washington as chief of the Bureau of Provisions and Clothing: "I am glad you take such a hopeful view of our national prospects . . . but my own opinion is that no nation ever came safe and sound through such a confounded difficulty as this of ours." To so close a friend Hawthorne could admit that he did not even want the Union restored; "amputation seems to me much the better plan, and all we ought to fight for is, the liberty of selecting the point where our diseased members shall be lopt off. I would fight to the death for the Northern slave-states"—Maryland, Virginia, Kentucky, Missouri—"and let the rest go." But the issue was a sorely vexing one: he was finding it difficult to concentrate on his "usual trash and nonsense" during such times as these, even if lately, "as the autumn advances, I find myself sitting down to my desk, and blotting successive sheets of paper, as of yore. Very likely I may have something ready for the public, long before the public is ready to receive it."

That was in mid-October 1861; and indeed the public of the time was abundantly distracted, while Hawthorne withdrew to his sky parlor to re-create Concord village of an earlier day. His unfolding story lets us date the earlier day precisely: April 18, 1775. The three young people, Robert, Rose, and Septimius, on the threshold of a world-changing encounter sit conversing under the sun's warmth about, among other things, the then-current tensions with England. But "Our story is an internal one," the author interrupts his narrative to remind us, "dealing as little as possible with outward events, and taking hold of these, only where it cannot be helped, in order by means of them to delineate the history of a mind bewildered in certain errors." Even so, it would be necessary, however briefly, to describe "the circumstances of the time in which this inward history was passing."

The very night, then, of the day when the story opens, horsemen would be heard shouting "Alarm! Alarm!" as they galloped past farmhouses alongside this same Lexington Road. The drum would beat, and in the darkness farmers would hastily gather. Tomorrow morning's sunlight would bring with it wild excitement, as armed men in groups hurried along the usually empty highway. "It was a good time, everybody felt, to be alive in," as Hawthorne describes the momentous dawn: "a nearer kindred, a closer sympathy from man to man, a sense of the goodness of the world, of the sacredness of country, of the excellence of life, and yet its slight account, compared with any truth, any principle." April 19, 1775: looking back on what Samuel Adams had called a glorious morning for America, this later observer more carefully writes of the "ennobling of brute force" then, "the feeling that had its godlike side; the drawing of heroic breath amid the scenes of ordinary life, so that it seemed as if they had all been transfigured since yesterday. Oh, high, heroic, tremulous juncture, when man felt himself almost an angel, on the verge of doing deeds that outwardly look so fiendish; oh strange rapture of the coming battle." And he goes on in the draft of his story: "We know something of that time now; we that have seen the muster of the village soldiery on meeting-house greens, and at railway stations; and heard the drum and fife, and seen the farewells, seen the familiar faces that we hardly knew, now that we felt them to be heroes, breathed higher breath for their sakes, felt our eyes moistened; thanked them in our souls for teaching us that nature is yet capable of heroic moments; felt how a great impulse lifts up a people, and every cold, passionless, indifferent spectator, lifts him up into religion, and makes him join in what becomes an act of devotion, a prayer, when perhaps he but half approves."

From a grand historical instance, in Concord at the colony's moment of rupture with England, the story of *Septimius Felton* sets out; but as always with Hawthorne, the history that matters will be internal, psychological rather than sociological: "the history of a mind bewildered in certain errors." For one of the three friends discovered conversing together in early spring sunlight is obsessed with the idea of defeating death, of living forever. Thoreau years earlier had told Hawthorne—as much as the present owner knew of his homestead's history—about a previous tenant at the Wayside who thought that he would never die; and around that hint the author was forming his new romance. This, too, he would struggle with extensively enough so that 448 pages of a different volume, 13, in the *Centenary Edition* of Hawthorne's works, are needed to contain the Septimius portions of the so-called "Elixir of Life Manuscripts." A man wants to live forever and comes upon the means to do so. To what purpose? Will the consequences be benevolent or otherwise?

And was all this scribbling but "trash and nonsense" anyway?—as he had described it to Bridge in mid-October. One thing was certain: no part of it would be ready to publish in the *Atlantic* any time soon; "for," the author wrote Fields peremptorily, "I don't mean to let you have the first chapters till I have written the final sentence of the story."

Much about these struggles of Hawthorne in wartime, in his sky parlor attempting to craft his romances, seems in its own way heroic. To be sure, the motivations to succeed up there were strong: he needed the money for his family, and he hoped that a completed novel would allow for a salubrious voyage back to England, back among friends where his health had thrived. So he kept at his labors as well as he could, filling foolscap through the fall and into winter despite the many distractions of the war, despite his lassitude, despite persisting dissatisfactions with the results of all his efforts.

Bridge wrote early in the new year 1862 urging his friend to come for a visit to Washington. There were reasons to stay where he was. "I am not very well," Hawthorne replied to the invitation, "being mentally and physically languid; but, I suppose, there is about an even chance that the trip and change of scene might supply the energy I lack. Also, I am pretending to write a book, and though I am nowise diligent about it, still each week finds it a little more advanced; and I am now at a point where I do not like to leave it entirely. Moreover, I ought not to spend money needlessly, in these hard times; for it is my opinion that the book-trade, and everybody connected with it, is bound to fall below zero, before this war, and the subsequent embarrassments, come to an end."

For such solid reasons as those Hawthorne should stay at home. Yet he was tempted, "greatly tempted by your invitation"—and, in the end, he went.

33

TOURING WITH TICKNOR

*A*gain his publisher Ticknor traveled with him. During an earlier spring, at the start of Franklin Pierce's presidency in 1853, those two had journeyed together to Washington as Hawthorne was preparing to assume his diplomatic post overseas. His consular duties in Liverpool were to have made the author and his family financially secure, but they had failed to do so. In midtenure, Congress had reduced the official compensation; additional remunerative fees had amounted to less than anticipated; the expenses of living in England had proved more than predicted; and a long sojourn in Italy afterward had exacted its costs as well. So here was the former consul, not rich at all, returning to Washington nine springs later during another presidency and again with William Ticknor, although this time for purposes quite different. This time, while watching his expenditures carefully, Hawthorne meant to get as close as he could to the Civil War, economizing all the while by staying with Commodore Horatio Bridge, friend since their Bowdoin days, and trusting that the change of scene would benefit an ailing author's health.

He and Ticknor took the train out of Boston on a cold clear Thursday morning, March 6, 1862. Whatever the calendar said, the day was still wintry; hills beyond the city were covered with snow, and ponds out the window frozen. Winter persisted through Worcester and Springfield and down into Connecticut; but in New York, where the author chose to linger a day or two, snow had given way to streets deep in mud and slush. New Jersey furnished further hints of a changing season, and by the time the travelers had reached Philadelphia over the weekend, the air had turned balmy. "We had met the Spring half-way, in her slow progress from the South; and if we kept onward at the same pace, and could get through the Rebel lines," Hawthorne wrote wistfully, in that era when seasons imposed sharper contrasts than now, "we should soon come to fresh grass, fruit-blossoms, green peas, strawberries, and all such delights of early summer."

Of the war, New York City had provided much talk but few signs: only some military goods in shop windows—"swords with gilded scabbards and trappings, epaulets, carabines, revolvers"—and at the station, on the train, the occasional officer returning from furlough. But from Philadelphia onward, soldiers were much in evidence. Between Baltimore and Washington guards stood at all the depots along the line; and between depots, on the hillsides, were clustered weather-beaten tents with smoke-blackened peaks bespeaking the stoves within. "At several commanding positions we saw fortifications, with the muzzles of cannon protruding from the ramparts, the slopes of which were made of the yellow earth of that region, and still unsodded." Until such inflamed times as these, as the author reflected, all the forts in America through a long era of peace had been grass-covered. Now, in addition to raw earth ramparts, wherever the train stopped this far south appeared throngs of soldiers, some entering the cars in hopes of finding up-to-date newspapers for accounts of the battle between the *Merrimack* and the *Monitor*, fought only the day before.

The travelers reached Washington at six in the evening, Monday, March 10, just too late to witness a grand spectacle that Ticknor, with one of his sons at the front, had been eager to see. That very day the Army of the Potomac, sixty thousand strong, had at last decamped from Washington and crossed the river headed for the Rebel fortifications at Manassas, close by Bull Run and the scene of the humiliating northern defeat nine months before. Nine long months had passed while the Union commander, the meticulous George B. McClellan, had been drilling and training his troops against so formidable a foe. At last the Federals had moved out, this very day bound the twenty miles south to wreak vengeance in the first major action in the East since the Bull Run disaster. And hardly were the troops gone before rumors began drifting back to Washington, soon after Hawthorne's arrival: "The vast preparation of men and warlike material," as he would recount the event, "the majestic patience and docility with which the people waited through those weary and dreary months,—the martial skill, courage, and caution with which our movement was ultimately made,—and, at last, the tremendous shock with which we were brought suddenly up against nothing at all!" For by then the Rebels had withdrawn from their Manassas fortifications to take up positions elsewhere, leaving behind no more than Quaker guns, wooden logs protruding to mock an overwary foe. "It was," Hawthorne would write in echo of the prevailing northern disgust, "as if General McClellan had thrust his sword into a gigantic enemy, and beholding him suddenly collapsed, had discovered to himself and the world that he had merely punctured an enormously swollen bladder."

During his visit, the author would get a glimpse of that Little Napoleon, young Major General McClellan, thirty-five years old, in his camp at Fairfax Seminary nearby. The general's headquarters, as Hawthorne described it, were located on a slight rise; and over a broad plain adjacent, a division of ten or twelve thousand men was mustering for review as the author and his group approached. "By-and-by we saw a pretty numerous troop of mounted officers, who were congregated on a distant part of the plain, and whom we finally ascertained to be the Commander-in-Chief's staff, with McClellan himself at their head. Our party managed to establish itself in a position conveniently close to the General, to whom, moreover, we had the honor of an introduction; and he bowed, on his horseback, with a good deal of dignity and martial courtesy."

Dignity had been the very ingredient lacking, earlier in the tour, during Hawthorne's encounter with President Abraham Lincoln, at the White House on March 13. That soon after their arrival, he and Ticknor had managed to attach themselves to a deputation from a Massachusetts whip factory bent upon presenting the president with a commemorative whip, handsomely encased. Faithful to their Thursday appointment, the deputation had appeared at the Executive Mansion punctually at nine o'clock, but not so the president. Mr. Lincoln had sent word that he was eating breakfast and would come down as soon as he could. "His appetite, we were glad to think, must have been a pretty fair one; for we waited about half an hour in one of his ante-chambers, and then were ushered into a reception-room, in one corner of which sat the Secretaries of War and of the Treasury"—Mr. Stanton and Governor Chase—"expecting, like ourselves, the termination of the Presidential breakfast." A couple of people in working garb added to the heterogeneity of the group, "mostly unknown to each other, and without any common sponsor, but all with an equal right to look our head-servant in the face." And it was that face precisely—that "very remarkable physiognomy," as Hawthorne denoted it—that the author had been particularly eager to behold.

"By and by there was a little stir on the staircase and in the passage-way, and in lounged a tall, loose-jointed figure, of an exaggerated Yankee port and demeanor, whom (as being about the homeliest man I ever saw, yet by no means repulsive or disagreeable) it was impossible not to recognize as Uncle Abe." Despite the man's Kentucky birth and western rearing, he appeared to Hawthorne, a veteran of seven years overseas, to be "the essential representative of all Yankees, and the veritable specimen, physically, of what the world seems determined to regard as our characteristic qualities." The reserved New Englander hardly knew what to make of this manifestation of a chief executive, after his close familiarity with that other, entirely proper presidential specimen General Franklin Pierce. As for Lincoln, "There is no describing his lengthy awkwardness, nor the uncouthness of his movement; and yet it seemed as if I had been in the habit of seeing him daily, and had shaken hands with him a thousand times in some village street." If forced to guess such a person's livelihood, this visitor would have supposed him to be a country schoolmaster. "He was dressed in a rusty black frock-coat and pantaloons, unbrushed, and worn so faithfully that the suit had adapted itself to the curves and angularities of his figure, and had grown to be an outer skin of the man. He had shabby slippers on his feet. His hair was black, still unmixed with gray, stiff, somewhat bushy, and had apparently been acquainted with neither brush nor comb that morning, after the disarrangement of the pillow." Looking more closely: "His complexion is dark and sallow, betokening, I fear, an insalubrious atmosphere around the White House; he has thick black eyebrows and an impending brow; his nose is large, and the lines about his mouth are very strongly defined"—as coarse a set of features, in short, as could be met with anywhere in America, so Hawthorne thought, yet redeemed withal by a countenance both serious and kindly, and "an expression of homely sagacity, that seems weighted with rich results of village experience." Indeed, "on the whole, I liked this sallow, queer, sagacious visage, with the homely human sympathies that warmed it; and, for my small share in the matter, would as lief have Uncle Abe for a ruler as any man whom it would have been practicable to put in his place."

On such a one the present deputation was duly bestowing its ivory-handled, ornamented whip, along with a hint as to the use to which the president might wish to put the instrument, in thrashing Rebels. But President Lincoln rose to the occasion of a small but delicate moment. Briefly he flourished the gift as though touching up a pair of horses, then diplomatically replied "that he accepted the whip as an emblem of peace, not punishment." Thus felicitously the interview ended, and "we retired out of the presence in high good-humor, only regretting that we could not have seen the President sit down and fold up his legs (which is said to be a most extraordinary spectacle), or have heard him tell one of those delectable stories for which he is so celebrated."

In what (to his surprise) turned out to be a monthlong stay in Washington, Hawthorne saw much else of interest. Gazing on the various public buildings, he judged them the equal of any in Europe, particularly the Capitol, with its new, elaborate dome, far more striking than the plain round Bulfinch dome that had topped the structure in Pierce's time. He ventured outside the city, traveling on one occasion with a party by rail as far as the site, at Harpers Ferry, of old John Brown's abortive raid to free slaves two years earlier. On the morning of this later, less ambitious venture, rain had started to fall, and all day long it poured. The village, when the sightseers finally reached it along the upper course of the Potomac, was discovered clinging forlornly to a steep hillside. A shabby brick church, one small shop with nothing for sale, the brick ruins of the United States armory: "The brightest sunshine could not have made the scene cheerful, nor have taken away the gloom from the dilapidated town." A corporal guided the party to the little building that old Brown had made his fortress and where he had been temporarily imprisoned after the marines under Colonel Robert E. Lee had stormed the place. "It is an old engine-house, rusty and shabby, like every other work of man's hands in this God-forsaken town," used now as a jail for Rebel prisoners, with whom Hawthorne and his party paused to exchange a not unfriendly word or two.

On another day, and in a different direction, the author with Ticknor, Bridge, and others ventured by sea the 150 miles to Fortress Monroe and Newport News. As at Harpers Ferry, the celebrated, budget-conscious author was traveling as an invited guest, thus spared the cost of the passage. When they arrived, the party found the bay before the fortress thronged with transports and ships of war all flying the Union flag—"'Old Glory,' as I hear it called these days." The visitors were welcomed aboard the flagship of the fleet, the forty-gun frigate *Minnesota*, and shown every part of the vessel. Yet with all her up-to-date improvements, the *Minnesota* and her like would never fight another battle. The reason lay nearby, "the strangest-looking craft I ever saw," as Hawthorne described it. "It was a platform of iron, so nearly on a level with the water that the swash of the waves broke over it, under the impulse of a very moderate breeze; and on this platform was raised a circular structure, likewise of iron"—the whole not like a vessel at all, rather like a machine, like a gigantic rat trap. "It was ugly, questionable, suspicious, evidently mischievous,—nay, I will allow myself to call it devilish; for this was the new war-fiend, destined, along with others of the same breed, to annihilate whole navies and batter down old supremacies. The wooden walls of Old England cease to exist and a whole history of naval renown reaches its period, now that the Moniter comes smoking into view; while the billows dash over what seems her deck, and storms bury even her turret in green water, as she burrows and snorts along."

Again, as with the *Minnesota*, Hawthorne's party was invited aboard this harbinger, the ironclad *Monitor,* and given a tour, surprised at the spaciousness of the quarters within. Much in his travels south surprised the author, while furnishing matter to ponder. ("There will be other battles," he was thinking of this present phenomenon, "but the Millennium is certainly approaching, because human strife is to be transferred from the heart and personality of man into cunning contrivances of machinery, which by-and-by will fight out our wars with only the clank and smash of iron.") So the effect of his venturing down from his sky parlor and away from his hillside had turned out to be in every way stimulating. After a month of sightseeing, Hawthorne would arrive back in Concord with his health invigorated and his spirits much improved.

Moreover, he had been keeping a notebook and meant to write up his impressions as an article for Fields's *Atlantic*. That should pay for the trip; and meanwhile, spring had come to Concord in the author's absence, and his family when he did get home were on hand to greet him ecstatically. On April 11, the day after his return, Sophia wrote of the household's being "in a state of full paean. Rose burst out into an original song last evening just as she was going to bed in the tune of 'John Brown' whose 'soul is marching on'—all in reference to Papa's going and returning from Washington. And I helped and sung too, and as we completed each verse, we both almost expired with laughter at our own fun. Just so crazy with joy are we."

Down the road from the Wayside all this while, on Main Street beyond the Milldam in Concord village, another household was enduring an attenuated sorrow. Ever since the first of the present year 1862, the Thoreau family had been tending their Henry in his mortal illness. He was forty-four.

In truth, the life that was ending seemed hardly to have amounted to much. During the course of it, Henry Thoreau had written a couple of books, the first of which he had himself paid to have published, obliged later to store the unsold bulk in the family attic. Ticknor & Fields had finally published the second book, after many rewritings. Describing the author's earlier, two-year retreat in the woods, *Walden* had fallen far short of commercial success. Besides those two works, this surveyor, handyman, and observer of nature had lectured some, written some essays, and kept manuscript journals aplenty, out of which on his sickbed he had lately been fashioning a few articles that would appear posthumously in the *Atlantic*. But townsfolk seemed less likely to remember Thoreau's writings than his contrariness and his idling ways. Julian Hawthorne would recall the man sourly enough, and Julian's sister Rose in maturity, when she thought of Thoreau, pictured first his enormous eyes, which had frightened her dreadfully as a child: "The unanswerable argument which he unwittingly made to soften my heart towards him was to fall desperately ill. During his long illness," she would recall, "my mother lent him our sweet old music-box, to which she had danced as it warbled at the Old Manse, in the first year of her marriage."

Mrs. Hawthorne understood their neighbor better than did Rose or Julian. The day after his passing—Thoreau finally died, of tuberculosis, on May 6, 1862, serenely at nine in the morning, his mother, sister, and aunt Louisa all close by—Sophia would write sadly, "On Friday Mr. Thoreau's funeral is to take place. He was Concord itself in one man—and his death makes a very large vacuum. I ought to be at his funeral for the sake of shewing my deep respect and value for him to others, though I could much better mourn him at home." She, her husband, and their children did attend the funeral. Hawthorne had admired Thoreau as a man "of thought and originality," and while living abroad he had taken pains to recommend *Walden* highly to his English friends. Both writers, in fact, had known what it was to spend time alone, if for their different reasons. "I suppose," Hawthorne's wife would record of Thoreau after his death, "he believed that beasts and reptiles, birds and fishes fulfilled their ends, and that man generally came short. So he respected the one and avoided the other."

Even so, despite the man's solitariness and cantankerousness in life, the church at his funeral was full. Alcott, a regular visitor at the sickbed through recent months, of course was there with his wife and daughters. As superintendent of the local schools, he had dismissed classes for the day, so that many schoolchildren were able to attend the services as well. Thoreau had always liked young people, and had thought very highly of Alcott: "He is perhaps the sanest man," he had said, "and has the fewest crotchets, of any I chance to know—the same yesterday and tomorrow." Of course such a friend was on hand to mourn Thoreau's passing. And Emerson was there and spoke at length. "The country knows not yet, or in the least part, how great a son it has lost," the eulogist remarked. It was a note that a few other prescient friends would strike, Alcott's daughter Louisa for one, then in her late twenties and hardly far forward yet with her career as an author. "Though he wasn't made much of while living," she wrote to a mutual acquaintance, "he was honored at his death"; and soon she would compose a poem, "Thoreau's Flute," which Mrs. Hawthorne was so taken with that she sent it to the Fieldses, urging them to publish it in the *Atlantic*. The poem did appear in those pages as an early specimen of the literary gifts of Louisa May Alcott. Meanwhile, that young woman felt sure that, despite the brevity of her friend's life, his days would bear fruit in time; "perhaps," she wrote, "we should know a closer relationship now than even while he lived."

A century would elapse before the truth of her insight came to be widely realized, a full century before the woodland idler had been elevated by slow degrees into the loftiest ranks of world literature.

34

WAR MATTERS

When Hawthorne had first come to know Thoreau two decades earlier, in 1842, he had invited Emerson's then handyman to dinner with him and his wife, newlyweds who had moved into the Manse the month before. After the dinner, the host had written bluntly in his journal that this new acquaintance, this Mr. Thorow, was "as ugly as sin, long-nosed, queer-mouthed." It was Hawthorne's invariable practice to observe closely and set down the truth as he saw it. But the truth was seldom simple. Thoreau's homeliness, he had gone on to say, was somehow "of an honest and agreeable fashion, and becomes him much better than beauty." Similarly President Lincoln, these twenty years later, appeared to the truth teller to be "about the homeliest man I ever saw, yet by no means repulsive or disagreeable." In fact, "I liked this sallow, queer, sagacious visage . . . and, for my small share in the matter, would as lief have Uncle Abe for a ruler as any man whom it would have been practicable to put in his place."

Returning home after meeting the president in the spring of 1862—the spring when Thoreau died—Hawthorne in the sky parlor set about composing an article for the *Atlantic* that would describe his recent trip to Washington. In the article, he tried hard to tell the truth, at a time of national crisis when truth was a commodity not always in demand. "Chiefly About War Matters" he called his essay, "by A Peaceable Man." After reading it, Fields of the *Atlantic* professed to like it hugely. "But," the editor went on with regret, "I am going to ask you to change some of it if you will." His colleague Ticknor had agreed, he said: the author should omit all references to "Uncle Abe." Call him "the President" through-out, and delete any mention of that gentleman's gawky uncouth-ness. "England is reading the Maga. now," Fields wrote, "& will gloat over the monkey figure of 'Uncle Abe' as he appears in yr. paper." The editor was speaking of course not personally, but pro-fessionally. Personally he found the piece a capital one—yet cer-tain parts about southerners further on should be changed as well. "Pray you ameliorate your description of the President, and change the other passages I have marked. . . . The whole article," he ended, "is piquant & tip top in all other respects."

Hawthorne would do it—he was, Fields later concurred, "the most good-natured and the most amenable man to advise I ever knew"—but he didn't care for the changes. The author wrote back that he had removed the entire Lincoln interview, since he felt unable to alter it satisfactorily. Cut it all out; but in doing so, the editor should know that he was deleting "the only part of the ar-ticle really worth publishing. Upon my honor, it seems to me to have a historical value—but let it go." The omission should be in-dicated with dashes and an explanatory note. As for the rest of what Fields had marked, Hawthorne had modified that part, so that "I cannot now conceive of any objection to it." But "What a terrible thing it is," he wrote after making the changes, "to try to let off a little bit of truth into this miserable humbug of a world!"

"Chiefly About War Matters" appeared in the *Atlantic* for July 1862. "There is no remoteness of life and thought," the article be-gins, "no hermetically sealed seclusion, except, possibly, that of the grave, into which the disturbing influences of this war do not pene-trate." Of course long ago the crisis had knocked at the author's cottage door "and compelled me," he goes on, "reluctantly, to sus-pend the contemplation of certain fantasies, to which, according to my harmless custom, I was endeavoring to give a sufficiently life-like aspect to admit of their figuring in a romance." At first it had seemed a pity that a writer, with no pretensions to being either soldier or statesman, "should be debarred from such unsubstan-tial business as I had contrived for myself, since nothing more genu-ine was to be substituted for it. But I magnanimously considered that there is a kind of treason in insulating one's self from the universal fear and sorrow, and thinking one's idle thoughts in the dread time of civil war." So, like others, this Peaceable Man had devoted hours to newspapers and the clicking telegraph, "until, after a great many months of such pastime, it grew so abominably irksome that I determined to look a little more closely at matters with my own eyes."

He had accordingly traveled to Washington and its vicinity, from which trip he had just returned. But the record of what a Peaceable Man had seen there would not always conform with conventional views, nor were all of his opinions about the war complacent ones. As a result, editorial notes occasionally intrude upon the account to vindicate a more orthodox viewpoint. When, for example, Hawthorne describes his visit to the Capitol and its impressive new dome as seen from outside, a note interrupts before any mention can be made of less impressive matter inside the building: *We omit several paragraphs here, in which the author speaks of some prominent Members of Congress with a freedom that seems to have been not unkindly meant, but might be liable to misconstruction. As he admits that he never listened to an important debate, we can hardly recognize his qualification to estimate these gentlemen, in their legislative and oratorical capacities.* " The article resumes in the Peaceable Man's voice: "We found one man, however, at the Capitol, who was satisfactorily adequate to the business which brought him thither"—"however" suggesting the *in*adequacy of statesmen alluded to in the paragraphs omitted. (Indeed, Hawthorne had written Fields from Washington of his disillusionment with the conduct of the war seen up close; "Things and men look better at a distance than close at hand.")

Again, the Peaceable Man is considering the attitude of southern citizens in the capital. It was not hard to imagine, he says, how unwelcome a southern army would be in a Massachusetts town; hence there seemed little to wonder about in noting the sullen glances so frequently cast on federal troops in Washington. Nor does he stop there. "It is a strange thing in human life," he goes on, developing a Hawthornean paradox, "that the greatest errors both of men and women often spring from their sweetest and most generous qualities"; thus many attractive, impulsive southern people will have joined the rebellion not through any burning love of the secessionist cause but for no better reason than that, forced to choose between conflicting loyalties to state and nation, they chose the one lying nearer the heart. "There never existed any other

Government against which treason was so easy, and could defend itself by such plausible arguments as against that of the United States." For, unlike in other countries, we here have two allegiances, of which for most people in that different era the one to the state would have felt much closer than any to a far-off federal entity. And thus hordes of decent nineteenth-century folk, loyal to their native states, had been converted into traitors, "who seem to themselves not merely innocent, but patriotic, and who die for a bad cause with as quiet a conscience as if it were the best"—all because this country is too vast "to be taken into one small human heart." So kill such of those as we must, the author concludes, but afterward bury them honorably in the native soil that they loved. The sentiment provokes a dry editorial comment: *We do not thoroughly comprehend the author's drift in the foregoing paragraph, but are inclined to think its tone reprehensible, and its tendency impolitic in the present stage of our national difficulties."*

The Peaceable Man was no doubt similarly impolitic in what he had to say about the Union's enemies whom he had encountered face to face. He had looked upon some twenty prisoners of war incarcerated in the dingy enginehouse at Harpers Ferry; and a pitiful vacant-eyed lot they had appeared, good-humored enough in their bumpkinlike way, and without "a trace of hostile feeling in the countenance, words, or manner of any prisoner there." True, nothing about those poor wretches resembled their sturdier and far more intelligent rural counterparts in New England; nor did such abject specimens seem to have "the remotest comprehension of what they had been fighting for, or how they had deserved to be shut up in that dreary hole." To the visitor's way of thinking, the best justification for the present war was that it might free such lowly southern peasants from a thraldom that rendered them scarcely a part of responsible humanity. Meanwhile, it appeared downright absurd that such brutelike creatures should regard the Union forces as their enemy, inasmuch as whatever might benefit them depended first of all on slavery's termination; "for thence would come the regeneration of a people,—the removal of a foul scurf that has overgrown their life, and keeps them in a state of disease and decrepitude, one of the chief symptoms of which is, that, the more they suffer and are debased, the more they imagine themselves strong and beautiful." The paradoxes, including one's apparent enemy being in fact one's friend, appeared to illustrate a lasting truth. "No human effort, on a grand scale, has ever yet resulted according to the purpose of its projectors. The advantages are always incidental. Man's accidents are God's purposes. We miss the good we sought, and do the good we little cared for." Which conclusion provokes yet another editorial response at the foot of the appropriate column: *"The author seems to imagine that he has compressed a great deal of meaning into these little, hard, dry pellets of aphoristic wisdom. We disagree with him. The counsels of wise and good men are often coincident with the purposes of Providence; and the present war promises to illustrate our remark."*

Yet it is the Peaceable Man's thoughts about John Brown that awaken the most indignant counterassertion. The glimpse of Brown's makeshift fortress at Harpers Ferry, turned into a jail for rebel prisoners, causes the author to utter an opinion widely held only south of the Mason-Dixon Line. "I shall not pretend to be an admirer of old John Brown," he admits to a readership who generally did admire that martyr's soul, which was marching on; "nor did I expect ever to shrink so unutterably from any apophthegm of a sage, whose happy lips have uttered a hundred golden sentences, as from that saying, (perhaps falsely attributed to so honored a source,)"— alluding to his neighbor Emerson, who had spoken thus two years earlier, around the time of Brown's hanging—"that the death of this blood-stained fanatic has 'made the Gallows as venerable as the Cross!'" On the contrary, the Peaceable Man asserts that "Nobody was ever more justly hanged. He won his martyrdom fairly, and took it firmly." More than that, "any common-sensible man, looking at the matter unsentimentally, must have felt a certain intellectual satisfaction in seeing him hanged, if it were only in requital of his preposterous miscalculation of possibilities"—to which outrageous opinion the editorial voice erupts in shocked dismay: *"Can it be a son of old Massachusetts who utters this abominable sentiment? For shame!"*

Julian Hawthorne's schoolmaster, Frank Sanborn, who had vigorously supported John Brown since meeting the abolitionist back in 1857, would soon be encountering Hawthorne's dismissive judgment of his hero in the *Atlantic,* as would some thirty thousand other northern and mostly Republican readers of the magazine, including many loyal villagers besides Sanborn in predominantly antislavery Concord, where Brown's daughters attended school and the old warrior himself had twice been welcomed. One such reader was Moncure Conway, a native Virginian who had earlier left plantation life to study at Harvard. There that enlightened young southerner, coming under Emerson's influence, was confirmed in his antislavery views. This short while later, Conway would encounter "Chiefly About War Matters" and be shocked to read at the foot of its printed columns the "terrible editorial comments" challenging assertions throughout the article. The young man happened at the time to be living in Concord, so he hurried with the magazine to Emerson's home, alarmed about the consequences of such editorial aspersions cast on their neighbor Mr. Hawthorne. "Emerson," according to Conway, "read the censorious notes and quietly said, 'Of course he wrote the footnotes himself.'"

He had. Even through the high emotions of wartime, Hawthorne had been able—as he always seemed able—to see both sides of a given issue. Accordingly, he had created his conventional editor to give voice to the contrasting viewpoint: the skeptic balanced by the prim loyalist. In acknowledgment of just this trait of her husband's—this double-visioned trait that had allowed him to compose his profound tales and novels—Sophia had written during his recent visit to Washington: "If it were not such a bore, I could wish thou mightest be President through this crisis, and show the world what can be done by using two eyes, and turning each thing upside down and inside out before judging and acting."

The image of Hawthorne as our wartime president must be left for a worshipful wife to embroider; doubtless the nation was better off with the president it had—whom, incidentally, Sophia at about this time was pronouncing to be no less than "a jewel. I like him very well," she wrote of Lincoln in July. "I think a man shows strength when he can be moderate at such a moment as this. Thou hadst better give my high regards to the President."

Just then, the president thus esteemed would have been struggling, among his many other cares, with the abundant complexities concerning slavery foisted upon him through the early months of 1862. Earlier, Hawthorne like other citizens had wondered what the war was being fought for: was it to hold the Union together? "If we pummel the South ever so hard, they will love us none the better for it." Yet President Lincoln would admit publicly of no doubt about our national purpose. Whatever the consequences of the bloody war in progress, the North's *purpose* in waging it was clear; and it had nothing to do with freeing slaves, or with lifting from the backs of such pitiful, scarcely human whites as Hawthorne had seen imprisoned in Harpers Ferry the degradations incident upon a foul, inhuman labor system. "If I could save the Union without freeing *any* slave I would do it," Lincoln would write the editor Horace Greeley this same summer; "and if I could save it by freeing *all* the slaves I would do it; and if I could do it by freeing some and leaving others alone I would also do that." The war, then, was being fought precisely to save the Union.

Yet the truth was more complicated. To win the war, the North needed to hold the border slave states, Kentucky and Missouri, which had not yet joined the Confederacy and were contiguous to the crucial Ohio and Mississippi Rivers. Declare the aim of the war to be the freeing of slaves, and those border states would go over to the Rebels. Hence, Lincoln's unambiguous assurances to Greeley in August 1862. He was fighting to preserve the Union—even if in the course of the preceding month he had already broached to two of his cabinet ministers, to Secretary of State Seward and Secretary of the Navy Welles, initial thoughts about issuing an emancipation proclamation, an executive order that would free all slaves in the states in rebellion.

The truth is complex. As social legislation, such a drastic move would be challenged in the courts and likely declared unconstitutional. But as a war measure, issued solely to defeat the Rebels, the executive decree could not be overruled. And it was true that without the labor of their slaves supporting the war effort, the Confederates were doomed. So free the slaves not for their own sake but to defeat the South, denying the rebellion a critical resource. Yet if the president up North should proclaim all slaves in rebel territory emancipated, horrendous bloodshed might well ensue, as those same slaves, freed, rose up in fury, slaughtering their oppressors. And if it didn't incite a bloodbath, at best the proclamation would set a vast army of freedmen trudging northward; and what was to be done with all those liberated bondsmen? With such societal questions, along with his weighty military ones, the president was currently contending. Lincoln could no more envisage blacks living peacefully alongside whites in the North than could most other Caucasians of his time, abolitionists included. Like almost everyone else, he regarded African Americans as naturally, irremediably separate from whites. What could be done, then, with all those liberated slaves, childlike, unskilled, scarcely educable? Put them in the army perhaps, in service positions behind the lines; or colonize them in foreign lands. Even this late Lincoln clung to colonization as the best solution. Yet whatever is done with them, an honest view will have to agree that, if any group stands to benefit from this war, "it will not be the present generation of negroes, the childhood of whose race is now gone forever, and who must henceforth fight a hard battle with the world, on very unequal terms."

Such a rigorous insight as that, from "Chiefly About War Matters," was hardly agreeable to northern opinion in 1862, in the midst of national turmoil. War breeds myth, with evil assuming external, identifiable form: the enemy is over there, wickedness made visible, as amid cheers and tears we, the good, accompany our boys marching heroically off to the village depot. About the actual war keep silent: the actual war that Rebecca Harding Davis was to describe with the clarity of vision of Hawthorne himself (whom she much admired)—"the filthy spewings of it; the political jobbery in Union and Confederate camps; the malignant personal hatreds wearing patriotic masks, and glutted by burning homes and outraged women; the chances in it, well improved on both sides, for brutish men to grow more brutish, and for honorable gentlemen to degenerate into thieves and sots." Such honesty of statement uttered in wartime offends a populace's vociferous patriotism. Davis set down her authentic observations about the actual Civil War only later; but Hawthorne's views were entered on the record at the time, and his views on slavery had been known generally for a decade, since the publication in 1852 of his *Life of Franklin Pierce*. He had been aware back then that his pronouncements on the national agony were costing him hundreds of friends, offended by an opinion that slavery's horrors should be left for Providence to deal with in its own time and way. In the decade since, enmity between North and South had only intensified, until now it had erupted in open warfare, making temporizing views all the more obnoxious. And now came this "extraordinary paper by Hawthorne in the Atlantic! It is pure intellect," wrote one reader uncomprehendingly, "without emotion, without sympathy, without principle . . . as unhuman and passionless as a disembodied intelligence."

It was more than that. "Chiefly About War Matters" is an artist's characteristic effort to render truth in its complexity. Evil, even in wartime, is not elsewhere, in southern homes and campgrounds. It lies, awaiting its moment, among the intricacies of every human heart. The author had implied as much in "Earth's Holocaust" twenty years before. Nor was it that he failed to thrill now with news of each northern triumph or grieve with every defeat. But the war was so horrible, its ends so obscure, its means so corrupting and drastic. On the very day after Hawthorne's departure from Washington to return home to Concord had come news of a federal victory in Tennessee, where Grant had met the rebel Albert S. Johnston in a two-day battle, but at a ghastly cost. Twenty-four thousand soldiers lay dead or had been wounded or were missing at Shiloh. *Shiloh* is Hebrew for "place of peace." One additional casualty on that ill-named battlefield was any hope that the war, which both sides had entered in full confidence of their possessing the right, would be short-lived.

35

FAMILY MATTERS

*I*f Hawthorne's views on the war offended his abolitionist relatives and neighbors in Concord and farther afield, his wife insisted that she cared not at all about other people's thoughts on
the matter. "Is that plain?" Sophia had written her sister Elizabeth
Peabody in early days of the war. "I do not care at all what any one
thinks of his opinions, as I wrote you plainly from England. He can
take care of himself very well." And, she had added, "I must say,
for it is the truth, that if you and all the world *thought* my husband proslavery, I should be perfectly indifferent. My only interest would be whether he truly were so or not." Of course he was
not; Hawthorne and his wife both deplored slavery. But the times
were such, in the summer of 1862 and on through a dark fall and
winter of Union defeats at Cedar Mountain, at the Second Battle
of Bull Run, at Fredericksburg, later at Chancellorsville, that nothing less than strident patriotism appeared to suffice.

"What gloomy times are these politically," Sophia wrote in the
summer, at the start of that long misfortune. "We suddenly seem
to have utterly collapsed and the South is rampant over us." And a
little later: "I think of Mrs. Holmes and of Mrs. Storer with such
deep sympathy that I have no spirits in these last days—and alas!
Mrs. Holmes and Mrs. Storer are but two of the thousands of
mothers, wives, sisters, who now hang suspended over an abyss of
sorrow. In all time was never such a war as this."

This whole year long she kept a pocket diary, so that by means
of Sophia's brief notations we may follow the Hawthornes in their
comings and goings throughout 1862. On May 9, for example: "Per-

fect south west day. Mr & Mrs Fields came to Mr Thoreau's funeral. They came first to see us and then dined and took tea at Mr
Emerson's. The funeral services were in the church. Mr Emerson
spoke. Mr Alcott read from his writings & Mr Reynolds read from
the bible & prayed. The body was in the vestibule covered with wild
flowers. We went to the grave. Thence my husband & I walked to
the Old Manse & monument." From such staccato entries stirs forth
one day in Concord in a vanished spring: May loveliness, reunion
with friends, the solemnity, the walk to the Manse, and sharp
memories awakened, of Thoreau in his twenties, of young hours
on the river in the *Pond Lily.*

Nationally the times were gloomy, but there were private joys
nonetheless. "Una's party took place to-night. Papa illuminated it
with his presence." That entry occurs exactly a month later, on
June 9, noting a delayed birthday party for Una, turned eighteen
in March, and for Rose, eleven in May. The rain had poured down,
yet the storm outdoors had only served within the Wayside to
heighten the pleasures of music and color and joy. "I only wish
you could have seen the groups of school girls—so pretty as they
all were with rosy cheeks and laughing eyes & lovely rich braided
hair and bouquets of brilliant flowers in their hands and boddices."
Much of the downstairs had been cleared of furniture to make room
for the five sets of dancers. Roses were everywhere. "Through the
pouring rain Mrs. Emerson sent a huge basket full; and Una put
on her gymnastic dress of short tunic and trowsers and gathered
herself—in the flood—two large baskets at Mr. Bull's & besides
there was a third which Mr. Bull (a rose fancier) sent afterwards
of white and pink moss-rose buds!"

Vases had been hired from the china shop, and the short-
stemmed roses were spread out on dishes. In the midst of the festivities, Hawthorne himself came down from his tower to see,
appearing, "in the gay throng, like a grand Olympian, descended
to a 'Paradise of children' in a golden age." Interestingly, Sophia
tells us that many of the young people had never so much as
glimpsed the shy author, "and were glad enough, and greatly surprised—and at the end, they tried to get up courage to go and bid
him good night." A guest was overheard saying, "Oh how I want to
shake hands with Mr. Hawthorne but I am afraid." Judge Hoar's
son chided the girl: "Oh don't be afraid—I am going to. It is proper

and he is not a bear. He will not bite." Thus Sam Hoar had stepped forth and performed the social courtesy, and others followed, "and they all got hospitable smiles," Sophia reported, "and seemed hugely pleased." In fact, everybody, she was certain, "had what the guests called 'a splendid time.'"

Other splendid times intervened despite the war. At Mr. Sanborn's academy, Julian was to recall later, "every week there was a school-dance, and, twice or thrice a year, a grand picnic, not to mention other jollifications; and in these Hawthorne's girls took part." Earlier, Julian and Rose had attended a masquerade ball, he as the Earl of Leicester, with Sophia diligently at work for days on elaborate costumes; and later, in this village long active in the anti-slavery cause, would take place an impressive fair to benefit black orphan children, for which Sophia and her offspring labored weeks to produce items to be auctioned off: hand-decorated Egyptian vases, a cologne bottle, Tennyson verses artfully illuminated. All the while, the Hawthorne young were surrounded by friends to fill out their teas and charades and skating parties, including the Alcott girls next door, Edward and Edith Emerson down the road, and the Mann cousins adjacent to Mr. Sanborn's school beyond the Milldam. Sophia for her part almost daily exchanged visits with her sister Mary Mann, whose frequent houseguest was their other sister, Elizabeth, out from her rooms on Winter Street in Boston.

Sophia's at-home day for receiving visitors was Wednesday. For the rest, her pocket diary indicates hours abundantly filled, despite headaches that came and went. Outside was always work to be undertaken in the field across the road: weeding, harvesting the vegetable garden, gathering strawberries. On the hillside behind the house, trees called for pruning. Neighbor Alcott enjoyed helping with that. Indeed, the kindly Alcott made something of a pest of himself, and his wife had a way of inducing Sophia's headaches by relaying dire war news—General Banks's army completely destroyed!—that proved after an anguished day or two to have been quite false. She is "the most apalling sensationalist," Sophia groaned. "She frightens me out of my five senses from time to time with telling me one thing and another—and suggesting blood-curdling possibilities." To reciprocate the Alcotts' frequent visits (on one such Rose recalled that Mr. Alcott had read her parents a long poem of his own composition from which they never recovered: "it was like a moonlit expanse, quiet, somnolent, cool, and flat as a month of prairies"), Hawthorne on a single occasion did venture over to the Orchard House, a neighborly gesture awkwardly executed, as from the start he sat forward shifting in his chair in the parlor and watching the clock, obviously anxious to be gone.

Meanwhile, inside its walls as out, Mrs. Hawthorne's home was filled with nineteenth-century chores that pressed on every waking hour: the tending to both daughters' lessons, the sewing that never ended, the nursing of children in sickness, the recruiting of help, the perpetual dusting. Celia the maid "cleared the old attic to-day," Sophia noted of one instance. "I found my dear hanging astral, that lighted my husband in his study at the Old Manse." She must have gazed on that recovered object long and lovingly. Twenty years before, under the yellow light of this same lamp, newlyweds in quiet evenings had relished reading the whole of *Paradise Lost* aloud, the two of them surpassingly happy reading together all the plays of Shakespeare.

Even now, at the close of these present days, Hawthorne would come off his hill or down from his tower for evenings of reading to the family in proper Victorian fashion: novels of Scott, Victor Hugo, Charles Reade, Wilkie Collins. But mostly he appears to have remained alone, scarcely partaking of the downstairs activity that Sophia's pocket diary records. The author's life was returning to the isolation of his young manhood, solitary years after Bowdoin under the eaves on Herbert Street now replicated in days in his tower or alone pacing the path on the crest of his hill overlooking Concord.

Up there he found much to brood about. He had tried and failed to write his English romances. "The Present, the Immediate, the Actual, has proved too potent for me. It takes away not only my scanty faculty, but even my desire for imaginative composition." He was, moreover, worried like so many others about the war. The news was disheartening. "Lowell had a nephew (whom he dearly loved) killed, and another wounded, in one battle; and a son of Holmes received two wounds in the same. The shots strike all round us." Nor was Hawthorne's commitment to the northern cause sufficiently unclouded as to provide much comfort to his spirits. In the months ahead he would even write his English friend Henry Bright of having been accused publicly "of treasonable sympathies," although, he protested, "I sympathize with nobody and approve of nothing; and if I have any wishes on the subject, it is that New England might be a nation by itself." Still, momentous matters such as these could not be dispensed with so readily. In other moods Hawthorne, against an Englishman's ignorance and with a patriot's vigor, defended the federal course: "if we had not fought"—this also to Bright, who was deploring the war—"the North would unquestionably have lost its Capital, and its identity as a nation, and would have had to make an entirely new position for itself, and probably three or four separate positions. If we stop fighting at this juncture, we give up Maryland, Virginia, Kentucky, Missouri, all of which are fully capable of being made free-soil, and will be so in a few years, if we possess them, but not in a hundred years, if we lose them. We give up our Capital too, and retire under a load of disgrace, which, to my mind, would make national extinction the lesser evil of the two." Few in the war party could have put the matter better; and was an intelligent Englishman really incapable of seeing the justice of that point of view?

The war was much on Hawthorne's mind through these trying months, and his abandoned romances would have been a further source of distress, if only for the monetary implications; for always the author fretted about his family's welfare. "I expect to outlive my means and die in the alms-house," he confessed to Ticknor in days ahead. "Julian's college-expenses"—his son would be entering Harvard next year—"will count up tremendously. I must try to get my poor blunted pen at work again pretty soon." And yet he was not well. The brief lift of his spirits after the spring trip to Washington had hardly lasted into the fall. Hawthorne was not well, and in his dejection he would confess to Emerson, who had joined him in pacing the hilltop behind the Wayside: "*This path is the only remembrance of me that will remain.*"

All of his writing, he had come to feel, would perish and be forgotten. Push on with it, then, only for bread; it became harder and harder to pick up his pen. Occasionally, although less and less often, Hawthorne did forsake his solitude and venture into Boston to attend the Saturday Club. "The dinner-table," in any case, "has lost much of its charm since poor Longfellow has ceased to be there, for though he was not brilliant, and never said anything that seemed particularly worth hearing, he was so genial that every guest felt his heart the lighter and the warmer for him." As for the other members, all were breathing patriot fire; Emerson himself, so Hawthorne reported, was "as merciless as a steel bayonet." Longfellow, too: although the poet continued avoiding the club, Hawthorne did run into him at Ticknor's bookstore, "looking well in health and more cheerful than when I saw him last. . . . I asked him what he felt about the war, and find him immitigable for its continuance." Like the others, Longfellow was ready to fight the war to the death. "To say the truth," Hawthorne adds, "any man must be sensible of the impossibility of ever bringing it to an end except by completest victory or direst defeat."

Yet the initial exhilaration when the troops had mustered and bands had played had given way to grim resolution. At Ticknor's store, Hawthorne observed his friend closely. Longfellow's "hair and beard have grown almost entirely white, and he looks more picturesque and more like a poet than in his happy and untroubled days. There is a severe and stern expression in his eyes, by which you perceive that his sorrow has thrust him aside from mankind and keeps him aloof from sympathy."

It sounds rather like a character out of a Hawthorne tale, like Goodman Brown or Reuben Bourne grown old. It sounds like Hawthorne himself, whose sorrows were thrusting him aside from mankind, holding him aloof from the sympathy of the townspeople among whom he lived. Always beneath his hilltop Concord lay in view, outwardly scarcely changed from the village to which he had brought his bride. A bit larger now—the federal census of 1860 records its population at 2,246, including 14 free males and females of color—a bit more heterogeneous, with Irish at work on farms, in homes, and at Damon's mill. But the principal business remained farming; and lawyers, county officers, and newspapermen still lingered in the village for the district courts, even if the upper courts had moved on to Cambridge and Lowell. And if the railroad had altered the rhythm of lives to something quite different from what it had been when the Hawthornes had first arrived here, the antislavery spirit of the place hardly varied from those earlier times, only more intense now with the war raging and townsmen dying in the Union cause.

And still, Hawthorne's skeptical temperament would have held him back from participating with any zest in communal bellicosities.

Throughout his life he had held back, observing—all the more determinedly in these days when evil had been so confidently located at a distance well south of here. Besides, he was ill. By year's end, in early December 1862, Sophia was expressing her distress forthrightly. Having the day before been to Boston shopping, she entered a notation in her pocket diary for Thursday, December 4: "Fine day—but my husband quite ill. I feel all bruised with my Boston walking & standing from 10 to 3. Every thing seems sad when he is ill. I sewed all day for Rose to get her ready for her visit to E. Cambridge." But her husband was too weak even to climb the steep stairs to his sky parlor. He must work on the ground floor. To her other daughter, Una, absent in Beverly visiting Aunt Ebe, Sophia was obliged to write a week later: "Papa has not a good appetite, and eats no dinners except a little potato. But he is trying to write, and locks himself into the library and pulls down the blinds."

36

OUR OLD HOME

L ocked in there, he was working neither on tales nor on romances. During these months Hawthorne had fallen into writing nonfiction, in part because he did it easily and very well, in part because he had an accumulation of observed material to draw upon, in part because Fields was paying him to make the effort. "Chiefly About War Matters" had furnished one specimen of such fare, a factual essay "of the photographic kind" describing his recent trip to Washington. That had appeared in the *Atlantic* for July 1862; and three months later appeared another essay from "A Peaceable Man" that opened with a headnote: "MY DEAR EDITOR,—You can hardly have expected to hear from me again, (unless by invitation to the field of honor,) after those cruel and terrible notes upon my harmless article in the July Number. How could you find it in your heart . . . to treat an old friend and liege contributor in that unheard-of way?" Despite such ill-treatment (recalling that the sly Hawthorne had himself written the anonymous footnotes), the author would demonstrate his sweetness and placability by sending along another article, describing a Warwickshire town, "in which, I trust, you will find nothing to strike out."

"Leamington Spa" constitutes one of what would total twelve sketches developed from the notebooks that the author had kept during his residence of four years and longer in England. Ten of the essays appeared in the *Atlantic* between October 1860 and August 1863. Together, all twelve at Fields's urging would be made into a book, called *Our Old Home,* published in September 1863.

It is a wonderful book. A Hawthorne devotee describes it as charming, delectable: "The execution is singularly perfect and ripe; of all his productions it seems to be the best written"—which is saying a great deal of a writer whose style is all but unfailingly superb. "At every step there is something one would like to quote—something excellently well said." Moreover, "the lightness, the fineness, the felicity of characterisation and description," that same critic goes on to specify, "belong to a man who has the advantage of feeling delicately." Indeed, the traits of sensitive perception beautifully expressed strike the modern reader of *Our Old Home* every bit as freshly and forcefully as they did that earlier discriminating critic Henry James.

But Hawthorne's picture of mid-nineteenth-century England exhibits virtues beyond style and sensitivity. Three might be mentioned. *Our Old Home* is filled with humor, all the more remarkable considering the taxing circumstances under which the essays were written, in the midst of worries about health, about family, about income, about the war. From the opening pages to the very last, the book stirs pleasure with its frequent, delightful wit—from an early description of furnishings in the consul's office, including a "fierce and terrible bust of General Jackson, pilloried in a military collar which rose above his ears," set alongside a New Testament for administering oaths, "greasy, I fear, with a daily succession of perjured kisses," right down to the final image of the tables at a London civic banquet roaring and thundering applause before falling silent, while the painfully shy consul rises dutifully to his feet, never having stood in a posture "of greater dignity and peril" and thus deeming it "sage policy here to close these Sketches, leaving myself still erect in so heroic an attitude," his speech left unrecorded.

In addition to abundant humor, *Our Old Home* gratifies us with its vigorous patriotism. Invariably treated with personal kindness during his years in England, Hawthorne was nevertheless annoyed by English condescension to his native land; and his irritation grew intense with British sympathy for the Confederate side in the war raging as he wrote his essays. Yet let the English disdain their former colonies as they will. For all their stupidity in driving those colonies to independence, what seems folly may have been fate "or, rather, the Providence of God, who has doubtless a work for us to do, in which the massive materiality of the English character would have been too ponderous a dead-weight upon our progress." For America is the land of progress. Of course Hawthorne's views of England are ambivalent: much that he saw there he loved. And yet this England, our old home, is stultified by class, by tradition, by the stale burden of history that lies upon it. America, land where victims of despotism find refuge, is by contrast full of opportunity and change; and "let us," Hawthorne urges, "welcome whatever change may come—change of place, social customs, political institutions, modes of worship—trusting that, if all present things shall vanish, they will but make room for better systems, and for a higher type of man to clothe his life in them, and to fling them off in turn."

That progressive quality was what most notably distinguished these exuberant United States, the world's best hope, from hidebound England: the freedom here for humanity to grow unpinched by feudal strictures, unencumbered by the titles and scepters of privilege—in a unique experiment over which the Civil War, all the more lamentably, was just then posing its threat to end humanity's single greatest attempt at governance.

But if the patriotism in *Our Old Home* gratifies as its humor delights, the book's compassion all the while reveals Hawthorne's deepest nature. His heart was large enough, he said, to take in only New England; and indeed that heart did seem (along with those of most of his countrymen) unable fully to embrace the sufferings of slaves in the South—as we perhaps, with our own geographic limitations, may fall short in empathy for, say, the suffering Tutsis. But in face-to-face encounters Hawthorne's feelings were acute, as disclosed in his essay "Outside Glimpses of English Poverty," in which he writes movingly of the destitute on the streets of Liverpool. The rich may seek to build lives that wall out the poor, but "How superficial are the niceties of such as pretend to keep aloof! Let the whole world be cleansed, or not a man or woman of us all can be clean." The author returns feelingly to nature's forgotten ones, to the wretched discards in life, the pitiful children. "Unless these slime-clogged nostrils can be made capable of inhaling celestial air," he writes, "I know not how the purest and most intellectual of us can reasonably expect ever to taste a breath of it. The whole question of eternity is staked there. If a single one of those helpless little ones be lost, the world is lost!"

Hawthorne's own Rosebud, his youngest child, eleven years old as he was writing "Outside Glimpses of English Poverty," would grow up to devote much of her adult life to tending destitute, shunned, and disfigured cancer patients, a commitment of such selflessness that by early in the twenty-first century she had become the subject of canonization proceedings in the Roman Catholic Church, to which religion she had converted in 1891. "My own convictions about human duties towards human suffering were clearly formed in youth," this Mother Teresa–like figure would explain, "by countless passages read in the works of Nathaniel Hawthorne." More specifically, Rose Hawthorne Lathrop cited, as the source of a life truly saintly, a passage from this same sketch by her father in *Our Old Home,* on the English poor.

By the summer of 1863, with the collection of essays being made ready for publication at Ticknor & Fields, its author had settled on the dedication. The choice seemed obvious. Hawthorne would dedicate *Our Old Home* to the man who had made his family's stay in England possible; the book could not have been written without the kind offices of Franklin Pierce. But it was more than that. After Pierce had left the presidency, he and his wife (Mrs. Pierce bearing locks of hair from poor Bennie and her other precious dead) had set off on extended travels around Europe, in the course of which they had visited Rome just at the time of Una's near-fatal illness. For a month in the spring of 1859 the Pierces had lingered, and the general had called upon his distressed friend every day, sometimes twice a day. "I shall always love him," wrote Hawthorne gratefully, "the better for the recollection of these dark days." Indeed, Sophia reported that General Pierce had come to comfort them in Rome as often as three times daily: "I think I owe to him, almost, my husband's life. He was divinely tender, sweet, sympathizing, and helpful."

Of course *Our Old Home* should be dedicated to Franklin Pierce. Yet these several years later, in the midst of civil war, the former president had become a figure ever more widely despised in the North. Nor had the politician's behavior of late been circumspect; too much seemed at stake for that. His friend Hawthorne might settle for—indeed, welcome—an America disembarrassed of the slave states, shrunk to a more morally defensible size; but for

Pierce the Union was sacrosanct. And the appalling Lincoln's suspension of habeas corpus in the course of this avoidable war, his arresting of obstreperous legislators, his promulgation of policies defying the Constitution and alienating the South beyond all chance of reconciliation struck the Union-loving Pierce as naked despotism. Forthwith he made his views on such incendiary matters known, despite cries of treason each time he did so.

"It is the opinion of wiser men than I am in the 'Trade,'" the editor Fields wrote Hawthorne on July 15, 1863, "that the Dedn. & Letter to F.P. will ruin the sale of yr. book. I tell you this, in season that you may act upon it if you elect so to do. A large dealer told me he shd. not order any copies, much as his customers admired yr. writings, and a very knowing literary friend of yours says it will be, in these days, the most damaging move you could possibly make. So, this is what I feared. Now you must decide whether you will risk the sale of 'Our old Home' by putting a friend's name to it."

With Hawthorne in such grim days—husband, father of three, ill, and his resources dwindling—money was always an issue; he had taken to writing essays because romances had proved no longer within his ability and because Fields was offering a hundred dollars each, sometimes more, for his sketches of English life. On his editor's latest advice he pondered deeply, smoked cigars over it, and considered how far he could go in acceding to it. "I find," he concluded, "that it would be a piece of poltroonery in me to withdraw either the dedication or the dedicatory letter." If, Hawthorne went on to explain to Fields, Pierce was so thoroughly hated that the very mention of his name would be enough to sink the volume, "there is so much the more need that an old friend should stand by him. I cannot, merely on account of pecuniary profit or literary reputation, go back from what I have deliberately felt and thought it right to do; and if I were to tear out the dedication, I should never look at the volume again without remorse and shame. As for the literary public, it must accept my book precisely as I think fit to give it, or let it alone."

The dedication reads: "To FRANKLIN PIERCE, AS A SLIGHT MEMORIAL OF A COLLEGE FRIENDSHIP, PROLONGED THROUGH MANHOOD, AND RETAINING ALL ITS VITALITY IN OUR AUTUMNAL YEARS, This Volume is Inscribed By NATHANIEL HAWTHORNE." It is dated: "THE

WAYSIDE, July 2d, 1863." On that same day, of course unknown to the author, General Longstreet's Confederate forces were attempting to break the federal line in the vale between Little and Big Round Tops, at sunset succeeding in holding the field at Devil's Den and the Peach Orchard on the outskirts of Gettysburg. Two days later, at high noon in Capitol Square in Concord, New Hampshire, former president Pierce was rising as principal speaker at a large Democratic rally, where he set about once more attacking President Lincoln for his "unconstitutional, arbitrary, irresponsible" use of power. This war, cried Pierce, was "fearful, fruitless, fatal"; with the president's policies of "emancipation, devastation, subjugation, it cannot fail to be fruitless in everything except the harvest of woe which it is ripening for what was once the peerless Republic." Hardly was the orator done, in the course of a five-hour rally with his lifelong friend Nathaniel Hawthorne seated beside him on the platform, when the first telegraphic word of a great Union victory at Gettysburg began passing through the audience, negating any such counsels of anguish as had just been uttered, on a day of triumph that would, moreover, see Vicksburg in the West yield to Grant's relentless encirclement, a success that—in the words of the current president, whom Pierce had condemned as of "limited ability and narrow intelligence"—permitted the Father of Waters to flow henceforth unvexed to the sea.

That Independence Day in Concord, New Hampshire—Hawthorne's fifty-ninth birthday—would strip off the last tattered remnants of Franklin Pierce's political respectability. The author might better have chosen a different occasion on which to pay his intimate friend a visit. Nor was the timing improved when his publishers released *Our Old Home* two months later. In mid-September a new volume by Nathaniel Hawthorne, dedicated to Franklin Pierce, was appearing in the bookstores. And on the same day, September 19, Union troops downriver from Vicksburg having discovered in their searches through Jefferson Davis's Mississippi plantation an earlier letter from Pierce to his former secretary of war, the *New York Evening Post* saw fit to publish the shocking document. Sophia first insisted that the letter was a forgery. But it wasn't. Pierce back in January 1860, when war fever raged in the final days of Buchanan's administration, had written his former cabinet secretary and mainstay of his own administration that he, Jefferson Davis, should be

the statesman leading the Union through its present peril. Moreover, Pierce had recklessly suggested that Americans still valued
the Constitution and its sanction of slavery in numbers sufficient
that, if secession did come, fighting would occur not south of the
Mason-Dixon Line but in towns and cities north of it.

That sounded close to encouraging rebellion. Elizabeth Peabody
had pleaded with her brother-in-law to reconsider his dedication,
but Hawthorne was not to be dissuaded. It "can hurt nobody but
my book and myself," he had responded firmly. "I know that it will
do that, but am content to take the consequences, rather than go
back from what I deliberately judge it right to do." As for Peabody's
fears that he would be thought to disapprove of the war, the author admitted to feeling "that the war will only effect by a horrible
convulsion the self-same end that might and would have been
brought about by a gradual and peaceful change," even while he
insisted that no one wished for northern victories more fervently
than he did. Meantime, Harriet Beecher Stowe was writing Fields
in November: "Do tell me, if our friend Hawthorne praises that arch
traitor Pierce in his preface . . .—what! Patronise such a traitor to
our faces!—I can scarce believe it"; even as Emerson, the mild-
mannered Emerson, was indignantly cutting the noxious dedication out of his copy of *Our Old Home*.

37

LAST TRAVELS

*T*hose were Hawthorne's sincere beliefs by then: that the war had been preventable, that its ends would have been achieved providentially in any case, but that once entered upon it must be fought through at whatever terrible cost. He was not alone in thinking thus; yet his was by no means a popular position, certainly not in abolitionist Concord when coupled with friendship for Franklin Pierce. Indeed, only a very few nationwide—among them Annie Fields, Gail Hamilton, and Jessie Frémont—would venture to express admiration for the Pierce dedication as a tribute to a lifelong affection. For many northerners, its opening pages alone had rendered Hawthorne's splendid new book little more than a scandalous notoriety.

The notoriety of *Our Old Home,* in fact, did lead finally to respectable sales, although not enough to ease the author's worries about his family's financial well-being. For years Hawthorne had dreaded—"if I die," as he said, "or am brain-stricken"—the prospect of leaving his loved ones beggars. He had taken the post in Liverpool precisely to obviate such a possibility, which a decade later, in the fall of 1863, in failing health and with his editor dismal about sales for this latest work, seemed all the more likely to follow upon a lifetime of writing. "I wonder how people manage to live economically. I seem to spend little or nothing, and yet it will get very far beyond the second thousand, for the present year." The author must try once more to compose a romance, make yet a third attempt at that most remunerative of the very few options lying before him. Accordingly in the fall he set to work, again gathering together his familiar, recalcitrant materials: the bloody footstep, the American claimant, the elixir promising youth and eternal life, and beside a Salem graveyard a house within which an ancient apothecary moves about with the care that the preternaturally aging Hawthorne himself must display now in shuffling through the Wayside.

"I do not find Mr. Hawthorne very well," Sophia wrote, "—or rather he is in too negative a state to resist damp and the world's jar. I am afraid that Concord is not the best place for him. . . . He takes cold every day (All this is sacred confidence) and has a slight feverishness with it." Her letters to Annie Fields and others during this autumn of 1863 and into the winter make for doleful reading: her husband's negativism, the ill-defined lassitude that has over-taken him, his daylong reclinings on the couch or sittings huddled before the fire, the occasional outbursts of alarming symptoms— nosebleeds, faintness, stomach upsets. "Tomorrow," nevertheless, "he says he shall go into his study and write, for he wishes to be ready with his Chapter for Mr. Fields."

That first chapter of *The Dolliver Romance* was delivered to the editor on a solemn occasion. On December 4, 1863, Fields's wife Annie was noting in her diary that Hawthorne had "passed the night with us; he came to town to attend the funeral of Mrs. Franklin Pierce. He seemed ill and more nervous than usual. He brought the first part of a story which he says he shall never finish. J. T. F. says it is very fine, yet sad." And two days later, on Sunday, De-cember 6, "Mr. Hawthorne returned to us. He had found Gen-eral Pierce overwhelmed with sadness at the death of his wife and greatly needing his companionship, therefore he accompanied him the whole distance to Concord, N. H." As for his chapter, the author "thought so little of the work himself as to make it impos-sible for him to continue until Mr. Fields had read it and expressed his sincere admiration. . . . This has given him better heart to go on with it."

Yet he could not go on. By February of the new year 1864 Hawthorne had given up the effort entirely. Fields had already announced the new romance in the *Atlantic*. "If you choose," the author wrote disconsolately, "you may publish the first chapter as an insulated fragment, and charge me with $100 of overpayment. I cannot finish it, unless a great change comes over me; and if I make too great an effort to do so, it will be my death; not that I should care much for that, if I could fight the battle through and win it, thus ending a life of much smoulder and scanty fire in a blaze of glory."

But he no longer had the strength for such a battle. Ticknor in this sad crisis made a suggestion. Perhaps the publisher and his dear friend Hawthorne should undertake another trip southward, in the direction of spring and balmy weather. Sophia seized gratefully on the plan. Those same two companions had traveled to Washington in 1853 and again in March only a couple of years ago, and during both trips Hawthorne had seemed to thrive. Moreover, his publisher had accompanied the family on the voyage to Liverpool; in no one's hands could Mrs. Hawthorne entrust her husband with more confidence. Thus on Sunday, March 27, she was accompanying her patient on the train into Boston, to deliver him into the care of Fields and Ticknor on Washington Street.

Fields took the ailing author home to Charles Street across the Common. "I was greatly shocked," the editor wrote later, "at his invalid appearance, and he seemed quite deaf. The light in his eye was beautiful as ever, but his limbs seemed shrunken and his usual stalwart vigor utterly gone." In the evening Hawthorne appeared a bit brighter, and at breakfast next morning "he spoke of his kind neighbors in Concord, and said Alcott was one of the most excellent men he had ever known. 'It is impossible to quarrel with him, for he would take all your harsh words like a saint.'" But for all that morningtime effort at cheer, Fields's guest was "evidently broken and dispirited about his health."

He and Ticknor set out nonetheless, traveling by rail as far as New York City and putting up at the Astor House. The publisher wrote faithfully back to Mrs. Hawthorne. Her husband, she could thus report, "was very tired the last forty miles—but had then retired with hope for a good night. This was Tuesday night 29th. Mr. Ticknor said he would write again the next day. How kind he is. I bless GOD for him at this serious juncture."

But the travelers had strayed into dreadful weather. In New York storms raged, so that their stay had to be extended, the two in their hotel while the rain poured down. March 30: "A worse than a northeaster has prevailed here to-day. I have hardly been out of the house; Mr. Hawthorne not at all. But we have been very comfortable within. He needed the rest, and the storm seemed to say that both he and I must be content." April 3, against expectations still imprisoned at the Astor House: "12 o'clock noon. Your letter has just arrived. The mail was very late. I handed it to our 'King,' and he read it with interest and delight, and is now writing an answer. I assure you he is much improved, but he is yet very weak. The weather has been as bad as possible. . . . I cannot now say," wrote Ticknor, "where we go next, as I shall be governed by what shall seem best for him. We shall float along for a while. Probably to Philadelphia tomorrow. I will keep you posted."

But the storm's relentlessness detained them where they were. Meanwhile, on the 5th, Sophia in Concord was writing to Hawthorne's friend Bridge, who had seen the notice in the *Atlantic* revoking the promise of a new romance. No, that was no author's dodge; "Mr. Hawthorne," she explained, "has really been very ill all winter, and not well, by any means, for a much longer time; not ill in bed, but miserable on a lounge or sofa, and quite unable to write a word, even a letter, and lately unable to read. I have felt the wildest anxiety about him." No spirits, no appetite, very little sleep. "The state of our country has, doubtless, excessively depressed him. His busy imagination has woven all sorts of sad tissues. You know his indomitable, untamable spirit of independence and self-help. This makes the condition of an invalid peculiarly irksome to him."

Yet by now the invalid was all but utterly dependent on others, on the good Mr. Ticknor for one, who before the 7th had at last got his charge as far as Philadelphia. That was a Thursday. "You will be glad to hear," the publisher assured Mrs. Hawthorne from the Continental Hotel there, "that your patient continues to improve. He wrote to you yesterday. He reads the papers, and sleeps well. The first real sunshine since we left Boston came upon us yesterday." Indeed, this morning Hawthorne had said at breakfast "he was feeling much better. Now, I don't know exactly what next, but, if he is inclined, I shall go to Baltimore. But it is not best to lay out a business plan, or feel that so much must be done in a given time. I tell him we will float along and see what 'turns up.' One thing is certain, it has been altogether too stormy to try the sea."

The two had talked earlier of sailing into the cheering warmth of the Gulf Stream and on to Havana; but actually, the wretched weather had got even Ticknor, hearty at fifty-three, down these last few days—bestowed on him a cough and, he confessed, a case of the blues. By the weekend the publisher had taken to bed himself, and Hawthorne in the adjoining room had been driven to send news, Saturday evening, back to Fields. "I am sorry to say," the invalid wrote with an effort we cannot know, "that our friend Ticknor is suffering under a severe billious attack since yesterday morning. He had previously seemed uncomfortable, but not to an alarming degree. He sent for a physician during the night." The doctor had pronounced the case one of bilious colic, and as bad as he had seen. Whereupon, wrote Hawthorne, he had belabored his patient "with pills and powders of various kinds, and then proceeded to cup, and poultice, and blister, according to the ancient rule of that tribe of savages. The consequence is, that poor Ticknor is already very much reduced, while the disease flourishes as luxuriantly as if that were the Doctor's sole object."

That same Saturday evening, April 9, these two New England visitors were to have been guests at the elegant private residence of a Mr. Joseph Harrison, a local friend of literature. Neither of course appeared, nor was an explanation offered. The next morning, another guest at the reception, a magazine publisher named Childs, took it upon himself to call at the Continental Hotel. This George William Childs went directly to Hawthorne's room and knocked. Receiving no answer, he opened the door. The author was pacing the carpet in a daze. "Hawthorne, how are you? Where is Ticknor?" A mumbled response spoke of their having taken him away. "What do you mean?" cried Childs. "I can't understand you." "Well"—the voice sounded bewildered—"it is too bad, he my best friend on whom I depended, coming here for my benefit, to please me." Presuming that illness was clouding the author's mind, Childs hurried down to the hotel office and asked the clerk, Mr. Duffy, what was the matter.

He was told that Mr. Ticknor had died that morning. The publisher's body was already at the undertaker's. The shocked Childs returned to Hawthorne in his room and begged him to be calm; he would look after him. Ticknor's eldest son was sent for. A telegram was dispatched to Fields. Accounts, however, of those hours and days in the confusion that followed disagree on several points. Arrangements were made to embalm the body; and according to Childs, Hawthorne lingered in Philadelphia a few days under his care, before Bishop Howe accompanied him back to Boston. Neither Fields for his part, nor Julian Hawthorne, nor Mrs. Hawthorne at the time or later, nor for that matter the unpublished recollections of Howe himself mention Childs or the bishop in this connection, an odd omission if those reputable gentlemen had in fact so significantly aided Hawthorne at a moment of deepest distress. Julian in his biography writes of his father's having to "carry out arrangements, among strangers, and when weighed down not only by physical weakness, but by heavy grief for loss of his friend. A more untoward event—one more fatal in its consequences upon him—could scarcely have occurred." According to his son, it was Hawthorne who telegraphed the dreadful news home, who arranged for the body to be prepared for transportation in care of Ticknor's son, and who then set out, presumably alone, on the "melancholy and grievous journey" to return to Boston.

In any event, he made his way somehow to Charles Street, to the home of his friends the Fieldses. They found the stricken author nervous, excited, and uncharacteristically talkative. Providing him with what comfort they could, they got him off as soon as possible on his way home to Concord.

Sophia had been lying down on a couch at the Wayside, "feeling quite indisposed." She heard outside the sound of a step on the piazza; it was her husband, not at all expected that day. Having found no carriage at the depot, Hawthorne had walked the long distance across the village, an effort that had left him covered in sweat. "I was frightened out of all knowledge of myself," Sophia wrote, "—so haggard, so white, so deeply scored with pain and fatigue was the face—so much more ill he looked than I ever saw him before." Terrified, she led her husband inside, where he could at last give way to his feelings, especially about those final, dreadful hours alone with "most excellent, kind Mr. Ticknor. It relieved him somewhat to break down as he spoke of that scene and of Howard Ticknor. Did he tell you? But he was so weak and weary he could not sit up much—and lay on the couch nearly all the time in a kind of uneasy somnolency not wishing to be read to even— not able to attend or fix his thoughts at all."

It had been a ghastly mistake, Hawthorne was murmuring; he, not Ticknor, should have died. Sophia was frantic; she hardly knew what to do. Her husband remained distraught in the days ahead.

He could not rest, could not walk ten minutes without needing to sit down, and thus was unable to get sufficient fresh air. "And his horror of Hotels," she reported, "and Rail cars is immense, and human beings beset him in cities."

In such dire circumstances General Pierce extended his skilled help, that widower who had tenderly nursed an invalid wife through so many years. His was the kindest of offers shaped into an admirable plan. He and Hawthorne would ride up into New Hampshire together. "I think," wrote Sophia, clutching at hope, "the serene jog trot in a private carriage into country places, by trout streams and old farm houses—away from care and news, will be very restorative. The boy-associations with the General will refresh him. They will fish and muse and rest and saunter upon horses' feet and be in the air all the time in fine weather."

And all the time, for all her gratitude, a grieving wife was struggling to understand the perplexities of her beloved husband's predicament. "He is indeed *very* weak," she wrote desperately to Annie Fields. "I hardly know what takes away his strength."

38

RELEASE

*H*awthorne's illness remained undiagnosed in his lifetime. Because of an aversion that the treatment of poor Ticknor at the last had intensified, the author steadfastly refused to allow doctors to attend him. Nevertheless, Dr. Oliver Wendell Holmes did find occasion socially, at Mrs. Hawthorne's entreaty, to look his friend over in a casual way; according to that physician, Hawthorne was suffering from "'boring pain,' distension, difficult digestion, with great wasting of flesh and strength." Sophia had spoken repeatedly of her husband's weight loss and of his increasing feebleness: "It almost deprives me of my wits to see him growing weaker with no aid. He seems quite bilious—and has a restlessness that is infinite." Pierce also, on their forthcoming trip together, would observe the patient's excessive restlessness, "whether in bed or up"— as well as his general helplessness, his difficulty in walking and in using his hands. Such symptoms, along with others on record, have encouraged later professional opinion to identify gastrointestinal cancer as the disease afflicting a body in such marked decline.

In his debility, whatever its cause, the author left Concord a final time on May 11. A few days earlier, Julian, now enrolled at Harvard, had come over from Cambridge for an hour's visit with his family. He had found his father sitting in the bedroom upstairs; "my mother and my two sisters were there also. It was a pleasant morning in early May." The boy came bearing some collegiate request, which Hawthorne granted. The visit ended. Julian bade his family good-bye and, at the door, paused. His father "was standing at the foot of the bed, leaning against it, and looking at me with a smile. He had on his old dark coat; his hair was almost wholly white, and he was very pale. But the expression of his face was full of beautiful kindness,—the gladness of having given his son a pleasure, and perhaps something more, that I did not then know of. His aspect at that moment, and the sunshine in the little room, are vivid in my memory. I never saw my father again."

Once more Sophia would accompany her husband to Boston; and from there, with Pierce, he set out northward by train, doubtless knowing he was dying and choosing to do so in a way that spared his family's witnessing the prolongation. In *Blithedale* he had written, "How many men, I wonder, does one meet with, in a lifetime, whom he would choose for his death-bed companions!" Now two companions since youth were venturing by rail to Andover, then on to Concord, New Hampshire, where, after a delay for weather, they set out in the general's carriage behind two horses and traveled slowly through Franklin, through Laconia, on to the center of the state, to the village of Plymouth, which they reached at six on Wednesday evening, the 18th. There they put up at the local inn, the Pemigewasset House.

For the Union cause, this same spring day was ending in the midst of discouraging times. After Gettysburg and Vicksburg, the North's battlefield successes had proven infrequent; the South was fighting grimly on. And ever since Shiloh the casualties had been monstrous: twenty-six thousand at Antietam, eighteen thousand at Fredericksburg, thirty thousand at Chancellorsville, more than forty-three thousand at Gettysburg. The slaughter had continued: at Chickamauga, in the Wilderness, at Spotsylvania. "I propose," Grant had written ten days ago, "to fight it out on this line if it takes all summer." But would the North tolerate the gore-smeared struggle that long? Let the erring sisters go. And could Lincoln's administration even win reelection in the fall to pursue the war? Privately, the president himself would soon be answering that question in the negative.

Meanwhile the bloodletting appeared unstanchable on this evening of May 18 as, far off in Plymouth, New Hampshire, Hawthorne after a daylong carriage ride was taking a bit of toast and tea and retiring early. Pierce would occupy the room adjoining, with the door between the two rooms left ajar.

But how would Sophia—who only a month before had written: "He is my world and all the business of it"—how would that adoring wife survive such a loss? And would Hawthorne's family be beggared, as he had feared, and what would become of the children? Rose, we have seen, would end her days ministering to impoverished, disfigured victims of incurable cancer, a life of veritable saintliness after the early death of her only child and the end, through death before the century turned, of an unhappy marriage to a brilliant alcoholic. She herself would live until 1926. Her brother Julian would live longer, into the 1930s, his Harvard years having petered out without his graduating, his professional life filled with scribbling that produced some twenty novels along with much else, his private life providing through two marriages an abundance of progeny, and his old age besmirched by a yearlong prison term served in the federal penitentiary at Atlanta for financial irregularities involving a Canadian mining enterprise (of which transgression the convict unflaggingly asserted his innocence). Una, the beautiful infant grown into fragile adulthood, would live only to her early thirties, engaged twice but never married, a most handsome, arresting woman, tall, red-haired like her sister, and fated to suffer at least one further nervous breakdown in her brief lifetime. At her mother's death, in a London suburb in 1871 (six years before her own, at thirty-three), it would be Una—the rebellious Una—who would hover at her side, clutching Sophia's delicate hand.

By the time of Mrs. Hawthorne's death, her husband's demise had slipped seven years into the past: that evening at the Pemigewasset House that had turned into the dark, small hours of the following morning, May 19, 1864. Through those hours Pierce had left his light on, his bed hardly six feet from Hawthorne's in the other room. The general could see that his friend slept soundly, manifesting none of the restlessness of earlier evenings; he was grateful for that. Hawthorne lay on his side facing the door, a hand under his cheek, his eyes closed. Pierce dozed off. Later a barking dog woke him; it was still dark, and to his surprise Hawthorne had not moved. The general rose, took the few steps into the other room, and touched his friend, so peacefully at rest that the bedclothes had not been disturbed. In Sophia's words: "He fell asleep softly, and waked in the heavenly world, without a sound or a struggle, and without the pain of bidding us farewell. No one needed to close his eyes, for he closed them himself. He was very grand and beautiful as he lay there, they told me."

The body reached Concord on Saturday, the 21st, and was taken to the Unitarian church. By then Julian had met with General Pierce in Boston and learned the details of his father's last hours (the childless Pierce would thereafter act as surrogate father to Hawthorne's son, furnishing Julian with counsel and financial support until the former president's own death five years later). Telegrams had been sent to Fields and to Emerson. "My sister came to tell me," Sophia wrote afterward. "I would not believe it. I only said 'No no no—It is not so—do not tell me so.'" And Una had said: "Oh Mamma, Papa has gone." The family assembled at the Wayside. The church was filling with flowers, Hawthorne's favorite lilies of the valley: "In every window was a tall vase—All along the galleries were rows of vases and the pulpit was covered, and crosses made of white flowers were hung on each side." Their fragrance was everywhere.

The funeral occurred on Monday, the 23rd, on a glorious spring day with fruit trees abloom all over the village. Some of the most notable figures in American literary culture attended, among them Emerson, Longfellow, E. P. Whipple, Lowell, Alcott, and Dr. Holmes, as well as Agassiz, Judge Hoar, and the attorney George Hillard; Hillard would serve as executor. At the funeral General Pierce sat with the family. In front of the pulpit was the coffin, on which was laid the single manuscript chapter of Hawthorne's last romance, as well as two wreaths, of tea roses and orange blossoms, and of apple blossoms from the orchard at the Old Manse. James Freeman Clarke, who twenty-two years earlier had married Nathaniel Hawthorne and Sophia Peabody in the front parlor at 13 West Street, Boston, delivered the eulogy. "God placed him here," the Reverend Mr. Clarke said, "to glorify New England life and pour over it the poetical beauty which was in his heart." And he went on: "I know of no other thinker or writer who had so much sympathy with the dark shadow, that shadow which the theologian calls sin, as our friend. He seemed to be the friend of all sinners, in his writings."

Those writings the author himself had at the end judged more ephemeral than the path that his tread had worn along the hillcrest behind the Wayside. He had summed them up dismissively as much smolder and scanty fire, without even the final glory of a last romance that he had hoped would be his best. And maybe Hawthorne had died in good time. The Civil War would end by forging a nation unlike any in which this regionalist had felt at home: an industrial nation, corporate, continental, pounded out of the huge wealth of land and textiles and railroads. In the war's aftermath, southern chivalry and all the airy romance of Sir Walter Scott would be discredited; and realism, so foreign to Hawthorne's own literary method, would reign triumphant through long decades ahead.

Alcott lamented the fair presences that one by one were fading from sight: "Thoreau, once the central figure in our landscape, has disappeared from it, and Hawthorne no longer traverses his hill-top near my house," so often seen up there "screened behind the shrubbery and disappearing like a hare into the bush when surprised." Hawthorne, wrote Alcott in his odd, memorable way, has gone "where he is now surpriseless by us." And Emerson would record in his journal, "Yesterday, May 23, we buried Hawthorne in Sleepy Hollow, to a pomp of sunshine and verdure, and gentle winds. . . . I thought there was a tragic element in the event, that might be more fully rendered,—in the painful solitude of the man, which, I suppose, could not longer be endured, & he died of it." To the grieving widow Concord's sage would write, perhaps rather too candidly, "I have had my own pain in the loss of your husband. He was always a mine of hope to me, and I promised myself a rich future in achieving at some day, when we should both be less engaged to tyrannical studies and habitudes, an unreserved intercourse with him. I thought I could well wait his time and mine for what was so well worth waiting. And as he always appeared to me superior to his own performances, I counted this yet untold force an insurance of a long life."

Hawthorne's life had ended, instead, at fifty-nine. But "superior to his own performances": would Sophia have welcomed Emerson's implicit denigration of her husband's achievement here at the last? It is a fact—with the solemn procession having left the church to ascend to the new cemetery at Sleepy Hollow, to a hillock there that Hawthorne in life had particularly favored, where beside the new-dug grave the Reverend Mr. Clarke will offer a final prayer—it will be a fact that the writings of Nathaniel Hawthorne (unlike so many of his contemporaries and near contemporaries, unlike Irving or Cooper or Bryant, unlike Melville and Thoreau, unlike Longfellow and all the other trinomial Brahmin poets) will, from that vernal moment to this, never suffer an eclipse of fame. Hawthorne at his death, whatever he or Emerson might think of his achievement, was admired as among the very greatest of America's literary figures; and in our own time, as for every intervening generation, he has retained that lofty standing. Indeed, his work speaks to us in the twenty-first century with perhaps a special pertinence. His life's solitude gave birth to creations that provide an alienated age with meanings even richer than the more communal Victorians would have extracted from them, and his flights of imagination may appeal with particular savor to those among us who have learned to taste the wonders of magical realism. Assuredly the depth of Hawthorne's psychological penetration and his understanding of evil and loneliness provide resonances so insistent in post-Freudian days that we may well marvel how our more innocent forebears—before world wars, before genocides—were able to appreciate this profound and subtle stylist adequately.

Sophia after the funeral would live only for her children. Friends noted, however, the remarkable composure with which she accepted her loss. Her faith had proved formidable. "When I see," she wrote immediately afterward, "that I deserved nothing and that my Father gave me the richest destiny for so many years of Time— to which Eternity is to be added, I am struck dumb with an ecstasy of gratitude, and let go my mortal hold with an awful submission, and without a murmur." To Annie Fields she would write mystically of standing on the shores of a sapphire sea, opaline waves lapping gently at her feet and sweeping gently over golden sands. "My darling has gone over that Sapphire sea, and these grand soft waves are messages from his Eternal Rest."

Soon enough she would follow after him, but for now she was living for the children. And in the months and years ahead Sophia found as occupation a task of particular attractiveness. The massive notebooks that her husband had kept through much of his life—the American notebooks, the English notebooks, the French and Italian notebooks—she settled down to prepare for publication. Not only did that happy labor provide needed income for her family; it also allowed her to revisit a treasured past in her husband's company. "It is a vast pleasure to pore over his books in this way," she wrote Horatio Bridge in November 1865. "I seem to be with him in all his walks and observations. Such faithful, loving notes of all he saw never were put on paper before. Nothing human is considered by him too mean to ponder over. No bird, nor leaf, nor tint of earth or sky is left unnoticed. He is a crystal medium of all the sounds and shows of things, and he reverently lets everything be as it is, and never intermeddles, nor embellishes, nor detracts. . . . It is only the great masters in any art," she concludes, "who trust to truth."

Indeed those same notebooks would appear to constitute another of Hawthorne's superlative achievements. In addition to the tales, the novels, the rich nonfiction of *Our Old Home*, there remains from his life's work this huge repository of nineteenth-century observation and insight. For all her exuberance, Sophia hardly exaggerates its merit, as a single random specimen must suffice to corroborate.

"To sit down," a living consciousness had written on a certain Saturday in the fullness of life, twenty years before his death, "in a solitary place (or a busy and bustling one, if you please) and await such little events as may happen, or observe such noticeable points as the eyes fall upon around you. For instance, I sat down to-day— July 27th, 1844, at about ten o'clock in the forenoon—in Sleepy Hollow, a shallow space scooped out among the woods." Just turned forty, Hawthorne was then living with his wife and four-month-old daughter at the Manse. Before him in his present solitude was this geologic opening, "pretty nearly circular, or oval, and two or three hundred yards—perhaps four or five hundred—in diameter." A decade and more would pass before the concavity was made into the town cemetery. For now, nearby were surrounding woods, and a cornfield, and a pathway that knotted oaks overshadowed. Hawthorne would take note of it all: the twigs and decayed leaves on the pathway, the bird chirpings overhead, the "cheerful, sunny hum of the flies . . . so gladsome that you pardon them their intrusiveness and impertinence." In fact, at this instant a fly was "intent upon alighting on my nose. In a room, now—in a human habitation—I could find in my conscience to put him to death; but here we have intruded upon his own domain, which he holds in common with all other children of earth and air—and we have no right to slay him on his own ground."

But there was so much more to see in one quiet interlude, an inexhaustible panorama: last year's acorn cups strewn about, suggesting table services at fairy banquets, oak balls that kittens love to play with on the carpet, mosses. "And how strange is the gradual process with which we detect objects that are right before the eyes; here now are whortleberries, ripe and black, growing actually within reach of my hand, yet unseen till this moment. Were we to sit here all day, a week, a month, and doubtless a lifetime, objects would thus still be presenting themselves as new, though there would seem to be no reason why we should not have detected them all at the first moment." The shadow of a bird flits across a patch of sunlight on the ground. The blue sky, the fragrance of white pine, a breeze sighing with hardly imaginable gentleness, a red squirrel shrilly chirruping—and suddenly a mosquito, about which instinct prevails over "all the nonsense of sentiment; we crush him at once, and there is his grim and grisly corpse, the ugliest object in nature." Then comes the striking of the village clock, and a cow bell tinkling, and the whistle of a locomotive, telling its story of "busy men, citizens, from the hot street."

Yet look even closer at hand. Mushrooms. A colony of anthills. Like some malevolent giant, the observer dribbles grains of sand over the entrance of an ant dwelling. "And, behold, here comes one of the inhabitants, who has been abroad upon some public or private business, or perhaps to enjoy a fantastic walk—and cannot any longer find his own door. What surprise, what hurry, what confusion of mind, are expressed in all his movements! How inexplicable to him must be the agency that has effected this mischief. The incident will probably be long remembered in the annals of the ant-colony, and be talked of in the winter days, when they are making merry over their hoarded provisions."

All of Hawthorne's wonderful achievement would seem to be here in microcosm: the sharp observation, the freshness of insight, the recognition of truth's complexity, the incipient compassion, the wit, the stylistic charm, the story forming that involves dark fate. Yet, he concludes, "how narrow, scanty, and meagre, is this record of observation, compared with the immensity that was to be observed, within the bounds which I prescribed to myself. How shallow and scanty a stream of thought, too,—of distinct and expressed thought—compared with the broad tide of dim emotions, ideas, associations, which were flowing through the haunted regions of imagination, intellect, and sentiment, sometimes excited by what was around me, sometimes with no perceptible connection with them. When we see how little we can express, it is a wonder that any man ever takes up a pen a second time."

To our benefit, this man, Nathaniel Hawthorne, did take up his pen again and wrote *The Scarlet Letter,* wrote *The House of the Seven Gables,* here having used it to record a single Concord day, now long dead, that the wonder of his art keeps miraculously alive.

NOTES

The frequently cited *Centenary Edition of the Works of Nathaniel Hawthorne* is here identifed as C, followed by volume and page numbers separated by a colon; thus, C15:637 refers to volume 15, page 637. Citations from Hawthorne's fiction are from the more accessible Library of America editions, identified as *Novels* and as *Tales and Sketches*. Other abbreviated citations are expanded in the Works Cited section (pp. 325–30).

Page

1 WEDDING IN BOSTON

3 "sensibility to feminine influence": Hawthorne, *The House of the Seven Gables*, in *Novels*, 473.

4 "that barrel of old Madeira": J. Hawthorne, *Hawthorne and Wife*, 1: 144. Details of the bet are in Bridge, *Recollections*, 47–48. In Bowdoin usage, Cilley's "chum" meant roommate.

5 "a carriage will call for you": C15:637.

5 "Sarah and the cook Bridget": Sophia Hawthorne's diary, 8/10/42; quoted at C15:639 n. Cornelia is Cornelia Park, another Boston friend.

5 "It seemed miraculous": Quoted in Mellow, *Hawthorne*, 197.

6 "as happy as people can be": C15:639 (7/10/42).

8 "your kiss would sanctify me": C15:339 (8/23/39).

8 "the ethereal dainties": C8:316 (8/5/42).

2 THE MANSE AND HISTORIC CONCORD

9 "wrinkles and gray hairs": C8:383 (4/26/43). When the Hawthornes lived there, the Ripley place was known as the Parsonage. After the author's departure from Concord, the publication of *Mosses from an Old Manse* affixed to the house the name that, oversimplifying, I use here throughout.

9 "universally respected and loved": Jarvis, "Ripley," 8:121.

9 "a description of our house": C8:323 (8/8/42).

11 "six myles of land square": Keyes, 570 (from the Act of Incorporation, 9/2/1635).

12 "a resolute and warlike spirit": Emerson, *Complete Works*, 11:68.

12 "alarmed by the ringing of ye Bell": W. Emerson, *Diaries*, 71.

13 Hoar's address: "Concord Monument," [Concord] *Yeoman Gazette*, 6/8/37: Typescript copy in Concord Free Public Library Special Collections.

13 "Breakfast with General Washington": W. Emerson, *Diaries*, 77.

14 "My dear, strive for Patience": W. Emerson, *Diaries*, 115 (9/23/1776).

3 AN END TO SOLITUDE

17 Hawthorne's injury: Elizabeth Manning Hawthorne to J. T. Fields, 12/70; Stewart, "Recollections," 319. On the Mannings, see Pearson, "Hawthorne and the Mannings."

17 Hawthorne's class standing: Bridge, *Recollections*, 33.

18 "what pursuit in life I was best fit for": J. Hawthorne, *Hawthorne and Wife*, 1:96.

18 "How proud you would feel": C15:139 (3/13/21).

18 "Our Native Writers": the text of Longfellow's address is in Higginson, *Longfellow*, 30–36.

19 "my destiny decided." J. Hawthorne, *Hawthorne and Wife*, 1:96.

19 "my 'twice-told' tediousness": C15:249 (3/7/37).

20 "I have made a captive of myself": C15:251 (6/4/37).

20 "utterly unlike every one else": Elizabeth Hawthorne to J. T. Fields, 12/26/70. Stewart, "Recollections," 325. Hawthorne's own account of the family's domestic isolation—taking meals separately behind locked doors and the like—is given, as his sister-in-law recalled it years later, in Pearson, "Elizabeth Peabody on Hawthorne," 266–67.

20 superior feelings of the Hawthornes: Lathrop, *Memories*, 6.

21 "'A writer of story-books!'": Hawthorne, *The Scarlet Letter*, in *Novels*, 127.

21 "grow like vegetables": To George Hillard, 7/16/41; C15:550.

21 Hawthorne's notebooks: Citations from C8:24, 23, 29–30, 229.

22 "You are . . . a puzzle to me": From George Hillard, after publication of *The Scarlet Letter* (1850); Lathrop, *Memories*, 121–22.

22 "without making . . . the slightest impression": Hawthorne, "Preface," *Twice-Told Tales*, in *Tales and Sketches*, 1150.

23 "lionize in a small way": J. Hawthorne, *Hawthorne and Wife*, 1:98.

23 "he did not realize how intently": Pearson, "Elizabeth Peabody on Hawthorne," 265.

23 "a seclusion . . . as deep as my own": C15:494 (10/4/40).

24 Hawthorne's love letters: C15:291, 511 (1/13/41), 357 (10/23/39), 495 (10/4/40).

25 "looking like the angel of the Apocalypse": To Mary Foote, 7/5/42; Lathrop, *Memories*, 49.

25 "Her interest has been very great": Lathrop, *Memories*, 49 (7/5/42).

4 CONCORD IN THE FORTIES

26 "sovereign power over everybody": Pearson, "Elizabeth Peabody on Hawthorne," 273.

27 "translucent with lovely expressions." J. Hawthorne, *Hawthorne and Wife*, 1:49.

27 "a great deal of quiet beauty": C8:321–22 (8/7/42).

27 Concord in the 1840s. The description draws principally on Keyes, "Concord," Jarvis, *Reminiscences*, Fischer, *Concord*, and Gross, "Transcendentalism," passim.

28 "a strip of sky": C8:321 (8/7/42).

29 "Blood, Flint, Willard, Meriam": Emerson, *Complete Works*, 11:30, 84–85.

30 "the invincible men of old": Emerson, *Complete Works*, 11:76.

31 "ignorant, low lived, unambitious": Horace Hosmer's opinion, as quoted in Gross, "Transcendentalism," 372; Thoreau, *Walden*, 329.

32 "put on an aspect of welcome": C8:322.

5 VISITORS AT THE MANSE

33 "confiding love of so rare a being": J. Hawthorne, *Hawthorne and Wife*, 1:251.

33 Description of Hawthorne: Fields, *Yesterdays*, 42; J. Hawthorne, *Hawthorne and Wife*, 1:120–21, 460; Lathrop, *Memories*, 200; Pearson, "Elizabeth Peabody on Hawthorne," 264–65; Turner, *Hawthorne*, 402.

34 he listened "devouringly": Pearson, "Elizabeth Peabody on Hawthorne," 266.

34 "a dozen of the villagers": Curtis, "Hawthorne," 45.

34 "always more at ease alone": J. Hawthorne, *Hawthorne and Wife*, 1:327.

34 "His vocation is to observe": To Mary Peabody, 10/9/42; quoted in Hurst, "Chief Employ," 46.

35 "Words with him are worlds": To Mrs. Peabody, 9/3/43; quoted in Hurst, "Chief Employ," 47.

35 "as happy as people can be": C15:639 (7/10/42).

36 "do not put it off so long": C15:641 (8/2/42).

36 "a man with a wife and a household": C8:334 ff (8/15/42).

37 "melancholy shadow of a man": To Sophia Hawthorne, 8/26/43; C15:700.

37 "the people had got into church": C8:335. On the ghost stories with the Hillards, see also Hawthorne, "The Old Manse," in *Tales and Sketches,* 1135.

39 "The stage for Concord": C15:643 (8/15/42).

6 MARGARET FULLER AND HENRY THOREAU

40 "the view is so peaceful": Myerson, "Fuller," 324–25 (8/20/42).

40 "'she came in so beautifully'": Sophia to Mrs. Peabody, 8/22/42; quoted in Gordan, "Hawthorne," 203.

41 "joy and superabundant life": *Memoirs Ossoli,* 1:203.

41 "The house within I like": Myerson, "Fuller," 325 (8/20/42).

42 "the power of so magnetizing others": *Memoirs Ossoli,* 1:65.

42 "never wished to leave this earth": Myerson, "Fuller," 324–25 (8/20/42).

43 "matters of high and low philosophy": C8:340 (8/22/42).

43 "What a happy, happy day": Myerson, "Fuller," 325 (8/21/42).

43 "Mr. Thorow dined with us": C8:353–54.

44 "no occupation . . . that suits him": To Epes Sargent, 10/21/42; C15:656.

44 "a sort of Indian life": C8:324 (9/1/42).

45 "My life, my life—": Thoreau, *Journal,* 1:371 (3/11/42). On John Thoreau's death, Robinson, *"Warrington,"* 12.

45 "keen and delicate observer of nature": C8:354 (9/1/42).

45 "I dined with the Hawthornes": Myerson, "Fuller," 339.

46 "I felt embarrassed": Myerson, "Fuller," 331.

46 "a thorough talk with Lidian": Myerson, "Fuller," 340.

7 HAWTHORNE AND EMERSON TOGETHER

47 "about 20 miles": Emerson, *Journals,* 8:273, 275.

49 "it is a sacred emblem": Emerson, *Nature,* in *Essays and Lectures,* 29.

49 "there was no inside to it": Emerson, *Journals,* 7:21 (6/38).

49 "a very pleasing fact": Porte, *Emerson Journals,* 288 (9/42).

49 "He seems to fascinate Mr. Emerson": J. Hawthorne, *Hawthorne and Wife,* 1:271.

50 "listen to Mr Emerson more worthily": C15:380 (12/2/39).

50 "everlasting rejecter": C8:357 (9/2/42).

50 "so simple, so without pretension": Hawthorne, "The Old Manse," in *Tales and Sketches,* 1146.

50 "faculty of seeing in the dark": James, *Hawthorne,* 394.

50 "no other world can show us": Hawthorne, "The Hall of Fantasy," in *Tales and Sketches,* 743–44.

51 "my father's name & history": Emerson, *Journals,* 8:273.

53 "as a model farm": Emerson, *Journals,* 8:274.

53 "passionless security": Hawthorne, "The Canterbury Pilgrims," in *Tales and Sketches,* 165.

53 "faded from my memory": C8:362 (10/10/42).
53 "like a day of July": Emerson, *Journals*, 8:274–75.
53 "I never had a home before": C8:362 (10/10/42).

8 FIRST FALL AT THE MANSE

54 "drip-drip-dripping": C8:348 (8/28/42).
54 "all gloom is but a dream": C8:351 (8/30/42).
55 "few purer and more harmless": C8:329 (8/10/42).
55 "figuring dithyrambic dances": Lathrop, *Memories*, 52–53.
56 "If you like skating": C15:664.
57 "my whole soul burns . . . for it": To his father, 12/5/24. S. Longfellow, *Life*, 1:53.
57 "speak anything but English": Quoted in Arvin, *Longfellow*, 28.
57 "Why do I travel?": Thompson, *Young Longfellow*, 234 (7/20/36).
58 "a young man after all": Wagenknecht, *Mrs. Longfellow*, 32 (7/31/36).
59 "He is a strange owl": To George Washington Greene, 10/22/38; Longfellow, *Letters*, 2:107.
59 "grand fellow": Quoted in Arvin, *Longfellow*, 53.
59 "expression even in that": Thompson, *Young Longfellow*, 258.
59 "The lady says she *will not!*": To George Washington Greene, 7/23/39; Longfellow, *Letters*, 2:159–60.
59 "Thou foolish woman": Quoted in Wagenknecht, *Longfellow Portrait*, 226 (5/18/38).
60 "deep unutterable eyes": Longfellow, *Hyperion*, in *Prose Works*, 2:164, 160.
60 "Some praise, and others condemn": To his father, 9/1/39; Longfellow, *Letters*, 2:168.
60 Longfellow would never write poetry again. "My poetic career is finished. Since I left America I have hardly put two lines together." Longfellow to his sister Elizabeth, 3/29; S. Longfellow, *Life* 1:168. The heavy demands of Longfellow's teaching are indicated in Hatfield, 65–66, and passim.
60 "the most unpleasant melancholy": Arvin, *Longfellow*, 49–50.
61 "any one can be *perfectly* well": To Charles Sumner, 9/17/42; S. Longfellow, *Life*, 1:417.
61 "the great event of my marriage": C15:662 (11/26/42).
61 "your writing poems about Slavery": C15:664–65 (12/24/42).

9 HAWTHORNE'S WRITING

62 "a rich warble from a bird": To Mary Foote, 12/18/42; Lathrop, *Memories*, 51.
62 "a Christian going to rest": To Louisa Hawthorne, 1/4/43; C15:666.
62 "the river is still frozen": C8:365–66 (3/31/43).

63 "most polished exertions": J. Hawthorne, *Hawthorne and Wife*, 1:159 (4/19/37).

64 "deepest associations . . . saddest thoughts": G. P. R. James, *Foreign and Colonial Quarterly Review*, Oct. 1843; in Crowley, *Critical Heritage*, 94.

64 "a little trade of gingerbread": Hawthorne, "The Old Apple-Dealer," in *Tales and Sketches*, 714, 719.

64 "the actual circumstances of life": Hawthorne, *Tales and Sketches*, 7 (from the first sentence in "The Hollow of the Three Hills," perhaps Hawthorne's earliest story to be published).

64 "the latter part of the last century": Hawthorne, "The Birthmark," in *Tales and Sketches*, 764, 769, 766, 778, 780, 778.

65 "and ruins it entirely": C8:165.

66 "Do not repent": Hawthorne, "The Birthmark," in *Tales and Sketches*, 780.

66 "more than mortal perfection": C8:184.

66 "in the city, it is death": Hawthorne, "The New Adam and Eve," in *Tales and Sketches*, 748, 756, 759.

67 "an annoyance, not a trouble": C8:367 (3/31/43).

10 TWO MORE WEDDINGS

69 "there being an inward inquietness": C8:368 (4/7/43).

69 "Indian-like sort of fellow": To Epes Sargent, 10/21/42; C15:656–57.

70 "high and classic cultivation": C8:369 (4/7/43).

70 "to our own landing-place": C8:378–79 (4/11/43).

71 "a sunbeam in his face": C8:371–72 (4/8/43).

71 "sweetest little bedfellow": C8:374 (4/9/43).

72 "yes, within an hour": C8:379 (4/11/43).

72 "darlings had to sit up straight": Quoted in Ronda, *Peabody*, 292.

73 "the reformation of the world": To Samuel J. May, 9/22/48; Messerli, *Mann*, 441.

74 "first rate genius": To Horace Mann, 3/3/38; Peabody, *Letters*, 199.

74 "something nearer home to duty": Mann to Elizabeth Peabody, 3/10/38; Messerli, *Mann*, 345.

75 "so full of joy & tenderness": Elizabeth Peabody to Rawlins Pickman; quoted in Ronda, *Peabody*, 209. On the wedding and departure, Messerli, *Mann*, 384–85.

75 "a Longfellow knock or ring": S. Longfellow, *Life*, 1:418 (9/28/42).

76 "suitors manifold": To George Washington Greene, 10/22/38; Longfellow, *Letters*, 2:106.

76 "comfort me, Mr. Longfellow": Wagenknecht, *Mrs. Longfellow*, 83.

76 "Day of light and love!": Journal entry, 5/10/44 (first anniversary); Thompson, *Young Longfellow*, 337.

76 "what is there to tell": To Martha Gold, 5/16/43; Wagenknecht, *Mrs. Longfellow*, 84.

77 "famine somewhere in my heart": To Tom Appleton, 5/24/43; Wagenknecht, *Mrs. Longfellow*, 85.

77 "Oh, it was a beautiful scene": Anne Longfellow to Elizabeth Poore, 8/15/43; Thompson, *Young Longfellow*, 340.

77 "pleasant fields and lands of quiet": To Anne Longfellow Pierce, 5/21/43; Longfellow, *Letters*, 2:536.

11 RURAL UTOPIAS

78 "the sun & the evening sky": Emerson, *Journals*, 8:433 (7/8/43).

79 "the highest genius of the time": Emerson's journal, 1857; quoted in Sears, *Fruitlands*, 8.

79 "I have never seen his equal": Emerson's journal, 1856; quoted in Shepard, *Pedlar's Progress*, 493.

79 "I learned divine wisdom": Quoted in Shepard, *Pedlar's Progress*, 215.

79 "I ask and ask": Quoted in Shepard, *Pedlar's Progress*, 181.

79 "to truth is no age or season": Quoted in Shepard, *Pedlar's Progress*, 184.

80 "This is the birth of the rose": Quoted in Bedell, *Alcotts*, 123.

80 "This is worth thinking of": Peabody, *Letters*, 181 (8/7/36).

80 "the cause of popular culture": A. B. Alcott, *Journals*, 195 (3/47).

81 "the fruits of oppression and blood": Quoted in Sears, *Fruitlands*, 72–73.

82 "planting, ploughing, sowing": Lane to William Oldham, 6/16/43; quoted in Sears, *Fruitlands*, 24.

82 "We will see them in December": Emerson, *Journals*, 8:433 (7/8/43).

83 "Our house stands apart": C15:539 (5/3/41).

83 "industry without drudgery": George Ripley to Emerson, 11/9/40; Sams, *Brook Farm*, 6.

83 "very silent & diffident": George P. Bradford's description to Hannah Thomas, 6/15/41; Mathews, "Letter," 228.

83 "Think that I am gone before": C15:527 (4/13/41).

84 "the sense of perfect seclusion": C15:575 (9/22/41).

84 "labor is the curse of the world": C15:558 (8/12/41).

84 "a man who feeds pigs": To George Hillard, 7/16/41; C15:550.

84 "other plans for ourselves": C15:563 (8/22/41).

84 "I wonder, I wonder, I wonder": C15:613 (2/27/42).

12 SEEKING A LIVELIHOOD

86 "I live in an old parsonage": To Evert Duyckinck, 11/26/43; C16:9.

86 "in the glory of health": To Louisa Hawthorne, 1/4/43; C15:667.

86 "I danced before my husband": Lathrop, *Memories*, 52.

86 "learning to be happy": To Margaret Fuller, 2/1/43; C15:671.

86 "what is there to write about": C8:315 (8/5/42).

87 "we were lovers of it": Lathrop, *Memories*, 51.

87 "the magic of Shakespeare": To Mary Foote, undated; Lathrop, *Memories,* 75.

87 "she is always cheerful": C8:367 (3/31/43).

87 "blooming in his arms": Quoted in Stewart, *Hawthorne,* 63.

88 "I know not what to say": C8:390–91.

88 "you satisfy me beyond all things": Lathrop, *Memories,* 79 (12/19/44).

88 "at the head of American Literature": Orestes Brownson in *Boston Quarterly Review,* 4/42; in Crowley, *Critical Heritage,* 87.

88 "he is the most original": *Arcturus,* 5/41; in Crowley, *Critical Heritage,* 74.

89 "our delight to do him honor": *Graham's,* 4/42; in Crowley, *Critical Heritage,* 85.

89 "the blessedness of our condition": J. Hawthorne, *Hawthorne and Wife,* 1:280–81.

89 "all do wrong alike": C15:682 (3/25/43).

89 "a respectable support by my pen": To Horatio Bridge, 5/3/43; C15:688.

90 "an army of eager applicants": *Spirit of the Times,* 3/16/43; Thomas and Jackson, *Poe Log,* 407.

90 "I might have written more": C8:367 (3/31/43).

91 "she *would not* be ill here": C15:695 (7/9/43).

91 Emerson writes Thoreau: Thoreau, *Correspondence,* 117 (6/10/43).

91 "gambolling in the breeze": C8:396 (10/6/43).

92 "my little wife rounding apace": C8:393 (9/24/43).

92 "the Steamer had arrived": C16:3 (11/7/43).

92 "sit at the back-door in Concord": Thoreau, *Correspondence,* 131 (8/6/43).

92 "deadly cold instead of livingly cold": Lathrop, *Memories,* 65–66.

93 "not been so cold a January": To Mrs. Peabody, 2/4/44; J. Hawthorne, *Hawthorne and Wife,* 1:274.

13 UNA

94 "Such are the designs": Charles Lane to Thoreau, 6/43; Thoreau, *Correspondence,* 115–16.

94 "I hate her": L. M. Alcott, *Journals,* 45 (9/14/43).

95 "It was good fun": L. M. Alcott, *Journals,* 45 (10/12/43).

95 "I wish I was rich": L. M. Alcott, *Journals,* 46 (10/8/43).

95 "Mrs. Alcott has no spontaneous inclination": Charles Lane to William Oldham; quoted in Sears, *Fruitlands,* 120.

95 "Thereupon ensued endless discussions": Lane to William Oldham, 11/26/43; Sears, *Fruitlands,* 123.

96 "the exiles left their Eden": L. M. Alcott, "Transcendental Wild Oats," in Sears, *Fruitlands,* 173.

96 "conjugal and paternal instincts": Abba Alcott to Samuel May, 1/11/44; quoted in Bedell, *Alcotts,* 231.

96 "to hear Paul preach": Messerli, *Mann*, 408.
97 "I have not yet seen the baby": C16:15 (3/3/44).
97 "it does not sound prettily!": C16:20 (3/15/44).
97 "'so dirty a face'": C16:24 n. 2 (3/12/44).
98 "ought not . . . too early in a man's life": C16:22 (3/24/44).
98 "the rail-road will soon be opened": C16:21 (3/15/44).
98 "the sombre texture of humanity": C16:23 (3/24/44).
99 "thought her form so perfect": C16:57 (7/2/44).
100 "the most shy and silent of men": Wagenknecht, *Mrs. Longfellow*, 112 (5/25/44).
100 "I liked Mrs. Longlady": C16:37 (5/27/44).

14 WOMEN IN THE NINETEENTH CENTURY

101 Hawthorne's "capital story": Wagenknecht, *Mrs. Longfellow*, 110 (4/13/44).
101 Bonfire on the western prairies: Hawthorne, "Earth's Holocaust," in *Tales and Sketches*, 887, 888, 890, 892, 897, 898, 903, 906.
102 "a new manifestation is at hand": Fuller, *Woman*, 113.
103 "exceptions in great number": Fuller, *Woman*, 212, 215.
103 "let them be sea-captains": Fuller, *Woman*, 214–15.
103 "a most beautiful child": Berg and Perry, 81–82, 84, 85, 89. Sarah is Sarah Clarke, who had attended Hawthorne's wedding.
104 "mend his shirts & socks": To Mary Mann, 4/6/45; quoted in Hurst, "Chief Employ," 45.
105 "commotion about woman's rights": J. Hawthorne, *Hawthorne and Wife*, 1:257.
105 "Nature would take care of that": Fuller, *Woman*, 215.
105 "Next to little Waldo": Berg and Perry, 89 (7/17/44).
105 "at least, not deep yet": Berg and Perry, 108 (8/2/44).
106 "open for travel next week": *Concord Freeman* (6/14/44 and 6/21/44), 2.
106 "Free Trade and Teamsters' Rights": Wilinsky, "Impact," 2.
106 "*Railroad stock* is in demand": *Concord Freeman* (7/12/44), 2.
107 "pastoral life whirled past and away": Thoreau, *Walden*, 419.
108 "into the ash-heap": Adams, *Education*, 725, 724; quoted in Marx, 345.

15 THE NATION BEYOND CONCORD

109 Hume, Franklin, Jefferson. Gould, *Mismeasure*, 32–35, and passim.
110 "without the allegation of any crimes": Resolves of Massachusetts Legislature, 3/43; quoted in E. R. Hoar, "Hoar," 39.
111 "require the communication": S. Hoar, "Expulsion," 319 (11/28/44).
112 "troll his old head like a football": Emerson, "Samuel Hoar," in *Complete Works*, 10:438.
112 Reaction to Hoar's treatment. "At our town-meeting, last Monday, Hon.

SAMUEL HOAR addressed his fellow citizens, and gave an interesting narrative of his late visit to South Carolina." *Concord Freeman*, Friday, 12/27/44. "Massachusetts is ominously quiet on the subject of S. Carolina. . . . Boston is very cool & ignoring." Emerson to William Emerson, 12/31/44; Emerson, *Letters*, 3:275.

112 "Does S.C. warn us out": Emerson, *Journals*, 9:174, 161.

113 "a poor, blind Samson in this land": Longfellow, "The Warning," in *Poetical Works*, 23.

113 "as good as a crime for her": Caroline Sturgis to Margaret Fuller, 1/45; Dedmond, 231.

114 "N.Y. plan one of great promise": Berg and Perry, 118.

114 "what offices they may fill": Fuller, *Woman*, 158–59.

114 "Now that I stand a little apart": C16:73.

116 "an act so foolish and wrong!": To Mary Longfellow Greenleaf, 3/22/44; Wagenknecht, *Mrs. Longfellow*, 108.

116 "almost died a natural death": To Francis Lieber, 3/10/45; Wagenknecht, *Mrs. Longfellow*, 118.

16 LEAVING THE OLD MANSE

117 "indifferent to the comforts of his family": Simmons, "Fuller's Boston Conversations," 217–18.

118 "in peaceful relations to the soil": Quoted in Shepard, *Pedlar's Progress*, 389.

118 "most . . . docile of all pupils": Quoted in Shepard, *Pedlar's Progress*, 390.

118 "this halfgod driven to the wall": Emerson, *Journals*, 9:86.

118 "I borrowed an axe": Thoreau, *Walden*, 354, 334, 394.

119 "green sweet-corn boiled": Thoreau, *Walden*, 371.

120 "our yearly multiplying millions": As two examples of the large literature concerning Manifest Destiny, see Merk, *Destiny and Mission*, and Horsman, *Race and Manifest Destiny*.

120 Polk's inaugural address: Richardson, *Presidents*, 4:379–80.

121 "How his friends do love him!": J. Hawthorne, *Hawthorne and Wife*, 1:281. The date of the visit was 5/9/45.

122 "the butcher, the baker, the tailor": To Pomroy Jones, 6/28/45; C16:104.

122 "moving Heaven and Earth": To E. A. Duyckinck, 4/7/45; C16:87.

122 "the best writer of the day": Fuller, "American Literature," 374.

123 "the honor and truth of others": J. Hawthorne, *Hawthorne and Wife*, 1:286–87.

123 "the price of my board at table": C16:116 (8/24/45).

123 "a devilish ugly predicament": C16:120 (9/28/45).

124 "ten dollars in my pocket": To Horatio Bridge, 10/7/45; C16:122.

124 Hawthorne at the head of American literature: Orestes Brownson in *Boston Quarterly Review*, 4/42; in Crowley, *Critical Heritage*, 87.

124 "where I wasted so many years": To Horatio Bridge, 10/7/45; C16:122.

129 "Servitude in new England": Quoted in Bedell, *Alcotts,* 283.
129 "I am unable to advise Mr. Alcott": Quoted in Bedell, *Alcotts,* 311.
130 "I have bought a house in Concord": To Grace Greenwood, 4/17/52; C16:533.
130 "it makes some noise in the world": C16:461 (Lenox, 7/22/51).
130 "A good deal was accomplished": Lathrop, *Memories,* 189–90.
131 "each presenting a long bill": C16:544 (6/8/52).
131 "We like the house . . . very much": C16:555 (6/18/52).

18 RETURN TO CONCORD

132 "nothing prospers with me": To E. A. Duyckinck, 12/24/45; C16:136.
133 "a dreadful country for a poet": Quoted in Thompson, *Young Longfellow,* 317.
133 "happier if I could write": C16:215 (11/11/47).
133 "I am turned out of office!": C16:273 (6/8/49).
133 "corruption, iniquity and fraud": Quoted in Hoeltje, "Writing," 338. A thorough treatment of the dismissal is in Nissenbaum, "Firing."
134 "not good for me to be here": C16:278 (6/12/49).
134 "the darkest hour I ever lived": C8:429 (7/29/49).
134 "He writes immensely": To Mrs. Peabody, 9/27/49; quoted in Stewart, *Hawthorne,* 93–94.
134 Hillard's letter: From Boston, 1/17/50; J. Hawthorne, *Hawthorne and Wife,* 1:354–55.
135 "justly a matter of shame": C16:309–10.
136 "either very good or very bad": Fields, *Yesterdays,* 49–50.
136 Reception of *The Scarlet Letter:* Crowley, *Critical Heritage,* 11.
136 "even *one* penny a volume": Lathrop, *Memories,* 270 (4/14/54).
137 "out of the beaten track": To William Pike, 9/2/51; C16:480.
137 "it has sold finely": To William Pike, 7/24/51; Lathrop, *Memories,* 152.
138 "for a menagerie of cattle": Sophia to Mrs. Peabody, 6/6/52; quoted in Hurst, "Chief Employ," 50.
138 "echoes were fairly roused": Lathrop, *Memories,* 191.
139 "I spend delectable hours there": To G. W. Curtis, 7/14/52; C16:567–68.
139 "the scenery of Concord": To G. W. Curtis, 7/14/52; C16:568.

19 CONCORD IN THE FIFTIES

140 "pres de l'entre du Vilage": Wheeler, *Concord,* 110.
140 Concord in the 1850s: In addition to sources cited for chapter 4 (at page 305), works drawn upon include Robinson, *"Warrington,"* Scudder, *Concord,* Gougeon, *Hero,* and Wheeler, *Concord.*
142 "the greatest blessing of this age": To Anne Longfellow Pierce, undated (spring 1847); Wagenknecht, *Mrs. Longfellow,* 129–30.

142 "one well-conducted institution": Thoreau, *Walden*, 416.

143 "Good-bye, John, etc.": C8:194 (2/19/39).

143 Irish population in Boston: von Frank, *Burns*, 38.

144 "mingle . . . in the political contests": Messerli, *Mann*, 449.

145 "corroborated by the authentic reports": Richardson, *Presidents*, 4:636.

146 "Politics . . . the topic of this country": Quoted in Holt, *Crisis*, 120.

147 "to his son to fix his shirt collar": *Middlesex Freeman*, 7/2/52.

20 TWO NOVELS

148 "without precedent in the history": *Middlesex Freeman*, 6/11/52.

149 "the highway of ordinary travel": Hawthorne, "Preface," *The Blithedale Romance*, in *Novels*, 633.

150 "truth of the human heart": Hawthorne, "Preface," *The House of the Seven Gables*, in *Novels*, 351.

150 "into and through them": J. Hawthorne, *Hawthorne and Wife*, 1:458.

151 "mistook for an angel of God": Hawthorne, *The Blithedale Romance*, in *Novels*, 679.

152 "the most perfect in execution": *Graham's*, 9/52; in Crowley, *Critical Heritage*, 256.

152 "finest imaginative writer": [Henry F. Chorley], *Athenaeum*, 7/10/52; in Crowley, *Critical Heritage*, 245.

152 "feeble, timid-looking woman": To Mary Longfellow Greenleaf, 4/53; Wagenknecht, *Mrs. Longfellow*, 193.

152 "mother to seven children": To Sarah Hale, in 1850; quoted in Hedrick, *Stowe*, 198.

152 "dry as a pinch of snuff": To Eliza Cabot Follen, 2/16/53; quoted in Hedrick, *Stowe*, 239.

153 "wicked fugitive slave business": To Catharine Beecher, undated (1850 or 1851); quoted in Hedrick, *Stowe*, 204.

154 "what yet remains untold": Stowe, "Concluding Remarks," *Uncle Tom's Cabin*, 513.

154 "How she is shaking the world": Wagenknecht, *Longfellow Portrait*, 113.

154 "the largest sum of money": Quoted in Hedrick, *Stowe*, 221. For a contemporary account of the extraordinary publishing efforts to keep up with the demand for *Uncle Tom's Cabin*, see Harry Franko, "Uncle Tomitudes," in *Putnam's* (1853); quoted in Pattee, *Fifties*, 135–36.

155 "too humble to think of doing good!": C18:116 (10/8/57).

156 "the tendency of all your fortunes": C16:545 (6/9/52).

21 HAWTHORNE AND SLAVERY

157 "one happy or comfortable moment": C16:545 (6/9/52).

158 "a mere country lawyer": C16:546 (6/9/52).

158 "the great subject of variance": To Franklin Pierce, 7/5/52; C16:561.

158 "sympathy for the slaves": To Zachariah Burchmore, from Lenox, 6/15/51; C16:456.

160 "an altogether odious set of people": Emerson, *Journals*, 9:120.

161 "do more to abolish Slavery": Porte, *Emerson Journals*, 329 (spring–summer 1844).

161 "the whip applied to old men": Emerson, *Complete Works*, 11:104. See also Harding, *Days*, 174–75; Gougeon, *Hero*, 70–85.

162 "I will not obey it, by God": Emerson, *Journals*, 11:412.

162 Fugitive Slave Act: The complete text is readily available online, at, for example, the Avalon Project of Yale Law School, www.yale.edu/lawweb/avalon/fugitive.htm.

162 that "filthy enactment": Emerson, *Journals*, 11:412.

162 "this Fugitive Law cornered me": To Zachariah Burchmore, 6/15/51; C16:456.

22 DEATH BY WATER

164 "being Minister to Russia": J. Hawthorne, *Hawthorne and Wife*, 1:453 (7/1/52).

164 "a life the solitude of which": J. Hawthorne, *Hawthorne and Wife*, 1:436.

165 "something may intervene": C16:555 (6/18/52).

165 "astonished to see Mr. Pike get out": J. Hawthorne, *Hawthorne and Wife*, 1:455–56.

167 "a blow that struck him to the heart": J. Hawthorne, *Hawthorne and Wife*, 1:456–57.

167 "methinks it is the ugliest": Hawthorne, *Novels*, 837.

167 "a Miss Hunt, about nineteen years old": C8:261–67 (7/9/45). Additional details about Martha Hunt are in Curtis, "Hawthorne," 55–60.

168 "Hold on! You have her!": Hawthorne, *Novels*, 836.

169 "These characters . . . are . . . fictitious": Hawthorne, *Novels*, 634.

169 "My life at Rome is . . . all I hoped": Quoted in Watson, *Fuller*, 39.

170 "a baby . . . alive to confirm it!": To Emmeline Austin Wadsworth; Wagenknecht, *Mrs. Longfellow*, 159.

170 "artificial and imitative": Fuller, "American Literature," 365.

171 "Her life was romantic & exceptional": Emerson, *Journals*, 11:259. Mrs. Barlow is Almira Penniman Barlow.

23 CREATING A LIFE

173 "the necessity of going to Salem": C16:585.

174 "so obscure as he certainly was": To Horatio Bridge, 10/13/52; C16:604.

174 Pierce's life: Besides Hawthorne's *Life of Pierce*, principal sources include Nichols's *Pierce*, Gara's *Presidency*, and von Frank's *Burns*.

176 "paltry Franklin Pierce": Emerson, *Journals*, 15:60 (5/24/64).

177 "made a kind of sunshine": Hawthorne, *Life of Pierce*, 87. My description of the biography draws upon Warner's "Making of the President."
177 "what wretched things men perpetrate": To Elizabeth Peabody, 10/8/57; quoted in Idol, "Peabody," 44.
177 "every slave knocked on the head": To Charles Eliot Norton, 11/10/50; Parkman, *Letters*, 1:79.
178 "for the sake of the slave!": J. Hawthorne, *Hawthorne and Wife*, 1:483.
178 "mistiness of a philanthropic theory": Hawthorne, *Life of Pierce*, 105.
179 "We are politicians now": C16:588 (8/25/52).
179 "With no very remarkable talents": Bridge, *Recollections*, 74 (12/25/36).
179 "Nothing can ruin him": C16:606 (10/13/52).
179 "He does the thing he finds right": J. Hawthorne, *Hawthorne and Wife*, 1:464 (9/10/52).

24 DAYS AT THE WAYSIDE

180 "not one word on the subject": J. Hawthorne, *Hawthorne and Wife*, 1:484.
181 "rather folly than heroism": C16:605 (10/13/52).
182 "ten years happier in time": J. Hawthorne, *Hawthorne and Wife*, 1:467.
182 "He turned back and walked with us": Lathrop, *Memories*, 190–92 (6/6/52).
183 "beginning to take root here": C16:602 (10/5/52).
183 "several more lives to live": Thoreau, *Walden*, 579. On Thoreau and Julian, Harding, *Days*, 308–09.
184 "They never will be arbitrary facts": To Mrs. Peabody, 7/18/52; C16:574. See also Pearson, "Elizabeth Peabody on Hawthorne," 276.
184 "it was almost appalling": J. Hawthorne, *Hawthorne and Wife*, 2:371.
184 "the very gayest person I ever saw": To T. W. Higginson; Higginson, *Life*, 254.
185 "brought up in the worst way": Quoted in Herbert, *Beloved*, 211 (10/51).
186 "the highest, wisest, loveliest thing": From Lenox, 1850; J. Hawthorne, *Hawthorne and Wife*, 1:373.
186 "it is now too late in life": To C. H. Peirce, 11/4/52; C16:616.
187 "any sacrifice to the right": To Dr. Peabody, 5/53; J. Hawthorne, *Hawthorne and Wife*, 2:12.

25 TO WASHINGTON

188 "the blessing you have been to us": Undated, from Lenox; J. Hawthorne, *Hawthorne and Wife*, 1:378.
188 "God cannot trifle!": Lathrop, *Memories*, 199.
189 Bennie's death: Nichols, *Pierce*, 224–25; *Boston Atlas*, 1/7/53 (vol. 30, no. 162), 2.
190 Pierce's inaugural address: Richardson, *Presidents*, 5:197–98, 201–02.

191 "hundreds of log cabins": Charles Mason's diary, as quoted in Nichols, *Pierce*, 313.

192 "I do not think of going to Washington": To Charlotte M. Bridge, 2/7/53; C16:634.

192 "another suit on the stocks": C16:658.

193 "precisely what was needed": Ticknor, *Hawthorne*, 6–7.

193 "off in a dark rain this morning": Lathrop, *Memories*, 208.

193 "applicant for one of the offices": To C. H. Peaslee, 4/13/53; C16:673, 674.

193 "Why did I ever leave thee": C16:675 (4/17/53).

194 "Hawthorne is quite a lion": Ticknor, *Hawthorne*, 44 (4/22/53).

194 "awaited a school-boy's homage": Mitchell, *Works*, 15:150–51.

195 "free to leave by Saturday": C16:679 (4/28/53).

195 "Kiss them all for me": From Philadelphia, 4/19/53; C16:677.

195 "I love them all": C16:679 (4/28/53).

26 DEPARTURE FOR EUROPE

196 "I read the history of the day": To Mrs. Peabody; Lathrop, *Memories*, 209.

196 "This is the sweetest place": To Mrs. Peabody, 4/29/53; Lathrop, *Memories*, 211.

197 "I burned great heaps of old letters": C8:552.

197 Hawthorne's replies to Sophia's letters: C15:333 (8/8/39), 475 (6/22/40); C8:373 (4/9/43); C16:233 (7/5/48).

198 "the cares of life lightened": To Thomas G. Appleton, 6/21/53; Wagenknecht, *Mrs. Longfellow*, 194.

198 "his personality was most radiant": Lathrop, *Memories*, 213.

199 "do not speak . . . of obligation": J. Hawthorne, *Hawthorne and Wife*, 1:355.

199 "it has never been out of my mind": Clark, *Auction*, 45 (8/9/53).

200 "how many things I have to do": C16:695.

200 "dinner vanishes into thin air": Longfellow, *Letters*, 3:387 (6/30/53).

201 The Hawthornes at Halifax: Sophia's notebook, aboard *Niagara*, 7/8/53; J. Hawthorne, *Hawthorne and Wife*, 2:16.

27 ONCE MORE TO CONCORD

205 "a very sensible woman": Ticknor, *Hawthorne*, 53 (7/22/53).

206 "between a longing and a dread": To James T. Fields, 12/30/59; C18:214.

208 "the forlornness of the little cottage": Lathrop, *Memories*, 421.

208 *"some victory for humanity"*: Mann, *Mann*, 575.

209 "Una did the hugging & kissing": To Miss Rawlins Pickman, 7/10/60; C18:301–02 n.

210 "their heads were silver white!": Downs, "Mr. Hawthorne," 99.

210 "Everybody was reading it": Howells, *Literary Friends*, 56.
210 "the depths of our common nature": Preface to *The Snow-Image*; Hawthorne, *Tales and Sketches*, 1154.
211 "the notices have been very kind": To James T. Fields, 4/26/60; C18: 271–72.
211 "I am not a melancholy man": C18:334 (11/5/60).
212 "a banquet in my honour!": To William Ticknor, 6/28/60; C18:301.
212 "schoolboy's Blue Monday": Quoted in Tryon, *Parnassus*, 248.

<h2>28 ALTERING THE WAYSIDE</h2>

213 "I am not a melancholy man": C18:334 (11/5/60).
213 "a demand for further elucidations": Hawthorne, *Novels*, 1239–42.
214 "I like to be praised too much": C18:262 (4/6/60).
214 "'The thing is a failure'": J. Hawthorne, *Hawthorne and Wife*, 2:238.
214 "with a wing of a house to build": From Rome, to William D. Ticknor, 3/4/59; C18:164.
215–16 Howells' visit: Howells, *Literary Friends*, 50–51, 47, 55.
217 "how everybody loves, *adores* him!": Lathrop, *Memories*, 428.
217 "at home in one dull spot": C18:380 (5/26/61).
217 "seems to be the Roman fever": C14:495 (11/2/58).
218 "It is almost the worst trial": Quoted in Herbert, *Beloved*, 256 (4/3/59).
218 "No one shared my nursing": To Elizabeth Peabody, 7/3/59; quoted in Herbert, *Beloved*, 250.
218 "I can give her to Him": J. Hawthorne, *Hawthorne and Wife*, 2:210.
219 "he is going to talk to Papa": To Richard Manning, 7/20/60; C18:309 n.
219 "I keep very jolly": To Richard Manning, 7/25/60; C18:309–10 n.
219 "fearful attacks of *dementia*": To Reverend William James, 12/21/60; quoted in Turner, *Hawthorne*, 431.
219 "good news of Una": C18:327 (10/9/60).
220 "that miserable Roman fever": To Francis Bennoch, 12/17/60; C18: 352–53.

<h2>29 CONCORD IN THE SIXTIES</h2>

221 "It is long since he had it": To Una Hawthorne, 12/19/63; J. Hawthorne, *Hawthorne and Wife*, 2:333.
223 "I am sick and sorrowful": S. Longfellow, *Life*, 2:246.
223 "The law must be executed": Quoted in Gara, *Presidency*, 107.
223 "windows of every office . . . full": Letter of Ann W. Weston, 6/5/54; quoted in von Frank, *Burns*, 210.
225 "infernally disagreeable country": To William D. Ticknor, early 1856; quoted in Arvin, *Hawthorne*, 229.
225 "free soilers, pro-slavery men": To William D. Ticknor, 10/10/56; quoted in Hall, *Critic*, 152.

225 "If he should swamp himself": C18:127–28 (11/5/57).

225 "I shall delight to assist him": A. B. Alcott, *Journals,* 328 (6/28/60).

225 "his drawbridges up": A. B. Alcott, *Journals,* 336 (2/17/61).

225 "no objection to the Governor": To Horatio Woodman, 11/5/60; C18:336.

227 "the date of a new Revolution": S. Longfellow, *Life,* 2:347.

227 "St. John the Just": L. M. Alcott, *Journals,* 95 (12/59).

227 "he is an Angel of Light": Thoreau, "Plea," 416.

228 Attempted abduction of Sanborn: His own account, written forty-one
years later, is in the *Middlesex Patriot,* Concord, Mass., vol. 2, no. 15,
for 3/29/1901. Concord Free Public Library Special Collections. See also
Sanborn, *Recollections,* 1:208–18; Scudder, *Concord,* 223–24.

30 SECESSION

229 Hawthorne's "remarkable personal beauty": Sanborn, *Hawthorne,* 55.

230 "I left out the first and best": Sanborn, *Hawthorne,* 11–12 (9/3/60). For
Concord in 1860, see, in addition to sources cited earlier (pp. 305, 313),
Gordon, "Concord," passim.

230 "brought up in the worst way": Quoted in Herbert, *Beloved,* 211 (10/51).

231 "Her friends feel very anxious": To Benjamin Smith Lyman, 9/18/60;
C18:317 n.

232 "no rights and no duties": To William Ticknor, 2/10/60; C18:227.

232 "a general smash?": C18:341.

232 "Secession is ... revolution": Richardson, *Presidents* 5:626, 634
(12/3/60).

233 "still have her rocks and ice": To Francis Bennoch, 12/17/60; C18:353.

233 "not bate one jot of its manhood": Quoted in Arvin, *Longfellow,* 134.

234 "We do not belong together": To Henry Bright, 12/17/60; C18:355.

234 "in print and accessible to the public": To Nathaniel P. Paschall, 11/16/
60. Lincoln, *Works* 4:141–42.

235–36 Lincoln's first inaugural: Lincoln, *Works* 4:262–71.

31 PATRIOTIC AMERICANS

237 "an excellent institution": To Henry Bright, 12/17/60; C18:355.

238 "the Fury of Hubbab": To Annie Fields, 1/61; Stewart, "At Wayside,"
263.

238 "we verge to a conclusion": To Annie Fields, 5/61; Stewart, "At Wayside," 264.

238 "as much ... as Papa can afford": Quoted in Lothrop, *Wayside,* 113
(6/5/61).

238 "A quire of paper on my desk": C18:363 (2/16/61).

238 "Surrender of Fort Sumter": A. B. Alcott, *Journals,* 338.

239 Concord's military muster: E. Emerson, "Hoar," 53–54; Reynolds, *Papers,*
247–48; Scudder, *Concord,* 228–29.

239 "one of my High Contracting Powers": To Annie Fields, 5/61; Stewart, "At Wayside," 272.

239 "Who could write stories": Quoted in Hedrick, *Stowe*, 301 (11/21/61).

240 "He says he sees nobody": A. B. Alcott, *Journals*, 339 (5/22/61, 5/23/61, 5/24/61).

241 "We never were one people": C18:381 (5/26/61).

241 "Ticknor's looks dark and dreary": Quoted in Tryon, *Parnassus*, 252.

241 "So much for war and books": Tryon, *Parnassus*, 252–53 (5/18/61).

241 "all literature loses its taste": S. Longfellow, *Life*, 2:365 (4/30/61).

242 "the uttermost desire of my heart": Wagenknecht, *Mrs. Longfellow*, 112 (5/28/44).

242 "the redemption of the country": Quoted in Arvin, *Longfellow*, 134.

243–44 Fanny Longfellow's death: The account is drawn from chapter 8, "Chariot of Fire," in Edward Wagenknecht's compilation of Mrs. Longfellow's letters and journals, which includes the letter to her sister Mary Appleton Mackintosh of 7/5/61, the final letter, to her son Ernest, of 7/7/61, and letters after her death from Cornelius C. Felton to Charles Sumner, dated 7/10/61, 7/19/61, and 7/21/61. Wagenknecht, *Mrs. Longfellow*, 239–45.

244 "gone but a little while before me": Winthrop, "Appleton," 300–01.

244 "this blackest of shadows": C18:391.

245 "the light went with her": Quoted in Williams, *Longfellow*, 81.

32 IN THE SKY PARLOR

247 "better have suffered ten defeats": To James Russell Lowell, 7/23/61; C18:394.

247 "so hopeless, so unstrung": To "My Dearest Husband," 7/25/61; J. Hawthorne, *Hawthorne and Wife*, 2:283.

247 "not much more discontented": C18:396–97 (4/28/61).

247 "made of hot molten metal": To Rose Hawthorne, 8/5/61; C18:399–400.

249 "vague unchronicled time": C12:441.

250 "never . . . in such a sad predicament": C12:220, 266, 286.

250 "Now dip your pen": C18:409 n. (9/18/61).

250 "that sweet genial time of year": C13:3.

251 "hopeful view of our national prospects": C18:412 (10/12/61).

251 "Our story is an internal one": C13:15–16.

252 "high, heroic, tremulous juncture": C13:17.

253 "the final sentence of the story": C18:408 (10/6/61).

253 "tempted by your invitation": To Horatio Bridge, 2/13/62; C18:427.

33 TOURING WITH TICKNOR

255 "all such delights of early summer": Hawthorne, "War Matters," 44. The description of the trip to Washington is taken from this source.

256 "up against nothing at all!": Hawthorne, "War Matters," 45.

256–57 Interview with Lincoln: Fields, *Yesterdays*, 99–101.

258–59 Trips to Harpers Ferry and Newport News: Hawthorne, "War Matters," 52–59.

259 "the clank and smash of iron": Hawthorne, "War Matters," 49.

260 "Just so crazy with joy": To Annie Fields, 4/11/62; Stewart, "Last Illness," 306.

260 "lent him our sweet old music-box": Lathrop, *Memories*, 420. For Julian's mature, hostile opinion of Thoreau as of 1898, see Harding, *Days*, 309.

261 "He was Concord itself": Quoted in Stewart, "Wayside," 273.

261 "of thought and originality": To Henry Longfellow, 11/21/48; C16: 248.

261 "man generally came short": Stewart, "Wayside," 273.

261 "the same yesterday and tomorrow": As recorded in the original manuscript of *Walden* (not in the final version); quoted in Shepard, *Pedlar's Progress*, 403.

261 "how great a son it has lost": Quoted in Harding, *Days*, 467.

261 "he was honored at his death": To Alfred Whitman, 5/11/62; Schlesinger, "Alcotts," 375.

262 "a closer relationship now": To Sophia Ford; quoted in Harding, *Days*, 468.

34 WAR MATTERS

263 "as ugly as sin": C8:353–54 (9/1/42).

263 "queer, sagacious visage": Fields, *Yesterdays*, 99–100.

264 "tip top in all other respects": Quoted in C18:458 n. (5/21/62).

264 "most amenable man to advise": Fields, *Yesterdays*, 98.

264 "the only part . . . worth publishing": C18:461 (5/23/62).

264 "Chiefly About War Matters": Citations from Hawthorne, "War Matters," 43, 46, 48–49, 55, 56, 54.

265 "better at a distance than close": C18:446 (4/2/62).

268 "'he wrote the footnotes himself'": Conway, *Hawthorne*, 204.

268 "be President through this crisis": Lathrop, *Memories*, 438 (3/15/62).

268 "I like him very well": Lathrop, *Memories*, 438.

268 "If we pummel the South": To Horatio Bridge, 5/26/61; C18:381.

269 "If I could save the Union": Lincoln, *Works*, 5:388 (8/22/62).

270 "a hard battle with the world": Hawthorne, "War Matters," 50.

270 "The filthy spewings of it": Davis, *Gossip*, 34.

271 "passionless as a disembodied intelligence": G. W. Curtis to Charles Eliot Norton, 6/26/62; quoted in Aaron, *Unwritten War*, 51.

271 Casualties at Shiloh: Long, *Civil War*, 196.

35 FAMILY MATTERS

272 "Is that plain?": Quoted in Ronda, *Peabody*, 270 (1861).

272 "What gloomy times are these": To Annie Fields, 6/62 and 7/62; Stewart, "Wayside," 272.

273 "to the Old Manse & monument": Woodson, "Diary," 300.

273 "Una's party took place to-night": Woodson, "Diary," 305.

273 "Mrs. Emerson sent a huge basket full": Stewart, "Wayside," 268–71.

274 "other jollifications": J. Hawthorne, *Hawthorne and Wife*, 2:267.

274 "the most apalling sensationalist": Stewart, "Wayside," 272 (5/26/62).

275 "flat as a month of prairies": Lathrop, *Memories*, 415.

275 "my dear hanging astral": Lathrop, *Memories*, 433.

275 "The Present, the Immediate, the Actual": Dedicatory Letter, *Our Old Home*, C5:4.

275 "The shots strike all round us": To Henry Bright, 11/14/61; C18:422.

276 "I sympathize with nobody": C18:543 (3/8/63).

276 "national extinction the lesser evil": C18:420 (11/14/61).

276 "I expect to outlive my means": Ticknor, *Hawthorne*, 305 (7/63).

276 "*the only remembrance of me*": Emerson, *Journals*, 15:60.

276 "Longfellow has ceased to be there": To Henry Bright, 11/14/61; C18:421–22.

277 "merciless as a steel bayonet": To Henry Bright, 3/8/63; C18:544.

277 "immitigable for its continuance": To Henry Bright, 3/8/63; C18:545.

278 "my husband quite ill": Woodson, "Diary," 320.

278 "he is trying to write": J. Hawthorne, *Hawthorne and Wife*, 2:326 (12/11/62).

36 OUR OLD HOME

279 "those cruel and terrible notes": C5:408.

280 "it seems to be the best written": James, *Hawthorne*, 432, 436.

280 "bust of General Jackson": C5:8, 9, 345, 60, 299, 282.

282 "My own convictions about human duties": Quoted in Maynard, *Fire*, 258.

282 "I shall always love him": C14:518 (4/19/59).

282 "He was divinely tender": To Elizabeth Peabody, 7/3/59; Lathrop, *Memories*, 371.

283 "opinion of wiser men than I": Quoted in C18:587 n. (7/15/63).

283 "a piece of poltroonery": C18:586 (7/18/63).

284 "fearful, fruitless, fatal": Quoted in Nichols, *Pierce*, 522.

284 "limited ability": Quoted in Nichols, *Pierce*, 521.

284 Pierce's letter to Davis: Nichols, *Pierce*, 510–11, 525; Ronda, *Peabody*, 281; Gara, *Presidency*, 178.

285 "judge it right to do": C18:590 (7/20/63).

285 "that arch traitor Pierce": Quoted in C18:516 n. (11/3/63).

37 LAST TRAVELS

286 "if I die . . . or am brain-stricken": To Horatio Bridge, 4/13/55; Bridge, *Recollections,* 146.

286 "spend little or nothing": To James T. Fields, 10/24/63; C18:606.

287 "Concord is not the best place": To Annie Fields, 10/63; Stewart, "Last Illness," 307.

287 "he wishes to be ready": C18:614 (11/29/63).

287 "the funeral of Mrs. Franklin Pierce": Howe, *Hostess,* 57–58 (12/4/63 and 12/6/63).

288 "much smoulder and scanty fire": To James T. Fields, 2/25/64; C18:641.

288 "dispirited about his health": Fields, *Yesterdays,* 117.

288 "I bless GOD for him": To Annie Fields, 3/31/63; Stewart, "Last Illness," 309.

288 "A worse than a northeaster": Ticknor, *Hawthorne,* 313–15.

289 "The wildest anxiety about him": Bridge, *Recollections,* 189, 191 (4/5/64).

289 "too stormy to try the sea": J. Hawthorne, *Hawthorne and Wife,* 2:342–43 (4/7/64).

290 "Ticknor is already very much reduced": C18:651 (4/9/64); Tryon, *Parnassus,* 275–76.

290–91 Childs's account: C18:652 n.; Derby, *Authors,* 344–46; Schubert, "Death of Ticknor," passim. (Absurdly, because of a falling-out after Hawthorne's death between Mrs. Hawthorne and the Fieldses, Julian's subsequent biography of his parents omits any mention through its two volumes of the editor who had done so much to advance his father's career.)

291 "A more untoward event": J. Hawthorne, *Hawthorne and Wife,* 2:343.

291 "deeply scored with pain and fatigue": To Annie Fields, 4/64; Stewart, "Last Illness," 309–10.

292 "They will fish and muse and rest": To Annie Fields, undated (late April?); Stewart, "Last Illness," 311.

38 RELEASE

293 "wasting of flesh and strength": Holmes, "Hawthorne," 99.

293 "a restlessness that is infinite": To James T. Fields, undated (early May?); Stewart, "Last Illness," 311.

293 "whether in bed or up": To Horatio Bridge, 5/21/64; Bridge, *Recollections,* 177–78. Pierce's account to Fields, dated 5/19/64, is in C18:656 n.

293 Diagnosis of Hawthorne's illness: Baym, *Hawthorne's Career,* 251; Wineapple, *Hawthorne,* 370–71.

294 "His aspect at that moment": J. Hawthorne, *Hawthorne and Wife,* 2:345–46.

294 "his death-bed companions!": *Novels,* 667.

294 Battle casualties: Long, *Civil War,* 268 (Antietam), 296 (Fredericksburg), 348 (Chancellorsville), 378 (Gettysburg).

295 "He is my world": To Annie Fields, 4/64; Stewart, "Illness," 310.

295 Hawthorne's children in adulthood: See Bassan, *Hawthorne's Son*, 213–20 (for Julian's crime and punishment) and passim; Hull, "Una Hawthorne," passim; J. Hawthorne, *Hawthorne and Wife*, 370 ff. (for Una's account of her mother's death); and Maynard, *A Fire Was Lighted*, passim.

295 "He fell asleep softly": To Anne O'Gara, 9/4/64; Bassan, "New Account," 563.

296 "I only said 'No no no'": To Anne O'Gara, 9/4/64; Bassan, "New Account," 563.

296 "crosses made of white flowers": To Anne O'Gara, 9/4/64; Bassan, "New Account," 564.

296 "the friend of all sinners": Boston *Evening Transcript*, 5/24/64; *Nathaniel Hawthorne Journal* (1972), 260. A facsimile of the Reverend James Freeman Clarke's eulogy is at this site, 259–61.

297 "disappearing like a hare": A. B. Alcott, *Journals*, 364; Wagner, "Pine and Apple Orchard," 40.

297 "the painful solitude of the man": Emerson, *Journals*, 15:60.

297 "superior to his own performances": Lathrop, *Memories*, 455–56 (7/11/64).

298 "my Father gave me the richest destiny": Quoted in Stewart, "Last Illness," 312.

299 "He is a crystal medium": Bridge, *Recollections*, 193–94 (11/7/65).

299 "To sit down . . . in a solitary place": C8:245–50.

Works Cited

THE LIST CONTAINS ONLY WORKS REFERRED TO IN THE NOTES.

Aaron, Daniel. *The Unwritten War: American Writers and the Civil War*. New York, 1973.

Adams, Henry. *The Education of Henry Adams*. In *Novels, Mont Saint Michel, The Education*. New York: Library of America, 1983.

Alcott, Amos Bronson. *The Journals of Amos Bronson Alcott*. Edited by Odell Shepard. Boston, 1938.

Alcott, Louisa May. *The Journals of Louisa May Alcott*. Edited by Joel Myerson, Daniel Shealy, and Madeleine B. Stern. Boston, 1989.

Arvin, Newton. *Hawthorne*. Boston, 1929.

———. *Longfellow: His Life and Work*. Boston, 1963.

Bassan, Maurice. *Hawthorne's Son: The Life and Literary Career of Julian Hawthorne*. Columbus, Ohio, 1970.

———. "A New Account of Hawthorne's Last Days, Death, and Funeral." *American Literature* 27 (1956): 561–65.

Baym, Nina. *The Shape of Hawthorne's Career*. Ithaca, 1976.

Bedell, Madelon. *The Alcotts: Biography of a Family*. New York, 1980.

Berg, Martha L., and Alice de V. Perry, eds. "'The Impulses of Human Nature': Margaret Fuller's Journal from June through October 1844." *Proceedings of the Massachusetts Historical Society* 102 (1990): 38–126.

Bridge, Horatio. *Personal Recollections of Nathaniel Hawthorne*. New York, 1893.

Centenary Edition of the Works of Nathaniel Hawthorne. Edited by William Charvat et al. 20 vols. Columbus, Ohio, 1962–88. In notes abbreviated as C, with volume and page number:

    5: *Our Old Home*
    8: *The American Notebooks*
   10: *Mosses from an Old Manse*
   12: *The American Claimant Manuscripts*

13: *The Elixir of Life Manuscripts*
14: *The French and Italian Notebooks*
15: *The Letters, 1813–1843*
16: *The Letters, 1843–1853*
18: *The Letters, 1857–1864*

Clark, C. E. Frazer, Jr., ed. *Hawthorne at Auction: 1894–1971.* Detroit, 1972.

Conway, Moncure D. *Life of Nathaniel Hawthorne.* New York, 1890.

Crowley, J. Donald, ed. *Hawthorne: The Critical Heritage.* New York, 1970.

Curtis, George William. "Hawthorne." In *Literary and Social Essays.* New York, 1895.

Davis, Rebecca Harding. *Bits of Gossip.* Boston, 1904.

Dedmond, Francis B. "The Letters of Caroline Sturgis to Margaret Fuller." In *Studies in the American Renaissance,* edited by Joel Myerson, 201–51. Charlottesville, 1988.

Derby, J. C. *Fifty Years Among Authors, Books and Publishers.* New York, 1884.

Downs, Annie Sawyer. "Mr. Hawthorne, Mr. Thoreau, Miss Alcott, Mr. Emerson, and Me." *American Heritage* 30:1 (1978): 94–105. Text edited by Walter Harding from an original manuscript in the Concord Free Public Library Special Collections.

Emerson, Edward A. "Ebenezer Rockwood Hoar." In *Memoirs of Members of the Social Circle in Concord, Fourth Series,* 1–130. Cambridge, Mass., 1909.

Emerson, Ralph Waldo, *The Complete Works of Ralph Waldo Emerson.* 12 vols. Centenary Edition, Boston, 1904: "Samuel Hoar," 10:435–48; "Historical Discourse at Concord, on the Second Centennial Anniversary of the Incorporation of the Town, September 12, 1835," 11:27–86; "Address: Emancipation in the British West Indies," 11:99–147.

———. *Essays and Lectures.* New York: Library of America, 1983.

———. *Journals and Miscellaneous Notebooks.* Edited by William Gilman et al. 16 vols. Cambridge, Mass., 1960–82.

———. *The Letters of Ralph Waldo Emerson.* Edited by Ralph Rusk. 6 vols. New York, 1939.

Emerson, William. *Diaries and Letters of William Emerson, 1743–1776, Minister of the Church in Concord, Chaplain in the Revolutionary Army.* Arranged by Amelia Forbes Emerson. N.p.: privately printed, [1972].

Fields, James T. *Yesterdays with Authors.* Boston, 1872.

Fischer, David Hackett, ed. *Concord: The Social History of a New England Town, 1750-1850.* Waltham, Mass., 1983.

Fuller, Margaret. "American Literature." In *The Writings of Margaret Fuller,* edited by Mason Wade, 358–88. New York, 1941.

———. *Woman in the Nineteenth Century.* In *The Writings of Margaret Fuller,* edited by Mason Wade, 105–218. New York, 1941.

Gara, Larry. *The Presidency of Franklin Pierce.* Lawrence, Kans., 1991.

Gordan, John D. "Nathaniel Hawthorne: The Years of Fulfilment, 1804–1853."

Bulletin of the New York Public Library 59 (1955): 154–65, 198–217, 259–69, 316–21.

Gordon, Jayne K. "Concord and the Great Rebellion, 1861–1865: The Impact of the Civil War on One New England Town." 1989. Unpublished typescript by the director of the Orchard House. In the Concord Free Public Library Special Collections.

Gougeon, Len. *Virtue's Hero: Emerson, Antislavery, and Reform.* Athens, Ga., 1990.

Gould, Stephen Jay. *The Mismeasure of Man.* New York, 1981.

Gross, Robert A. "Transcendentalism and Urbanism: Concord, Boston, and the Wider World." *Journal of American Studies* 18 (1984): 361–81.

Hall, Lawrence Sargent. *Hawthorne: Critic of Society.* New Haven, 1944.

Harding, Walter. *The Days of Henry Thoreau.* Princeton, 1965.

Hatfield, James Taft. *New Light on Longfellow.* Boston, 1933.

Hawthorne, Julian. *Nathaniel Hawthorne and His Wife.* 2 vols. Boston, 1885.

Hawthorne, Nathaniel. "Chiefly About War Matters." *Atlantic Monthly* 10 (1862): 43–61. The text is available, as well, in *The Complete Writings of Nathaniel Hawthorne,* Old Manse Edition, 22 vols. 17:361–420. Boston, 1900.

———. *Life of Franklin Pierce.* In *The Complete Writings of Nathaniel Hawthorne,* Old Manse Edition, 22 vols. 17:75–193. Boston, 1900.

———. *Novels.* New York: Library of America, 1983.

———. *Tales and Sketches, A Wonder Book for Girls and Boys, Tanglewood Tales for Girls and Boys.* New York: Library of America, 1982.

———. *The Works of Nathaniel Hawthorne.* See *Centenary Edition of the Works of Nathaniel Hawthorne.*

Hedrick, Joan. *Harriet Beecher Stowe: A Life.* New York, 1994.

Herbert, T. Walter. *Dearest Beloved: The Hawthornes and the Making of the Middle-Class Family.* Berkeley, 1993.

Higginson, Thomas Wentworth. *Henry Wadsworth Longfellow.* Boston, 1902.

———. *Part of a Man's Life.* Boston, 1905.

Hoar, Ebenezer Rockwood. "Samuel Hoar." In *Memoirs of Members of the Social Circle in Concord, Third Series.* Cambridge, Mass., 1907.

Hoar, Samuel. "Samuel Hoar's Expulsion from Charleston: A Reprint of Senate Document No. 4, Commonwealth of Massachusetts, 1845." *Old South Leaflets,* 21st series, no. 40 (1903): 313–32.

Hoeltje, Hubert J. "The Writing of the Scarlet Letter." *New England Quarterly* 27 (1954): 326–46.

Holmes, Oliver Wendell. "Hawthorne." In *Atlantic Monthly* 14 (1864): 98–101.

Holt, Michael. *The Political Crisis of the 1850s.* New York, 1978.

Horsman, Reginald. *Race and Manifest Destiny: The Origins of American Racial Anglo-Saxonism.* Cambridge, Mass., 1981.

Howe, M. A. DeWolfe. *Memories of a Hostess . . . Drawn Chiefly from the Diaries of Mrs. James T. Fields.* Boston, 1922.

Howells, William Dean. *Literary Friends and Acquaintance.* Edited by David

Hiatt and Edwin Cady. Vol. 32 of *The Howells Edition, the Approved Text of the Modern Language Association of America.* Bloomington, Ind., 1968.

Hull, Raymona E. "Una Hawthorne: A Biographical Sketch." *Nathaniel Hawthorne Journal* 6 (1976): 87–119.

Hurst, Luanne Jenkins. "The Chief Employ of Her Life: Sophia Peabody Hawthorne's Contribution to Her Husband's Career." In *Hawthorne and Women: Engendering and Expanding the Hawthorne Tradition,* edited by John L. Idol and Melinda M. Ponder, 45–54. Amherst, 1999.

Idol, John L., Jr. "Elizabeth Palmer Peabody: A Tireless Hawthorne Booster." In *Hawthorne and Women: Engendering and Expanding the Hawthorne Tradition,* edited by John L. Idol and Melinda M. Ponder, 36–44. Amherst, 1999.

James, Henry. *Hawthorne.* In *Literary Criticism: Essays on Literature—American Writers, English Writers,* 315–457. New York: Library of America, 1984.

Jarvis, Edward. "Ezra Ripley, D.D., 1778–1842." In *Annals of the American Pulpit,* 9 vols., edited by William B. Sprague, 8:121–25. New York, 1859–69.

———. *Traditions and Reminiscences of Concord, Massachusetts, 1779–1878.* Edited by Sarah Chapin. Amherst, 1993.

Keyes, John S. "Concord." In *History of Middlesex County,* 3 vols., edited by D. Hamilton Hurd, 2:570–612. Philadelphia, 1890.

Lathrop, Rose Hawthorne. *Memories of Hawthorne.* Boston, 1897.

Lincoln, Abraham. *The Collected Works of Abraham Lincoln.* Edited by Roy P. Basler. 9 vols. New Brunswick, 1953–55.

Long, E. B., and Barbara Long. *The Civil War Day by Day: An Almanac 1861–1865.* Garden City, N.Y., 1971.

Longfellow, Henry Wadsworth. *The Letters of Henry Wadsworth Longfellow.* Edited by Andrew Hilen. 6 vols. Cambridge, Mass., 1966–82.

———. *The Poetical Works of Longfellow.* Cambridge Edition. Boston, 1975.

———. *Prose Works.* 2 vols. Boston, 1886.

Longfellow, Samuel. *Life of Henry Wadsworth Longfellow, with Extracts from his Journals and Correspondence.* 2 vols. Boston, 1886.

Lothrop, Margaret M. *The Wayside: Home of Authors.* New York, 1940.

Mann, Mary P. *Life of Horace Mann.* Boston, 1865.

Marx, Leo. *The Machine in the Garden: Technology and the Pastoral Ideal in America.* New York, 1964.

Mathews, James W. "An Early Brook Farm Letter." *New England Quarterly* 53 (1980): 226–30.

Maynard, Theodore. *A Fire Was Lighted: The Life of Rose Hawthorne Lathrop.* Milwaukee, 1948.

Mellow, James R. *Nathaniel Hawthorne in His Times.* Baltimore, 1980.

Meltzer, Milton, and Walter Harding. *A Thoreau Profile.* New York, 1962.

———. *Memoirs of Margaret Fuller Ossoli.* 2 vols. Boston, 1852.

Merk, Frederick. *Manifest Destiny and Mission in American History: A Reinterpretation.* New York, 1963.

Messerli, Jonathan. *Horace Mann: A Biography.* New York, 1972.

Mitchell, Donald G. [Ik Marvel]. *The Works of Donald G. Mitchell.* 15 vols. New York, 1907.

Myerson, Joel. "Margaret Fuller's 1842 Journal: At Concord with the Emersons." *Harvard Library Bulletin* 21 (July 1973): 320–40.

Nathaniel Hawthorne Journal 1972. Edited by C. E. Frazer Clark, Jr. Washington, D.C., 1973.

Nichols, Roy Franklin. *Franklin Pierce: Young Hickory of the Granite Hills.* Philadelphia, 1958.

Nissenbaum, Stephen. "The Firing of Nathaniel Hawthorne." *Essex Institute Historical Collections* 114 (1978): 57–86.

Parkman, Francis. *Letters of Francis Parkman.* Edited by Wilbur R. Jacobs. 2 vols. Norman, Okla., 1960.

Pattee, Fred Lewis. *The Feminine Fifties.* New York, 1940.

Peabody, Elizabeth Palmer. *Letters of Elizabeth Palmer Peabody.* Edited by Bruce A. Ronda. Middletown, Conn., 1984.

Pearson, Norman Holmes. "Elizabeth Peabody on Hawthorne." *Essex Institute Historical Collections* 94 (July 1958): 256–76.

———. "Hawthorne and the Mannings." *Essex Institute Historical Collections* 94 (July 1958): 170–90.

Porte, Joel, ed. *Emerson in His Journals.* Cambridge, Mass., 1982.

Reynolds, Grindall. *A Collection of Historical and Other Papers.* Concord, Mass., 1895.

Richardson, James D. *A Compilation of the Messages and Papers of the Presidents, 1789–1897.* 10 vols. [Washington], 1899.

Robinson, William S. *"Warrington" Pen-Portraits: A Collection of Personal and Political Reminiscences from 1848 to 1876.* Boston, 1877.

Ronda, Bruce A. *Elizabeth Palmer Peabody: A Reformer on Her Own Terms.* Cambridge, Mass., 1999.

Sams, Henry W., ed. *Autobiography of Brook Farm.* Englewood Cliffs, N.J., 1958.

Sanborn, Franklin B. *Hawthorne and His Friends: Reminiscences and Tribute.* Cedar Rapids, Iowa, 1908.

———. *Recollections of Seventy Years.* 2 vols. Boston, 1909.

Schlesinger, E. B. "The Alcotts Through Thirty Years." *Harvard Library Bulletin* 11 (1957): 363–85.

Schubert, Leland. "Hawthorne and George W. Childs and the Death of W. D. Ticknor." *Essex Institute Historical Collections* 84 (1948): 164–68.

Scudder, Townsend. *Concord: American Town.* Boston, 1947.

Sears, Clara Endicott, compiler. *Bronson Alcott's Fruitlands, with Transcendental Wild Oats, by Louisa M. Alcott.* Boston, 1915.

Shepard, Odell. *Pedlar's Progress: The Life of Bronson Alcott.* Boston, 1937.

Simmons, Nancy Craig. "Margaret Fuller's Boston Conversations: The 1839–1840 Series." In *Studies in the American Renaissance,* edited by Joel Myerson, 195–226. Charlottesville, 1994.

Stewart, Randall. "The Hawthornes at the Wayside, 1860–1864: Selections from Mrs. Hawthorne's Letters to Mr. and Mrs. Fields." *More Books: The Bulletin of the Boston Public Library,* Sept. 1944: 263–79.

———. "Hawthorne's Last Illness and Death: Selections from Mrs. Hawthorne's Letters to Mr. and Mrs. Fields." *More Books: The Bulletin of the Boston Public Library,* Oct. 1944: 303–13.

———. *Nathaniel Hawthorne: A Biography.* New Haven, 1948.

———. "Recollections of Hawthorne by His Sister Elizabeth." *American Literature* 16 (1944–45): 316–31.

Stowe, Harriet Beecher. *Uncle Tom's Cabin, or Life among the Lowly.* In *Three Novels.* New York: Library of America, 1982.

Thomas, Dwight, and David K. Jackson. *The Poe Log: A Documentary Life of Edgar Allan Poe, 1809–1849.* Boston, 1987.

Thompson, Lawrance. *Young Longfellow, 1807–1843.* New York, 1938.

Thoreau, Henry David. *The Correspondence of Henry David Thoreau.* Edited by Walter Harding and Carl Bode. New York, 1958.

———. *Journal.* 4 vols. Edited by John C. Broderick. Princeton, 1981–92.

———. "A Plea for Captain John Brown." In *Collected Essays and Poems,* 396–417. New York: Library of America, 2001.

———. *Walden.* In *A Week on the Concord and Merrimack Rivers, Walden, or Life in the Woods, The Main Woods, Cape Cod.* New York: Library of America, 1985.

Ticknor, Caroline. *Hawthorne and His Publisher.* Boston, 1913.

Tryon, W. S. *Parnassus Corner: A Life of James T. Fields.* Boston, 1963.

Turner, Arlin. *Nathaniel Hawthorne: A Biography.* New York, 1980.

von Frank, Albert J. *The Trials of Anthony Burns.* Cambridge, Mass., 1998.

Wagenknecht, Edward. *Longfellow: A Full-Length Portrait.* New York, 1955.

———, compiler. *Mrs. Longfellow: Selected Letters and Journals of Fanny Appleton Longfellow (1817–1861).* New York, 1956.

Wagner, Frederick. "All Pine and Apple Orchard: Hawthorne and the Alcotts." *Essex Institute Historical Collections* 118 (1982): 31–41.

Warner, Lee H. "Nathaniel Hawthorne and the Making of the President— 1852." *Historical New Hampshire* 28 (Spring 1973): 20–36.

Watson, David. *Margaret Fuller: An American Romantic.* Oxford, 1988.

Wheeler, Ruth R. *Concord: Climate for Freedom.* Concord, Mass., 1967.

Wilinsky, John. "The Impact of the Railroad on Concord, Massachusetts, 1844–1887." Typescript dated 12/1/1975. In Concord Free Public Library Special Collections.

Williams, Cecil B. *Henry Wadsworth Longfellow.* New York, 1964.

Wineapple, Brenda. *Hawthorne: A Life.* New York, 2003.

Winthrop, Robert C. "Memoir of the Honorable Nathan Appleton." *Proceedings of the Massachusetts Historical Society,* ser. 1, vol. 5 (1860–62): 249–308.

Woodson, Thomas, James A. Rubino, and Jamie Barlowe Kayes. "With Hawthorne in Wartime Concord: Sophia Hawthorne's 1862 Diary." In *Studies in the American Renaissance,* edited by Joel Myerson, 281–359. Charlottesville, 1988.

Acknowledgments

Over several years, Leslie Perrin Wilson, curator, and her assistant, Joyce Woodman, have made me welcome among the subterranean treasures of the Special Collections at the Concord Free Public Library in Concord, Massachusetts. Both Leslie and Joyce have been unfailingly supportive in sharing with me their vast knowledge of the history of a remarkably well documented American village. Similarly, the Boston Athenaeum with its obliging staff has furnished—for this book as for earlier ones—an invaluable sanctuary for writing and research. The scholarship on Hawthorne and the century in which he lived is of course immense; after many years of reading in it, I've profited in ways that my Notes and Works Cited only very partially disclose. Thus I offer a blanket expression of thanks here for the stimulation and insight that historians and literary critics of that earlier age have provided. I thank, in addition, my editor at Grove Press, Joan Bingham, and her assistant, Lindsay Sagnette, as well as two friends whose interest was instrumental in converting the notion of a book on Hawthorne into *Hawthorne in Concord*: David Michaelis and Herman Gollob. Finally, my wife listened appreciatively to each chapter of the book as it was written, offering keen suggestions that I invariably acted upon. For that, as for much else in forty-five happy years of marriage, I bless my good fortune while expressing to her, if not for the first time, my gratitude and love.

INDEX